ReFocus: The Films of Albert Brooks

ReFocus: The American Directors Series

Series Editors: Robert Singer, Frances Smith, and Gary D. Rhodes

Editorial board: Kelly Basilio, Donna Campbell, Claire Perkins, Christopher Sharrett, and Yannis Tzioumakis

ReFocus is a series of contemporary methodological and theoretical approaches to the interdisciplinary analyses and interpretations of neglected American directors, from the once-famous to the ignored, in direct relationship to American culture—its myths, values, and historical precepts.

Titles in the series include:

ReFocus: The Films of Preston Sturges
Edited by Jeff Jaeckle and Sarah Kozloff

ReFocus: The Films of Delmer Daves
Edited by Matthew Carter and Andrew Nelson

ReFocus: The Films of Amy Heckerling
Edited by Frances Smith and Timothy Shary

ReFocus: The Films of Budd Boetticher
Edited by Gary D. Rhodes and Robert Singer

ReFocus: The Films of Kelly Reichardt
E. Dawn Hall

ReFocus: The Films of William Castle
Edited by Murray Leeder

ReFocus: The Films of Barbara Kopple
Edited by Jeff Jaeckle and Susan Ryan

ReFocus: The Films of Elaine May
Edited by Alexandra Heller-Nicholas and Dean Brandum

ReFocus: The Films of Spike Jonze
Edited by Kim Wilkins and Wyatt Moss-Wellington

ReFocus: The Films of Paul Schrader
Edited by Michelle E. Moore and Brian Brems

ReFocus: The Films of John Hughes
Edited by Timothy Shary and Frances Smith

ReFocus: The Films of Doris Wishman
Edited by Alicia Kozma and Finley Freibert

ReFocus: The Films of Albert Brooks
Edited by Christian B. Long

edinburghuniversitypress.com/series/refoc

ReFocus:
The Films of Albert Brooks

Edited by Christian B. Long

EDINBURGH
University Press

Edinburgh University Press is one of the leading university presses in the UK. We publish academic books and journals in our selected subject areas across the humanities and social sciences, combining cutting-edge scholarship with high editorial and production values to produce academic works of lasting importance. For more information visit our website: edinburghuniversitypress.com

© editorial matter and organization Christian B. Long, 2021, 2023
© the chapters their several authors, 2021, 2023

Edinburgh University Press Ltd
The Tun—Holyrood Road
12 (2f) Jackson's Entry
Edinburgh EH8 8PJ

First published in hardback by Edinburgh University Press 2021

Typeset in 11/13 Ehrhardt MT by
IDSUK (DataConnection) Ltd

A CIP record for this book is available from the British Library

ISBN 978 1 4744 3425 6 (hardback)
ISBN 978 1 4744 3428 7 (paperback)
ISBN 978 1 4744 3426 3 (webready PDF)
ISBN 978 1 4744 3427 0 (epub)

The right of the contributors to be identified as authors of this work has been asserted in accordance with the Copyright, Designs and Patents Act 1988 and the Copyright and Related Rights Regulations 2003 (SI No. 2498).

Contents

List of Figures	vii
Notes on Contributors	ix
Acknowledgments	xi
1 Introduction *Christian B. Long*	1

Part I   Brooks as Media Critic

2 Your General Humor Buildup: Constructing Albert Brooks *J. D. Connor*	51
3 The Counterculture Squared: Albert Brooks's *Saturday Night Live* *Jeff Menne*	78
4 Irony Ends in Why *Thomas Britt*	94

Part II   Brooks as Auteur

5 When Success is Failure *Christian B. Long*	119
6 *Modern Romance*: Albert Brooks's Anatomy of Love *Enid Stubin*	136
7 Easy Riders, Raging Yuppies: *Lost in America* and the Work of the Professional-Managerial Class *Derek Nystrom*	150
8 Defending *Purgatorio*: Dante, Brooks, and Finding One's Celestial Place *Frank Percaccio*	171
9 Albert Brooks Channeling the Feminine *Rebecca Bell-Metereau*	189

Part III Brooks as Cultural Figure

10 Finding Brooks: Animating the Baby Boomer Generation
in *Finding Nemo* 211
Dietmar Meinel

11 Debt, Payback, and Economics in Nicolas Winding Refn's *Drive* 226
Tom Ue

Bibliography	241
Filmography	252
Recordings	254
Television	255
Writing	257
Index	258

Figures

1.1	*Taxi Driver* "*We* are the people" or "We *are* the people"	12
1.2	*Lost in America*: dropping out responsibly	24
1.3	A face that registers "all the known emotions"	26
2.1	Albert Brooks's 1973 *Joke* mandala	65
2.2	Ad Reinhardt's 1956 *Joke* mandala	68
3.1	Not live television, A Film Written and Directed by Albert Brooks	87
4.1	Albert Brooks displays the Ettinauer camera, a "startling breakthrough" in observational recording	97
4.2	David Howard (Brooks) proposes a "bold experiment" to get his money back and create positive advertising for Las Vegas	106
4.3	Albert Brooks revives "Danny and Dave" for a new audience in Delhi	112
5.1	Dr. Yaeger (Charles Grodin), matador	121
5.2	Beatrice (Debbie Reynolds) sneaking into the frame	128
5.3	David (Brooks) takes the job in New York and finds his nemesis Brad there	133
6.1	Robert (Brooks) and Mary (Kathryn Harrold) on a date, breaking up again	138
6.2	"I don't want a Quaalude"	139
7.1	The exemplary consumer at his real job: David (Brooks) in his office, discussing the Mercedes leather for his new car	155
7.2	"I didn't have any problems"	159
8.1	Judgment City, soul processing center	174
9.1	"Such a sensitive man"	193

9.2	Watching Daniel (Brooks) watch Julia (Meryl Streep) watching her life	198
9.3	Food as one of the mediators of John (Brooks) and Beatrice's (Debbie Reynolds) relationship	200
10.1	Marlin the clownfish (Brooks) tells a joke	219
10.2	Marlin (Brooks) lies to Dory (Ellen DeGeneres) to get through the jellyfish	220
11.1	The handshake between Bernie (Brooks) and Driver (Ryan Gosling) from their different viewpoints	230
11.2	The handshake between Bernie (Brooks) and Driver (Ryan Gosling) from their different viewpoints.	231

Notes on Contributors

Rebecca Bell-Metereau is Professor of English at Southwest Texas State University, San Marcos and the author of *Transgender Cinema* (2019) and *Hollywood Androgyny* (1985).

Thomas Britt is Associate Professor of film at George Mason University. He has made nine documentary films, including *Lost in Winesburg* (2008), *A Short Film About Touring* (2012) and *Unpredictable* (2011). He is also a writer for *PopMatters*.

J. D. Connor is Associate Professor of Cinematic Arts at the University of Southern California. He is the author of *Hollywood Math and Aftermath: The Economic Image and the Digital Recession* (2018) and *The Studios after the Studios: Neoclassical Hollywood, 1970–2010* (2015).

Christian B. Long works in the Graduate School at the University of Queensland. He is the author of *The Imaginary Geography of Hollywood Cinema, 1960–2000* (2017) and co-editor of *Film and the American Presidency* (2015).

Dietmar Meinel is Assistant Professor at the University of Duisburg-Essen Institut für Anglophone Studien and the author of *Pixar's America: The Reanimation of American Myths and Symbols* (2016).

Jeff Menne is Associate Professor of English and Screen Studies at Oklahoma State University and the author of *Post-Fordist Cinema: Hollywood Auteurs and the Corporate Counterculture* (2019) and *Francis Ford Coppola* (2014).

Derek Nystrom is Associate Professor of English at McGill University. He is the author of *Hard Hats, Rednecks, and Macho Men: Class in 1970s American Cinema* (2009).

Frank Percaccio is Associate Professor of English at CUNY-Kingsborough Community College.

Enid Stubin is Associate Professor of English, CUNY-Kingsborough Community College.

Tom Ue is Frederick Banting Postdoctoral Fellow in the Department of English at the University of Toronto Scarborough. He is the author of *Gissing, Shakespeare, and the Life of Writing* (Edinburgh University Press, forthcoming) and *George Gissing* (forthcoming), and the editor of *George Gissing, The Private Papers of Henry Ryecroft* (Edinburgh University Press, 2020).

Acknowledgments

Robert Singer, Gary Rhodes, Frances Smith, and Richard Strachan showed enormous patience, as well as unflagging good humor, while the book was coming together. The contributors showed similar patience and humor. I owe them all a great deal of thanks for making this book come true. In particular, Rebecca Bell-Metereau for helping me at a tough point of chapter-shepherding, Derek Nystrom for his feedback on the introduction, and J. D. Connor for answering a call from the blue.

An earlier version of "When Success Is Failure" appeared in *Senses of Cinema* Issue 80 (2016), and I am grateful for their allowing me to use it in this collection.

Thanks to Kirstin Woodward, Diana Marsh, Marly Dein, and Angie Kahler, who are great colleagues. Thanks to Alison Pike and Kate Swanson, who let me take a few months off for a fellowship in Vienna. Thanks to Monika Wittmann, Leopold Lippert, and my students at University of Vienna for a sublime last hurrah of university teaching.

Thanks to Jay, Mook, Blake, Jono, Jackson, Jimmy, Gaveril, Matty, Josh, AJ, Adam, Cameron, Rickie, Aaron, Nick, Yungy, and Eddie at Southside Eagles Football Club. Thanks to Mark Maguire, who has been my friend in football stadiums in Christchurch, Bray, Barcelona, Vienna, Milan, and who knows where next. Thanks to Dr. Rasha Al-Tameemi for keeping me from breaking down entirely. Thanks to Dr. Carolyn DeWytt for getting a handle on my epilepsy.

I miss my sisters, Colleen, Killian, and Megan, and wish that I could see them more often, as well as the people who come with them: Piper, Wren, Rachel, Grace, Dave, Matt, and Max. The Clements—Bruce and Ellen, Becca and Thea, Matt, Kate, Luke, and Madison—are a wonderful family to have joined. Thanks to our two cats Archie and Ozzie, who are near-constant sources of amusement and affection.

Superlatives and expressions of thanks can't get close to how much I love Jennifer Clement.

CHAPTER 1

Introduction

Christian B. Long

The film may be called *Finding Nemo* (Stanton and Unkrich, 2003), but the two characters who appear on screen the most are the forgetful blue tang Dory, voiced by Ellen DeGeneres, and Marlin the clownfish, voiced by Albert Brooks.[1] The Nemo in need of finding is the only survivor of an attack by a barracuda that killed more than four hundred of his siblings as well as his mother. The attack leaves Marlin a terrifically worried single parent, which may go some way to explaining why Marlin is a clownfish who isn't funny. On Nemo's first day of school, Marlin meets some of the other parents, and when asked to tell a joke, explains that, "Clown fish are no funnier than any other fish." Marlin then proves as much, mangling the set up to a joke about a mollusc and a sea cucumber. Soon after, Marlin tells the forgetful Dory, "If this is some kind of practical joke it's not funny. And I know funny. I'm a clown fish." Evidently, funny does not include impressions, as Marlin finds the school of fish "impressions" of a swordfish, lobster, octopus, and ship nothing but a waste of time. If Dory's defining character trait is an inability to remember anything until it's narratively and emotionally necessary, Marlin's defining trait is to be earnest rather than funny until it is narratively and emotionally necessary. The not-funny clownfish telling a joke well registers Marlin's growth. Only after rescuing Nemo (with the help of Dory and the ragtag group of dentist's office aquarium dwellers) can Marlin tell the sea cucumber joke he failed to deliver earlier.

Marlin represents something like a career achievement award for Brooks, introducing him to a new audience in a way that honors his earlier work. *Finding Nemo* offers a series of echoes to Brooks's career as a stand-up comic and filmmaker. Brooks's stand-up material in the late 1960s and early 1970s, both on stage and in appearances on late-night talk shows, engaged with the form of stand-up, including the practical means to perform impressions. And clowns, if not clownfish, figure in the Albert Brooks persona: the story behind his leaving stand-up features performing for an audience dressed as clowns (more on Brooks's stand-up career later). In his films leading up to *Finding Nemo*, Brooks showed his ability to play the straight man to: an omni-competent Meryl Streep in *Defending Your Life* (Brooks, 1991), a humorously confused Brendan Fraser in *The Scout* (Ritchie, 1994); an understated Debbie Reynolds in *Mother* (Brooks, 1996); and a scenery-chewing Sharon Stone in *The Muse* (Brooks, 1999), all of which readied him to play against DeGeneres's charming and cheerful gormlessness. Even though most of the family and child audience may not have consciously registered it, Albert Brooks in fact offered the ideal voice for Marlin. Based on the persona created throughout his career, a flustered, often too earnest clown who isn't funny *is* Albert Brooks. Or at least "Albert Brooks."

This volume makes the case that Albert Brooks merits not only a wider readership/viewership, both critical and popular, but also that Brooks offers a useful lens through which to engage American film and culture since the late 1960s. In the rest of this introduction, I offer a brief Brooks biography, then move to his start in show business as a stand-up comic to begin to identify the ideas and concerns that appear in his work. Then I transition to his actor-for-hire work on television and in film, further developing what an Albert Brooks appearance tends to signify. Then I draw these threads together by working through the films he wrote and directed. I suggest that an intertextual framing perspective—what we might call "Brooks tropes"—consistently appears throughout his films, from his debut feature *Real Life* (1979) to his last film as a writer-director, *Looking for Comedy in the Muslim World* (2005). Providing this overview of Brooks's career will, for the most part, work through the popular press's coverage of Brooks and his work, as Brooks has, until this volume, attracted no dedicated critical attention in academic film studies (or cultural studies). This introduction will establish the general outlines of the public persona of "Albert Brooks," which infuses a paradoxical approach to comedy—one we might describe as coyly subversive and conservatively radical—and the ten chapters that follow will further elaborate on the cultural significance of Brooks as a persona, a filmmaker, performer, and symptomatic cultural figure.

BORN INTO COMEDY

There are a few things that everyone seems to know. Abraham Lincoln was born in a log cabin. Shakespeare left his wife his second-best bed. The toilet flushes in the other direction in Australia. Albert Brooks was born Albert Einstein. Albert Brooks grew up in showbiz, the son of a singer and actress,

Thelma Goodman, and a comic, Harry Einstein, which may explain the name Albert Einstein. Early in his career Harry worked with Eddie Cantor and Al Jolson, and under the stage name Parkyakarkus appeared in small roles in a number of films as a source of ethnic dialect humor. Harry Einstein died after having a heart attack on stage, at a roast of Lucille Ball and Desi Arnaz, when Albert was 11 years old and his brother, Bob Einstein (stage name Super Dave Osborne) was 16. Young Albert Einstein went to Beverly Hills High School, where he was friends with Rob Reiner, son of the comedian Carl Reiner, who is said to have told Johnny Carson that a very young Albert was the funniest person he knew. Upon graduating from high school, Albert went to Carnegie Institute of Technology, where he briefly studied acting.

Albert began working as a stand-up comic, releasing two albums in the 1970s, *Comedy Minus One* (1973) and *A Star Is Bought* (1975), both of which self-consciously play with the conventions of comedy on the radio and the stand-up comedy album.[2] Side one of *Comedy Minus One* takes the standard approach, a recorded routine that features observational bits, such as the life of an opening act, prank call radio bits like "Kooky Krazy Kalls," as well as more conceptual material like "Rewriting the National Anthem." On side two the live audience disappears altogether for the tutorial "Comedy Minus One." In a manner akin to the Music Minus One recording series, Brooks and the listener at home collaborate to deliver a comedy routine. The lines the album listener should deliver were printed on the album case, turning the packaging itself into a script. Like many comics, Albert is the butt of his own jokes in the more or less traditional bits on the album, but the "Comedy Minus One" routine changes his relationship to his audience. In the routine, Albert plays the straight man, delivering all of the set-up lines. However, as a whole "Comedy Minus One" is a comedy routine designed literally to have no laughs, but rather to make the audience inhabit the role of comic.

A Star Is Bought shows a similar interest in the form of comedy, tied to a desire to find an audience, leading Brooks to imagine a number of routes to success and fame that a comic like him might take. The first track explains that each track is "individually designed for different kinds of radio stations," from country to classical to blues. And so, with the help of Linda Ronstadt, Rob Reiner, Harry Shearer, Peter Tork, and Mickey Dolenz, among others, Brooks records not a stand-up album—there is no stand-up comedy on the album—but rather a comedy concept album rooted in radio comedy. As a comic, "Brooks is not like Carlin, Klein or Pryor (and certainly not like Cheech and Chong), who bring humor to fairly ordinary situations (though Brooks does that too); Brooks's strength is in the unexpected twist of an already bent imagination."[3] Unlike the two biggest major stand-up stars of the 1970s—Richard Pryor and George Carlin—neither Kaufman nor Martin nor Brooks did explicitly political/topical comedy, although their critiques of the show-bizzing of American culture certainly had a political cast to them. Pryor in particular stands out as a comic who created characters and mined his personal experiences to wrestle with the racial politics of the contemporary United States in a way that drew in massive audiences. One of post-war comedy's major figures, Lenny Bruce, faced obscenity trials for his stage routines, consistently confronted square society, and had both a biopic (*Lenny* (Fosse, 1974)) and a biopic-within-a-biopic (*The Stand-Up* in *All That Jazz* (Fosse, 1974)) made about him. George Carlin's "Seven Words You Can't Say on Television" on *Class Clown* followed up Bruce's on-stage routines on obscenity to great notoriety and acclaim. In a more narrative vein, Richard Pryor put a very human face on suffering and indicted the white power structure in doing so. In "Wino and Junkie," the latter, unable to find work and stuck in a world of violence and distrust, asks Wino for advice on how to deal with the white man. Pryor ends the routine with Wino admitting, "I know how to deal with him. That's right. That's why I'm in the position I am today." Carlin and Pryor, like Bruce before them, rooted their work in their sociopolitical moments, but Brooks took a different path and made a different subject his own. Both *Comedy Minus One* and *A Star Is Bought* establish a baseline for Brooks's career in comedy, a career that insistently and critically engages with comic form as both a method and a subject.

The sort of meta-comedy Brooks was writing and performing in the 1970s was finding a wider audience. Much like Brooks, Andy Kaufman confronted the formal constraints and conventions of comedy. Kaufman has also had biopics made of his life, and at least one cultural studies book on his work, Florian Keller's *Andy Kaufman: Wrestling with the American Dream*. Steve Martin is, like Brooks, a comedian who went on to success in film, television, and literature. Like Kaufman, Martin has been the subject of a detailed academic analysis, in Tracy Wurter's "Comedy Jokes: Steven Martin and the Limits of Stand-Up Comedy," which uses Martin to understand changes in comedy in the 1970s.[4] In Wurter's account of Martin, strictly political readings "do not account for how Steve Martin's stand-up—eschewing direct social content in favour of an overabundance of formal signifiers—worked to affect its audience or why he became such a big hit in the second half of the 1970s."[5] Wurter's analysis of Martin sees two key formal concerns leading to a thematic one: his troubling of the comedian figure and of comedy itself lead to an engagement with a broader cultural meaninglessness.

A stand-up comic presents a slightly different kind of performer compared other entertainment figures. David Marc makes an odd choice to describe what makes comedians different as performers. He argues that, "Good actors can be singled out of bad plays; good singers can put over bad songs. But in the case of the stand-up comedian, there is no dividing medium from message."[6] At this point, Steve Martin appears and unsettles Marc's otherwise compelling case: "When performing stand-up comedy, Steve Martin is Steve Martin is Steve Martin."[7] As a stand-up working in meta-comedy, Steve Martin is "Steve Martin," "a performer who would be purely funny based on verbal and visual symbols of comedy but entirely devoid of topical content. Within this context, Martin's character would not be funny if he was entirely successful. His attempts at joking must fail, at least most of the time."[8] In other words, a meta-comic ticks all the boxes of how a comic should perform, and in doing so chooses a funny failure. This sort of stand-up "represents a unique instance in the possible interactions between audience and performer: the audience is not laughing with the comic, or at the jokes, or even at themselves; they are laughing at comedy itself."[9] This view of comedy turns many of Steve Martin's bits into a version of Noam Chomsky's grammatically correct but nonsensical sentence "Colorless green ideas sleep furiously"; the zany Groucho glasses and arrow through the head on the cover to *Let's Get Small* might be formally or technically correct, but they are not particularly meaningful.[10]

This turn to meaninglessness pushes against a common thread in considerations of stand-up comedy, in that it presents the comic as a cultural critic, a figure who mines their culture's shortcomings for materials. But for a meta-comic like Steve Martin, as Wurter sees it,

> stand-up comedy does not ultimately lead to some deeper social meaning but rather plays with the idea of entertainment ... Rather than a throwback to simple vaudevillian laughs or safe, middle-of-the-road comedy, Martin can be seen as the first major American stand-up star to make his audience laugh at stand-up comedy itself.[11]

Rather than a social life under examination, Martin's comedy examines the spectacle of it all, the showbiz nature of so much of contemporary life. While Guy Debord published *La société du spectacle* in 1967, Wurter sees this redefinition in American comedy occurring in 1974 and 1975, with the commercial pay-off coming slightly later: in 1977 *Let's Get Small* hit the top-ten album chart, and in 1978 *A Wild and Crazy Guy* went platinum, and saw Martin's self-aware novelty song "King Tut" become a top twenty hit. As Thomas Britt will explore in his chapter, Albert Brooks has often found himself ahead of the comedy game. His stand-up albums, obsessed as they are with comic form and showbiz conventions, came out in 1973 and 1975, perhaps a little too early to catch the wave Martin rode to massive success.

Not that Albert Brooks was an unsuccessful comic performer in the 1970s. On the contrary: Brooks was a frequent guest on late-night talk shows and was even offered the "permanent host" position of *Saturday Night Live*, a job he would turn down to make short films, which Jeff Menne analyses in his chapter. Brooks does not occupy a central place in most accounts of *Saturday Night Live* or the history of stand-up, but he certainly has his champions. In the lead-up to two for-hire works coming out in 1983—*The Twilight Zone: The Movie* (Landis, 1983) and *Unfaithfully Yours* (Zieff, 1983)—Paul Slansky profiled Brooks for *Playboy*. An anecdote that Slansky uses to set up a discussion of Brooks's uncompromising approach to comedy neatly links showbiz and meaninglessness, both in Brooks's material and life:

> In 1975, *Time* called Brooks "the smartest, most audacious comic since Lenny Bruce and Woody Allen." Wary of too much success too soon, he was determined to keep control of his career. He was on the verge of signing to star in *Our Man in Ra-taan*, a sitcom about a TV newsman stationed in Africa, when a network executive asked him, "What do you see for this character in five years?" "Suicide," Brooks replied, and abandoned the project.[12]

The ability to walk away from a sure thing—a comic getting their own sitcom is a sure sign of having "made it"—testifies to Brooks's dedication to his craft. It's a fair reading; for all of his self-aware slapstick (about which more soon), Brooks is a serious comedian. As Slansky observes,

> Steve Martin was the guy with the arrow through his head who said, "Excuse me." Chevy Chase smirked and fell down a lot. Cheech and Chong did dope jokes, George Carlin said dirty words and Andy Kaufman seemed to think that the point of performing was to make people nervous about laughing. For those of us who took comedy seriously in the Seventies, though, there was only the holy trinity: Richard Pryor, Lily Tomlin and Albert Brooks.[13]

A similar connection of Brooks and smartness comes in Matt Zoller Seitz's obituary for another comic, Garry Shandling. Seitz writes that Shandling's comic persona, "fused Jack Benny's unctuous neediness, Charles Grodin's dour certitude, Albert Brooks' self-lacerating intellectual discomfort, and Warren Beatty's dashing Hollywood satyr act, and added shadings from Shandling's own personality."[14] In discussions of Brooks as a comic, the terms writers use to describe him—serious, intellectual, avant-garde, cerebral deconstruction of the creative process—all push the writerly aspects to the fore, even though that writer was also a performer who knew his material and its form.

Brooks promoted *Comedy Minus One* on *The Tonight Show*, one of his frequent mass-audience venues while Johnny Carson was the host. In a 1973 episode, Brooks, seated in a leather chair, addresses the crowd with some sad news. "Here I am, five years into my career," he says, "and I have no more material left."[15] He waits for the laughter and applause to die down and then adds, "It surprised the hell out of me . . . I think there's more inside of me. There has to be more bits in here. It's just at this time in my life, it's so deep that I'd do injury to myself to go and get it." His confession about not having any material then segues into a shameless bit of promotion for his album, which he pulls out from the chair and describes as, "the album with the mirror on the back and the script in the middle. How are people gonna know it's maybe the funniest record ever made, and it's on ABC Records and GRT tapes if you don't go out and tell them?" Brooks had an audience laughing at the form of the talk show visit to promote new material, as well as the tendency of performers to want to play their new material instead of "the hits." After this meta-comedy set-up, Brooks then explains what he would never do to get laughs, which is pander to the audience's baser tastes by dropping his pants or drawing a funny face on his chest or taking a pie in the face or breaking an egg over his head or getting spritzed in the face with water, all slapstick gags that he performs. The audience laughs riotously and continuously throughout the entire bit that denies that the very things getting laughs are the sorts of things that Albert Brooks would do to get laughs. And here Brooks compounds the false humility of never going for easy laughs with a solemn promise. He makes a serious face behind the whipped cream and begins solemnly, "But ladies and gentlemen, this isn't the real me. This isn't what I'm about." His voice gets more insistent and he starts speaking faster as he builds to the end of the monolog:

> If I have done nothing else here tonight, I'd like to have at least instilled a trust between you and me. Me as a comedian and you as an audience. A trust that lasts throughout my career and throughout your lifetimes. A trust that you know that if you see my name in *TV Guide*, if you see it in the record stores, you see it on a bus, you know that work's gone behind it. That quality's gone behind it. Because this.

And then he gestures at his half-naked whipped cream-covered body, "This isn't me." The audience-pleasing (we might say pandering) slapstick gags Brooks uses resemble the cover to Steve Martin's top-ten-selling 1977 album *Let's Get Small*, which acts as both a sight gag and a preview of Martin's material. Martin wears an avalanche of cheap bits: piling balloon animals, bunny ears, Groucho glasses, and an arrow through the head in an overdetermined display of "goofy fun." Meta-comedy thus lets Brooks have it both ways, moving from no material to the most hackneyed of material to an admission and critique of the hackyness of the material he just performed, all demonstrating for the audience that even "without material," when Albert Brooks performs, he delivers.

Ten years later, on a 1983 *Tonight Show* appearance, Brooks again took fairly hacky material—impersonations a few years past their sell-by date—and by using overstated prop and physical humor redeems and nails the bit.[16] He produces a picnic basket filled with what he calls a prototype of an impersonator kit that will allow anyone at home to perform these impersonations. Building on his interest in the comic potential of the pseudo-scientific as seen in *Famous School for Comedians* and again in *Real Life*, Brooks explains that "we have seven scientists, three doctors we've employed for the last five years, and they have come up with a way for you to impersonate great people." This research, in an echo of "Comedy Minus One," makes it possible for anyone to perform impersonations if they have the right food. Brooks produces a lemon slice, which he sucks vigorously, to produce the facial tics and voice of Clark Gable. He subsequently cuts up a baked potato, first to do Burt Lancaster, and then, with the addition of ground pepper, to do Curly from the Three Stooges. The routine depends not on the quality of Brooks's impersonations, but on his descriptions of how food can produce the desired performance: "this [lemon's] a little green so it's going to be bitter. That's for Gable in his thirties, when he was 30 to 35. Older Gable, older lemon," and "pepper's good for everyone, it says Brando, Sullivan, et al." Brooks's physical business goes beyond interactions with the food. He repeatedly stacks the food containers on Johnny's desk and shuffles them around as they teeter and nearly fall, juggling the "as hot as you can stand it" baked potato in an extended set-up. In other words, that Brooks barely bothers to do actual impersonations (except for the Curly) and the performers impersonated were no longer major stars (though Lancaster was still working), does no harm to the bit. Instead, the performance adds increasingly absurd demystifications of the mechanics of comedy to build to an almost childish climax of a Curly impersonation, which almost anyone can do without a baked potato and ground black pepper.

In spite of his propensity for pushing comic form to the fore of his work and his excursions into absurdity and slapstick, both on record and on television, Brooks is less often compared to a radio comic like Jack Benny or even a fellow meta-comic like Steve Martin, but rather the stand-up turned writer-director Woody Allen. In *Seriously Funny: The Rebel Comedians of the 1950s and 1960s*, Gerald Nachman categorizes Brooks as one of "Allen's gifted comic children."[7] On the one hand this is chronologically fair, as Allen got his start writing for television comedy shows in the 1950s and his three stand-up albums in the late 1960s precede Brooks's albums. But on the other hand, Allen did more traditional stand-up—his albums are recordings of live sets—whereas Brooks did not. The formal and thematic connections between Allen and Brooks are less certain than their ethnic connection, as both are Jewish. The Allen-Brooks connection continues into Brooks's film work, which the first section of the collection will investigate in some detail.

If, as John Limon writes in *Stand-Up Comedy in Theory, or, Abjection in America*, "stand-up is the resurrection of your father as your child," a better comic connection for Brooks is his actual father, who found minor fame as the "ethnic comedy" figure Parkyakarkus.[18] Albert resurrects his father in his stand-up and film work, returning frequently to the comic who, like Harry Einstein, dies on stage. Further, Harry Einstein's pantomime Greek identity resembles the blackface of his early collaborators, Eddie Cantor and Al Jolson, both of whom worked in blackface. As Michael Rogin's analysis shows, the ability to take off blackface (as well as Greekness), enabled Jewish American performers' assimilation by showing their whiteness could be covered up and removed.[19] In the resurrection of his father and comedic fathers, Albert Brooks's Jewishness is paradoxically both resurrected and covered up to assert an over-orthodox identification with American middle-class whiteness, rather than Jewishness, and drives Brooks's career in stand-up, film, and television, as a comic who asserts deep, but ironized, patriotism and shamelessly chases mainstream—which is to say WASP establishment—success and acceptance.

Brooks's upending of his middle-class whiteness provides the biggest laugh in a Chris Rock-hosted sketch for the 2005 Oscars.[20] In the pre-taped bit for the live show, Rock went to a Magic Johnson Theatre to see if Hollywood was indeed out of touch with its audience. Rock asks a number of African American moviegoers, "What was your favorite movie this year?" Instead of the Oscar-nominated films—*Sideways* (Payne, 2004), *Finding Neverland* (Forster, 2004), *Million Dollar Baby* (Eastwood, 2004), *The Aviator* (Scorsese, 2004), or *Ray* (Hackford, 2004)—the African American moviegoers Rock interviews name *AVP: Alien v Predator* (Anderson, 2004), *Saw* (Wan, 2004), and *Chronicles of Riddick* (Twohy, 2004) as the year's best. Then Rock asks them if they've seen some of the films nominated for Best Picture. *Sideways* draws three noes. As does *Finding Neverland*. As do *Million Dollar Baby* and *The Aviator*. Then he asks, "Did you see *White Chicks*?" The three yes responses are all very enthusiastic: "Oh yeah; I love *White Chicks*"; "Yes, I love that movie"; "Yeah I seen that. That was good." Next, Rock interviews Albert Brooks, the first white person to appear in the segment. The set-up to the joke establishes Brooks as the very audience member that the Academy Awards has in mind with its nominations:

Rock. Did you see *Sideways*?
Brooks: Yes.
Rock. Did you see *Finding Neverland*?
Brooks. Yes, I did.
Rock. Did you see *Million Dollar Baby*?
Brooks. Oh yes.

Brooks delivers each affirmative directly to Rock, with a minimum of energy and inflection. Finally, Rock asks Brooks, "Did you see *White Chicks*?" Brooks turns to the camera and yells, "Best movie of the year! They got robbed!" The first joke of the segment—that Black and white audiences prefer different films—gives way to a second joke—different taste regimes value different sorts of films—which in turn gives way to the third and biggest joke, that the extra-white and square Albert Brooks, in spite of the "rules" set up in the joke, loves *White Chicks*. What looked like a straightforward bit about the difference between white and Black movie audiences becomes a slightly more pointed critique of the economy of prestige, thanks to the change in direction from set-up to punchline that Albert Brooks and his comic career, persona, and performance make possible.

The sort of meta-comedy Albert Brooks wrote and performed in the 1970s found a much larger audience in the late 1990s and eventually offered an established niche for both alt-comics and mass-audience comics in the twenty-first century. Fox tried to compete with the Big Three networks in the late 1980s and 1990s on the back of comedy programs such as *In Living Color*, and *The Ben Stiller Show*, which it picked up from MTV. Both the cast and writers of *The Ben Stiller Show* went on to long and successful careers in comedy, not just Ben Stiller and Judd Apatow, but also Janeane Garofalo, David Cross, and Bob Odenkirk. In a *New York Times Magazine* article that describes *The Ben Stiller Show* as a kind of Gen-X *Your Show of Shows* comic-talent-incubator, former cast member Dana Gould explains that the cast of *The Ben Stiller Show* all shared the opinion that "Albert Brooks was the funniest person on the planet. We all wanted to become him, to write and direct and act in really harshly funny movies."[21] The article's writer David Handelman then notes that the cast and writers "haven't achieved Brooks' stature yet—only Stiller has directed films ('Reality Bites,' 'The Cable Guy'), and he didn't write them," an assessment that would eventually become inoperable with the appearance of the Judd Apatow school of comedy that began with *Freaks and Geeks* (1999–2000) and *Undeclared* (2001–2) on television and then *The 40-Year-Old Virgin* (Apatow, 2005) and *Knocked Up* (Apatow, 2007) on film.[22] Apatow acknowledged the importance of Brooks to his work, not only by calling his work "like the Torah to me," but also in casting Brooks as the father of his frequent stand-in, Paul Rudd, in *This Is 40* (2012).[23] If Ben Stiller, to some degree, and Judd Apatow, to a greater degree, are Brooks's main inheritors in film, a great deal of the alt-comedy school of performers certainly continue the meta-comedy that Brooks helped to develop in the 1970s. To name one, in *Waiting for 2040*'s "Feminist Dick Joke" (2014), Hari Kondabolu first tells a dick joke, then backs up to explain the joke's construction and how his word choice sought to create a more inclusive dick joke, and finally imagines possible avenues to critique his joke's political shortcomings.[24] In television, the Adult Swim show *Tim and Eric Awesome Show, Great Job!* (2007–10) from Tim Heidecker and Eric Wareheim shows a similar propensity to revel in the formal aspects of comedy like *A Star Is Bought*—in their case the lo-fi aesthetic of local television, celebrity appearances, and surreal digressions.

But Albert Brooks never really became a star. If a star is "like us, only more so," Brooks is "like us, only too much so." A profile in *People* magazine at the time of *Real Life*'s release looks less like a promo feature on the film and Brooks and more like a way for Brooks (and his friends) to engage with the form of a celebrity story. Reflecting on his youth, Brooks's deadpan registers even in print: "I was the class clown, the school clown, the city clown, the clown of the year. I guess many people thought of me as a clown."[25] Brooks the adult appears almost unknowable: "Secretive (even his friends don't know the occupation or last name of the lady named Bonnie he's dated for two years) and solitary ('Sometimes I don't get out of bed all day'), he doesn't smoke, drink or eat meat. 'I'm a bland freak,' he says. 'I love bland foods.'"[26] His collaborator Monica Johnson, "one of the few to penetrate Albert's privacy" to say, "'He's got one egg in the refrigerator, laundry all over. It's kind of sad—this genius roaming around in a cave. I looked in his closet once,' she continues, 'and there are two plaid shirts, a plaid bathrobe and a clown suit. It's a very arresting sight.'"[27] In the face of the common identity of performers who don't exist except when they're on stage, the on-stage Brooks pulls apart the way performing on stage creates a joke, a comic routine, and a comic performer, effectively erasing himself, leaving no one to make a star. The article ends with an attempt to make the case for Brooks as someone worth paying attention to, and does so with Brooks's attention to the intellectual and formal aspects of comedy: "'Nobody would ever take comedy seriously before,' observes Brooks, adding, 'I think the term "comedian" has come up in the world in the last five or six years.' Indeed, along with Lily and Richard, Woody Allen, Steve Martin, not to mention his old Saturday Night colleagues, Brooks is one of the reasons."[28] The *People* story performs a version of Brooks's meta-comedy; to understand Brooks it is necessary to consider not just product but also process, how show business does and doesn't function. These concerns and the persona that emerges out of them appear throughout Brooks's films, not only those he wrote, directed, and performed in, but also those in which he performed in as an actor-for-hire. And since Brooks is more likely to be recognized for his work for other filmmakers, it's best to start with his for-hire work.

ALBERT BROOKS AS AN ACTOR-FOR-HIRE

Though he worked as a stand-up and appeared on late-night talk shows both to perform and to promote his material, Albert Brooks claimed not to want to be a comedian. In a *Playboy* article from 1973, Brooks claimed that when he was on tour, opening for Richie Havens and Neil Diamond, he wasn't doing what he wanted; "I wanted to be an actor . . . And I certainly didn't want to be on the road."[29] After making a half dozen guest appearances on television shows in the late 1960s and early 1970s, including *The Odd Couple* and *The Dick Van Dyke Show*, and appearing in his short films for *Saturday Night Live*, Brooks made his film debut as the Palantine for President campaign worker Tom in Martin Scorsese's *Taxi Driver* (1976).[30] Amidst the film's tension, Brooks's Tom offers a release valve in his displays of unrequited attraction to Betsy and in his workplace frustrations. In an interview during a retrospective at Lincoln Center, Brooks described the Tom-Betsy relationship as, "I liked her; she didn't like me. A recurring theme for the rest of my life."[31] *Taxi Driver* not only set in motion Brooks's on-screen romantic identity, but also his professional one. In a scene reminiscent of Bob Newhart's telephone call routines, Tom argues with the company that made the campaign buttons over a change in where the emphasis is placed, shifting the campaign's overall message:

> Our slogan is "We are the people," and "are" is underlined. These new buttons have "we" underlined. That reads "*We* are the people." There's a difference. "We *are* the people" is not the same as "*We* are the people."

Brooks pauses and then delivers the funniest line in the exchange: "Let's not fight." Here Brooks's frustration seems ready to boil over at any moment, but he remains professionally passive-aggressive. He ends the conversation by using a combination of verbal acuity and money: "Look, we'll make it real simple. *We* won't pay for the buttons. *We* throw the buttons away." Tom represents something like a toothless, comic version of Travis Bickle facing down the scum of the office supply world, and also a Newhart-like "straight man who gets laughs all on his own."[32]

Figure 1.1 *Taxi Driver* "*We* are the people" or "We *are* the people"

J. Hoberman sees the film as a high-water mark for all involved, writing that, "Certainly no one connected with *Taxi Driver* ever again reached such heights" adding, "although Albert Brooks became a significant filmmaker in his own right." But for the most part, discussions of *Taxi Driver* pay little attention to Brooks. Peter Bradshaw offers one sentence, that Brooks gives "a great, overlooked performance as the nervy and nerdy researcher Tom"; Leonard Quart, Gretchen Schwartz, and Roger Ebert write about *Taxi Driver* in detail without mentioning Brooks at all.[33]

After a well-regarded performance in a very well-received film, Brooks did not get a role in someone else's movie for four years, when he very briefly appeared in *Private Benjamin* (Zieff, 1980), in which he dies while consummating his marriage to Judy Benjamin (Goldie Hawn).[34] Another three years passed until his appearance in *Twilight Zone: The Movie*, in which he is killed by something really scary before the credits run, and *Terms of Endearment* (James L. Brooks, 1983), in which he plays the off-screen voice of Aurora Greenway's (Shirley MacLaine) husband Rudyard. After less than ten minutes of on-screen time between 1980 and 1983, Brooks appeared in the poorly received Dudley Moore picture *Unfaithfully Yours*. Vincent Canby called Brooks's performance "attractive," which was some of the rare praise the film found.[35]

After being good in a poor movie, Brooks was, by all accounts, great in a good movie, *Broadcast News* (James L. Brooks, 1987).[36] His Oscar-nominated performance as Aaron Altman found him "very close to stealing" the film from under its Oscar-nominated leads, Holly Hunter and William Hurt, to say nothing of Joan Cusack and Jack Nicholson (Thomas Britt's chapter considers James L. Brooks's film as a key film in understanding Albert Brooks as a comic performer and persona).[37] Aaron Altman represents what might be described as the best-known instance of the Albert Brooks Persona to appear in a Brooks film, except the writer-director is not Albert, but by James L. (no relation). This combination of critical and box office success means that *Broadcast News* represents the most recognizable and memorable Albert Brooks performance to a wide audience. While not quite John Cassavetes acting in films like *The Dirty Dozen* and *Rosemary's Baby* before making *Husbands* and *Minnie and Moskowitz*, Brooks's success in *Broadcast News* opened up a potential one-for-them-one-for-me template that Brooks might pursue in Hollywood.

However, in a repeat of his experience after the success of *Taxi Driver*, Brooks did not appear in another filmmaker's project until seven years after *Broadcast News*. These next two films did not find much success. In the first, he once again worked with James L. Brooks in *I'll Do Anything* (1994), a Hollywood satire that began life as a musical but, after test screenings, became a non-musical.[38] *I'll Do Anything* was a box office flop that didn't do that well with critics either. Brooks garnered praise for his performance as the film producer Burke Adler, in terms of both his performance of interiority—"Brooks is an expert at portraying neurotic frustration"—and physicality—"a rambunctious cartoon."[39] Stanley Kaufman doesn't mention Brooks in his scathing review of the film, which may be testament to the soft spot Kaufman has for him.[40] He also starred in *The Scout*, the first film to cast Brooks as something like a parental figure.[41] In its first half (roughly) *The Scout* feels quite a bit like an Albert Brooks film, owing to its script by Brooks and his frequent writing partner Monica Johnson (Rebecca Bell-Metereau analyses the importance of Johnson to Brooks's career in her chapter). Exiled to Mexico by New York Yankees management, Al updates the Yankees GM Ron Wilson, with a set-up: "Yesterday I saw a game played by five men, two women, a child, and a goat at third base." Ron eagerly replies, "Really? Was the goat any good?" Of course, Al doesn't sign the goat but rather Steve Nebraska, a troubled man-child who can hit and pitch like a modern-day Babe Ruth. Roger Ebert's one-and-a-half-star review begins with the assessment "Rarely does a movie start high and go downhill so fast," but admits that in its opening twenty-five minutes, the film is "brilliant."[42] Much of the credit goes to Brooks; both Ebert and Peter Rainer of the *Los Angeles Times* describe Brooks as the funniest man in movies/America, "when he has the right material."[43] *The Scout* falls apart almost completely in its third act, the product of studio input according to Brooks. As he told Judd Apatow:

> I wrote this movie with Monica Johnson called *The Scout* that Michael Ritchie directed. I can't stand the way it ends, and it was a fight that I lost. I yelled so loud at Peter Chernin, I never worked at Fox again. I lost my temper. I went crazy, and I said, "Look, you're not the one in the paper getting . . ." And, sure enough, *The New York Times*, it was like the reviewer was listening. She said, "I'm so surprised that Albert Brooks would end a movie this way." And I'm going, "Albert Brooks didn't end a movie this way!"[44]

Much like *I'll Do Anything*, *The Scout* was a failure at the box office and did little to expand Brooks's appeal as someone to cast as the lead in a major picture.

Brooks, always billed as A. Brooks, was cast frequently, over many years, in multiple roles, on *The Simpsons* to great success. For anyone who listened to his radio-humor-informed stand-up, the suitability of voice-over work to Brooks's talent would have been obvious. Brooks first appeared in season one (1990) as Jacques, Marge's lothario bowling instructor who defines brunch— "it's not quite breakfast, it's not quite lunch, but it comes with a slice of cantaloupe at the end. You don't get completely what you would at breakfast, but you get a good meal"—with the utmost sincerity through a thick if inconsistent French accent.[45] Later, in season five (1993) Brooks voiced self-help guru Brad Goodman.[46] In *Planet Simpson*, Chris Turner gives an extended analysis of Brooks as Brad Goodman that is worth quoting at length for its attention to Brooks's voice-acting range and ability:

> He gave a sappy, superficial life to Brad Goodman, Springfield's briefly beloved self-help guru. Brooks went for the subtle, slow-burn lampoon rather than broad caricature: his Goodman doesn't ooze insincerity, he just lightly dribbles it . . . Goodman barks, then rapidly reins himself in and continues expounding pop-psychologically. For a moment, his voice hints at self-important rage before returning to polished professional empathy—in the process telling us far more about Goodman's brand of bullshit than a cartoony explosion of anger would have. Through a dozen little touches like these, Brooks created a timeless *Simpsons* character.[47]

The performance that rivals Brad Goodman for quality came in season eight (1996), when Brooks appeared as the Bond-villain-like Hank Scorpio.[48] Turner calls Hank Scorpio Brooks's "real masterwork," and singles out Hank's exit from a scene: "his voice bubbling over with compassion . . . Scorpio tosses a grenade for emphasis . . . 'Homer,' he adds, still empathetic, 'on your way out, if you wanna kill somebody, it would help me a lot.' On the basis of his delivery of this line alone, Brooks' place in *Simpsons* history is secure."[49] Brooks as a comic writer roots a great deal of his humor in the idiolect of the American professional-managerial class (Derek Nystrom places Brooks in the professional-managerial class in his chapter) and the madnesses and hierarchies embedded in it, "his voice mov[es] effortlessly from the we're-all-pals folksiness of the modern executive ('At Globex, we don't believe in walls') to the psychopathic posturing of a James Bond villain bent on world domination (which turns out to be his true goal)."[50]

A combination of frustration and occasional mania over work, usually professional-managerial concerns, represents a significant part of Brooks's career as a voice-over actor-for-hire. After his work in *Terms of Endearment*, and success with *The Simpsons*, Brooks appeared as the depressed tiger Jacob in *Doctor Dolittle* (Thomas, 1998), the businessman in *The Little Prince* (Osborne, 2015), and Tiberius the grumpy red-tailed hawk in *The Secret Life of Pets* (Renaud and Cheney, 2016). Brooks was cast as the anxious single clownfish parent Marlin in the massive box office success *Finding Nemo* (and its sequel *Finding Dory* (Stanton and MacLane, 2016), a film that Dietmar Meinel analyses in depth in his chapter. Brooks also voiced Russ Cargill, a variation on Hank Scorpio, in *The Simpsons Movie* (Silverman, 2007).[51] This attraction and repulsion to professional mores appears in his work in Steven Soderberg's *Out of Sight* (1998), in which Brooks plays Richard Ripley, whose mansion holds a cache of valuable diamonds.[52] In the longest scene Brooks shares with George Clooney, two versions of investment in professional identity and their form of charisma play out. The incredibly charming Jack (Clooney), shot in low angles, always smiling and angling his eyes upward, draws you in. Jack immediately understands that the diamonds are hidden not in a safe, but a fish tank. Jack's a good working thief. Conversely, Richard/Brooks, always shot from above while he half-slouches on expensive furniture, is abrasive and pushes away, spitting out thanks to his former jail cellmates who compliment his house and incredulous that Jack would bear a grudge over a condescending job offer as thanks for help while in prison. Richard is a boss until the end.

Brooks finally played a serious dramatic leading role in Christine Lahti's *My First Mister* (2001).[53] The film got fair reviews, with some mention of Brooks's being "quieter and more relaxed than usual" "in a nice, quietly uncharacteristic performance."[54] At the other end of the tonal spectrum, Brooks starred alongside Michael Douglas in the loud, broad, ill-considered box office failure *The In-Laws* (Fleming 2003), a remake of the 1979 Arthur Hiller movie with Peter Falk and Alan Arkin.[55] In the Alan Arkin role Brooks does as well as he can. Mick LaSalle's review admits that "it's always a pleasure to watch Brooks get mentally tortured."[56] For the purposes of this collection, a second bit of LaSalle's praise for Brooks deserves attention: he writes that Brooks plays Jerry "with his patented misery, dread and disdain."[57] At the time *The In-Laws* was released, Brooks had appeared in fewer than twenty films, and in more than half of them he was in a supporting role at most. But in those few film performances Brooks established a recognizable, "patented" identity.

With LaSalle's invocation of the Brooks persona being well established by 2003, the assessment *TV Guide* made of Brooks's casting on the show *Weeds* (2005–12) rings true: "They wanted a 'name' and they got one."[58] Brooks played Lenny Botwin, the father of Nancy Botwin, the suburban widow drug dealer's father-in-law. Brooks's performance has something familiar at its base: a frustration with his surroundings and an armor of ironic distance. Two factors are new: drugs and Jewishness. Outside of some Quaaludes in *Modern Romance* (covered in Enid Stubin's chapter), drugs don't play a big part in Brooks's films. Similarly, jokes about Brooks's Jewishness are not a staple in his thirty-some other roles. But his *Weeds* appearance—probably thirty minutes of screen time total—features pervasive drug references and stereotypical notions of Jewishness. He complains that his son didn't marry a doctor; he speaks some Yiddish, calling his son a gonif, his grandson a schmendrick, and translates his dying mother's Yiddish last words; and he sits shiva for his dead mother. In his last episode, the Jewish humor starts to curdle: he sends his "shiva goy" to buy a lottery ticket with the numbers tattooed on his mother when she was in a concentration camp; he describes the appeal of his house as "we're a block from the beach. There's a charter school right down the street. There isn't a shvartsa in sight"; he tells his grandson that genocide "must never again happen *to Jews*. What do I give a shit about other places?" The credits to his final episode even feature a star of David turning into a pot leaf and chapter titles with Hebrew letters. Brooks appears to be enjoying his chance to play a character who is barely likable even compared to his family members who smother old women in their sleep. The character Lenny retains an ironic distance from pretty much everything that's happening, balancing getting laughs with playing the necessary foil and heel to Nancy. In a scene in which he recalls his mother before she was dying and bedridden, Lenny tells his grandsons, "It's a shame you boys never got to know her," with sadness and regret in his voice. After a very brief pause he begins the next sentence brightly: "But you can blame your mother for that!" A four-episode guest spot on a cable television program seems to be the fulfilment of Brooks's dream in the early 1970s: he'd finally become an actor, someone who could take the material given to him and make it better through his performance.

In his mid-sixties Brooks appeared in a number of dramatic supporting roles, appearing in *Drive* (Refn 2011), *A Most Violent Year* (Chandor 2014), and *Concussion* (Landesman 2015) (Tom Ue's chapter considers late-career Brooks in detail).[59] Being cast against type as the tough gangster Bernie Rose in *Drive* brought Brooks a great deal of acclaim, and he won a raft of awards for his performance, including the African American Film Critics Association, New York Film Critics Circle, and National Society of Film Critics award for best supporting actor, among others. The Oscar eluded him—he wasn't even nominated.[60] Not that he dwelt on it. On Oscar night 2017, when the Best Picture Oscar was briefly and erroneously given to *La La Land* (Chazelle, 2016) instead of *Moonlight* (Jenkins, 2016), Brooks tweeted out, "Because of tonight's horrible Oscar mistake I have retained a lawyer to see if I won for DRIVE."[61] Scott Tobias does not see Bernie as a departure from Brooks's career, writing that:

> It's a mistake to think of Brooks as some weak-willed neurotic, given to the sort of mild self-effacement associated with Woody Allen or other screen comics of that ilk. From the beginning of his career as writer-director-star—and often in roles for hire—Brooks has committed to putting himself under harsh light, mercilessly exposing his own characters for their vanity, jealousy, cruelty, and compromise.[62]

No moment in the film captures this lack of self-effacement than one of its most obvious: when Driver meets Bernie. As Bernie waits to shake his hand, Driver says, "my hands are a little dirty," to which Bernie replies "so are mine." The timing of Brooks's delivery changes the line from a punchline into a threat. Through such slight changes to his timing and delivery, Brooks creates a performance in which, "there's no self-deprecation, no neuroses, no eagerness to please or make himself understood. He's simply the type of person who can stab a guy with a fork without thinking twice about it."[63]

Judd Apatow's *This Is 40* features Brooks in a role that makes him a father to multiple generations of comic performers.[64] In addition to his older, grown son Pete played by Apatow stand-in Paul Rudd, Brooks also has a set of toddler triplets (whom he commands to perform as the Three Stooges) he admits he can't tell apart. In Brooks's work, pathos can often seem far away. It may be that because Brooks often plays a supporting character, and it's hard to pity characters like Aaron Altman, who bemoan the unfairness of life in such selfish terms. But there is a sadness in both the character and Brooks's performance of *This Is 40*'s Larry, an old man screaming at the planes that fly over his house every eight minutes to "drop something valuable!" Not entirely comfortable with his grown son but financially dependent on him, Larry tells Pete "your mother wanted you aborted" to stop Pete from cutting off financial support. Dismissive of an even younger generation of "his own," to the point of jokingly yelling "line up for murder," *This Is 40* shows Albert Brooks's slightly uneasy relationship with the comic generations that followed him. In the case of Rudd/Apatow, both *The 40-Year-Old Virgin* and *Knocked Up* made more money on their own than all of Brooks's movies combined. As for the toddlers, for some reason Brooks is still around, suddenly finding himself with identical kids in a pool, unable to tell one from the other, as if they were all clownfish with identical markings.

The list of filmmakers with whom Brooks has worked is impressive: Oscar-winners James L. Brooks, Christine Lahti, Sidney Lumet, Martin Scorsese, and Steven Soderbergh, Oscar nominee J. C. Chandor, and Cannes award-winner Nicolas Wending Refn. Box office successes Michael Ritchie (in the 1970s), John Landis (the 1980s), Judd Apatow (the 2000s), Chris Renaud, (the 2010s), and Pixar/Andrew Stanton (the 1990s–2010s). And *The Simpsons* during their 1990s heyday. Outside of the critical box office success stories, Brooks has worked with Andrew Fleming, the director of interesting if flawed comedies like *Dick* (1999) and *Hamlet 2* (2008), steady studio hands Betty Thomas and Howard Zieff, and investigative reporter turned director Peter Landesman. With perhaps the exception of *Drive* and *A Most Violent Year*, all of Brooks's actor-for-hire work establishes a screen persona of a middle-class, professional-managerial type, and develops further contours to that identity as his career progresses. I would now like to turn to a more detailed consideration of Albert Brooks films and the persona that they create for their writer-director-star, and why that persona offers useful entry points to understanding Hollywood film and American culture from the 1970s through the 2010s.

ALBERT BROOKS AS A WRITER-DIRECTOR-ACTOR

It's a little difficult to define exactly what kind of comedy Albert Brooks's films are. Meta-comedy? Anti-comedy? Romantic comedy? Comic horror? Brooks was the lead—or at least the co-lead—in every film that he wrote. Writing for and then directing himself makes Brooks's films function as star vehicles. As Frank Krutnik writes in his introduction to *Hollywood Comedians, the Film Reader*, "All Hollywood star vehicles must mediate between a fictionally specific character identity and a star image that circulates beyond the boundaries of the particular film, and beyond cinema itself. Comedian comedy exacerbates this tension, however, because its prime rationale is to provide a show-case for the star performer."[65] From the early 1970s Brooks developed a persona, and that persona recurs throughout his actor-for-hire work. In his own films, the identity first established in *A Star Is Bought* and *Comedy Minus One* and *Tonight Show* appearances remains, with further shadings appearing with each new film. As Thomas Britt's chapter will make clear, Brooks was always a little ahead of the comedy game. He was, according to Tom Teicholz,

> the first of his contemporary comedians to play an eponymous lead character. Since then, a number of actors and celebrities, such Kareen [sic] Abdul Jabbar in Airplane or Neil Patrick Harris in the Harold and Kumar series, have played themselves, and a generation of stand-ups such as Garry Shandling, Jerry Seinfeld, Larry David and, more recently, Amy Schumer, Abbi Jacobson and Ilana Glazer play versions of themselves on screen. But Brooks was there first.[66]

So first we must ask, who was Albert Brooks playing? One of his strongest partisans, Scott Tobias, describes the figure that emerges out of Brooks's film performances of himself:

> "Albert Brooks" seems like its creator's worst image of himself—that of a callow entertainer who pretends to genius, but will happily do what it takes to reach a large, adoring audience instead. In that respect, it's a mark of Brooks' integrity that he's never really reached that audience himself, perhaps because he so doggedly resists their affection.[67]

Obviously, the resistance to affection within the films generates its own kind of appeal that has, in fact, created an adoring audience (however small it may be compared to his contemporaries). But he'd really rather have a larger audience even though it would certainly make him even more miserable. What prevents this from happening is that Brooks has a way of "bringing . . . every weakness into the light."[68] Gavin Smith described the Brooks persona as "smugly self-confident, oblivious to its own absurdity . . . supremely assured yet inept."[69] That is to say, the Albert Brooks Persona is not flawed at the beginning and improved or at least polished at the end. He remains deeply imperfect and unaware (with the exception of *Defending Your Life*, although he's dead when he learns), a version of *Seinfeld*/Larry David's "No hugging. No learning" motto *avant la lettre*.

Such a persona—"a guy who's smart, sarcastic, self-obsessed and all too well aware that he inspires complete indifference in most people"—creates problems in categorizing Brooks films.[70] What Krutnik calls comedian comedy, "deals consistently with relations between norms and deviance. Generally cast as an outsider or misfit in some way, the comedian presents a spectacle of otherness by serving as a conduit for energies that are marginal, non-normative or antisocial."[71] The exact opposite is the case with Brooks. Without fail he appears as the opposite of an outsider or misfit, as someone deeply invested in the maintenance of norms. Even his rebellion is by the book, as in *Lost in America* (Brooks, 1985). Dave Kehr offers one possible explanation why Brooks can be so rule-bound and yet at the center of a comedian comedy:

> Brooks always appears in his films as a character who makes his living from the manipulation of reality—a documentary filmmaker, a feature film editor, two advertising men. Yet it is the ultimate impermeability of reality, its stubborn resistance to change and influence, that brings his characters low, throwing off the rhetorical structures they have tried to project upon it.[72]

Someone involved in the manipulation of reality has to know what the agreed-upon reality of the world is. Furthermore, a good filmmaker will know the way to make a classical Hollywood picture but can do something else. In my discussion of *The Scout* above, I noted that Roger Ebert and Peter Rainer called Brooks the funniest man in movies. Dave Kehr was way ahead of them. Writing in 1991, at the release of *Defending Your Life*, Kehr wrote, "That Albert Brooks is the funniest American alive isn't a proposition that needs much arguing. The evidence is on the screen."[73] Kehr makes the case for Brooks as a great director who makes comedies:

> But that Brooks is also a filmmaker of great formal innovation is less obvious. He has probably done more to alter the basic grammar of American film than any director since John Cassavetes, though his contributions are anything but flashy and conspicuous. Brooks' originality, in fact, lies in the opposite direction, in the stripping away of all artifice, of all traditional rhetoric, of all the enforced rhythms and familiar structures of film comedy.[74]

James Slaymaker, writing almost thirty years later, offers an enumeration of Brooks's directorial signature:

Clumsy motion within banal, enclosed spaces; long takes that call attention to their own duration; avoidance of non-diegetic sound; minimalist compositions; off-rhythms; sluggish (though precise) comic pacing; and a lack of reaction shots and/or reverse angles.[75]

The two scenes that showcase this style are his argument with Linda at the Hoover Dam in *Lost in America* and his conversation with his State Department handler at the Taj Majal in *Looking for Comedy in the Muslim World*.[76] A single minute-long tracking shot follows Brooks, his assistant Maya, and Stewart as they walk past the Taj Majal, Stewart offering extensive notes, Brooks resisting them, and no one ever looking at the mausoleum that takes up the background. In addition, the expense and trouble of going on location to the Hoover Dam or to the Taj Majal and wrangling all the tourists to make sure that a long take in long, traveling shot comes off—rather than to show off the gorgeous location—plays a joke on the institutional reasons to film on location, foremost among them, the location's visual and cultural appeal. The scenes seem to be dialogue-driven, but the contrast between the amount of dialogue and almost total lack of location-shot spectacle is a consistently deployed bit of comic media critique. The mismatch of the sort of filmmaker who would make such films and a studio comedy director is the ongoing friction of Brooks's career, both in aesthetic and box office terms.

Writing in the early stages of Brooks's film career, Paul Slansky bemoaned

> The fact that Brooks' admirers think he's a genius is irrelevant to the oilmen, real-estate tycoons and soda bottlers who now run the studios. To them, he is merely unbankable . . . Brooks has avoided the pitfalls of mass acceptance by avoiding that acceptance. At 35, after 16 years in the business, he is still not quite a star.[77]

Brooks never quite managed to be a star, but he kept finding work because his presence offered something to films that other performers didn't. In what follows I provide a brief overview of his short films for PBS and *Saturday Night Live*, his feature films *Real Life, Modern Romance, Lost in America, Defending Your Life, Mother, The Muse, Looking for Comedy in the Muslim World*, his novel *Twenty Thirty: The Real Story of What Happens to America*, and his Twitter account to describe the Albert Brooks Persona. This persona provides an access point to the political undercurrents of his work and their overall meaning in American culture, which the eleven chapters in this collection consider in more depth.

Brooks's first film was for PBS; working from an article he wrote for *Esquire*, he made "Albert Brooks' Famous School for Comedians" for *The Great American Dream Machine* series in 1972 (Jeff Menne's chapter deals with

Brooks's short films in detail).[78] The film opens with Brooks directly addressing the camera and turning to the "camera two" position ahead of cuts. The trade school that Brooks offers a filmed tour of breaks comedy into component parts. The pie-throwing class, for example, shows how to execute the gag well. The sequence presents comedy training as a version of the gladiator training sequence in *Spartacus* (Kubrick, 1960), with the instructor showing the three highest-comedy-value places to hit someone, marking his student's neck "3," cheek "2," and nose "1." This combination of an abstract approach to the craft and careful attention to film form (and film history) continues throughout Brooks's career. A few years later Brooks was offered the permanent host position at *Saturday Night Live* (*SNL*), which he turned down. Instead of performing live in New York, he wrote and directed six short films for the show. In the short "Sick in Bed," Brooks calls in sick from doing a short film, and in doing so runs through a native advertising routine for his own record and also wonders what the difference is between roasted and broasted (broasted is fried under pressure). While the "Mid-Season Replacement Shows" short is clearly about the finished product in the entertainment industry, "Sick in Bed" goes behind the scenes to the degree that Albert singles out a film processor, not exactly the first job that comes to mind in film production, for special attention. "Sick in Bed" works a lot like Brooks's "no new material" routine in that he makes a show of not just the material performed, but of the process required to get there, which tends to be a little less polished than what ends up on screen. The process is polished by experts "The National Audience Research Institute," in which Albert uses the scientific method to be sure audiences will like his routines.[79]

Like "Famous School for Comedians," and his *SNL* shorts "Mid-Season Replacement Shows" and "The National Audience Research Institute," *Real Life* (1979), shows a sustained interest in the scientific verification of comedy and the behind-the-scenes aspects of the media industry.[80] A comic response to the 1973 television show *An American Family*, which followed the Loud family through their daily routine and eventual breakdown, *Real Life* begins with Albert Brooks explaining the film's genesis as a combination of social science and entertainment—a search for "the one family unit that could reflect day-to-day living in contemporary America and, at the same time, hold a motion picture audience completely spellbound"—and speculating on how this advance in science and film could "not only have a chance at winning an Oscar, but possibly a Nobel Prize too. Ooh. It gives me the chills." On the one hand, such a dream is ridiculous on its face. However, in the context of *An American Family*, about which the anthropologist Margaret Mead claimed "may be as important for our time as were the invention of drama and the novel for earlier generations: a new way to help people understand themselves," the joke is more strongly rooted in 1979's media-literate reality than that of 2020.[81] With what

Janet Maslin describes as "absolute insincerity and irrational good cheer"[82] Brooks establishes his character as someone who dreams of achievement as if it is his right, and prestige, abilities, and temperament be damned. Dreams of Nobel Prizes disappear from Brooks's works after *Real Life*, but the middle-class arts worker who believes in the American myth of success remains (this idea is further developed in the chapter "When Success is Failure.") Writing in the week before the 2016 US presidential election that put a reality show star to the White House, Tom Teicholz praises the far-sightedness of the film:

> Yet if we see humor in the self-seriousness of the participants and delight in the outrageousness of their antics, if we see the irony in the genre's ability to produce stars (and even presidential candidates!) and acknowledge it as part of "show business" — then we'd do well to recall that these insights have already been abundantly elucidated in Albert Brooks' prescient 1979 debut feature film, *Real Life*.[83]

It may have been less than successful as a Hollywood production, but as a prescient piece of media criticism *Real Life* delivered. Although *Real Life* made almost no money at the box office, it slowly gained recognition as one of the very first, and accordingly, significant mockumentary films, and a degree of critical regard followed. The critic Jonathan Rosenbaum included *Real Life* in his "Alternate One Hundred" response to the AFI's Top 100 films list from 1999.[84] And so in the first decade of his career, Brooks's 1970s films set the baseline for his persona, a professional, middle-class media worker driven to succeed and a believer in a scientific approach to his chosen field. The romantic problems were soon to come.

After burning down a house to save his movie, Brooks's second film, *Modern Romance*, took that unsettling darkness even further.[85] Gavin Smith and James Slaymaker both register the unsettlingly obsessive nature of Robert Cole (Brooks), with Smith describing the film as "A truly terrifying comedy."[86] Scott Tobias compares Robert Cole (Brooks) to "Jake LaMotta in *Raging Bull*, only his inner turmoil manifests itself in stalking and passive-aggression instead of bloody fisticuffs. Both films are insightful about men's ugliest, most primal feelings about women, and both are equally bruising."[87] *Modern Romance* contrasts the lightness of its (apparent) genre, the romantic comedy, with the wages of the lessons the genre imparts. Slaymaker roots the discomfort in Brooks's performance in the way the genre has informed expectations of gender performance:

> Bob's absolute lack of self-awareness blinds him to just how creepy and domineering his actions truly are, as well as the role social conditioning plays in enabling men like Bob to indulge in their worst tendencies

without facing significant consequences—a form of social conditioning Brooks connects to the gender imbalance endemic in the romantic comedy genre, which the structure of *Modern Romance* slyly subverts."[88]

Or, as *The Onion* sums up a common reading of the rom-com: "Romantic-Comedy Behavior Gets Real-Life Man Arrested."[89] In his performance of Robert,

> Brooks doesn't shy away from the fact his character is a shit, but the portrait of his grief, paranoia, and the nature of a romantic rebound is effectively painful nevertheless. The director himself is a suffocating onscreen presence, from the way his character looks at Mary to the way he naturally speaks: Brooks talks from the back of his mouth rather than from the tongue—a kind of negative energy source, a hole that sucks the dryness from a room. It's very claustrophobic."[90]

Such a combination of abstract engagement with the gender politics of a genre and a performance calibrated to unsettle and disturb make *Modern Romance* what J. Hoberman calls a "feel-bad" movie "that would seem to verge on anti-entertainment."[91] The couple doesn't get together—or at least stay together—at the end. Going past deferral of pleasure to denial of it may have contributed to the film's trouble at the box office.

Lost in America is Brooks's best-known film, a film that wasn't too ahead of the curve like *Real Life* or antagonistic to a Hollywood audience like *Modern*

Figure 1.2 *Lost in America*: dropping out responsibly

Romance, but still pushed the edges of Hollywood comedy. David and Linda Howard are both successful professionals. He's in advertising; she's in personnel. Infuriated after being passed over for a promotion, David convinces Linda to sell their house, buy a Winnebago, and hit the road like *Easy Rider*. Among *Lost in America*'s key images is the sight of a biker giving the waving David the finger, resolutely refusing his gesture of solidarity. In brief, David and Linda (mostly David) believe they can have it all, the freedom of a job-free life on the road but the cushion of a lot of money in the bank. David claims that "I can be more responsible because I'll be in a position of responsibility."

But even after he gets passed over for promotion and quits, as does Linda, "[t]hey can't drop out of society. They *are* society."[92] David spends most of the movie delivering "splendidly stupid soliloquies and delightful self-deception," putting the contradictions of middle-class life in the 1980s on harsh display.[93] In a discussion of Las Vegas on film, in the section "Snobs," John Powers singles out *Lost in America* for its ability to see the way Las Vegas stages one aspect of American class politics clearly:

> those with social pretensions have always looked down on the city, viewing it as something of a game preserve for proles. Since American ideology discourages overt references to class, the movies have largely overlooked such snobbery. The one exception is Albert Brooks' great comedy *Lost in America* . . . [with] the casino manager, smiling with amused, almost admiring disbelief that this coddled middle-class twit thinks that he can talk his way out of anything.[94]

Derek Nystrom's chapter covers a great deal of ground with regards to class politics in the film, so I will briefly note that class dynamics in the form of David's haughty snobbery are never far from the surface, even on superficial matters such as Brad's bad suit or Mercedes leather as opposed to real leather, or the social hierarchy of the right and wrong sorts of gamblers.

Writing in 2014, Nathan Rabin makes the case for a career-retrospective box set for Brooks, placing him alongside Elaine May as comic directors who deserve greater respect and a place in the pop canon.[95] In an answer to Rabin's prayers, *Lost in America* was added to the Criterion Collection in July 2017. In the essay for the film's release, Scott Tobias argues that, "the Brooks of *Lost in America*, and *Modern Romance* and *Real Life* before it, has no interest in ingratiating himself with the audience, which may explain why these movies struggled so much at the box office."[96] After securing critical regard with his first three films, Brooks wrote his most financially successful film, the post-mortem romantic comedy *Defending Your Life* (Frank Percaccio's chapter analyses the film in concert with Dante's *Purgatorio*).[97] In it, Brooks plays the ad man Daniel Miller, who dies in a car accident on his birthday and finds himself in the antiseptic afterlife of Judgment City, where he must watch movies of his life as part of the "examining period" to determine if he can "move forward," which is to say use more than three percent of his brain and overcome fear. In an afterlife run "along the lines that would be recommended by a good MBA program," Daniel learns about not just the life that just ended, but also his previous lives. Playing a dead character doesn't change the broad outlines of the Albert Brooks Persona. Daniel shows a keen interest in what the rules and workings of the examination system are, asking what the normal or required actions are to move forward.

On his second night in Judgment City, Daniel meets Julia (Meryl Streep), a woman who died in a pool accident. Meryl Streep was the first significant star cast in a Brooks film; *Defending Your Life* came during the five years when Streep showed she could do comic roles—*She-Devil* (Seidelman, 1989), *Postcards from the Edge* (Nichols, 1990), *Death Becomes Her* (Zemeckis, 1992)—and action roles—*The River Wild* (Hanson, 1994)—just as well as dramatic roles. As Julia, Streep "softens her thespian exoskeleton for a surprisingly engaging performance"[98] and has "never been more natural."[99] The script (Brooks working without his usual writing partner Monica Johnson) makes Julia almost unbelievably kind, generous, and fearless. Though both Brooks and Streep are known for their cerebral qualities, the physical performances were noted at the film's release. Often shot in soft lighting with a touch of backlighting to give her a slight halo, Streep's Julia frequently laughs with such force that it jolts Daniel out of his usual slumped posture and furrowed brow. As for Brooks, "he's a virtuoso of facial reactions. As he battles two judges and a determined

Figure 1.3 A face that registers "all the known emotions"

prosecutor for his spiritual life, he seems to register all the known emotions; embarrassment happens to be his specialty."[100]

While it doesn't take much imagination to see the appeal of a Meryl Streep comedy-romance to an adult audience, *Defending Your Life* had a broader appeal, at least in test market showings. In a twenty-five-year anniversary piece, Brooks recalls that:

> All of my movies had to go through the normal testing processes, and I never got *E.T.*-type test scores. From *Real Life* to *Modern Romance*, some of the cards were like, "What's wrong with this person?" So it was funny because [*Defending Your Life*] got like a B+ overall, but it got an A+ from young people.[101]

If Brooks made inroads with a younger audience with *Defending Your Life*, his next film, appears to have sought out a different audience: those familiar with 1950s and 1960s Hollywood cinema. In *Mother* (1996) Brooks plays a middle-aged science-fiction writer going through a second divorce.[102] He moves back in with his mother, convinced that only by sorting out his relationship with her can he hope to have successful relationships in the future. The casting for the role of his mother, Beatrice Henderson, was offered to Doris Day and Nancy Reagan, neither of whom had been on screen in more than twenty-five years. Both Day and Reagan turned the role down and Debbie Reynolds, who had spent the last twenty or so years performing on stage and in small roles on television, got the part (and a Golden Globe nomination). Among the top 100 box office films of 1996,[103] only one featured a woman older than Reynolds in a significant role: Lauren Bacall in *The Mirror Has Two Faces* (Streisand, 1996). There were plenty of men around Reynolds's age, including Robert Redford (as a romantic lead) in *Up Close and Personal* (Avnet, 1996). While Brooks delivers a number of one-liners, he mostly plays straight man to Reynolds's performance. David Canfield writes that:

> Over her career, Reynolds proved herself not just as a movie star with killer singing chops and dancing skills. She also proved to be a great—perhaps even underrated—film actress. There's no better example than *Mother*... Reynolds is unsparing in capturing that understated menace, while also careful in getting to the heart of it.[104]

John may have the more obvious gotcha lines, but it's Reynolds's combination of slightly overstated Studio-era dialogue delivery and subtle physical performance that carries the film. At a shopping trip to the Golden Gate Galleria mall, John says he wants to go to a store called, "Tell It All. You go in and you tell them your most personal secrets." Beatrice looks at him suspiciously and says, "you're joking." When John replies with a "yeah" that talks down to her, Beatrice, never taking her look away from John, says, "if only your writing were that real," before exposing a tiny grin a moment before a cut. The withering sarcasm directed at John's professional competence gives the scene its laugh, but the grin at the end shows that Beatrice—who will be shown to have given up a writing career when she became a mother—shows that the barb isn't entirely personal; writing good dialogue for a character could be her business too.

A two-hander starring someone who hasn't been on screen in a couple of decades is not your average follow-up to your first (very modest) hit, nor is the trailer to *The Muse* your average trailer.[105] Albert walks out in front of a large movie screen, introduces himself, and starts to describe the film and the trailer in a single minute-and-fifteen-second take in a long long shot. The science of comedy returns, as Brooks explains that he worked with NASA, The National Institute of Human Behavior (from *Real Life*), and Harvard night school to create a trailer style that could capture how funny *The Muse* is. What follows is a sped-up version of the film with Brooks providing matching cartoonishly fast gibberish dialogue and commentary like "gee, Sharon's good there." Albert wraps up the trailer with a hard sell:

> Now according to our researchers, you should not only want to see this film in real time, you're actually going to have to. Your brain is now in what science calls a wound state. If you don't see this material slowly, you could go insane, or die, or even worse.

The trailer may be the least-cut trailer of the 1990s, with only four cuts in two and a half minutes if we don't count the hyper-sped-up film that Brooks narrates. It also operates almost entirely in long shots, without any close-ups, and only a single, second-long medium shot. Deploying his full arsenal of scientifically based comedy, radio-show-style humor, and formal convention avoidance, Brooks promises a self-aware film business satire, which is what *The Muse* is.

The Muse is also a testament to Brooks's strange position in Hollywood, well regarded by peers for his talent but distrusted by the studios because his movies don't make any money. Sharon Stone was a recent Oscar nominee for *Casino* looking to show she could do comedy, and Jeff Bridges was by the late 1990s already in the "when will he win an Oscar" stage of his career. Rob Reiner, James Cameron, and Martin Scorsese all provide cameos as themselves, or at least the versions of themselves who need a muse to continue to succeed in Hollywood. Fellow actors and directors all seemed to be happy to sign on to a Brooks film. Paramount, on the other hand, dropped *The Muse* after another backstage Hollywood comedy, *Burn Hollywood Burn* (Hiller/Smithee 1997), did very poorly at the box office. The explanation that the genre was out of fashion partially explains the decision; Brooks's track record of modest at best box office results explains the rest.

The Muse explains Hollywood success as the product of working with a muse (Stone). Steven Phillips's (Brooks) screenwriter friend Jack (Bridges) has had a string of successes working with her, as have directors like Scorsese and Cameron. Because Steven is less willing to give his muse the extravagant gifts she requires, he doesn't meet with Steven Spielberg but rather his cousin Stan Spielberg. Decoupling success from talent and merit, *The Muse* is a gentle satire on Hollywood. The frequent comparison for *The Muse* is Robert Altman's *The Player* (1992), but Mike Higgins argues that "Brooks can only yet dream of Altman's complexity and assurance."[106] Coming almost a decade later, "to say that [*The Muse*] is the best satire Hollywood has produced in years only shows the unwillingness of Steven's hated studio executives to produce comedies that are more strongly spiced."[107]

While the trailer for the film continues Brooks's fascination with the faux-quantification of comedy and shows some formal daring, the tone of *The Muse* was softer than Brooks's previous films. Whereas the film editor Robert Cole in *Modern Romance* had a small dingy apartment, Steven in *The Muse* has a large and nicely decorated house in Pacific Palisades (probably in the same neighborhood as Larry David). Steven has been financially and professionally successful, but that success moves further into the past every day, something Josh, the producer at Paramount tells him right before he releases Steven from his three-picture deal. Every time one of his friends or colleagues mentions a success—usually thanks to Sarah the muse—pain flashes across Steven's face. At least Daniel Miller died a comically undignified death, run over by a bus while searching the footwell of a BMW for a CD case. In the end, *The Muse* considers the pains of relative affluence. Coming from someone from "a long line of comic auteurs willing to play protagonists subject to wild humiliation,"[108] the humiliation of an awkward interview with Steven Spielberg's nephew or of becoming the and-one of his newly successful-in-business wife is much less pointed.

After *The Muse* Brooks appeared in a big Hollywood action comedy, *The In-Laws*, and had his greatest box office success as the voice of Marlin in *Finding Nemo*. After these two major Hollywood productions he made his last film as a writer-director-star (at the time of writing). Brooks began his directing career playing a showbiz version of himself, "Albert Brooks," in *Real Life* and he didn't return to that character until what Scott Tobias called the "misunderstood 2005 flop, *Looking For Comedy In The Muslim World*."[109] Like *The Muse*, *Looking for Comedy in the Muslim World* gently satirizes Hollywood and has "Albert Brooks" facing many of the same questions of relative affluence. However, *Looking for Comedy in the Muslim World* critiques US foreign policy in a way that is rare in Hollywood movies. To begin with, the Hollywood satire *Looking for Comedy in the Muslim World* mocks the way Brooks doesn't quite fit in Hollywood by showing the entirety of his audition for Penny Marshall's planned remake of *Harvey*: in sixty seconds Brooks enters, tries to ingratiate himself with Marshall, fails, and leaves without the role. (Penny Marshall's in-film assessment aside, Brooks's experience in one-person phone-call scenes and radio comedy point towards an interesting performance against an imaginary rabbit). Left without any positive job prospects, Albert takes an interview with the State Department for a job determining what makes the Muslim world laugh. With a 500-page report hanging over his head, Albert goes to India accompanied by two State Department flacks, hires an assistant, and tries to discover what makes people laugh.

Formally speaking, the editing of concert films creates an affinity between performer and audience. The comedian performs, and the reaction shots of the audience show laughter and enjoyment. *The Original Kings of Comedy* (Lee, 2000) and *Blue Collar Comedy Tour: The Movie* (Harding, 2003) both create an affinity between performers and audience, even though one is directed by the film-school-trained, prestige-film maker Spike Lee and the other by the reality-television-trained C. B. Harding. Brooks as a director does the opposite in *Looking for Comedy in the Muslim World*. He creates a debacle of a performance in its setting, an auditorium with house lights that resemble daylight; in editing, cutting to bewildered and silent audience members; and in misfiring dialogue, when the audience members who do connect with the performer/Albert on stage, find their suggestions ignored completely. In an Albert Brooks movie, affection is never a two-way street in comedy performances; comics all die alone. The comedian dying on stage cut against a blank-faced audience is a consistent throughout Brooks's work—from his first film *Real Life*'s opening number through *Defending Your Life*'s visit to Judgment City's comedy club to his last film. Only after sneaking across the India-Pakistan border to perform around a campfire with a group of hash-smoking Pakistani comics does Brooks allow himself a friendly audience. In a nice bit of career symmetry, after word gets out of his border-crossing performance—not just to Pakistani and Indian intelligence, but also to Al Jazeera—Albert gets excited and returns to the dream first mention in *Real Life*: "Oh my God! Do you know what this means? . . . This is how you win a Nobel Prize." A comedian who is not funny, having discussions of "bombing" with Iranian men, plays a role in escalating tensions to put India and Pakistan on the brink of nuclear exchange, then goes home. The film ends in the relative affluence of his Los Angeles home, and while a strings version of "America the Beautiful" plays, his wife toasts him as "the Henry Kissinger of comedy," the model for the Nobel Prize winner Albert would be for his efforts. *Looking for Comedy in the Muslim World* tries very hard, in not just its stand-up comedy scenes but nearly all its scenes to refuse any affinity between performers and audience, to the point of its ending of nuclear war as the logical consequence of American blundering on the subcontinent.

Perhaps unsurprisingly, *Looking for Comedy in the Muslim World* did poorly at the box office and its reviews were mixed. Most reviews, after making some sort of statement about how a Brooks movie is welcome at any time, spend a lot of time looking for and at the film's comedy. The review from *Entertainment Weekly*'s Owen Gleiberman provides a harsh one-sentence summary: "Albert Brooks journeys to India and Pakistan to learn what makes the Muslims of the world laugh, but the film lacks a genuine — or funny — point of view."[110] The film gets called "only half of a good comedy,"[111] "decidedly hit-and-miss,"[112] and "an extended joke that drags on."[113] Roger Ebert offers the faint praise, "I liked the movie. I smiled a lot."[114] A. O. Scott, who five years later made a video praising *Lost in America*, writes that *Looking for Comedy in the Muslim World* "tiptoes across a minefield of political sensitivities on its way to a handful of pretty good jokes. Unfortunately, there are not quite enough of those to carry an audience through 98 minutes."[115] It could be that Brooks made a covertly overtly political movie, and that did not compute for most critics. Too accustomed to Brooks's deconstruction of generic convention and film form, we might say cultural politics, an Albert Brooks movie with an interest in geopolitics seems unreadable. Peter Travers writes that "Brooks makes sure the joke is always on the obtuse version of himself that he's playing, and by extension every American who stays willfully blind to other cultures."[116] Scott Tobias argues:

> What critics didn't understand about the film is that its barbs are aimed more at the Brooks persona than anything to do with politics or even cultural differences. The mission of the title is as hilariously compromised as the movie-within-a-movie in *Real Life*, and entirely a reflection of "Albert Brooks" narcissism and lack of integrity. (The fact that he doesn't really go deep into the Muslim world is a feature, not a flaw.)[117]

In such a reading, Brooks's earlier work makes the political critique of *Looking for Comedy in the Muslim World* both possible and even more forceful. James Slaymaker spells out this critique in some detail:

> Brooks sees the U.S. not as a global superpower built on imperialistic violence, but a benevolent force concerned with establishing stability and order. It is this narrow-minded worldview which blinds Brooks to the true nature of the quest he's been assigned, whose true aim is not to heal the rift between different cultures but rather to employ soft power as a means to enable America's cultural and economic expansion and the protection of its strategic global position. Fortunately, the real Brooks is scathingly critical of such ethnocentrism, and the result is his darkest, most haunting work."[118]

To make a film darker than *Modern Romance* represents something of an accomplishment. This is not to say that *Looking for Comedy in the Muslim World* is Brooks's best work. Rather it represents what might have been had Brooks pursued a late-career turn that combined his interest in comic form with more overtly political subject. There have been no new Albert Brooks movies, political or not, but there have been an Albert Brooks novel, *Twenty Thirty: The Real Story of What Happens to America*, and @AlbertBrooks on social media, both of which engage with US politics quite directly.

NOVEL AND TWITTER

Brooks films are West Coast films. He gets as far as Arizona in *Real Life* and *Lost in America*, but *Modern Romance*, *Defending Your Life*, *Mother*, *The Muse*, and *Looking for Comedy in the Muslim World* are all set California. And outside of Beatrice Henderson's house in the Bay area, California here means Los Angeles. Brooks makes the earthquake-driven destruction of Los Angeles the centerpiece of his first novel, *Twenty Thirty: The Real Story of What Happens to America* (hereafter *2030*).[119] Mike Davis writes that, "The obliteration of Los Angeles ... is often depicted as, or at least secretly experienced as, a victory *for* civilization."[120] In the frequent novels and films that imagine it, the apocalypse would make the greatest improvement to Los Angeles. But whereas the bulk of Los Angeles-destroying narratives purge the United States of a poisoned appendage, Brooks imagines a United States already in severe decline and an earthquake that demands lateral thinking if the city—and by extension the nation—is to be salvaged. Los Angeles doesn't slide into Arizona Bay, but its near-apocalyptic destruction creates a dystopic zone within an already-decaying United States.

Brooks's United States teeters on the cusp of becoming a former global hegemon, and a Los Angeles earthquake instigates the end game. *2030*'s vision of the future speaks to the tensions of domestic politics in the Obama era it was written in—health care costs, crumbling infrastructure, and debt: "It had always been warned that the giant debt would fall to them, but until it actually did, young people still held out hope for the American dream. Once they were being taxed higher, earning less, and receiving less government assistance than their parents, the resentment level soared."[121] In Brooks's fictional world, "almost three trillion dollars was just going to pay the *interest* on the national debt. There was no longer room for any meaningful programs; it seemed that the president's job was just to keep the ship afloat."[122] The decline of the USA in *2030* owes quite a bit to the discovery of a cure for cancer, which makes an aging population live even longer and absorb more and more resources. Eighty-year-old Brad Miller, born in 1950, worries less about cancer than where he'll live after his townhouse is destroyed. Curing cancer has the side effect of creating political gridlock in Washington DC because the not-quickly dying off Baby Boomers are old people—which is to say reliable voters—and demand a greater share of the nation's resources, which means that the nation's infrastructure is falling apart even without earthquakes.

Such a vision of what the Boomers have wrought resembles the future the National Commission on Fiscal Responsibility and Reform (Simpson-Bowles for the sake of brevity) wants the United States to avoid:

> Over the long run, as the baby boomers retire and health care costs continue to grow, the situation will become far worse. By 2025 revenue will be able to finance only interest payments, Medicare, Medicaid, and Social Security. Every other federal government activity—from national defence and homeland security to transportation and energy—will have to be paid for with borrowed money.[123]

In *2030* infrastructure, in particular the transportation infrastructure, plays a key role in recovering from the near-apocalyptic earthquake. The desire to get the highways of Los Angeles rebuilt, up, and running—ideally without traffic jams—represents *2030*'s concrete measure for successful disaster recovery. The rebuilt transportation infrastructure in *2030* seems to offer an index to the nation's return to health. In this regard, *2030* stands out from the rest of Brooks's work, which focuses intently on his characters' interpersonal relations, not the broader social and economic world.

In typical Brooks fashion, a wish fulfilled leads to misery. In *2030* cancer has been cured and middle-class Boomers can look forward to living close to forever. And that's just the start of the problems. In other words, *2030* is a dystopian novel. The dystopia Brooks imagines wrestles with the abstract concept of debt, and to do so needs to give debt and its effects a concrete form. For individuals like Kathy, unexpected medical emergencies lead to debt and poverty. The people of Los Angeles and the United States as a collective experience debt in the form of a major earthquake's effects on Los Angeles, in particular its freeways. Like most dystopias, *2030* responds to the multiple crises of its cultural and political moment. As M. Keith Booker argues,

> dystopian literature generally also constitutes a critique of existing social conditions or political systems, either through the critical examination of the utopian premises upon which those conditions and systems are based or through the imaginative extension of those conditions and systems into different contexts that more clearly reveal their flaws and contradictions.[124]

In a non-dystopian form, Raymond Chandler's novels revealed the flaws and contradictions of mid-century Los Angeles. As Fredric Jameson writes in *Archaeologies of the Future*,

> What interested Chandler was the here and now of the daily experience of the now historical Los Angeles: the stucco dwellings, cracked sidewalks, tarnished sunlight, and roadsters in which the curiously isolated yet typical specimens of an unimaginable Southern Californian social flora and fauna ride in the monadic half-light of their dashboards. Chandler's problem was that his readers—ourselves—desperately need not to see that reality.[125]

Along similar lines, while readers may desperately need not to see the reality of contemporary Los Angeles' decay, Brooks limits his scope to a few key elements of the built environment—Brad's ruined condo and the completely destroyed freeway system, in particular—to register concretely a sense of the experience of national decline. Brooks in *2030* piles a few of the key crises of early twenty-first-century America—rising medical costs, debt, the government's inability to lead natural disaster recovery—on top of each other, using an earthquake in Los Angeles to heighten the flaws of the current system.

After eight chapters of introducing a dystopian United States, more than ten percent of the novel, Brooks introduces a localized catastrophe. Brooks does not destroy Washington DC, where the newly elected first Jewish president Matthew Bernstein oversees a sclerotic government. Instead, he destroys Los Angeles. The USA is dystopian, and Los Angeles only more so.[126] The Big One hits and

> Los Angeles was not prepared for this [earthquake]. No city could be. No freeway was drivable, no buildings were okay, and many came down completely. Ninety-eight percent of the property in Los Angeles County was severely damaged.[127]

The literary and film destruction of Los Angeles, for someone like Mike Davis, throws into relief the shifting racial anxieties of US and Angeleno life. Brooks keeps racial anxieties muted to concentrate on issues of age and class. The earthquake in *2030* does not lead to a blasted hellscape or race war in Los Angeles, but rather imagines how things could get appreciably—materially—worse than the already-described USA of *2030*, both in Los Angeles and nationwide.

Brooks took up writing *2030* in the wake of the 2008 global financial crisis (GFC), and discussions of debt, both public and private, occupied minds in Washington. The novel begins with Brad Miller's eightieth birthday party, attended by superannuated Baby Boomers who are "thin, healthy, all better looking than their parents were at forty."[128] Those additional years mean greater Social Security and non-cancer-related health care expenses, many of which are, for the rich, cosmetic and/or recreational. "But as advanced as science was becoming," Brooks writes, "no one had come up with a debt machine."[129] Or, more accurately, a debt-paying (or debt-forgiving) machine. The dangers of debt and Social Security's sustainability were of sufficient public concern after the GFC that in February 2010 President Obama organized Simpson Bowles to find a "bipartisan" solution to the problem. The Commission's mission included, "stabiliz[ing] the debt-to-GDP ratio at an acceptable level once the economy recovers" and to "propos[ing] recommendations that meaningfully improve the long-run financial outlook, including changes to address the growth of entitlement spending."[130] The Simpson-Bowles report makes its grim diagnosis in the language of responsibility:

> we spent the past eight months studying the same cold, hard facts. Together, we have reached these unavoidable conclusions: The problem is real. The solution will be painful. There is no easy way out. Everything must be on the table. And Washington <u>must</u> lead.[131]

As is usually the case in post-Reagan American politics, everything on the table when it comes to social programs means cuts and means testing. Simpson-Bowles proposed to raise the retirement age to 67 in 2027 and 69 by 2075. In *2030* extended lifespans create significant economic and social costs that a make rebuilding a leveled Los Angeles impossible. But there is Chinese money and manufacturing. As Brooks imagines the president's assessment of the potential to rebuild Los Angeles by going into something like a public-private partnership with the PRC:

> But now all anyone could talk about was California and how great China was and how maybe China would build up the rest of the country. The idea of a new America had now become only about its buildings and infrastructure. It was like someone had detonated an intellectual neutron bomb. What happened to the new America that was going to let younger people breathe and dream and not be saddled with debt? Younger people now felt as if the earthquake had set them back even more.[132]

Though he roots the dystopia and near-apocalypse of *2030* America in the material, Brooks can't help but return to the psychological concerns that appear throughout his films full of editors and admen and filmmakers: dreaming.

The form that America's dreaming takes is an outlier in Brooks's work as well: sports. Beyond his abortive attempt at jogging in *Modern Romance*, Albert

Brooks's work doesn't go in for physical activity. But in *2030* sports rebind the nation, not movies.

> The opening of the new football stadium in downtown Los Angeles was a major event. It was a beautiful site with monorails providing transportation directly into the arena. And it was surrounded by ongoing constructions; new condominiums, office buildings, and three hotels that looked as though they would be finished within a year. It was the kind of downtown that Los Angeles had always dreamed about, but never could accomplish. The rest of the city was taking shape and it was equally magnificent. No other American city looked like it. Finally, America made a leap into the future. It had taken a disaster to make it happen, but it happened nonetheless, and the rest of the country was jealous.[133]

Dystopian narratives like *2030* are less about the future and more about the ability of the current moment, of contemporary structures of feeling to make life enjoyable (or bearable at worst). In *2030* the inadequacy of early twenty-first-century sociopolitical life appears in the form of a Simpson-Bowles Social Security Grand Bargain, plus the New Democrats/neoliberal public-private partnership applied on a supra-national level to make health care available to all, especially the young. If *Looking for Comedy in the Muslim World* showed "Albert Brooks'" optimism of the will, *2030* shows flashes of optimism, but mostly a pessimism of the will. The destruction of Los Angeles by a massive earthquake in the end represents a victory for civilization, and that victory ends up taking the form of a city that is simultaneously completely nationalized and completely privatized. Austerity and decline are the best-case scenario for our long dotage.

Brooks joined Twitter to promote his book, and soon started to use it for more than announcing events. Brooks is not as prolific a tweeter as many celebrities, with only around 3,900 tweets in eight and a half years. Before 2016, when he started posting more about the day-to-day events of US political life, Brooks tweeted out the anniversaries of his films' releases, one-liners, and complaints about the cable company. He also frequently thanked anyone who sweated a lot on camera for getting him a residual check. His updates on his career affirmed his persona of someone who ought to have had more success, whether his problems in getting movies made— "Just told the head of a major studio he was out of touch and over the hill. I then smiled and said April Second!"[134]—or with not getting nominated for awards—"Woke up excited. Tried on the tux. Prepared the speech. Realized I'm not nominated and now going back to bed."[135]—or being a forgotten part of something—"I thought the SNL reunion was in L.A. Shit."[136] Most of his movie-industry-related tweets fall in line with the mood Tobias sees across all of Brooks's work, "one of profound restlessness and dissatisfaction, often followed closely by the shame of leading a life of privilege and comfort and its never being enough."[137] From short films through feature films, both as an actor-for-hire and writer-director, the Albert Brooks Persona entails a "screen personality that epitomized the self-absorbed American middle class,"[138] in particular the professional-managerial-class worker with a fading belief in the potential for a scientific-technocratic approach to make life better (for himself mostly), tempered by a lifetime of experience that has taught him not to put much trust in institutions to behave as they "should." Something like a Larry David for the mores of corporate personhood.

With this persona in mind, it's interesting to think that Albert Brooks was considered for roles in *Dead Poets Society* (Weir, 1989), *Big* (Marshall, 1988) (it seems Penny Marshall never rated Brooks), *Pretty Woman* (Marshall, 1990), and *Boogie Nights* (Anderson, 1997), losing out to undeniably bigger stars every time: Robin Williams, Tom Hanks (though perhaps not at the time), Richard Gere, and Burt Reynolds. It's hard to see Brooks being suited to the inspirational John Keating, the genuinely innocent man-child Josh, or the slick master of the universe Edward Lewis. But Jack Horner in *Boogie Nights* makes sense as a continuation of Brooks's roles as someone involved in the creation of film who wants to make something substantial in spite of the obstacles his films of choice present.

Albert Brooks as a figure deeply invested in media making and media criticism makes up the first section of this collection. This section proceeds chronologically, starting with Brooks's stand-up career in the 1960s and 1970s, in J. D. Connor's chapter "Your General Humor Buildup: Constructing Albert Brooks." Connor places Brooks in conversation with movements not only in comedy, but also in contemporary US art, especially conceptual art. Over half a decade, Brooks constructed a New Comedy practice of unparalleled breadth that could bring together media-critical practices directed at magazine publishing, live performance, radio, and television, that could unite the subversive educational scenarios of the Famous School and the joke-mandala with the formal subversions of the animal "film" and the pseudo blooper. It had room for questions about the propositionality of the joke (or the work of art) alongside name-naming criticism of key players in the US media ecology. Its social commentary did not lie in a haughty assumption that "real" social problems could be reduced to the discourses of their appearance. Instead, Brooks took the real problems that confronted him, medium by medium, and found ways of opening up critical habitations that might simultaneously speak to their cultural typicality—contemporary television and radio—and their historical specificity. Connor shows that those habitations have specific occasions and conceptual consequences and that the passage between those scales is managed via a relentless reflexivity. That reflexivity has been seen as a limitation of Brooks's

TV-bit-based approach. But as the reflexive embodiment of a medium already at a fever pitch of reflection, Albert Brooks stood as a singular figure against the ground of US television.

Next, the section moves to Jeff Menne's analysis of Brooks's television work with *Saturday Night Live* in 1975. In "The Counterculture Squared: Albert Brooks's *Saturday Night Live*," Menne considers how Brooks's conflicts with producer Lorne Michaels and the films Brooks produced represent a key moment in the counterculture and the role the professional class would play not just in entertainment, but also in American political life from the 1970s onward. With Brooks's anxious conformity appearing only in prefilmed shorts, the more anti-statist energies of the live-in-New York performers appear both on screen and in production. The success of the show on television and some of its performers in film promoted not Brooks's anxious responsiveness to the requirements of his job—such as a comic pleasing an audience—but instead a posture of indifference toward work, and in doing so helped to put in place a structure of feeling that would accompany the economic restructuring of the neoliberal era. In the subsequent chapter, Thomas Britt provides an overview of Brooks's films' media critique. Brooks repeatedly makes films that place him inside the media as an embedded critic who believes in and is beholden to the system that he critiques, and Britt investigates how when critiques from the inside do not succeed in changing the system, Brooks turns to anti-humor as a kind of revenge against the media industry from which he can't extricate himself.

The next set of chapters takes an auteurist approach to Brooks's works. In a broad overview, Christian Long reads Brooks's films as investigations of the rhetoric of success, turning every win into a loss, rendering every success a kind of failure and vice versa. The next four chapters analyze the breadth of Brooks's career, offering extended attention to specific films to provide in-depth analyses of the forms that success and failure take in Brooks's films and the ways the two blur into each other. Enid Stubin traces the ways in which film editing and romance swirl around each other in *Modern Romance*. Through a close reading of *Modern Romance*, she tracks the overlaps and intersections of love and the perfectibility that movie-making holds out as possible. *Modern Romance*'s editing scenes, which show the negotiations required to create a film, provide a professional analog for Robert Cole's personal (but not private) emotional world. For a film professional like Robert, security and stability require working within and against the hierarchy of a studio that both thwarts and reflects the demands of love. Much the same is true in his relationship with Mary Harvard, showing how a self-reflexive film like *Modern Romance* deploys notions of aesthetic control in film making to understand life and love outside of business hours.

Derek Nystrom's chapter approaches *Lost in America* as a comedic investigation into the contradictions of middle-class life. Starting with the film's skewering of yuppie angst and its complicated relation to the hippie counterculture that somehow gave rise to, yet was also betrayed by, this newly discovered sociological group, Nystrom's chapter argues that *Lost* is ultimately about the difficulty of imagining professional labor that can generate value outside of the capitalist marketplace. Taking the film's recurrent allusions to *Easy Rider* as a form of meta-filmic commentary, Nystrom suggests that *Lost* serves as a meditation on Brooks's own efforts to pursue an alternative American cinema.

Frank Percaccio's comparative analysis of *Defending Your Life* and Dante Alighieri's *Purgatorio* reads both texts as cultural indicators of historicized perspectives representing our potential post-existence, a vision of the afterlife revealed. Different as they appear on the surface—vernacular Italian poetry and commercial, comedic film—each narrative contextualizes a belief system suggesting a higher plane of existence in which imperfect souls must glean wisdom from a past life and ultimately learn how they have erred. In *Purgatorio*, the soul embraces its sins, learns from them, atones, and thus moves closer to God, his love, and ultimately, Heaven. In *Defending Your Life*, Brooks's soul similarly has to achieve greater understanding to comprehend earthly missteps so he can truly understand his life and the universe, use more of his brain, and ultimately move onward, just as Dante and his fellow sinners wished to do.

Finally, Rebecca Bell-Metereau identifies the importance of collaborators to an auteur. Her chapter, "Albert Brooks Chaneling the Feminine," makes the argument that Albert Brooks's genius lies in his ability to internalize and value female perspectives. Historical analysis of his major films suggests that Monica Johnson, his co-author on many works, along with other powerful women like Meryl Streep, profoundly influenced his depiction of gender and life in general.

The last section considers Brooks not as a writer-director-actor, but rather as a performer who brings forty years of meaning to his roles, placing these films in a longer cinematic and cultural continuum. Dietmar Meinel's "Finding Brooks: Animating the Baby Boomer Generation in Finding Nemo" reads Albert Brooks through the lens of star studies with particular interest in his embodiment of the baby boomer generation to understand a shift in his persona from meta-comedy to sincerity. Voicing the animated clownfish Marlin, Brooks addresses the parents and grandparents, particularly the baby boomer generation, in *Finding Nemo*'s audience. In doing so, the chapter argues, Brooks-as-Marlin challenges the predominant cultural climate in post-9/11 America.

In the collection's last chapter, "Debt, Payback, and Economics in Nicolas Winding Refn's *Drive*," Tom Ue reveals how primary Bernie, the character Albert Brooks plays, is to *Drive*, notwithstanding his limited share of narrative time, and how Bernie makes pronounced the challenges of successfully reconciling with the story's criminal system. For Ue, Bernie's narrative offers fresh commentary on Driver's (Ryan Gosling) narrative, and by attending more closely to the mobster, we can learn more about both the central protagonist and his world. After establishing the dialogic relationship between the Driver and Bernie, Ue juxtaposes *Drive* with *The Godfather* (1972, 1974, 1990) to show how Refn's borrowings and exploration of similar concerns help us understand both Driver's and Bernie's positions to offer insights into the film's understanding of monetary exchanges and its criminal world.

CONCLUSION

That Brooks is deserving of greater attention and regard is a common thread in a lot of the popular engagements with his work. In 1985 Gerald Peary wrote that "Albert Brooks is a multitalented comic whose time for wider popularity has come." In 1999 Mike Higgins called Brooks an "unfairly neglected director." And in 2014 Nathan Rabin, as I've already noted, wrote "Incidentally, you know who else deserves a box set? Fucking Albert Brooks."[139] It's not likely that there will be another filmmaker like Albert Brooks, at least not out of Hollywood. In an interview with Jennifer Wood, Brooks locates his career in a particular industrial moment that does not seem like it will return:

> I don't know that, any of the films that I made, I could make today. I would have to find another way to do that. It's not just me saying, "It's that the movie business." I could convince financiers that America would like me, even if they didn't, but I never could convince somebody that Korea would love *Modern Romance*. I just couldn't do that. [Back then] I only had one country to lie about. Now, I'd have to say, "No, believe me, China's going to go nuts over this!"[40]

Here the common comparison of Brooks with Woody Allen runs aground. In terms of their place in the film industry, they are very different. Unlike Brooks and his six-year (and more) gaps between films, Allen has continued to make a movie a year, casting well-known stars, by moving to Europe, where his critical standing and relatively greater box office success means he can more easily secure financing. Allen's greatest box office success came from his forty-second movie as a director, *Midnight in Paris* (2011). The differences are also regional and cultural: Woody has New York and tourist Europe, twenties jazz, and jackets with patches on the elbows. Brooks has Los Angeles and ironically used Steppenwolf and Simon & Garfunkel, and "two plaid shirts, a plaid bathrobe and a clown suit." He never had a major hit of his own, but Albert Brooks is a Hollywood lifer. Though he has been in hits and critical favorites, it's lucky for Brooks that Hollywood film history is more than the box office top ten and the Oscars. His career-long engagement with middle-class professional-managerial life in America "mediate[s] between a fictionally specific character identity and a star image that circulates beyond the boundaries of the particular film, and beyond cinema itself."[41] Mediated through Brooks, technocratic utopianism in the late 1960s and early to mid-1970s, hyper-mediatized/reality television culture in the late 1970s, acquisitive yuppie life in the 1980s and early 1990s, the introspection (or navel-gazing) of late middle age in the 1990s, and finally the unwitting realization that middle-class professional-managerial sorts often make the world a worse place in the early 2000s, all show the changing beliefs and horizon of possibility for American culture's second- and third-place winners as something comic.

For Judd Apatow, Albert Brooks's films "are like the Torah."[42] This collection seeks to provide useful commentary on those works to further deepen our understanding and appreciation of Brooks, his work, and his place in American film and cultural history. This collection in its individual chapters and as a whole argues that Albert Brooks merits greater critical consideration. The eleven essays take the first steps towards a serious engagement with Albert Brooks's work as an actor-for-hire, a voice-over performer, and as a writer-director-actor as an entry point to analyze American culture, in the form of Hollywood as an industry and a workplace, how films teach us to see love and life, the contemporary art world, gender performance, Dante, success and failure, debt and doubles, generational identity, how comedy works and has changed in the twentieth and twenty-first centuries.

NOTES

1. Andrew Stanton and Lee Unkrich, dirs. *Finding Nemo.* 2003; Burbank, CA: Buena Vista/Pixar. DVD.
2. Albert Brooks, *Comedy Minus One*, Rhino/WEA B000008DSV, 1993, compact disc. Originally released in 1973. Albert Brooks, *A Star Is Bought*, Wounded Bird Records B06XKNZRMG, 2017, compact disc. Originally released in 1975.
3. Judith Sims, "Comedy Prof Albert Brooks Spits It Out," *Rolling Stone*, January 17, 1974. Available at <http://www.rollingstone.com/culture/features/comedy-prof-albert-brooks-spits-it-out-19740117> (last accessed December 27, 2020).
4. Tracy Wurter, "Comedy Jokes: Steve Martin and the Limits of Stand-Up Comedy," *Studies in American Humor* 3, no. 14 (2006): 23–45. Florian Keller, *Andy Kaufman. Wrestling with the American Dream* (Minneapolis: University of Minnesota Press, 2005).
5. Wurter, "Comedy Jokes," 24.
6. David Marc, *Comic Visions: Television Comedy & American Culture. Second Edition* (Malden: Blackwell, 1997), 11.
7. Marc, *Comic Visions*, 11.
8. Wurter, "Comedy Jokes," 27.
9. Wurter, "Comedy Jokes," 27.
10. Noam Chomsky and Daiv Lightfoot, *Syntactic Structures* (Berlin and Boston: De Gruyter Mouton, 2009), 15. "Second, the notion 'grammatical' cannot be identified with 'meaningful' or 'significant' in any semantic sense."

11. Wurter, "Comedy Jokes," 24, 27.
12. Paul Slansky, "Albert Brooks Is Funnier Than You Think," *Deadspin The Stacks*, May 9, 2014. Available at <http://thestacks.deadspin.com/albert-brooks-is-funnier-than-you-think-1573238010> (last accessed December 27, 2020).
13. Slansky, "Albert Brooks."
14. Matt Zoller Seitz, "Garry Shandling Was One of American Television's Greatest Artists," *Vulture*, March 24, 2016. Available at <http://www.vulture.com/2016/03/garry-shandling-american-tv-great-artist.html#> (last accessed December 27, 2020).
15. Johnny Carson, host and Albert Brooks, guest. *The Tonight Show*. Aired June 6, 1973, on NBC. Available at <https://youtu.be/nDO3IJKB-P8> (last accessed December 27, 2020).
16. Johnny Carson, host and Albert Brooks, guest. *The Tonight Show*, Aired February 24, 1983, on NBC. Available at <https://youtu.be/y7Q5T7hSa5Q> (last accessed December 27, 2020).
17. Gerald Nachman, *Seriously Funny: The Rebel Comedians of the 1950s and 1960s* (New York: Back Stage Books, 2004), 553.
18. John Limon, *Stand-Up Comedy in Theory, or, Abjection in America* (Durham, NC: Duke University Press, 2000), 27.
19. Michael Rogin, "Blackface, White Noise: The Jewish Jazz Singer Finds His Voice." *Critical Inquiry* 18, no. 3 (1992): 417–53, 447.
20. Chris Rock, host. *77th Annual Academy Awards*. Performed February 27, 2005, on ABC. Available at <https://youtu.be/JerPfHYro1U> (last accessed December 27, 2020).
21. David Handelman, "The Ambivalent-About-Prime-Time-Players," *The New York Times Magazine*, December 28, 1997. Available at <http://www.nytimes.com/1997/12/28/magazine/the-ambivalent-about-prime-time-players.html?pagewanted=all> (last accessed December 27, 2020).
22. Handelman, "The Ambivalent."
23. Judd Apatow, "Our Mr. Brooks," *Vanity Fair*, January 2013. Available at <http://www.vanityfair.com/hollywood/2013/01/albert-brooks-this-is-40> (last accessed December 27, 2020).
24. "A Feminist Dick Joke," Hari Kondabolu, Bandcamp, track 2 on Hari Kondabolu, *Waiting for 2040*, Kill Rock Stars, 2014.
25. Cheryl McCall, "Psst! Albert Brooks Isn't Kin to Mel Except in Comedy—he was Born, and Sort of Is, An Einstein," *People*, April 16, 1979. Available at <https://people.com/archive/psst-albert-brooks-isnt-kin-to-mel-except-in-comedy-he-was-born-and-sort-of-is-an-einstein-vol-11-no-15/> (last accessed December 27, 2020).
26. McCall, "Psst!"
27. McCall, "Psst!"
28. McCall, "Psst!"
29. Slansky, "Albert Brooks."
30. Martin Scorsese, dir. *Taxi Driver*. 1976; Culver City, CA: Sony Pictures Entertainment, 2004. DVD.
31. Scott Foundas and Albert Brooks, "An Evening With Albert Brooks," in *Film at Lincoln Center*, YouTube video, 1:02:14. Available at <https://youtu.be/ZgXN6venczo> (last accessed December 27, 2020).
32. Jason Zinoman, "No Real Hurry to Tell the Joke," *The New York Times*, May 26, 2014. Available at <https://www.nytimes.com/2014/05/27/arts/television/bob-newhart-master-of-the-one-sided-conversation.html> (last accessed December 27, 2020).
33. J. Hoberman, "35 Years Later, Taxi Driver Still Stuns," *Village Voice*, March 16, 2011. Available at <https://www.villagevoice.com/2011/03/16/35-years-later-taxi-driver-

still-stuns/> (last accessed December 27, 2020); Peter Bradshaw, "Taxi Driver review—Scorsese's sleaze is still the bee's Knees," *The Guardian*, February 10, 2017. Available at <https://www.theguardian.com/film/2017/feb/09/taxi-driver-review-scorseses-sleaze-is-still-the-bees-knees> (last accessed December 27, 2020); Leonard Quart, "A Slice of Delirium: Scorsese's 'Taxi Driver' Revisited," *Film Criticism* 19, no. 3 (1995): 67–71. JSTOR, available at <www.jstor.org/stable/44075823> (last accessed December 27, 2020); Gretchen Schwartz, "'You Talkin' to me?'": Robert DeNiro's Interrogative Fidelity and Subversion of Masculine Norms," *The Journal of Popular Culture* 41 no. 3 (2008): 443–66; Roger Ebert, "Taxi Driver," *RogerEbert.com*. Available at <https://www.rogerebert.com/reviews/great-movie-taxi-driver-1976> (last accessed May 26, 2020).

34. Howard Zieff, dir. *Private Benjamin*. 1980; Burbank, CA: Warner Home Video, 1997.
35. Vincent Canby, "Film—'Unfaithfully Yours,'" *The New York Times*, February 10, 1984, C7.
36. James L. Brooks, dir. *Broadcast News*. 1987; New York: Criterion Collection, 2011. DVD.
37. Vincent Canby, "Film: 'Broadcast News,' Comedy," *The New York Times*, December 16, 1987, C21.
38. James L. Brooks, dir. *I'll Do Anything*. 1994; Culver City, CA: Sony Pictures Home, 2003. DVD.
39. Jeff Strickler, "'I'll Do Anything' Has Split Personality," *Star Tribune*, February 4, 1994. 4E; Owen Gleiberman, "I'll Do Anything," *Entertainment Weekly*, February 4, 1994, 36. Available at <https://ew.com/article/1994/02/04/ill-do-anything-2/> (last accessed December 27, 2020).
40. Stanley Kauffman, "Messing Around," *The New Republic*, March 7, 1994, 30–1.
41. Michael Ritchie, dir. *The Scout*. 1994; Los Angeles: Twentieth Century Fox, 2001. DVD.
42. Roger Ebert, "The Scout," *RogerEbert.com*, September 30, 1994. Available at <https://www.rogerebert.com/reviews/the-scout-1994> (last accessed May 26, 2020).
43. Peter Rainer, "Movie Review: Brooks Hits Fly Ball in 'The Scout,' but Not Over Fence," *Los Angeles Times*, September 30, 1994. Available at <https://www.latimes.com/archives/la-xpm-1994-09-30-ca-44660-story.html> (last accessed December 27, 2020).
44. Apatow, "Our Mr. Brooks."
45. David Silverman, dir. *The Simpsons*, Season 1, episode 9, "Life on the Fast Lane." Aired March 18, 1990, on Fox. Brooks also appeared as Cowboy Bob in season 1.
46. Bob Anderson, dir. *The Simpsons*, Season 5, episode 7, "Bart's Inner Child." Aired November 11, 1993, on Fox.
47. Chris Turner, *Planet Simpson: How a Cartoon Masterpiece Documented an Era and Defined a Generation* (London: Ebury, 2004), 404.
48. Mike B. Anderson, dir. *The Simpsons*, Season 8, episode 2, "You Only Move Twice." Aired November 3, 1996, on Fox.
49. Turner, *Planet Simpson*, 405.
50. Turner, *Planet Simpson*, 404. Also, in season 16 (2005) Brooks made an appearance as Tab Spangler, camp counselor.
51. David Silverman, dir. *The Simpsons Movie*. 2007; Los Angeles: Twentieth Century Fox. DVD.
52. Steven Soderberg, dir. *Out of Sight*. 1998; Universal City: Universal Home. DVD.
53. Christine Lahti, dir. *My First Mister*. 2001; Los Angeles: Paramount, 2002. DVD.
54. Todd McCarthy, "My First Mister," *Variety*, January 18, 2001. Available at <https://variety.com/2001/film/markets-festivals/my-first-mister-1200466323/> (last accessed December 27, 2020); Keith Phipps, "My First Mister," *The AV Club*, March 29, 2002. Available at <https://film.avclub.com/my-first-mister-1798196050> (last accessed December 27, 2020).
55. Andrew Fleming, dir. *The In-Laws*. 2003; Sydney: Roadshow Entertainment. DVD.

56. Mick LaSalle, "Odd couple amplified / 'The In-Laws' remake brings wildly different dads together," *SFGate*, May 23, 2003. Available at <https://www.sfgate.com/movies/article/Odd-couple-amplified-The-In-Laws-remake-2646259.php> (last accessed December 27, 2020)
57. LaSalle, "Odd couple."
58. Jenju Kohan, series creator. *Weeds Season 4*. 2008; Sydney: Sony Home Entertainment, 2010. DVD. Michael Ausiello, "Weeds Scoop: Albert Brooks is Nancy's 'Dad'," *TV Guide*, April 14, 2008. Available at <https://www.tvguide.com/news/weeds-scoop-albert-8084/> (last accessed December 27, 2020).
59. Brooks also appeared in the as-yet-unreleased Louis C. K. film *I Love You, Daddy* (2017).
60. Nicholas Winding Refn, dir. *Drive*. 2011; Arundel, Australia: Pinnacle Films. DVD.
61. Albert Brooks, (@AlbertBrooks), February 27, 2017, "Because of tonights." Available at <https://twitter.com/AlbertBrooks/status/836085267639455748> (last accessed December 27, 2020).
62. Scott Tobias, "What 'Albert Brooks' says about Albert Brooks," *The Dissolve*, September 18, 2013. Available at <http://thedissolve.com/features/movie-of-the-week/162-what-albert-brooks-says-about-albert-brooks/> (last accessed March 17, 2017).
63. Tobias, "What 'Albert Brooks'."
64. Judd Apatow, dir. *This Is 40*. 2012; Sydney: Universal Sony Home Entertainment, 2013. DVD.
65. Frank Krutnik, *Hollywood Comedians: The Film Reader* (London: Routledge, 2003), 7.
66. Tom Teicholz, "When Reality Was a Joke: The Making of Albert Brooks' *Real Life*," *Los Angeles Review of Books*, November 5, 2016. Available at <http://blog.lareviewofbooks.org/arts-culture/film/reality-joke-making-albert-brooks-real-life/> (last accessed March 17, 2017).
67. Tobias, "What 'Albert Brooks'."
68. Tobias, "What 'Albert Brooks'."
69. Gavin Smith, "All the Choices: Albert Brooks interview," *Film Comment* 35, no. 4 (July–August 1999). Available at <https://www.filmcomment.com/article/all-the-choices-albert-brooks-interview/> (last accessed December 27, 2020).
70. Tom Tunny, "Video Reviews," *Sight and Sound*, January 1, 1998: 58.
71. Krutnik, *Hollywood Comedians*, 3.
72. Dave Kehr, "As A Director, The Comedian Turns Into A Ruthless Realist," *Chicago Tribune*, March 31, 1991. Available at <http://articles.chicagotribune.com/1991-03-31/entertainment/9101280875_1_modern-romance-first-short-film-comedy> (last accessed March 17, 2017).
73. Kehr, "As A Director."
74. Kehr, "As A Director."
75. James Slaymaker, "'To Err is Human, to Film Divine': The Films of Albert Brooks," *MUBI.com*, October 5, 2018. Available at <https://mubi.com/notebook/posts/to-err-is-human-to-film-divine-the-films-of-albert-brooks> (last accessed December 27, 2020).
76. Albert Brooks, dir. *Lost in America*. 1985; Pyrmont, Australia: Warner Home Video, 2003. DVD. Albert Brooks, dir. *Looking for Comedy in the Muslim World*. 2005; Burbank, CA: Warner Home, 2006. DVD.
77. Slansky, "Albert Brooks."
78. Albert Brooks, dir. "Albert Brooks' Famous School for Comedians." 1971; *The Great American Dream Machine*, S'More Entertainment, 2015. DVD.
79. Albert Brooks, dir. "Sick in bed." 1975; *Saturday Night Live: Season 1, 1975–1976*, Universal City, CA: Universal Pictures Home Entertainment, 2006. DVD. Albert Brooks, dir. "NBC Super Season." 1975; *Saturday Night Live: Season 1, 1975–1976*,

Universal City, CA: Universal Pictures Home Entertainment, 2006. DVD. Albert Brooks, dir. "The National Audience Research Institute." 1976; *Saturday Night Live: Season 1, 1975–1976*, Universal City, CA: Universal Pictures Home Entertainment, 2006. DVD.
80. Albert Brooks, dir. *Real Life*. 1979; Hollywood: Paramount Home Video, 2000. DVD.
81. Jeffrey Ruoff, "'Can a Documentary Be Made of Real Life?': The Reception of *An American Family*," in *The Construction of the Viewer: Media Ethnography and the Anthropology of Audiences*, ed. Peter Ian Crawford and Sigurjón Baldur Hafsteinsson (Copenhagen: Intervention Press, 1996), 270–96. Taken from Jeffrey Ruoff's website: <https://www.dartmouth.edu/~jruoff/Articles/RealLife.htm> (last accessed December 27, 2020).
82. Lawrence O'Toole, "Taking potshots at U.S. crockery," *Macleans*, March 26, 1979, 62–3, 62; Janet Maslin, "Screen: Albert Brooks Turns 'Real Life' Into Movie: Family is the Lens," *The New York Times*, March 2, 1979. Available at <https://www.nytimes.com/1979/03/02/archives/screen-albert-brooks-turns-real-life-into-moviefamily-is-the-lens.html> (last accessed December 27, 2020).
83. Teicholz, "When Reality."
84. Jonathan Rosenbaum, *Movie Wars: How Hollywood and the Media Limit What Films We Can See* (London: Wallflower, 2000), 105.
85. Albert Brooks, dir. *Modern Romance*. 1981; Culver City, CA: Sony Home Entertainment, 2006. DVD.
86. Slaymaker, "'To Err'"; Smith, "All the Choices."
87. Tobias, "What 'Albert Brooks'."
88. Slaymaker, "'To Err'."
89. *The Onion*, "Romantic-Comedy Behavior Gets Real-Life Man Arrested," April 7, 1999. Available at <https://local.theonion.com/romantic-comedy-behavior-gets-real-life-man-arrested-1819565117> (last accessed December 27, 2020).
90. Michael Pattison, "Albert Brooks' 'Modern Romance'," *MUBI.com*, February 17, 2017. Available at <https://mubi.com/notebook/posts/love-actually-close-up-on-albert-brooks-modern-romance> (last accessed December 27, 2020).
91. J. Hoberman, *Make My Day: Movie Culture in the Age of Reagan* (New York: The New Press, 2019), 16. The two movies Hoberman uses to exemplify the "feel bad" movie are *Blow Out* (Di Palma, 1981) and the Albert Brooks-starring *Taxi Driver*.
92. Scott Tobias, "*Lost in America*: The $100,000 Box," *The Criterion Collection*, July 25, 2017. Available at <https://www.criterion.com/current/posts/4760-lost-in-america-the-100-000-box> (last accessed December 27, 2020).
93. Gerald Peary, "Dropouts of the middle class," *Maclean's*, April 8, 1985, 62.
94. John Powers, "The Big Casino," *Sight and Sound*, November 1, 1996, 18–20.
95. Nathan Rabin, "*The Dissolve* on . . . the directors we want to get career-spanning box sets," *The Dissolve*, July 30, 2014. Available at <http://thedissolve.com/news/2856-the-dissolve-on-the-directors-we-want-to-get-caree/> (last accessed December 27, 2020).
96. Tobias, "*Lost in America*."
97. Albert Brooks, dir. *Defending Your Life*. 1991; Burbank, CA: Warner Home, 2001. DVD.
98. Desson Howe, "'Defending Your Life'," *Washington Post*, April 5, 1991. Available at <https://www.washingtonpost.com/wpsrv/style/longterm/movies/videos/defendingyourlifepghowe_a0b2e7.htm> (last accessed December 27, 2020).
99. Lou Cedrone, "'Defending Your Life' Albert Brooks' new movie is almost heaven," *The Baltimore Sun*, April 5, 1991. Available at <https://www.baltimoresun.com/news/bs-xpm-1991-04-05-1991095207-story.html> (last accessed December 27, 2020).

100. Howe, "'Defending'."
101. Jennifer Wood, "'Defending Your Life' at 25: Albert Brooks on Making a Comedy Classic," *Rolling Stone* March 22, 2016. Available at <www.rollingstone.com/movies/news/defending-your-life-at-25-albert-brooks-on-making-a-comedy-classic-178596> (last accessed January 7, 2021).
102. Albert Brooks, dir. *Mother*. 1996; Hollywood: Paramount Home, 2006. DVD.
103. "1996 Domestic Gross," *Box Office Mojo*. Available at <https://www.boxofficemojo.com/yearly/chart/?yr=1996&p=.htm> (last accessed December 27, 2020).
104. David Canfield, "*Mother*, Albert Brooks' Biting Mother-Son Comedy, Featured Debbie Reynolds' Last Great Performance," *Slate*, December 29, 2016. Available at <http://www.slate.com/blogs/browbeat/2016/12/29/debbie_reynolds_gave_one_of_her_greatest_performances_in_albert_brooks_mother.html?platform=hootsuite> (last accessed December 27, 2020).
105. Albert Brooks, dir. *The Muse*. 1999; Universal City, CA: Universal Home, 2010. DVD.
106. Mike Higgins, "The Muse," *Sight and Sound*, January 1, 2000, 99.
107. Raphael Shargel, "Confusing Success with Profit," *New Leader*, September 20, 1999, 20–1.
108. Shargel, "Confusing."
109. Tobias, "What 'Albert Brooks'."
110. Owen Gleiberman, "Looking for Comedy in the Muslim World," *Entertainment Weekly*, January 27, 2006. Available at <https://ew.com/article/2006/01/27/looking-comedy-muslim-world-2/> (last accessed December 27, 2020).
111. William Arnold, "Brook's 'Muslim World' Comedy is Hit-and-miss," *Seattle Post-Intelligencer*, January 19, 2006. Available at <https://www.seattlepi.com/ae/movies/article/Brook-s-Muslim-World-comedy-is-hit-and-miss-1193212.php> (last accessed December 27, 2020).
112. Peter Travers, "Looking for Comedy in the Muslim World," *Rolling Stone*, January 12, 2006. Available at <https://www.rollingstone.com/movies/movie-reviews/looking-for-comedy-in-the-muslim-world-128137/> (last accessed December 27, 2020).
113. Leah Rozen, "Picks and Pans Review: *Looking for Comedy in the Muslim World*," *People*, January 30, 2006. Available at <https://people.com/archive/picks-and-pans-review-looking-for-comedy-in-the-muslim-world-vol-65-no-4/> (last accessed December 27, 2020).
114. Roger Ebert, "Looking for Comedy in the Muslim World," *RogerEbert.com*, January 19, 2006. Available at <https://www.rogerebert.com/reviews/looking-for-comedy-in-the-muslim-world-2006> (last accessed May 26, 2020).
115. A. O. Scott, "Sometimes Politics Simply Won't Do." *The New York Times*, January 20, 2006. Available at <http://movies2.nytimes.com/2006/01/20/movies/20musl.html> (last accessed December 27, 2020).
116. Travers, "Looking."
117. Tobias, "What 'Albert Brooks'."
118. Slaymaker, "'To Err'."
119. Albert Brooks, *Twenty Thirty: The Real Story of What Happens to America* (New York: St Martin's, 2011).
120. Mike Davis, *Ecology of Fear: Los Angeles and the Imagination of Disaster* (New York: Metropolitan Henry Holt, 1998), 277, emphasis in original.
121. Brooks, *Twenty Thirty*, 19.
122. Brooks, *Twenty Thirty*, 19.
123. National Commission on Fiscal Responsibility and Reform. *The Moment of Truth* (Washington, DC: The White House, 2010), 11. Available at <https://web.archive.org/

124. M. Keith Booker, *Dystopian Literature: A Theory and Research Guide* (Westport, CT: Greenwood, 1994), 3.
125. Fredric Jameson, *Archaeologies of the Future: The Desire Called Utopia and Other Science Fictions* (London: Routledge, 2005), 287.
126. As I finish this collection in March 2020, it may be that the first Jewish president could inherit something similar.
127. Brooks, *Twenty Thirty*, 47.
128. Brooks, *Twenty Thirty*, 1.
129. Brooks, *Twenty Thirty*, 23.
130. Barack Obama, "National Commission on Fiscal Responsibility and Reform," in *Executive Order 13531 Sec. 4*. Available at <https://obamawhitehouse.archives.gov/the-press-office/executive-order-national-commission-fiscal-responsibility-and-reform> (last accessed December 27, 2020).
131. *Moment of Truth*, 6, emphasis in original.
132. Brooks, *Twenty Thirty*, 312.
133. Brooks, *Twenty Thirty*, 369.
134. Albert Brooks, (@AlbertBrooks), April 3, 2015, "Just told the head of a major studio." Available at <https://twitter.com/AlbertBrooks/status/583658577698557952> (last accessed December 27, 2020).
135. Albert Brooks (@AlbertBrooks), February 23, 2015, "Woke up excited." Available at <https://twitter.com/AlbertBrooks/status/569566721893408770> (last accessed December 27, 2020).
136. Albert Brooks (@AlbertBrooks), February 16, 2015, "I thought the SNL reunion was in L.A. Shit." Available at <https://twitter.com/AlbertBrooks/status/567130153646817280> (last accessed December 27, 2020).
137. Tobias, "*Lost in America*," *The Criterion Collection*, July 25, 2017. Available at <https://www.criterion.com/current/posts/4760-lost-in-america-the-100-000-box> (last accessed December 27, 2020).
138. Peary, "Dropouts."
139. Peary, "Dropouts," 62; Mike Higgins, "The Muse," *Sight and Sound*, January 1, 2000, 98–9; Rabin, "*The Dissolve*."
140. Wood, "'Defending'."
141. Krutnik, *Hollywood Comedians*, 7.
142. Apatow, "Our Mr. Brooks."

PART I

Brooks as Media Critic

CHAPTER 2

Your General Humor Buildup: Constructing Albert Brooks

J. D. Connor

RECEIVER WISDOM

In the context of the New Comedy of the 1960s and 70s, the received wisdom about Albert Brooks is that his principal aims were aesthetic, not political. As Richard Zoglin explains, "His comedy might have looked like a retreat from the social consciousness" of Lenny Bruce, George Carlin, Richard Pryor, or Robert Klein. "But Brooks was an artistic radical just the same." His stand-up was "Pirandellian . . . doubling back on itself, satirizing the very notion of being an entertainer—comedy *about* comedy." Zoglin's account of this era goes on to nuance that apparent break from politics, but his general sense remains that the Bruceans "were modernists, breaking down the traditional joke-joke monologue and inventing a new, more free-form kind of stand-up" while Brooks "was a postmodernist, resurrecting the old style and encasing it in irony and self-parody."[1] Or, as Brooks explained in a *Tonight Show* appearance on June 6, 1973, "It has been my passion forever, and ever, to pursue the field of comedy itself: to take it apart a bit, to bring it more to you people."[2]

The outlines of Brooks's early career—the pre-cinematic era—are well known. Unlike other stand-ups, he began by performing on television, not by touring or as part of an improv troupe. Only after his performance on the *Steve Allen Show* did he begin playing out, and that came to a halt in 1974 as a result of what Zoglin calls "a famous breakdown onstage in Boston."[3] By then he had already made his first short film—*Albert Brooks' Famous School for Comedians* (1971)—and would shortly make several more for the inaugural season of *Saturday Night Live*.[4]

Nearly every account of Brooks's stand-up career begins by emphasizing its ending. This makes the stand-up seem contingent and unwanted—even

Brooks seems to agree with this account, explaining that he really wanted to be an actor[5]—rather than the complementary offshoot of a unique mode of comedy that came to being on television. "Television," here, includes both the live or live-to-tape recording of performances before an audience for (later) broadcast *and* the threaded replay of pre-recorded shorts or telefilms like *Famous School*. In addition to those parameters of liveness-delay-recording, Brooks's television is marked by the rhythms of commercial breaks and possible interruptions, and so he anticipates both—by becoming the pitchman who would interrupt his own work and, when that isn't possible, by "obsessing" about the possibility of interruption, even going so far as to call NASA "to help him determine" whether the moon landing would pre-empt his debut on *Dean Martin Presents the Golddiggers* in the summer of 1969.[6]

At the core of Brooks's TV variety-show appearances—he did more than fifty in this era—is the send-up of the traditional bit.[7] Paul Slansky rattled off a few of these in a long *Playboy* profile: "the impressionist whose every imitation sounded like Ed Sullivan; the shadow artist with the broken hand who was reduced to portraying 'a bunny hiding behind a rock'; the mime who described everything he was doing in a French accent ('Now I am walking up ze stairs, now I am petting ze dog')."[8] Brooks did the mime bit on the *Steve Allen Show* in 1969. He was a terrible ventriloquist on *The Ed Sullivan Show* in 1971 and *The Flip Wilson Show* in 1972. He was by turns "an animal trainer . . . whose elephant has gotten sick at the last minute and ha[d] to be replaced by a frog," and a comedy version of a plate-spinner who had to keep half a dozen people laughing.[9] At the first *American Music Awards* in 1974 he was Carl Heller, a children's songwriter doing a lounge-y retrospective of his work. That oeuvre included both "Brush Your Teeth" and "Eat Your Beans, Please." They were the same song.[10]

The high-concept or one-man-sketch approach was so determining that it resulted in a modular style of comedy once Brooks actually went on tour. "At first he was so green that he would simply string a few of his TV bits together with perfunctory segues."[11] Yet rather than see the early career as the professional overcoming of those limits—to no one's great surprise, he did—we might see that half decade as the activation of an extended range of mediated performance and studio practices. That is, if Brooks's comedy came to being on television, it could not exist entirely there. The stand-up gigs would be performances that were defined *negatively*. They were "not television": live, yes, but not to tape, and not for broadcast. This may in fact be the standard stand-up situation, yet Brooks can barely imagine it. In "Memoirs of an Opening Act, Part I," a piece of stand-up recorded live for the album *Comedy Minus One* (1973) and thus already within the orbit of comedy-toward-recording, he imagines a fantasy broadcast of the event, a second scene, an elsewhere.[12] "By the way, you know this room is full, and I might—there's a camera up there, right now there's a Jewish audience in the Wilshire Ebell Theatre watching this. They do that on High Holidays. When the temple fills up they move into theaters." More biographical frameworks have excavated the specific Los Angeles Jewishness of the scene; I will keep the focus on the media configuration Brooks invokes.[13]

For Brooks's version of the New Comedy, the meta-turn is a medial turn. Instead of simply chronicling his early career—Zoglin has done an excellent job of that and there is no large, untapped archive of material that might supplement his account—I will consider a different set of relations for his work: presentation and context, scale and audience, markets and media.[14] In what follows, I turn to a limited selection of Brooks's work from the early 1970s in order to do two things with each. First, I place it in its media-cultural contexts. This is ordinary enough, but in the case of Brooks's comedy, those contexts have been ignored or all but erased by the modular integrity of the bit and a general critical emphasis on his meta stance.[15] As a consequence the *occasions* for his meta-comedy have been underthought, and once those occasions are restored, the precise stakes of his apparent turn away from immediate political engagement become clearer. Second, and far more speculatively, I link each of these pieces to cognate work taking place in then-contemporary US art, particularly to efforts to come to terms with mass media and media discourse over the long history of conceptual art. While these two approaches are in some ways complementary—they are both contextualizations, one toward the vernacular, one toward the artworld—they are intentionally asymmetrical in the roles they play in my overall reading. Explicating some of the referential ground of his bits restores a wider range of aims to Brooks's interventions; forging analogies to the artworld de-specifies his "postmodernism," his "deconstruction," his "meta" spin on the medium of comedy and the media as institutions. If Brooks's meta-comedy is a version of (institutionally acceptable) institutional critique, it should also be understood as an unheard voice in the debates around the idea that art is fundamentally propositional.[16]

This asymmetry captures at the level of methodology the peculiar historical configuration of the era coincident with and immediately surrounding Brooks's early career. There was so much art, particularly conceptual art, that was funny, deadpan, or po-faced. Alongside it, and evolving out if it, there was so much activist work, but activist work that had its roots or targets within its own socially proximate art institutions. Benjamin Buchloh's legendary essay "Conceptual Art 1962–1969: From the Aesthetic of Administration to the Critique of Institutions" captures the passage between those poles, but naturally enough without wondering about the comedic proximity of the work in question.[17] At the same time, the aim of cultural contextualization cannot simply be to match an object—or a creator—to a context and call it a day. By setting up two distinct poles of attraction, I place Brooks's work in a field of aspiration, underwritten and held in tension by broad cultural forces and small-c conceptual analogues. In that contextual field, the work has *options*, degrees of freedom and surprise that are, nevertheless, positionally visible from long-standing cultural or conceptual vantage points. This may seem like an overbuilt framework, but it has two important and immediate consequences. First, it provides sufficient interpretive ballast that the early Brooks material is not reduced to stuff he made along the way to the major works. Second, it hard-wires the scalar discrepancy between tight references or individual jokes and wider aesthetic stakes. If the framework does its job, it renders the large claims I will make about Brooks's significance not implausible, leaving the process of conviction to the readings themselves.

Those stakes are complicated by the supervening and evolving nature of US television. As the overwhelming focus of cultural diagnosis, television and its coverage of the political—the war in Vietnam, Watergate, the rising of suppressed populations, the articulation of state media support within a stalling market economy, and so much more—would seem to constrain the significance of any *merely* media-critical stance. Instead, I take Brooks's televisual era to be comedy's introjection of the TV and video art that are the subject of art historian David Joselit's *Feedback: Television Against Democracy*. Joselit understands TV as "the commercial doppelgänger of art's experimental advance toward information since the mid 1950s."[18] He contends that such doubling amounts to a complementary operation, ultimately with political consequences: "Art stands against television as figure stands against ground, and television, in its privatization of public speech and its strict control over access to broadcasting, stands against democracy." In Brooks's case, though, he "stands against television" as the figure against the ground upon which he stands (up).

That may seem too precious, but I mean it in particular ways. Within Joselit's recounting of "certain events in the video ecology of mid-century America that disrupted or reconfigured television's closed circuit," Michael Shamberg's career offers especially suggestive and coincident parallels with Brooks's.[19] Shamberg's path through the "video ecology" of the 1970s began with radical theoretical and activist work in *Guerrilla Television* (1971). He then played a key role at the video collective Raindance/*Radical Software* (1970–4) and the satirical *Top Value TV* (*TVTV*, 1972–7) before becoming a top-tier Hollywood producer with *The Big Chill* (1983).[20]

Brooks's career aligns almost too neatly. He debuted on *Steve Allen* in 1969; that year he was a member of the writers room for the TV series *Turn-On* (Friendly and Schlatter, ABC 1969).[21] And if his subsequent stand-up did not obviously "expose society's injustices or stick a thumb in the eye of the censors," *Turn-On* did.[22] The show's *Laugh-In* sensibility was grounded in the conceit that a computer was choosing segments for playback, almost at random, certainly not in the usual televisual order. Sketch fragments would play out in a white cube, Moog synth tones would bleep and bloop, live action would be punctuated with pop-up animation: A cartoon biplane would pass along the top of the screen trailing signs such as "Israel Uber Alles" and "Free Oscar Wilde." (We do not know who wrote what on the show.) *Turn-On* was so sexually frank that it was essentially canceled in the middle of its premiere on February 5, 1969. Some stations did not return to the broadcast after the first commercial break; others in Western time zones refused to show it; the second episode never aired.

To continue the parallel, Brooks's *TVTV* analogue was, of course, his work for *Saturday Night Live* in 1975. Like Shamberg he would then shift to Hollywood filmmaking. *Real Life* (1979) was his directorial debut, but *Broadcast News* (James L. Brooks, 1987) would be Brooks's most direct *Big Chill* complement; both co-starred William Hurt and both were "sophisticated and nuanced stor[ies] about the vulnerability of idealism."²³ As part of that depiction, *The Big Chill* "prominently features therapeutic uses of video," turning Shamberg's suggestion that the middle classes should "videotape and play back their own alienation" into "a feature of Hollywood entertainment." In contrast, Brooks's *Broadcast News* comes at the end of a decade of therapeutically inflected, media-political writing, directing, and acting: *Taxi Driver* (Scorsese, 1976; Brooks plays a political spin doctor), *Real Life* (comedian-documentarian), *Modern Romance* (1981; film editor), and *Lost in America* (1985; advertising executive). In *Guerrilla Television* Shamberg declared that "True cybernetic guerrilla warfare means re-structuring communications channels, not capturing existing ones," and his subsequent efforts attempted to put that claim into action, before settling on the "therapeutic" model of *The Big Chill*. Brooks's early work in contrast would test that claim: could one *capture* existing channels? Or would such "fantasies of revolution and subversion" be rendered "either cynically opportunistic or childishly naïve"?²⁴ What happens to art's "commercial doppelgänger" when it prominently features its own autocritique? Can you stand against the ground of television even as you enact television's most exemplary figures, most typical studio practices? Is such a tautological instantiation of televisuality critical at all?

To answer those questions, I highlight Brooks's relations to debates about teachability, audience membership, intermedial competition, and marketing—central topics in any history of US television. But rather than simply align Brooks with the video art versions of those debates—an alignment that would necessarily highlight Brooks's complicity with the mainstream media institutions throughout and likely lead to a judgment of the limitations of his critical stance—I highlight the ways in which his work brought central aspects of conceptual art to the fore. This, in turn, has the effect of broadening the ambit of the work. I proceed chronologically through four examples and relate each to a cognate artwork: the "Famous School for Comedians" to Dan Graham's *Homes for America* (1966); "Memoirs of an Opening Act, Part I" (1973) to David

Antin's "Talking at Pomona" (1972); a joke diagram from that same year to Ad Reinhardt's own *Joke* (1956); and the album *A Star Is Bought* (1975) to Richard Serra and Carlota Fay Schoolman's *Television Delivers People* (1973). This course will emphasize the diverse range of media channeled in Brooks's early work, from off-screen stand-up, to comedy albums, mock advertisements in print, audio, and audio-visual form; audio and audio-visual technical demonstrations; faux-documentaries and faux-news reports.

I. TEACHING

Albert Brooks' Famous School for Comedians appeared in *Esquire* in February, 1971.[25] An eight-minute film version aired on PBS's *The Great American Dream Machine* in October.[26] The original six-page feature was structured as a special advertising insert, putatively addressed to anyone who has had "a friend turn to you and say, 'You know something, [your name here], that was pretty funny. You should think about being a comedian.'" It combined attractive depictions of life at the school—students milling about the "Jack Klugman Comedy Research Center," sitting in classrooms practicing spit-takes, or choosing a favorite charity to support "in case they make it big"—with the five-minute "Comedy Talent Test" itself—multiple choice punchlines, fill-in-the-blank insults, a game where you are supposed to match individual facial features to the comedians they belong to. As editor Lee Eisenberg explained, Brooks "took complete control of the photography, he was exceptionally meticulous and hard to please with written copy. But we hope we gave him what he wanted."[27]

Brooks modeled the ad on those placed in magazines and sent via direct mail for artistic correspondence schools, and the most basic part of the gag was the assumption that there was a real Famous School for Comedians campus, "located on twenty-two gorgeous acres near Arlington National Park." There you could work on discrete comedy skills before returning to your life as the "funny one" of your friends back home. Part of what made the bit work for Brooks was the underlying pathos, the inevitable appeal of something like an official certification of your talent, identified via an art test, and the correlative instructional scene: if you can draw a pirate, why couldn't you learn to do it better? If you can tell a joke, why not work on making it funnier?

In the case of the school for comedians, though, what might seem implausible or useless—working with a drummer to help your timing—had a more caustic edge. Brooks's hucksterism was not simply a joke, it was a joke with a direct reference: The Famous Writers School (est. 1961). Like its elder sibling, the Famous Artists School (est. 1948), FWS advertised heavily and at its peak was supported by a staff of 800 commissioned salespeople. Just as the FAS sales pitch relied on the prestige of its "Guiding Faculty" including Norman

Rockwell, the FWS touted its ties to publishing legend Bennett Cerf, *Twilight Zone* creator Rod Serling, Iowa Writers Workshop head Paul Engle, and prolific romance writer and television host Faith Baldwin.

But what made the Famous School for Comedians topical was not simply the prominence of the Famous Writers School, but the latter's collapse. Its downfall was brought on by Jessica Mitford's devastating profile in the July 1970 issue of the *Atlantic*.[28] Her reportage detailed the exploitation of the students who enrolled while her interviews exposed the utter detachment of the "Guiding Faculty" from the actual work of the place. As Cerf explained to her—on the record!—"I know nothing about the business and selling end and I care less. I've nothing to do with how the school is run; I can't put that too strongly to you." As for the real desire of students for writing instruction that Brooks drew on, Cerf was dismissive: "Oh, come on, you must be pulling my leg—no person of any sophistication, whose book we'd publish, would have to take a mail-order course to learn how to write." Later coverage highlighted the enormous burdens placed upon the "Teaching Faculty," who had to grind through the enormous volume of submissions.[29] The school lurched through efforts at reform, promising to cease certain deceptive advertising practices. Still, the mea culpas and the new approach did not succeed. Famous Artists declared bankruptcy in February 1972.[30]

The details of that collapse—the prestige scam at the top and the crushing workload at the bottom—help explain two of Brooks's visual gags. In one photo, the nine "Advisory Faculty" are shown sitting around a sauna in towels. They are recognizable TV comics: Orson Bean, Totie Fields, and the Dean, Eddie Albert. The photomontage that places their heads on other bodies highlights their lack of connection to the school. Below that picture is a smaller one of "well known comedy writer and part-time professor Mordecai Hunter" in his office being buried under piles of assignments, "grading a student's test paper." The ad leaves its media criticism largely tacit. One would have to be a true contemporary, for example, to know that when Brooks dangles the possibility of being on the Ed Sullivan Show ("*Sunday night* at 8p.m. on CBS") he is demonstrating how far behind the times he is: the network had canceled the show and the slot was now occupied with the CBS Sunday Movie. Befitting his place in *Esquire*, Brooks presumes a sophisticated audience. Without the web of references, the joke is reduced to the more general one of the teachability of comedy and the callowness of the hard sell.

Part of the reason that immediate context has been lost despite the continuing success of the Famous School is that the specific cues were left out of the telefilm. That version was so successful that it was put forward for Emmy consideration, anthologized as part of *Great American Dream Machine*'s "best of" showings and its 1974 series retrospective, and picked up for theatrical distribution.[31] Where the *Esquire* ad quietly conveyed that students would not receive the ballyhooed personal attention they were promised by contrasting the Advisory Faculty having a schvitz with the overburdened Mordecai Hunter, the *GADM* film showed neither, concentrating on the classroom situations. Instead, it relied on the more structural opposition between its status as a long-form advertisement and its appearance on the non-advertising-supported Public Broadcasting System. The canniness of seeing through the ad's deceptions was displaced to the contextual unexpectedness of its appearance. Brooks's ad for the Famous School was as out of place as *Sesame Street*'s announcements that the episode had been brought to you by the letter W and the number 8.

Dan Graham's *Homes for America* first appeared in *Arts* magazine in the December 1966/January 1967 issue, which helped shape its reception as a sophisticated intervention in questions about the relationship between the artwork and its reproduction.[32] But he initially wanted it to appear, like the *Famous School*, in *Esquire*. As he explained, "My real interest was actually *Esquire* magazine, because *Esquire* magazine, which had the best writers, also had color features of the sterility of the suburbs, with kind of boring, formalistic photographers who would go and show the sterility of the suburbs."[33] At its aesthetic heart was the homology between the gridded layout of the piece and the gridded layout of the suburbs; at its sociological heart was the homology between the apparently automatic operation of the market and the affected affectlessness of the prose, that "aesthetic of administration" that Buchloh highlighted. "The owner is completely tangential to the completion of the project"; "Contingencies such as mass production technology and land use economics make the final decisions, denying the architect his former 'unique' role."[34]

In addition to this bureaucratic tone, the piece devoted much of its space to the limited array of model homes, their possible colors, and the combinatorics of mass production. At a certain point, such pseudo-documentation crosses the line between useful illustration and eye-glazing encyclopedism: "Each block of houses is a self-contained sequence—there is no development—selected from the possible acceptable arrangements." Here Graham lists forty-eight different permutations of four different models in groups of eight in two columns of twenty-four. On the left, each model is adjacent to a duplicate (AABBCCDD to DDCCBBAA) on the right there are no adjacent pairs (ABCDABCD to DCBADCBA). "As the color series usually varies independently of the model series, a block of eight houses using four models and four colors might have forty-eight times forty-eight, or 2,304 possible arrangements."[35] At that moment, the piece exemplifies the combination of "bureaucratic rigor and deadpan devotion" to process and permutation that Buchloh considers typical of conceptual art in the period. In *Arts* magazine, there was no doubt that the bureaucratese was part of the artistic project; in *Esquire* it would have been harder to tell, and the joke might have played better, and longer.

And had it played longer, it might have been more obvious that conceptual practices stand in a complex relationship to their own limits. Buchloh emphasizes conceptual artists' "acute sense of discursive and institutional limitations." They possess, for him, a "critical devotion to the factual conditions of artistic production and reception without aspiring to overcome the mere facticity of these conditions."[36] But where those limitations seem most galling and systemic, we find the emergence of humor out of that combination of "bureaucratic rigor and deadpan devotion." I want to insist on that twin development, in no small part because Buchloh's claims about the "obvious" limitation of the social aims of this art are rejected by the artists themselves: "Everybody thinks it's sociological. Buchloh thinks it's sociological critique of minimal art," Graham says. "It's not an analysis . . . It's not a study . . . It's a joke."[37]

Homes for America is legible as both sociological critique and joke, and the former has largely swamped the latter. But if we restore the dual reception of the piece, it becomes clearer that conceptual humor is a collateral product of the constraints on its social reckoning. Inverting each of those terms can illuminate Brooks's position: his social reckoning is the product of the liberated reflexivity of his humor. If he can joke about anything as long as it becomes a joke about comedy as such, then it is unsurprising that the specifics of his target—the Famous Writers School; the notion of comedy "instruction"—are lost to the formal innovation, just as Graham's humor was lost to its sociocritical reception. This is the risk that his accommodation to the antecedent form of the *Esquire* piece entailed; it's the risk that Graham wanted to run.

II. AUDIENCING

Early in *Comedy Minus One*, in "Memoirs of an Opening Act, Part I" Brooks notes that "concert halls have gotten too big anyway." He spends some time discussing how *this* arena isn't too big, and that even 4,000 people in Philharmonic Hall isn't too large. "After that . . . Grand Funk Railroad sold out Shea Stadium. David Cassidy sold out the Astrodome." Here, he diverts to jokes about Cassidy's young audience, the abundance of station wagons at the concert, and Ford's reliability issues before returning to the question of scale:

> It's getting worse. There's no building large enough. Three Dog Night just passed a law within their group, starting I think in two months, they will play no more buildings of any kind. They will just play states. Do thirty, thirty-two concerts a year. Stand in the middle of Kentucky and play. [guttural shout] Everyone pays that day! Appearing in Kentucky . . . Three Dog Night! [whiny singing] "Liar, liar."

> [obsequeiously] Eight fifty. [moan, then gruffly] I'm just goin' to Dayton! [guttural voice returns] You heard it, you pay it!

Brooks's gestures must have given more context—an extended palm for the $8.50, driving pantomime for the man going to Dayton—and his head and eyes would have made the hot-swapping between characters clearer. But the centerpiece of this joke is a philosophical question about what it means to be an audience. If you don't have a building you don't know you're at a concert, and while obviously that puts you in the world of people who are "overhearing" rather than "hearing," the situation is nevertheless governed not by an antecedent transaction (buying a ticket *to go to* a show) but by an experience: "You heard it, you pay it!" The problem, here, is the discrepancy between scale and audience—and the comedy of that point lies in the mismatch between the bare fact of a scalar relation "appearing in Kentucky" and the obligation to be an audience "You heard it, you pay."

Brooks is not finished.

> What could the ultimate of that be? They get on a jet plane in New York and fly to Los Angeles and play in the plane, let the military promote the concert, and have everyone in the country pay a dollar. "'Scuse me you two, see that plane?" [woman's voice] "Yes, we do." [Back to Brooks] "Two dollars." [Pompous man] 'Let me treat ya, honey."

The bit ends. The jet concert bears even less of a relationship to its audience than the Kentucky appearance: the music can't be heard, the performers can't be seen, and yet the price must be paid. To be an audience, here, is a matter of being administered as such, and the shift from a collective experience to an administrated collectivity is ludicrous.

Something nearly parallel preoccupies David Antin in his poem "Talking at Pomona." "Talking at Pomona," first published in the volume *Talking* and in *ArtForum* in 1972, is the first of Antin's "talk poems." These were, as Marjorie Perloff calls them, "experiments with controlled improvisation, recorded directly on tape" and then transcribed (albeit in complex ways). Just as Brooks is working through the social infrastructures of performing (buildings, audiences, scales, publics), so Antin is exploring the nature of different sorts of artmaking, particularly painting and sculpture.

Early on, Antin is discussing the notion that "sculpture articulates space"—a notion he has *already* marked off as old-fashioned. His example is putting a "non-committal cube" in a three-dimensional space, which is, he quickly says, like what happens in the Wallace Stevens poem, "Anecdote of the Jar." "I placed a jar in Tennessee" it begins, and the claim, elaborated in the poem, is that a new set of relations emerges as a result: "It made the slovenly wilderness/ Surround." The upshot—"It took dominion everywhere"—is a maximalist, modernist idea of relating. Antin reflects: "now putting a jar in tennessee is   after all an odd idea   merely because the scale of the jar and the scale of tennessee is discrepant   you have an idea of a relation between a geographical entity that isn't visible and something that is trivially handleable."[38] In patiently, deadpannily working through the actual situation of this jar, Antin does *not* note that placing a jar in Tennessee is not something that Stevens actually did *nor* that Stevens is writing a poem, which is (perhaps) what Antin is doing on stage and in transcription, *nor*, finally, that it would take a maximal claim like "placing a jar in Tennessee is sculpture" to bridge the gap between sculpture and poetry. All of that is tacit, and maybe not even intended. But it is that tonal combination—po-faced ordinary language reasoning backstopped by winking transcendence—that initially made the talk poems such a controversial practice.

Antin's audience surely laughed somewhere along here, a kind of bursting forth at the literalism of working through the discrepancy. Brooks's did as well. What makes Brooks's version more modally familiar as stand-up is the shift from narration to dramatization, the emergence of characters who have to make this mad "conceptual nexus" actually function: the ticket-taker, the man headed to Dayton, the couple unknowingly out on a date, and the military promoters. And the way we got to those characters was by building out from a delimited scene—a theater, then a hall, then an arena, finally beyond buildings to what Antin calls "a geographical entity that isn't visible." There, no longer in anything like the familiar participations of a concert, Brooks finds the edges of relation: "You heard it;" "See that plane?"

Not that Antin doesn't do that as well, albeit usually in reverse. In his Wittgensteinian mode, at just such points colloquy emerges: "one might say that sculpture's proceeding was to create a conceptual relation between spaces of a sort now you say 'what sort?' and they'd say 'well of an interesting sort'."[39] From "one might say" to the one who says it, or to *you* as the person enrolled in the process of *saying it*. And then we're off to the races again.

That interpellated *you* is the central figure in *Comedy Minus One*. Across the bottom of the album front we read "Introducing the Comedy Team of Albert Brooks and . . . (Over!)" while the back proclaims "You!" and features a mockup of a backstage dressing mirror with a sheet of mylar-like reflective material glued where the mirror should be. In the eponymous piece, "you" perform with a recording of Brooks by reading along with an included script. As Tim J. Anderson has noted, *Comedy Minus One* takes its place in a long history of "instructional records," most directly the "Music Minus One" series begun by the legendary Irv Kratka, but dating back to the Add-a-Part 78s of the 1940s.[40] But if *Comedy Minus One* takes its title from musical recordings made for musicians and aspiring singers, the dramatic structure owes more to "Co-Star: The

Record Acting Game." "Co-Star" was a series of fifteen LPs launched in 1958 in which well-known actors from Cesar Romero to Pearl Bailey to Tallulah Bankhead would perform one part in a scene and the listener—again working from an included script—would play along.[41] The temporal relationship of script and recording, and the emphasis on "read[ing] your lines at the proper pace so that the flow of the scene is natural and realistic," were much closer to Brooks's album than the play-along groupwork of "Music Minus One." If the Famous School offered a ludicrous group of exercises and techniques, and held out the promise of faculty feedback that would never come, Co-Star and *Comedy Minus One* at least delivered on what they offered: the chance to step out of the infinite audience and perform. There would be no feedback, but none was offered.

Yet the inclusiveness of Brooks's "you" is limited. "Memoirs of an Opening Act" begins by setting the context at Doug Weston's Troubadour in Hollywood where it is being recorded. Not, again, by specifying that they are at the Troubadour or noting the date, but by noting:

> There's mics all around here. There's a recording truck outside. A record is being made. There's nothing you have to worry about, just have a good time. Just don't identify your laughter. A lot of people like to [Booming laugh] '"Ha ha ha ha haaaa," said Bill Harrison of Phoenix.'

"Identified laughter" is the conceptual flipside to the imputed audience: the performance reaches out to anyone within earshot; the audience member has no similar recourse.

That asymmetry is, for Brooks, part of the scalar problem of individual identity subsumed within the national, and as is usual with Brooks, he explores the conceptual inverse at length in another piece, "Rewriting the National Anthem."[42] The set-up asserts that with things in the country "changing" (how is unspecified) the anthem will have to change as well. One might hire someone, but he quickly rejects Henry Mancini's version—"Big mountains, lots and lots of trees" to the tune of "Moon River"—in favor of the fairer process of holding open auditions. And with that as his concept, he is now able to work through an array of stereotyped characters arranged on axes that span from amateur to professional, from enthusiasts to critics. The opener, "Ted Rutherford," is a man unleashed—"Hey, World!" he begins—thrilled to have his chance at last. He is followed by a piano novice, equally thrilled to get both hands properly alternating, "Heart and Soul" style. When "LeRoy Williams" steps to the piano and announces he is from "any ghetto you choose" the audience already knows this is a different level of intensity. He picks out individual notes with his left hand, percussive and ominous before launching into the song "You jail, all your black—" At which point he is immediately and smilingly cut off like all the others. In dramatic contrast to Williams is 75-year-old Hal Carter from Michigan, who retains the current melody but replaces the lyrics with wholehearted praise for consumer society: "Let's give thanks for our lawns, and our two-car garages. Let's give thanks for TV!" The piece concludes with a Vegas lounge singer whose lengthy, maddening pre-song patter prevents him from ever getting to the point. "Would you get off the stage!" Brooks shouts in his stage-manager voice, whereupon Brooks does.

The exemplars of professional performance here—Mancini and the lounge singer—fail to adequately incorporate the vast "you" of the national audience. Even the *most* professional cannot manage anything more specific than "lots and lots of trees." Where Antin's "you" veers between the depersonalized interlocutor of analytic philosophy and the specified "you"s of his current audience, Brooks's songwriting hopefuls may be specified by region, age, ethnicity, professional status, and so on. That pluralization makes it harder to imagine any adequate result from the process. Yet at the end of the bit, when Brooks takes the direction he gives himself, his identity collapses into the persona of the lounge singer. That collapse both suggests that Brooks is an unspecified third professional, one capturing the diversity of the national audience by attempting to catalogue it directly and solves the problem of the utter impracticality of such a strategy. (He need not work through a million potential songs; he has found a way to end the bit.) "Rewriting the National Anthem," like "Memoirs of an Opening Act" pivots around questions of performance and scale, questions that are enlivened by the threat that individual identity poses to the adequate management of those scenarios. It may be unsatisfying or ludicrous to be "audienced" by an airplane flying overhead; it may be impossible to find a way to allow everyone to audition for the new national anthem. These are the antinomies of "dominion" and participation as Brooks sees it. And like his other interventions, they may be present in a variety of media—live in concert or on record—but they take their imbalance from the basic televisual situation.

III. CYCLING

The sort of intermedial competition behind the different incarnations of the Famous School, "Rewriting the National Anthem," or "Comedy Minus One" could reach a remarkable degree of intensity. In 1968, Mason Williams, head writer for *The Smothers Brothers Comedy Hour*, had a hit single with the instrumental "Classical Gas" (#2 on the Hot 100; #1 on Easy Listening). The song was buoyed by its repeated performance on the popular show. In addition to multiple live versions, Williams persuaded animator Dan McLaughlin to turn his pre-existing, experimental, "kinestatic" film *God is Dog Spelled Backwards* into a music video for the piece.[43] As in *God is Dog*, Williams's song would play under rapidly changing still images—"for the first time, all of 3000 years of Fine Art in 3 minutes."[44] *The Smothers Brothers* repeated the formula that fall when they aired Chuck Braverman's historical speed-run, *American Time Capsule*. Such music montages seemed to carry obvious ideological potential, whether for the left or right. Cuban director Santiago Alvarez's pro-Civil Rights short *Now!* (1964) relied on the technique to generate activist solidarity while Eugene Jones hoped to generate a reactionary irritation in his ads for Nixon's 1968 campaign that bore titles such as "Convention," "Failure," and "Crime."[45] These latter, all-but-avowedly fascist commercials promised "an honest look at the problem of order in the United States" and would eventually give rise to the stunning diagnostic montage in Alan Pakula's *The Parallax View* (1974).

Brooks's intervention came earlier than Pakula's and worked by undermining the standard technique. His connection to the popular source of these films, *The Smothers Brothers*, was personal and competitive—his brother Bob Einstein was in the writers room while Brooks was trying to make his way at *Dean Martin* and *Turn-On*. In Brooks's entry into the kinestatic canon, again set to "Classical Gas," the images in the film would survey animal life rather than Fine Art, only "the film had been lost in the mail, so he had to try to re-create it live" by "flipping madly through the pages of a Time-Life book on the animal kingdom; then, after exhausting the pages, he raced backstage to bring out props—a live dog, a beach ball (in lieu of a seal), even a can of sardines."[46] Writing about Brooks's performance at the Troubadour in Hollywood for *Billboard*, Bob Kirsch called the routine "undoubtedly" "the highlight of the act."[47]

Against the slickness of the professionals and ad men, Brooks offered a cheap, DIY substitute. But in that faltering assemblage, he brought together not simply music and photography but publishing (in its high-gloss, industrial middlebrow), animal training (and its failures), and industrial fishing. It was both a summa of the prevailing relations of nature and culture and a bathetic come-down from then-hip, image-overload aesthetics.

At the same time, watching Brooks "flip madly" through the book recast media intensity as personal desperation. That personalization could then appear to decontextualize the media critique, replacing the baring of the device with the baring of the soul, shifting attention from how the media does things *to you* to how you might participate, or try to. The same summer that Kirsch saw Brooks perform the animal "film," Brooks appeared again on *The Tonight Show* to work through the steps to telling a joke—"A good joke. It's not a bad joke." This is where he avows that it has been his "passion forever, and ever, to pursue the field of comedy itself" and he casts the bit as an explicit spin-off of his management of the Famous School, which is "operating, profiting I might add, on the East Coast." At the heart of his explanation, is a mad, spiraling

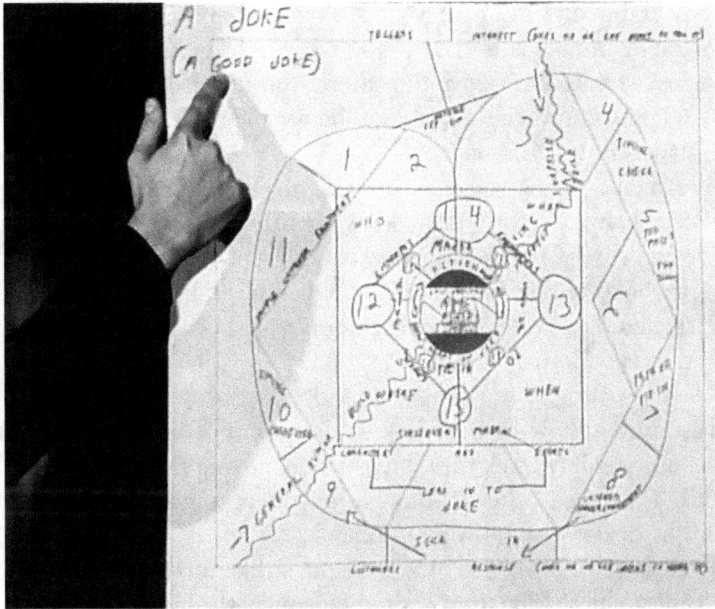

Figure 2.1 Albert Brooks's 1973 *Joke* mandala. Carson footage supplied courtesy of Carson Entertainment Group

diagram, a joke-mandala that he sets on an easel at the beginning, and that gets his first big laugh.

The mandala takes us from "steps one to twenty," an orderly progress belied by the actual delivery. What Brooks sets up as a set of interlocking aspects of the joke—timing checks, the dispensation of information, monitoring listener reactions—arrive as a manic cycling through voices and frameworks. Throughout the routine, levels of discourse collide and fracture as he jumps from meta-commentary to prosaic example. There are cues about what phase of the joke we are in, from the "outside setup" through the "suck in" to the "Actual. Heart. Of the Joke. Say it with me: Heart. Of. Joke." There are banalities derived from sales lingo about gauging the "Listener's Eagerness to Laugh" and the "Visible Listener Enjoyment. That's our VLE." There are bits and pieces of the jokes that are ostensibly being setup—non-existent jokes about, for example, "two hookers and turtle" or a woman with an eight-foot nose. He will suddenly gesture at the chart to underline a point only to leave the *Tonight Show*'s director behind. "People might want to look at the monitors in the studio, might want to look at your feet. Doesn't really matter." The dizzying diagram and the dizzying routine work in perfect sync:

> Presentational Voice: Now, between step 8 and 9 we have our "suck in." We call it a "suck in," that's the point in the joke where you wanna have

the guy trapped. I mean, if you don't have him trapped here, you're gonna be in trouble later. But if you do it right, nothing will drag him away. See, if you don't have him there, you never can be sure of him. And god only knows they leave right before the punch. [Places hands on hips; shakes head.] Oh, boy.

Aggro joke-telling voice: So his wife turned to him and said—

Voice change, slightly dismissive, slightly apologetic for cutting in: Oh, I gotta run. [Checks imaginary watch]

Aggro joke-telling voice, abashed: Okay, bye, thanks.

Presentational Voice: [Smiling] You're left with a punch in your pocket. No good. [fist extended]

Offered as a humor how-to, the joke-mandala is impossible to put into practice. No one could possibly track these steps while moving fluidly through the joke being told. The joke of the bit thus lies in the misapplication of analysis and action, in the discursive shuffling itself.

And yet there is a practice to it, a mandala-like invocation of simultaneity and cyclicality, a punchline that is simultaneously the big sell:

And at the same time from the very beginning your general humor buildup, it should be starting at the beginning of the joke and getting more and more, your surprise build [Finger tracking from the corners of the diagram; fist pumping] your rising interest, more and more, it joins now, you're ready to go into the punch, you got all their attention, then you go in, step 20, the actual punch [punching with left fist] you give it to 'em . . . You got 'em on the floor, you got 'em laughing if it's good enough. Start over with number one. Do it again.

That practice differentiates the mandala from analogous joke diagrams while grounding it in the temporal closures of the TV variety-show bit: the joke ends, the bit ends; both begin again, some other time, some other place.

As a diagram, Brooks's joke-mandala falls in the tradition of the diagrams popularized by Max Eastman in *Enjoyment of Laughter* (1936) and the mocking rejoinder to Eastman by Robert Benchley, "Why We Laugh—Or Do We?" published the next year in *The New Yorker*.[48] Indeed when Brooks heads over to the desk after his *Tonight Show* performance, Johnny Carson comments, "Haven't heard such a dissection since Max Eastman." Eastman had created his diagrams out of symbols for frustration and satisfaction arrayed on angular and dashed lines that would trace the joke's path. Benchley responded with something closer to Corporal Trim's walking stick flourish from *Tristram Shandy*. But where their diagrams both hew to the form of particular jokes and so meander, Brooks's traces the stages of the social relationship of joke-telling in general and so achieves the form of an emblem. As he narrates his way through the twenty steps, Brooks seems to tap into the most cant-ridden portions of Eastman's work, particularly the "Ten Commandments of the Comedic Arts," with its invocations of "interest" and "redeeming disappointments," or its discussion of timing: "Not only must the mind be genuinely on the way (plausibility), and the not-getting-there a genuine surprise (suddenness), but the surprise must come at the instant when the on-the-wayness is most complete, and the surprise most unexpected."[49] This is the sort of discourse that Benchley took on.

Yet Brooks's diagram is both a record of the joke's path and a map that at certain distances from the center arrays the fourfold relations of the joke (Who, What, When, Where) or spatializes the "Listener's/ Eagerness/ To/ Laugh." Relying on a broad assimilation of the mandala to popular culture, largely driven by psychedelic art and a fascination with Jungian analysis, Brooks was able to count on the immediate recognizability of his version, however lumpy and off-balance it might be.[50] At the same time, his mandala is wildly and illegibly over-labeled, linking its presentation to keyword-driven sales talk. That reflexive linguistic surplus aligns Brooks's diagram to Ad Reinhardt's *Joke*, a collage piece usually called *A Portend of the Artist as a Yhung Mandala* (1956). Reinhardt's "last" art-world cartoon, *Joke* is encrusted in puns and nonsense, pseudo-profundities and barbs directed at art-world institutions.[51] Offered without the benefit of live narration, *Joke* rewards deeper and deeper attention to both its arrangement and its linguistic inventions.

Brooks's hand-annotated visual aid is amateurish next to Reinhardt's precisely ruled version, a construction that offered "barely a trace of the artist's hand."[52] Just as his rushed kinestatic "film" undid the passivity such an image barrage might inspire, so Brooks's narrated mandala inspires a kind of manic processualism, the polar opposite of the contemplative stance the mandala should offer. Still, both artists' works participate in the stasis of cyclicality: Reinhardt to display a synchronic picture of the art system, particularly in its New York forms; Brooks to dwell on the iterative nature of the joke. In his notebook entry "Mandala," Reinhardt points to the figure's "Rules, regularities, symmetry" and adumbrates its conceptual positions:

Recoverable, repeatable circular time, transhuman
Starting over at beginning   non-historical
Eternal return, repetition   transmundane[53]

In *Joke*, Reinhardt takes that "transmundanity" and ironically applies it to the surface busy-ness of the art world, finding an assured, external point of view on the system. Brooks tries to find such a point but cannot locate any center that might hold. What might seem "transhuman" for Reinhardt is exhaustingly all-too-human for Brooks.

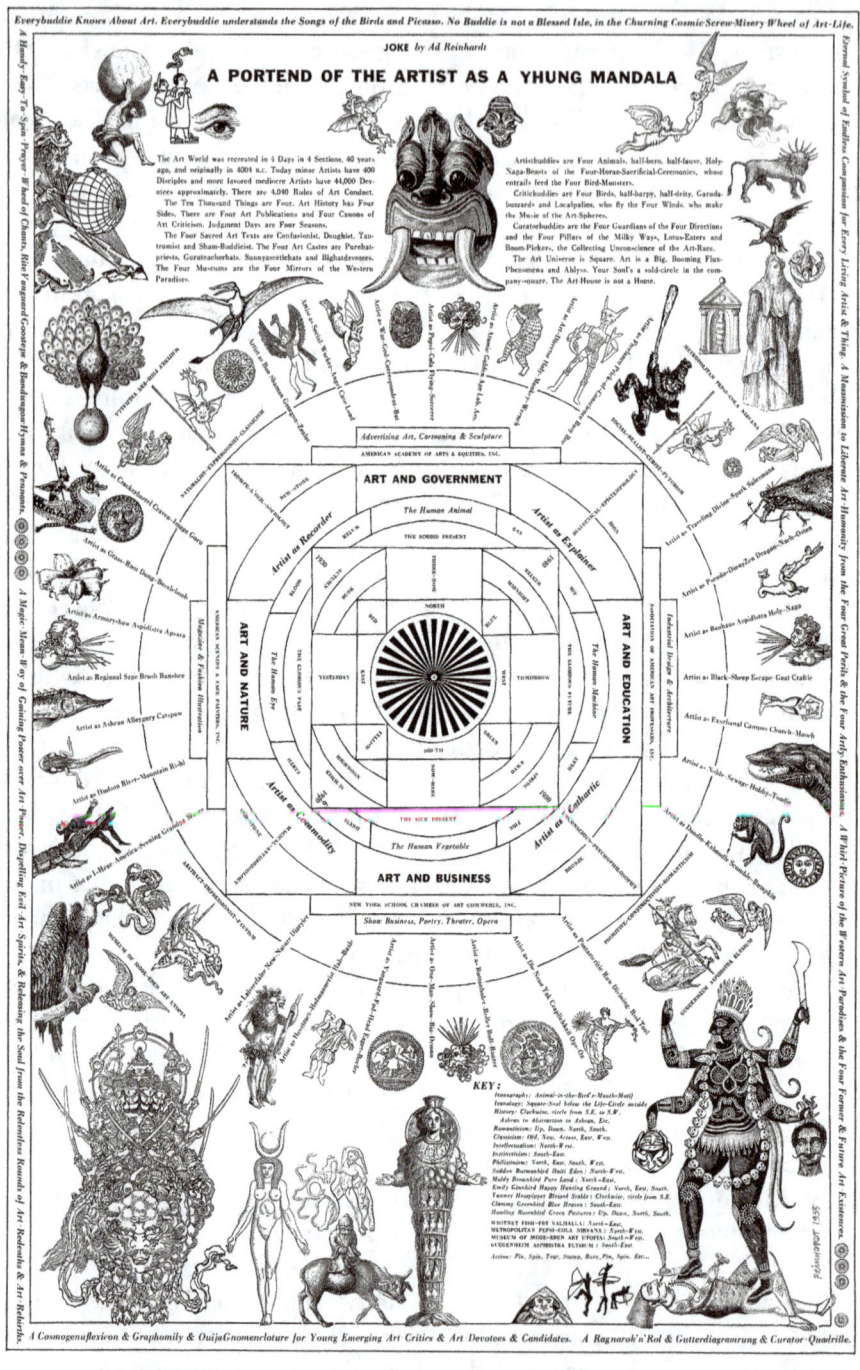

Figure 2.2 Ad Reinhardt's 1956 *Joke* mandala. © 2020 Estate of Ad Reinhardt / Artists Rights Society (ARS), New York

Seen one way and the joke-mandala is the most self-reflexive of Brooks's early comedy bits, the one that seems to have the weakest links to its medial surround. It is the height of "comedy about comedy," and if it has a social vector, it would seem to be, yet again, about the difference between amateurs with their hacky street jokes and professional analysts such as Brooks. But aligned with Reinhardt's *Joke* it becomes clear that it is not only about comedy but about the labor of explication. Where Reinhardt's painting, and his explication of it, amounted to an "extreme form of self-critical, perceptual positivism,"[54] his cartoons and collages were complementarily extreme forms of art-critical, conceptual mock-mysticism. And while it might be possible to make the aesthetic positions of the paintings and the collages cohere, the gap between the austere, cruciform monochromes and the baroque, mandalic or serial polylogues posed a problem that would require a tremendous amount of interpretive work to bridge. In this sense, Brooks's meta-comedy—comedy-critical, conceptual mock-formalism—lies close to Reinhardt's cartoons, but the interpretive work is foregrounded as the performer's own bodily enlistment in the project. Whether stumbling around onstage dripping olive oil from a sardine can or jabbing at the air to indicate where "the punch" belongs, Brooks centralizes the underlying media critique in his own physical situation. And that situation depends on the givenness of the constrained temporality of "the bit," the reliably ready-to-hand contextualization of his performance.

IV. BUYING

If the aim of Brooks's televisual era were to investigate and exhaust the possibilities of meta-comedy, then the joke-mandala might be its endpoint. If, as I have been contending, its aim is more properly to situate the New Comedy as both a form of media critique and as a source of conceptual innovation, then there might still be much to accomplish after the release of *Comedy Minus One*. Brooks followed the end of his live stand-up career with the album *A Star Is Bought* (1975).[55] While the title alludes to the perennial, tragic story of Hollywood success, *A Star Is Bought* is immersed in the media industrial landscape of US radio. Each featured track is directed at a particular pre-existing format: Country, Top 40, Talk, Classical, the "FM Undergound," and Nostalgia. And for each of those formats, the "song" aligns with a particular subgenre: the country song is the patriotic "Phone Call to Americans"; the Top 40 number is a novelty "Party From Outer Space"; the classical song is "Bolero," with new, hypersexual lyrics; the FM song is a blues performed with Albert King; and the nostalgia entry is a rediscovered Old-Time Radio comedy episode of *The Albert Brooks Show* from World War II. In this redoubled precision, *Star* converts "Rewriting the National Anthem" from a collection of social portraits ("state your name and where you're from") to a distribution of market segments. It is both a specification of the contents of those formats and a survey of the medium as a whole.

Star sets off each of its fictional format entrants with a narrated introduction—a clean break from the songs, unlike the discursive collisions of the joke-mandala bit. Overall, fifteen minutes (roughly one-third of the record's runtime) is devoted to intercalary talk. Each of those sections is named not for the format it introduces but for its place in the record's running order: "In the Beginning," "Near the Beginning," "The End of the First Beginning," "A New Beginning," "Call This Cut Three, Side Two." A stereo experiment from *Comedy Minus One* reappears here in the form of a "Promotional Gimmick." The aim is to pre-record "custom" announcements for every radio station in the country. Brooks explains that while visiting—and here he lists several cities and regions—he enjoys "the good sounds of K   the good sounds of W." After that, he lists half the alphabet in the left channel, half in the right. (The introduction usefully explains this is part of a copy-protection strategy.) Ostensibly, a radio station such as WOXY would choose the appropriate regional tag, cut the letters O, X, and Y out of Brooks's list, and then assemble its very own station ID. (How that would work with a record is less clear: they would need to use an intermediary tape source first, just as someone acting along with Brooks on *Comedy Minus One* would need a tape in order to review their performances.)

A station is formatted; a format is populated. The subgenres for each format are themselves mobilizations of clichés, none more explicit than the "Party From Outer Space," which sends up novelty "break-in records" that build imaginary interviews from snippets of other popular songs. "Near the Beginning" tells the story of Brooks's search for a Top 40 hit. He is initially steered to the break-in record by Peter Tork and Mickey Dolenz of The Monkees, who emphasize the genre as compensation for Brooks's lack of talent. But after consulting with intellectual property lawyer David Braun, he realizes that the expense and difficulty of pre-clearing the rights to popular songs will make the endeavor unprofitable and time-consuming. At this point, Brooks opts to write *fake* songs to splice into the record, becoming—at least in miniature—a Top 40 hit machine. The disdain Tork and Dolenz show for the novelty records pioneered by Dickie Goodman seems real, but the entire process that leads Brooks to "Party From Outer Space" is itself a pre-scripted, fake interview, one that Brooks's audience takes as part of a successful bit despite its (hidden) proximity to Goodman's hacky recordings.[56]

At that moment, *A Star Is Bought* seems like an endpoint to the bit-accumulation strategy. An album of styles, a meta-album of anthology tracks, *Star Is Bought* concludes with the narrator doing a series of impressions (Jimmy Cagney, Marlon Brando) that all sound just like him, a meta-turn on Brooks's own earlier failed impressionist bit. That is then followed by an unlisted track, a commercial for *The Best of Pardon My Boner! Vol. 8*, itself a parody of the Kermit Schafer *Pardon My Blooper!* series that had begun with *Radio Bloopers* in 1947 and was still going strong into the 1970s—Shafer would release a double album set (*Super Bloopers Vol. 1*) in 1974 that would receive international distribution through K-Tel.[57] In Brooks's commercial, the blooper itself comes from the "Pardon My Boner newsroom," in which the newscaster intones, "In Chicagoland today, a woman slipped and fell on the asshole. Asphalt. Oh shit, I said 'asshole.' Oh goddammit, I said 'shit.' Oh Jesus, I said 'goddammit.' Oh, nooo." [Laugh track.] Everything about it is phony: the newsroom, the blooper, the chain linking blooper-to-blooper-to-blooper, and the laugh track. It stands at the end of this fake-anthology record as another fake anthology. Its Chicago setting conjures the notorious "Uncle Don," blooper, a long-standing fake in which the host of a long-running children's radio program on WOR supposedly cursed into a hot mic. The blooper may or may not have existed, but that did not deter Schafer from "reconstructing" it and introducing it on *Vol. 1* as "a legend." In that version Don (not actually Don) sings his sign-off song, makes certain the show is off the air, and then announces, "I guess that'll hold the little bastards tonight." Schafer's synthetic version takes care to spatialize the recording engineer's assurance that they are no longer broadcasting, and drops "Don's" voice to the edge of audibility. In sending up *Pardon My Blooper!*, then, Brooks and co-producer Harry Shearer were recognizing a pro in action, but they were depending upon an audience's ability to see some vestige of critique that could differentiate their work from Schafer's.

Recognition of market clichés and differentiations underlies Brooks's critique of radio. In contrast, Richard Serra and Carlota Fay Schoolman's *Television Delivers People* relies on the unspecific nature of TV: "There is no such thing as mass media in the United States except for television," it declares.[58] First aired on March 3, 1973 *Television Delivers People* delivers its sharp media critique clearly, in simple rolling text set against a flat, chroma-key blue background. That baldness helps make the piece effective. Yet no one would confuse it with an ordinary TV program. It stands out precisely because of its visual banality, because it is very nearly a *non-program*. By contrast Brooks's *Famous School* film stood out not because it was an ad but because it was an ad within the context of PBS.

Yet Serra and Schoolman also add a musical soundtrack to the match the non-imagery. This insipid accompaniment is the crucial third element of the piece. Neither explicitly critical like the text nor neutrally administrative like the text's presentation, the "muzak" seems aggressively propagandistic, a too-obvious attempt to pacify the critical faculties aroused by the critique, a hand-tipping, slightly smirking acknowledgment that the system is busy hiding its operations under the light jazzy sounds of a bustling marketplace. As it happens, the soundtrack to *Television Delivers People* (at least the canonical version I have heard) is provided by the Manfred Minnich String Orchestra. *Television* includes two songs, "That's Why" and, five minutes in, "Beauty Salon," that appeared on a 1970 album recorded for Sonoton, a label that produced licensable music in a wide range of genres.

Yet in choosing licensable music that is muzak-*like* rather than, for example, rerecording actual muzak, Serra and Schoolman adhere to the usual copyright conventions and only perform their subversion of them. (Brooks, in contrast, fakes his thefts and announces his fakes.) Certainly their choice has not struck critics as in any way undercutting their media-critical bona fides. For in addition to being a corporate provider of canned music for commercial enterprises, by 1973 "muzak" had been a term of approbation for a decade or more.[59] Critics believe they hear "muzak," and muzak is what they disdain; but what they are not hearing is the silent operation of the system of intellectual property.

Still, the de-specificity of muzak (or string-heavy Easy Listening, which is here being mistaken for muzak) is crucially related to the work's invocation of mass media. Television in 1973 still operated according to what Richard A. Peterson and Russell B. Davis, Jr., contemporaneously dubbed "vertical" programming: given a competition for overall market share, networks varied their programming "greatly, both through the day and from week-day to weekend." And yet "at any one time in the schedule, however, the programming of each network was much like that of others."[60] The post-war arrival of television had captured much of the radio audience, and in response radio broadcasters moved away from vertically programmed networks to "horizontally programmed" stations that differentiated themselves from local competitors by adopting different formats—those formats that Brooks took as received categories in *Star Is Bought*. In this regard, radio was decidedly more advanced than television. TV was a truly "mass medium"—Serra and Schoolman were not wrong—while radio was entirely subsumed by formats. That historical shift would only come to television in the wake of the cable revolution, and even then it would be incomplete: the "major networks" continue to base their programming on dayparts. Within *Television Delivers People*, "massness" is *figured by* the muzak; radio, in contrast, as a formatted medium subject to *horizontal* differentiation seems more insidious, more aligned with Max Horkheimer and Theodor Adorno's analysis of genre and prestige differentiations in classical Hollywood: "Something is provided for all so that none may escape; differences are hammered home and propagated. The hierarchy of serial qualities purveyed to the public serves only to quantify it more completely."[61]

Yet even muzak was not what it had been by 1973. As Joseph Lanza and Hervé Venel variously explain, Muzak's model of mood management through "stimulus progression" was under assault. In place of background music that aimed to subliminally guide workers to greater productivity through the day, new competitors offered "foreground music" to enlist consumers in a company's particular brand identity. This changed the sort of music that one heard as well. The arrival of "foreground" music services such as Audio Environments, Inc. and Yesco put paid to Muzak's approach of remaking popular songs in 1,000-strings-of-death versions. The company struggled against its hipper, more formatted competitors, first by distributing original artist recordings rather than covers, then by launching its own foreground service in 1980 and eventually merging with Yesco in 1987.[62]

One line from *Television Delivers People* is true of network television and remains true of formatted radio: "In commercial broadcasting the viewer pays for the privilege of having himself sold." What Serra and Schoolman did not foresee was the resourcefulness of the market in periods of flux, the ability of the culture industry to generate sufficient differentiation that it might retain an audience ready to sneer at the *muzakification* of media. Brooks joked about the opposite, the possibility that the entire nation would be made an audience unwittingly, but he knew from his tours, his performances at the Troubadour, and his reflections on contemporary radio that such universalization was unlikely. Without doubting that consumers of commercial media bring themselves to market, or that stars long to be bought themselves, Brooks sought the contours of those exchanges—not simply in the demand that one pay for a ticket to a show one did not see, but in similar scenes of instruction, contemplation, close reading, and critical audition.

Over half a decade, Brooks constructed a mode of New Comedy practice with unparalleled breadth that could bring together media-critical practices directed at magazine publishing, live performance, radio, and television, that could unite the subversive educational scenarios of the Famous School and the joke-mandala with the formal subversions of the animal "film" and the pseudo blooper. It had room for questions about the propositionality of the joke (or the work of art) alongside name-naming criticism of key players in the US media ecology. Its social commentary did not lie in a haughty assumption that "real" social problems could be reduced to the discourses of their appearance. Instead, Brooks took the real problems that confronted him, medium by medium, activated by particular events (the collapse of FWS; the rise of kinestatic filmmaking) and found ways of opening up critical habitations that might simultaneously speak to their cultural typicality—contemporary television and radio—and their historical specificity. I have shown that those habitations have specific occasions and conceptual consequences and that the passage between those scales is managed via a relentless reflexivity. That reflexivity has been seen as a limitation of Brooks's TV-bit-based approach. But as the reflexive embodiment of a medium already at a fever pitch of reflection, Albert Brooks stood as a singular figure against the ground of US television. That differentiation was always in danger of collapsing. Brooks managed to sustain it through suddenness, surprise, speed, and a dedication to the display of intermedial collisions at every occasion.

NOTES

1. Richard Zoglin, *Comedy at the Edge: How Stand-up in the 1970s Changed America* (London: Bloomsbury, 2017), 110–11.
2. Johnny Carson. *Tonight Show*, guest appearance by Albert Brooks, aired June 6, 1973, on NBC. Available at <https://youtu.be/nDO3IJKB-P8> (last accessed December 28, 2020).
3. Zoglin, *Comedy at the Edge*, 110.
4. Jeff Menne discusses this in his chapter.
5. Zoglin, *Comedy at the Edge*, 117.
6. Zoglin, *Comedy at the Edge*, 123.
7. Paul Nanas, Brooks's long-time manager, email to author, August 14, 2018.
8. Paul Slansky, "Albert Brooks is Funnier Than You Think," *Deadspin*, May 9, 2014. Available at <https://thestacks.deadspin.com/albert-brooks-is-funnier-than-you-think-1573238010> (last accessed December 28, 2020).
9. Zoglin, *Comedy at the Edge*, 113.
10. Albert Brooks, "Albert Brooks as Carl Heller," *American Music Awards*. Aired February 19, 1974, on ABC. Available at <https://www.youtube.com/watch?v=r2Z6AfsNSJA> (last accessed December 28, 2020).
11. Zoglin, *Comedy at the Edge*, 116
12. Albert Brooks, *Comedy Minus One*, Rhino/WEA, 1993, compact disc.
13. Zoglin, *Comedy at the Edge*; Dave Nuttycombe, "Albert Brooks and the Rise of 'New Humor,'" *Vulture.com*, February 9, 2011. Available at <https://www.vulture.com/2011/02/albert-brooks-and-the-rise-of-new-humor.html> (last accessed December 28, 2020).
14. To anticipate: Despite the alliances between Brooks and other conceptual artists I will be calling Brooks's works works and not propositions à la Joseph Kosuth. That is because the aim of these performances and their records is to highlight the effort necessary to produce or procure the position from which the proposition has been made. When Benjamin Buchloh writes of the founders of Conceptual Art that "Their convictions were voiced with the (by now often hilarious) self-righteousness that is continuous within the tradition of hypertrophic claims made in avant-garde declarations of the twentieth century," he points to the possibility of an alternative temporality for the hilarious, namely, via the hypertrophic claims of advertising. That would of course provide the infradiscourse of Brooks's relentless pitching of himself and his projects. Buchloh follows that sentence by quoting Joseph Kosuth's prohibition against the notion of a "conceptual *work* of art" (108). Benjamin Buchloh, "Conceptual Art 1962–1969: From the Aesthetic of Administration to the Critique of Institutions," *October* 55 (Winter 1990): 105–43.
15. For an extensive consideration of stance in relation to West Coast art, see Jacob Stewart-Halevy, "California Conceptualism's About-Face," *October* 163 (Winter 2018): 71–101.
16. Kosuth, "Art after Philosophy"
17. Buchloh, "Conceptual Art 1962–1969."
18. David Joselit, *Feedback: Television Against Democracy* (Cambridge, MA: MIT Press, 2007), xi.
19. Joselit, *Feedback*, 85ff.
20. The collected works of Top Value Television are available at <www.tvtvnow.com> (last accessed December 28, 2020).
21. Ed Friendly and George Schlatter, *Turn-On*. Aired 1969, on ABC.
22. Zoglin, *Comedy at the Edge*, 111.
23. Joselit, *Feedback*, 101.
24. Joselit, *Feedback*, xii.

25. Albert Brooks, "Albert Brooks' Famous School for Comedians," *Esquire*, February 1971, 89–94.
26. "Wednesday's Television Programs," *Los Angeles Times*, October 20, 1971, G23. It doubtless aired on other dates and times on other PBS affiliates. *GADM* deserves to be much better known. A DVD anthology was issued in 2015 with an appreciative essay by David Bianculli. *Great American Dream Machine*, television program DVD. USA: PBS/S'More Entertainment, 2015.
27. Lee Eisenberg, "Back Stage with Esquire," *Esquire*, February 1971, 8.
28. Jessica Mitford, "Let Us Now Appraise Famous Writers," *The Atlantic Monthly*, July 1970. Available at <https://www.theatlantic.com/magazine/archive/1970/07/let-us-now-appraise-famous-writers/305319/> (last accessed December 28, 2020).
29. William W. Kiefer, "Writing Instructors Want Better Status, Conditions," *Hartford Courant*, August 12, 1971, 24.
30. The advertising pledge was announced in June 1971 and revised further in December; "Four Schools Agree to Shun Deceptive Advertising," *New York Times*, June 18, 1971, 32; "Famous Writers School Agrees To Substantial Revision of Ads," *New York Times*, December 14, 1971, 32. The bankruptcy declaration listed liabilities of more than $40 million and assets less than $28 million. *New York Times*, February 9, 1972, 61. It emerged from Chapter 11 bankruptcy in 1973. "From Paint to Pipe: FAS Draws up Plan for New Business," *Wall Street Journal*, November 28, 1975, 14.
31. "Rugoff in Short Pickup from Educational Video," *Variety*, December 22, 1971, 5.
32. Dan Graham, "Homes for America," *Arts*, December 1966/January 1967, 21–2. It was reprinted in altered forms many times. For the variants see Alexandra Wolf, "Dan Graham's *Homes for America* re:visited," *all-over*, 2015. Even the "facsimile" of the original version in Dan Graham, *For Publication* (Los Angeles: Otis Art Institute, 1975), 17–20, has been significantly rearranged.
33. Dan Graham and Sabine Breitwieser, "Dan Graham," *Museum of Modern Art Oral History Program*, November 1, 2011. Available at <https://www.moma.org/momaorg/shared/pdfs/docs/learn/archives/transcript_graham.pdf> (last accessed December 28, 2020). The discussion of the early work captures, in its meandering way, some of Graham's sense of the linkages between his diverse projects. For another take on *Esquire* see Peter Scott, "Grahamarama," *artnet*, July 7, 2009. Available at http://www.artnet.com/magazineus/features/scott/dan-graham7-7-09.asp (last accessed December 28, 2020). Brooks and Graham cross over in multiple ways, not simply their sense that *Esquire* was the logical place in which to launch a media critique. One of Graham's early and essential writings was about the *Dean Martin Show* (Dan Graham, "Dean Martin/Entertainment as Theater," *Rock My Religion* [Cambridge, MA: MIT Press, 1993], 56–65), originally appearing in 1969; it spawned Graham's performance piece *Lax/Relax*.
34. Graham, *Arts*, 22; Graham, *For Publication*, 20.
35. Graham, *Arts*, 22; Graham, *For Publication*, 18.
36. Buchloh, "Conceptual Art," 141.
37. Graham and Breitwieser, *Museum of Modern Art Oral History Program*, 9–10.
38. David Antin, *Talking* (Chicago: Dalkey Archive Press, 2001), 151.
39. Antin, *Talking* 151.
40. Tim J. Anderson, "Listening to the Promise of a Better You: Considering the Instructional Record," *Leonardo Music Journal* 26 (2016): 28–31. Irv Kratka, "Q + A," *Music Trades*, May 2015, 48–53.
41. Drew Friedman, "Co Star, The Record Acting Game," *drewfriedman* (blog), November 8, 2011. Available at <http://drewfriedman.blogspot.com/2011/11/co-star-record-acting-game.html> (last accessed December 29, 2020).

42. On the record *Comedy Minus One* and on a videotaped October 25, 1973 appearance on *The Flip Wilson Show* "Williams" is third.
43. Mason Williams, "Original Classical Gas Video '3000 Years of Art'." Available at <http://www.classicalgas.com/gasvideo.html> (last accessed June 2, 2020).
44. Mason Williams, "Classical Gas—3000 Years of Art," mp4 video, 3:11. Available at <https://www.youtube.com/watch?v=viyufRQKlto> (last accessed December 29, 2020).
45. "Convention," *The Living Room Candidate: Presidential Campaign Commercials 1952–2016*, (Astoria, NY: The Museum of the Moving Image, 2020), video 49 sec. Available at <http://www.livingroomcandidate.org/commercials/1968/convention#4019> (last accessed December 29, 2020); "Failure," *The Living Room Candidate: Presidential Campaign Commercials 1952–2016*, (Astoria, NY: The Museum of the Moving Image, 2020), video 4 min. Available at <http://www.livingroomcandidate.org/commercials/1968/failure#4009> (last accessed December 29, 2020); "Crime," *The Living Room Candidate: Presidential Campaign Commercials 1952–2016*, (Astoria, NY: The Museum of the Moving Image, 2020), video 1 min. Available at <http://www.livingroomcandidate.org/commercials/1968/crime#4023> (last accessed December 29, 2020).
46. Zoglin, *Comedy at the Edge*, 114. Brooks did a version on *The Tonight Show with Johnny Carson* that aired February 18, 1972. Based on that, there is no evidence that the book is from *Time-Life*, which does not seem to have published such a volume, but I have not been able to locate it. In any case, it has similarities to many lavishly illustrated animal books of the era. The book appears to be called simply *ANIMALS*. It features pictorial laminated boards and low-text, image-heavy two-page spreads throughout.
47. Bob Kirsch, "Talent in Action: Albert Brooks; Kenny Rankin," *Billboard*, July 21, 1973, 58.
48. Max Eastman, "To Diagram a Joke," *Enjoyment of Laughter* (New York: Simon & Shuster, 1936), 279–89; Robert Benchley, "Why We Laugh—Or Do We?" *The New Yorker*, January 2, 1937, 14.
49. Eastman, "To Diagram a Joke," 317.
50. The sources of the mandala in pop culture span a range of discourses: the religious, the psychedelic, the orientalist. See Rose Harris-Birtill, *David Mitchell's Post-Secular World: Buddhism, Belief, and the Urgency of Compassion* (London: Bloomsbury, 2019), 137–66; Daniel G. Noel, ed. "Jung's anti-modern art of the mandala," *Picturing Cultural Values in Postmodern America* (Tuscaloosa: University of Alabama Press, 1995). Available at <https://philpapers.org/rec/DOTPCV> (last accessed December 29, 2020). See the works by Allen Atwell, Lex de Bruijn, Hugo Mujica, and Usco in Robert E. L. Masters and Jean Houston, *Psychedelic Art* (New York: Grove, 1968).
51. Reinhardt would produce an update to a cartoon from fifteen years earlier: Ad Reinhardt, "How to Look at Modern Art in America," *ARTnews*, Summer 1961, 36–7.
52. Thomas Hess, *The Art Comics and Satires of Ad Reinhardt* (Rome: Marlborough, 1975), 23, cited in Prudence Pfeiffer, *Routine Extremism: Ad Reinhardt and Modern Art* (PhD diss., Harvard University, 2010), 104.
53. Ad Reinhardt, *Art-as-Art: The Selected Writings of Ad Reinhardt* (New York: Viking, 1975), 188.
54. Buchloh, "Conceptual Art," 111.
55. Albert Brooks, *A Star Is Bought*, Wounded Bird Records, 2017, compact disc.
56. For a discussion of Goodman's relationship to copyright, see Joanna Demers, *Steal This Music: How Intellectual Property Law Affects Musical Creativity* (Athens: University of Georgia Press, 2006), 76–8.
57. For photos of the sleeve and labels, see <https://www.discogs.com/Kermit-Shafer-Super-Bloopers-Vol1/master/478922> (last accessed December 29, 2020).

58. *Television Delivers People*, video installation created by Richard Serra and Carlota Fay Schoolman. Collected in *Surveying the First Decade: Volume 2*. USA: Video Data Bank, 2008.
59. Hervé Venel, *Triple Entendre: Furniture Music, Muzak, Muzak-Plus* (Champaign: University of Illinois Press, 2013), 47.
60. Richard A. Peterson and Russell B. Davis, Jr., "The Contemporary American Radio Audience," *Popular Music and Society* 3, no. 4 (1974): 299–313.
61. Max Horkheimer and Theodor Adorno, *Dialectic of Enlightenment*, trans. Edmund Jephcott (Palo Alto, CA: Stanford University Press, 2007), 97; translation modified in light of the earlier Continuum version, 123.
62. Venel, *Triple Entendre*, 71–3; Joseph Lanza, *Elevator Music: A Surreal History of Muzak, Easy Listening, and Other Moodsong* (Ann Arbor: University of Michigan Press, 2004), 219–20. For further considerations of Muzak, foreground music, and the manipulation of mood, see Paul Allen Anderson, "Neo-Muzak and the Business of Mood," *Critical Inquiry* 41 (Summer 2015): 811–40; Ronald M. Radano, "Interpreting Muzak: Speculations on Musical Experience in Everyday Life," *American Music* 7 (Winter 1989): 448–60; Jonathan Sterne, "Sounds like the Mall of America: Programmed Music and the Architectonics of Commercial Space," *Ethnomusicology* 41 (Winter 1997): 22–50.

CHAPTER 3

The Counterculture Squared: Albert Brooks's *Saturday Night Live*

Jeff Menne

There is a counterfactual history worth imagining, one in which late night television never became hip—no *Saturday Night Live* in the form we have come to know it, and no evolution of the form through *The Kids in the Hall* (HBO, 1988–93; CBS, 1993–5) and Jon Stewart and whatever comes next. This would be the history in which Albert Brooks was the permanent host of *SNL*, and week after week the show was framed by his effacing style rather than the free-form styles brought by the rotating cast of hipsters who hosted the first season—George Carlin, Robert Klein, Lily Tomlin, Richard Pryor, and so on. This history nearly came to pass. The story goes that in planning the show, Lorne Michaels and Dick Ebersol approached Brooks and asked if he would be its full-time host. Brooks suggested instead that he contribute short films to the show, Michaels and Ebersol accepted, and this was the situation for the first half of the debut season before the arrangement ended. "I sort of felt that I was the first stage of the rocket that went to the moon," Brooks has said, "I provided a service, I helped to get them off the ground, and about two miles up I was thrown into the ocean."¹ Hence the history we do have is one in which Brooks scarcely left his imprint on *SNL* and the show meanwhile revolutionized television comedy and hangs around today as an institution overseen by Lorne Michaels (more or less) alone.

It's easy to see, though, what drew Michaels to Brooks: they both favored a kind of meta-comedy whose target was the institutional framework of show business itself. *SNL*, for instance, would famously mock the commercials that necessarily interrupted its broadcast. In this and other gestures they could imagine they were biting the hand that fed them. But what distinguished Michaels and Brooks is perhaps more to the point. Brooks's comedy tended to satirize the institution not by being iconoclastic but by being obsequious. His running joke was that he recognized what was professionally required of him, and he tried conforming to it. This is one outcome of the new comedy, which can be traced from Lenny Bruce and Dick Gregory to George Carlin and Richard Pryor, but it's not the approach Michaels would pursue. My argument here will be that *SNL* was a key moment in the counterculture's accommodation to institutions, particularly in terms of the self-understanding of the professional class—the so-called new class—and by understanding the sensibility that *SNL* retailed, we get a sense of how the new class was politically redefined as the liberal consensus gave way to the conservative revolution. In this process, I'll argue, Michaels's proud iconoclasm laid a channel for the anti-statist energies animating the counterculture in a way that Brooks's anxious conformity never could, and this played out in terms of television and film, both their cultural meanings and their industrial norms.

To say that Albert Brooks was one outcome of counterculture comedy is to say that its satirical impulse could be reformist as much as radical. Whereas a publication like *The Realist* or a repertory like The Committee required alternative institutions, Brooks made his career within the mainstream institutions. He was born into a show-biz family, his father having featured on Al Jolson's and Eddie Cantor's radio shows, and he grew up a schoolmate of other show-biz kids, such as Rob Reiner and Larry Bishop. He made his name on variety and late-night shows such as *The Flip Wilson Show* and *The Tonight Show* with Johnny Carson, and many of his bits were deconstructive and self-aware. In a 1973 appearance on *The Tonight Show*, he confessed to the audience, "Here I am five years into my career, I have no more material left." But he's on TV anyway, he tells us, because that's the business. His record company insisted. "How are people gonna know," he says as he holds up his stand-up album, *Comedy Minus One*, "it's maybe the funniest record ever made, and it's on ABC records and GRT tapes, if you don't go on television?"[2] At bottom of the joke that he was an insider professionalized into the business was the premise that entertainment ineluctably *was* a profession, just like the others, with its own forms of training (its guilds and their apprenticeship system) and networks (cronyism, nepotism, etc.). The first short film Brooks made, in fact, *The Famous School for Comedians* (1972), was a mock commercial for those who were funny socially but wondered if they had "what it takes to become a professional."[3] On one hand, it sent up the Famous Artists School; on the other, it traded on the fact that acting academies and film schools had become a main path into the industry. What's significant for my purposes is that Brooks used film for this send-up which aired on *The Great American Dream Machine* (PBS, 1971–2): filming his comedy might let him stabilize his career, and the rhythms of his lifestyle too, because the medium was orderly and controlled unlike the chaotic and unpredictable nightclub circuit.

The essential difference between Brooks and Lorne Michaels, indeed, might be understood in terms of the ontologies of film and television—as per Herbert Zettl, the former was "medium dependent" and the latter "event dependent." Film, Zettl says, "affords us great control," TV does not.[4] Though Brooks and Michaels were both developing the idiom of meta-comedy, Michaels needed to present his in terms of lawlessness, as if to suggest that his knowing departure from the rules of comedy was fraught with risk. The audience would be on the edge of an event, not in the good hands of professionals. Brooks concedes that he missed this. He told Michaels and Ebersol that "this 'live' stuff" was "absolutely meaningless" to him. "I didn't see anything live," he told them, because he grew up on the West Coast and everything "was always tape-delayed." In this industrial configuration, people worked in a sustainable way. On *The Tonight Show*, Brooks explained, "If you were bad, you were bad; nobody did it over again. But you did it earlier. You didn't have to stay up until eleven-thirty."[5] But for Michaels *SNL*'s "liveness" would give it the look of an event, and producing such an event became an all-encompassing commitment for its cast and crew. There was no life outside it, and as Dick Ebersol put it, liveness was the alibi for this:

> You are asking them to work five or six days a week for 16 or 18 hours! At least they can go home to their wife or husband, whom they haven't seen for the better part of a week, and say, "Hey, I had to do it. The show airs on Saturday. It had to be right."[6]

Because "the cost in human lives is great," Michaels admitted, one had to think of it as something other than a job—a calling, a passion, a subversion of routine, what have you. "One of the reasons I was so curious about live television was hearing about *The Jack Parr Show* and *The Tonight Show*," Michaels said, "how they worked around the clock. It all seemed fairly romantic, which it is indeed." But if shooting "live on tape" was for Brooks an industrial concern—a less punishing lifestyle, more controllable work hours—liveness was for Michaels an aesthetic concern. It was formal; it produced a look. "I believed the show should look, for the first few times," he said, "as if the network had closed down for the night, and these guys had snuck into the studio."[7] What I will suggest in the following is that Brooks and Michaels, though their sensibilities seemed congruent, represented substantively different forms of comedy: Brooks derived his style from the counterculture, but rendered it "square" by pitching his work as a kind of industrial critique, which didn't sit well with *SNL*, since the show was in the end a form of aesthetic critique. The show's hipness, moreover, was predicated on an aesthetic critique that effectively left its industrial underpinnings untouched. Had Brooks fashioned the look of *SNL* we might imagine viewers would have seen nothing but these underpinnings.

DOMESTICATING THE COUNTERCULTURE

From the start the problem with making *SNL* hip was that it was on TV. The network presumed that the people the show would target would not stay home and watch it. But Ebersol knew that "the only way this show would work would be if the young embraced it... Johnny [Carson] was the most brilliant person in the world but his show wasn't for teenagers."[8] The baby boomers were the TV generation, in that they were raised on it, and because they had learned its conventions so thoroughly they were also the fiercest critics of the medium. This seems apt, in that they were also the most educated generation up to that point. Their education turned them into critics of the medium most familiar to them. Michaels has acknowledged the importance of the historical moment, and Marshall McLuhan, who—Michaels notes—was at University of Toronto at the same time he was studying there, had said that "we were leaving the industrial age and coming into the information age."[9] When the show later succeeded, it was received in these terms. TV critic Michael Arlen would commend it for dealing "with the morass of media-induced show-business culture that increasingly pervades American life."[10] Michaels was therefore at all times sensitive to the low regard in which TV was held and the difficult task he faced in trying to elevate it. In the spirit of the show, he made light of the medium. "We're still trying to figure out how to get these people into the little box," he joked with Tom Snyder in the run-up to the show's debut. Theodor Adorno had suggested in fact that the scale of the screen was directly proportional to our low regard for its stars. "The little men and women who are delivered into one's home become playthings for unconscious perception," he wrote, "They are, as it were, his property, at his disposal, and he feels superior to them."[11] Michaels knew in constructing the show that he had to address the reputation of TV. He nearly did not add John Belushi to the cast, as it happens, because he expressed the disdain of TV typical of his generation. "Belushi came in for a meeting with me," Michaels said, "and he was heavily bearded at the time. And he had this stance—he was a radical actor, he wasn't going to do television. And I said, 'Thank you very much, that's fine. Why are you here?' Well, he'd heard that I represented something new in television. But the more he would talk about how television was shit, the more I would say that I loved television."[12] The Adorno critique Michaels was trying to outrun was that TV "collapsed the distance between product and spectator," that by way of it the culture industry, which served up its offerings as commodities "simply by virtue of the function of advertising," had brought its peculiar forms of unfreedom into the space of the home.[13]

One form of this unfreedom—namely the FCC regulation of the airwaves—was the object of George Carlin's ridicule in his famous bit "Seven Dirty Words You Can Never Say on Television." The problem was not precisely that you could not say these words but rather that the prohibition on them was emblematic of the check that TV generally put on expressivity. Ebersol had struggled to court Richard Pryor for the show, for instance, because Pryor's agent said his client would "never be able to do what he does well on over-the-air television."[14] This suggests not simply obscene language but a whole social terrain of drugs, ghetto life, racialized policing, and so on. When the show had Carlin as its first host, indeed, the controversy was not over the obscene words he might say but whether or not he would wear a suit. NBC worried, Michaels claims, that it would lose affiliates if Carlin wore a T-shirt. Carlin got around the issue by wearing a three-piece suit with a T-shirt. *SNL*, it might fairly be said, opened up the expressive ambit of TV to include, as Michael Arlen would say, "important new trends in modern comedy" which, if denied, would have been "to deny people an important way of looking at and identifying with their world."[15] But the other form of unfreedom that TV spread—namely commodification—was more complicated because it could be redoubled in the very act of unbinding self-expression. A stock criticism of the counterculture is that it surrendered its political goals for cultural freedoms. David Gross, for one, has made this analysis in terms of the schematic difference between its politicos and the hippies. The politicos critiqued the hippies, Gross says, for their belief that "just *living differently*" would be enough to change the world." In this vein Yippie leader Jerry Rubin had argued that "*politics is how you live your life*, not whom you vote for." In Rubin's philosophy, the promiscuity of the counterculture lifestyle would immunize it against co-optation. "*We cannot be co-opted*," he claimed, "*because we want everything*."[16] The coherence of this philosophy is less important for my purposes than the kind of responses *SNL* mounted to it. There was the official response—let's say—and the Albert Brooks response.

The official response took the form of a mock commercial that ran in episode 2 (October 18, 1975).[17] Anne Beatts attributes the idea to writer Michael O'Donoghue. It begins on an empty frame of a faux brick wall streaked with yellow spray paint, with Jerry Rubin speaking in voice-over: "The 1960s, a time of change, a time of sharing, a time of growth." Bob Dylan's "Blowin' in the Wind" plays underneath his voice. Rubin steps into the frame and introduces himself, "Hi, I'm former Yippie leader Jerry Rubin, and I lived those years with you. Burning draft cards, liberating administration buildings, and of course, scrawling revolutionary slogans on the walls in spray paint." There are two important notes struck here: first, that Rubin is telling his audience he "lived those years with you," thus hailing the spectator as a thirty-something; and second, the consignment of the 60s to a closed past. The verdict of the Chicago Seven trial had only been rendered in February 1970. To imagine this period as that—a period, with its own integrity—is an act of fiat. There were good reasons, of course, to think of the 60s in the past tense: Saigon had fallen in April of 1975, thus ending the war that "the sixties" might be said to have been coextensive with, and in the coming year Apple Inc. would be founded and Jerry Rubin would become an early investor. Hence in this moment, it's plausible to say that the counterculture entrepreneur was shaping the legacy of the 60s more powerfully than were the marginalized politicos, and Rubin, who will notoriously be remembered for his transition from Yippie to Yuppie, was prominent in redefining the baby-boom revolution: "Wealth creation," he would say in the 80s, "is the real American revolution."[18] In the *SNL* commercial, Rubin is shilling for wallpaper. "Now the Berkeley Collection is capturing those colorful years," he says, and he offers a graffiti sentiment for aging hippies of all types ("the dissident," "the peacemaker," etc.) on "pre-trimmed, pre-pasted rolls of durable, decorator-approved wallpaper perfect for your den or recreation area." In this, *SNL* is making a pitch to an imagined audience of baby boomers who have aged into the job market and domestic life. They are staying home on Saturday nights; they have kids, after all. But this is not instant nostalgia. The tone is different, more self-aware. What it suggests is that the boomers were hip enough to be always-already in on their own commercial exploitation. In the final image, Rubin raises his fist and says, "Up against the wallpaper, [Bleep]," to signal that if "motherfucker" could not be said on air, *SNL* could skirt the prohibition by making viewers think the word themselves.

Albert Brooks's response, by contrast, is subtle, hardly political on its face, and certainly not defiant, but directed at the industrial structure behind *SNL* and TV generally. In Brooks's first *SNL* short, "The Impossible Truth," he sends up a *Ripley's Believe It or Not* (it "scans the globe looking for the events that will astound everybody") in newsreel form, featuring the story of a blind cab driver, a report on the country of Israel and the US state of Georgia agreeing to trade places, and a bit about the age of consent being lowered to seven in Oregon.[19] The jokes are not especially funny, in part because their comic motivations are so broad. The story about the cab driver is rooted in the sentiment that NYC cab drivers are so reckless they might as well be blind. Yet Brooks adds a little vinegar in his interview with the driver, asking him, "You still drive?" The driver brushes it off: "Damn right I still drive, what should I do, sit home and collect welfare?" And the bit about the age of consent in Oregon notes that "this progressive state" has changed its laws, which should be read as a swipe at the moral laxness of the left, but the result is a boost to the economy. "Businesses of all types report a surge in activity," says the voice-of-god narrator, while the depicted scene is of a Los Angeles casting agent visiting to recruit young female talent from the state. The bit turns inward, that is, on the meretricious character of the industry itself. The LA talent scout who would look for seven-year-old beauties is nonetheless an easy joke, one that has the markings of the Borscht Belt. What Brooks is targeting rather is the insipid presentation: the newsreel scanning of the globe, the voice-of-god, the amazing story, and so on. Here, we the audience are in on the joke because we are media-literate enough to groan at the hoariness of it all. In what seems a throwaway, then, we get the sting of the joke as its closing text scrolls: "It should be known that THE IMPOSSIBLE TRUTH is a fully copyrighted feature. Infringement of that copyright can lead to a long and costly legal battle that we will win." If the jokes within the film were designed to be broad and formulaic, it now becomes clear that the real joke is that even jokes as insipid as these have been propertized. True to Brooks's style, it is a joke on the form that jokes assume, and it plays on us only when we grasp that our consumption of such culture has enriched whoever has a license on it. It's not always clear what the politics of Brooks's material is, but its sensibility, in this instance and others, is at odds with the hipster immunization against class politics that was otherwise becoming the *SNL* signature. Elaborating a new style—in comedy and elsewhere—might be a professional prerogative, and might feel like an expressive freedom, but the copyright holders are still the same people. This is how Brooks would respond to Rubin.

LIVE FROM MADISON AVENUE

If the content of hipness was that it couldn't be co-opted, its form was liveness. In each the stress falls on celerity, on never being in the place one is expected to be. *SNL* could outrun co-optation by wanting everything, as the Jerry Rubin line goes. And formally, it could outrun regulation by being live and unpredictable. This, the Lorne Michaels line, will not withstand scrutiny. To wit, the reason Albert Brooks's "The Impossible Truth" was the first of his short films to run on *SNL* is that the one he first submitted, "Operation," was too long at thirteen minutes to layer in as a unit of programming. Michaels had asked Brooks to make films three minutes in length, Brooks had argued for five minutes, and Brooks's first endeavor was nearly three times that. The irony, I will show, is that the film is about professionalism, the very domain in which Brooks was failing Michaels by giving him a film that wouldn't neatly fit into television programming. The live unit, by contrast, was suppler. It could move with the moment. For instance, Billy Crystal had quit negotiating an appearance on the first show because none of his bits could be effectively fitted into a two-minute spot. Andy Kauffman, though, had bits of that kind. The improvisatory character of the show came from the fact that between dress and air, Michaels was combining the various units of programming to fit the total run time. Sketches that didn't come off in dress were dropped, Weekend Update jokes were written up to the last minute. Michaels could brandish this as the mark of the show's essential wildness. Before the first episode, he joked with Tom Snyder about George Carlin's seven words: "There is a six-second delay, but some of those words have eight or nine letters." *SNL*'s unfettered expressiveness was vouched in its liveness.

The liveness was a problem from the network's point of view. Robert Klein, who hosted the fifth episode, says that "everyone was quite terrified about the live television aspect of the show. Most people in that building at NBC in New York hadn't done a live show since *Howdy Doody*."[20] Strategically, this was at once the charm and challenge of shooting in New York. The city was the home of live TV, but no one any longer had the professional chops to do it. The infrastructure—both the studio and the crews—were not ready for live broadcast. Shooting live, in effect, induced a state of amateurism. Michaels has said that when he came to Rockefeller Center "there were deer running through the halls." He could choose any floor, and he chose Studio 8H, which in turn required $300,000 to refurbish and technologically outfit. Michaels was encountering the leftovers of a television industry that had by that time abandoned New York for Los Angeles, as Johnny Carson had in 1972, and he was able therefore to re-imagine the medium as though he were in the pioneering set of producers from the 50s first able to shape its look. He turned the infrastructural concerns, in short, to aesthetic purposes. "The show looks a little run-down and ragged," Michaels would say, "That's the look I wanted. Not terribly slick. It's what New York was at the time and still is, by and large. Deteriorated, run-down, and loved because of it."[21] Michaels wanted not to hoard this look and feeling—the look of Times Square in the 70s, the unruliness of CBGB's—but to deliver it into "the middle of the country," where, he concedes, "our strength has always been."[22] This finally is the value of the show's liveness, that it synchronizes New York City with the Central Time Zone, exporting wild, urban feeling into the safe-zone of the suburbs. That the time of Belushi's act, say, was simultaneous with the time of its reception was crucial to its effect. But herein, too, lies an irony: though the show styled itself an amateur siege on a bastion of professionalism, signaled in the name given its cast, the "Not Ready for Prime Time Players," the cast had in fact been trained in the technique—improv—that enabled the show to run live. The Not Ready for Prime Time Players were the ones with experience tailoring their work to the exigencies of the moment. Thus in the early going it may be said the cast were the only ones professionally credentialed, such as it was, to carry off a show of this kind.

Brooks's short film, "Operation," was simply a holdover by this standard.[23] In substance his film was telefilm, which is to say it was, like many other sitcoms, shot on film in Hollywood but intended for broadcast on TV. First, a word about the film, and its object of ridicule; and then, a word about its odd violation of the *SNL* sensibility. The film begins with Brooks directly addressing his audience. "So many of us go through life doing one thing, wanting to do something else," he says, "I'm one of those people. I'm a comedian, show business has been good to me, but quite frankly, if I had the grades in school, I would have become a surgeon." He tells his audience that he's doing something about it. He took out a classified in "ten of the nation's leading newspapers" which stated, "I, Albert Brooks, professional entertainer, wish to perform open-heart surgery, coronary bypass operation preferred." In return he offers to pay the patient $1,000 and there is a "good chance," he notes, that it will appear on national television. On August 31, he says, "a Ralph Porter of San Francisco" took Brooks up on the offer. He was the "logical choice," Brooks says, because he lived in the same state as him and "this pushed quite a few of the legal matters out of the way." And most gratifying to Brooks, he "happened to be a big fan, he was one of those 'anything you do is alright with me' kind of guys." In the premise, then, Brooks mixes a couple of jokes: one, that a move to relax professional standards is absurd, and two, that entertainers, if they be counted among professionals, are the most likely to confuse their specialized skill for a generalizable one. Both these concerns are tied to the historical moment. In the emergent politics of libertarianism, the goal was to beat back such state practices as occupational licensure, a hallmark of the professions, and let the marketplace select out the meritocratic in any given occupation. The Cato Institute, which had been founded a year earlier by Charles Koch and others, continues to track "Occupational Freedom" alongside "Labor-Market Freedom" state by state to this day to calculate its Human Freedom Index. In the same year as the Cato Institute's founding, libertarian philosophy was given the imprimatur of academic respectability by Robert Nozick's *Anarchy, State, and Utopia*, which was a rebuttal of John Rawls's liberal philosophy. Obviously Brooks's joke that anyone would allow a hobbyist to perform open-heart surgery on them is absurd on its face, but his quip that it was better to do this within California and avoid interstate licensing was surely targeting the anti-statist politics then gaining steam. California was a hotbed of competing political movements, thanks to Hollywood—Warren Beatty had served as an aide in George McGovern's 1972 presidential campaign, while Ronald Reagan served as the governor from 1967 to 1975. If Reagan was installing a libertarian ethos in the centers of state power in this moment, it was work he had already begun within Hollywood when as president of the Screen Actors Guild he used his authority to grant MCA a special waiver that would undermine the regulation of the industry.[24] Brooks's joke about California can be read, from our vantage, as a swipe at what we might call entertainment overreach, a process wherein the charisma minted in Hollywood's ambit was getting applied in unrelated fields.

From the absurd premise, Brooks sees the joke through in a deadpan and documentary treatment. In its observations it is meticulous. Details about the coronary artery are displayed by way of a model; Brooks has a dust-up with the surgeon assisting him, then learns he forgot to pull the saphenous vein from

Figure 3.1 Not live television, A Film Written and Directed by Albert Brooks

the leg for the bypass; and the function of the heart lung machine is shown. "Operation" anticipates the "Synchronized Swimming" mockumentary that Christopher Guest, Harry Shearer, and Martin Short made for *SNL* in 1984, and Rob Reiner's *This Is Spinal Tap* (Embassy, 1984), but those, it might be said, were punching down. It's in fact the case that Brooks's short film was able to run at all only because Reiner, his close friend, was the host that week and insisted on it. This seems right for Brooks, who had gotten breaks because his was a show-business upbringing. His first professional gig, after all, was nationally syndicated on *The Steve Allen Show*. In his strain of mockumentary, then, he was not punching down, but punching his class. What rankled Michaels, I propose, is that Brooks thematized class identity when *SNL* hipness depended on the show's indifference to such matters. Underneath this performative indifference, of course, was a respect for the commercial structure of television that Michaels was bound to keep up. In this respect the real problem with Brooks's "Operation" was that at thirteen minutes, it gave no quarter for commercials.

At that length, Michaels said, "it necessitated commercials in the middle and on either end" such that the film claimed "close to twenty minutes" for itself in total.[25] For all that Brooks's film was telefilm, it did not, as the products of that industry did, respect the beats of commercial television. The live unit was suppler, yes, but in the end it was not indifferent but in fact highly disciplined. You could comment on the disciplining function that commercials had, as Michaels would note. "To have eighteen minutes of commercials in your time," he remarked, "to not comment on commercials would be ridiculous."[26] You could use self-aware form to disclose its industrial constraints, that is, but you could not push through the form in order to rearrange the industry. A legendary *SNL* moment illustrates this fine distinction. When Elvis Costello performed on the December 17, 1977 episode (as a replacement for the Sex Pistols, it's worth noting) he struck up the song "Watching the Detectives" but famously interrupted his band by waving his arms.[27] He told the audience, "I'm sorry, ladies and gentlemen, there's no reason to do this song here." He then launched into the song "Radio, Radio." Rumor has it that Michaels, standing offstage, raised his middle finger to Costello for the duration of his performance. "It was a rough week," Michaels admits. "We always let the musical acts pick their own songs. But we spend a lot of time on rehearsals; we block out every camera shot, because every second counts."[28] For this, Costello was banned from the show for over a decade. This incident specifies the meaning of *SNL* liveness: it was a punk attitude, but highly professionalized. Brooks, it seems, gave the lie to the notion that film was the disciplined medium and liveness the anarchic event. On this count it's fair to say that Brooks's critique had substance where *SNL*'s was mere appearance.

A POLITICAL THEORY OF MEDIA

For the baby-boom generation, there had been a couple of ways to understand the set of strictures that television put on programming—one, historical, and the other, financial. Michaels tended to assess the low regard for television in terms of its place in the historical cycle of media forms. Quoting Edmund Carpenter (McLuhan's collaborator at University of Toronto), Michaels explained that "one medium, when it bears the burden of mass communication, liberates the ones that don't." In his moment, it was television that had liberated film. Hence everybody—Michaels included—wanted to become a film director. But Michaels was looking forward to "cable and video disc [liberating] television. And then there will be more freedom."[29] The financial structure of television, though, has meant that it might never enjoy the same freedoms as do other media that are sold directly to their markets. Films, that is, are sold directly to their audience, whereas in television the audience is sold to advertisers. Because the direct buyer is the advertiser, and their purchase is the attention of viewing audiences, a science of demographic study has attended the evolution of television. Television, in turn, has always had to bear this extra, bulky apparatus around it which has endeavored to represent audience taste. The last short film that Brooks made for *SNL*, "The National Audience Research Institute," takes this apparatus as its object, revealing that the effort to represent an audience statistically looks a lot like the bureaucratic state's efforts to represent the electorate statistically.[30]

In the film Brooks profiles a research institute outside Phoenix, Arizona, dedicated to studying what audiences like and why they like it. He wanders among mainframe computers and explains that though many performers say, "I don't care about the audience. If they don't like it fine. I've got my own style, my own bag, I'll wait for other audiences," he is more market sensitive. "I'm not that stupid," he says. "That's why I'm willing and able to change in any direction you choose." He claims to have come to the National Audience Research Institute with his own money and a $25,000 grant ready to undertake the most comprehensive analysis to date of an individual's act. Though he again seems to run together the professionalism of the arts with that of the sciences, we know that quantitative methodologies were used to determine television programming. Todd Gitlin notes that the "old movie studios used audience surveys," and still use them, "but the networks have been far more systematic in deploying the techniques of quantitative social science to try to predict the unpredictable."[31] For the movie studios it was often more a qualitative exercise—executives would attend a screening in the hinterlands, at some theater in Texas or Minnesota, and they would know by the feel of the room if the movie would be successful. The survey cards might refine their sense of why something worked, but it was famously intuitive. Hence moguls like Jack Warner based what would be the general response on whether he personally had to get up to use the bathroom multiple times, or Harry Cohn based it on whether "my fanny squirms." Television, by contrast, was measured by Nielsen Ratings, and its breakdown of demographic groups (affluence, age) set the price for blocks of time and quality of programming. Brooks makes light of the methodologies. In one scene he speaks with Brian Elsner, "one of the first men," he says, "to introduce computers into audience analyzation." Elsner tells him, "We have tons and tons of computer data. By the time we compile it and read it out, it's out of date—we can't even use it. It's embarrassing." Each test that Brooks documents seems equally meaningless, but he seems to dutifully attend them and trust that they will help him better design his product along the lines of audience taste. In one, he shows four people of varying ages sitting in recliners and listening to his comedy album. "On the surface, this test appears to tell nothing" he admits, "however, once the information was fed into a computer, the results were astounding." He does not reveal the "results" nor why they astounded him. After spending "millions of dollars on a testing program," he explains, the institute "can't divulge its secrets on national television."

Brooks is making fun of waste, surely enough, but with a kind of bonhomie that is absent otherwise in the *SNL* ethos. In the final scene, as Brooks walks away from the institute, he holds up the 822-page report they've given him. "I'm going to go on a vacation now and have somebody I trust put this into a synopsis I'll read." In an afterthought, he turns to the camera and says, "If you're going on a vacation, please have a nice one, too." He's playing the part of an oblivious executive so ensconced in his career that he can't imagine that his audience doesn't have a secretary too and won't be enjoying a nice vacation as he does. But the tone is gentle, in my reading, because he himself has built a career on something as unstable as audience taste, and he can in turn sympathize with the impulse to quantify that taste by way of analytics. If "nobody knows anything" is the only verity in Hollywood, according to screenwriter William Goldman, it's good to insulate oneself from the blunt force of this truth. Brooks doesn't believe in the efficacy of the project, it seems, but neither is he bent on tearing down an apparatus that supports so many careers.

But *SNL* was more savage about the institutional supports for entertainers. If they were to radicalize the industry, Michaels said, it "required not pandering, and it also required removing neediness, the need to please."[32] As Chevy Chase explained, "One of the things that made the show successful to begin with that first year and made me successful was this feeling of 'I don't give a crap'," which, he says, "came partially out of the belief that we were top of the minors in late-night television and that we wouldn't go anywhere anyway. So we had no set of aspirations in the sense that this would be a showcase that would drive us to bigger and better things."[33] Chase's take on the show is belied by the competition between cast members and writers, between Belushi and himself, for instance, by everyone's ongoing concern that their bits make the cut, and by the jokes they told about their precarity. In an interview in the week of the show's launch, Michaels joked of the cast, "We've got eight, and we're hoping for two to really work. Not all of these people will become stars." Chase, too, joked before the cast, "I can say without contradiction that I will be working every week as one of the stars on the show," but he said, turning to Dan Aykroyd, "Danny here, who is a funny fellow in his own right, will be on once in a while when we work his contract out." Treating their career ambitions as a joke was only a means of ironizing before the public what was happening backstage. Chase and Belushi both resisted contracts in the early stages, Chase successfully on the technicality that he was under short-term contract as a writer and thus entirely free as a performer, and Belushi until the night of the debut show, according to Bernie Brillstein, when NBC locked him into terms at the last minute.[34] So the "I don't give a crap" attitude was put on to dissimulate what were in fact career ambitions.

Doing one's job as though it were not in fact a job, but instead something more like a lark for which one could or could not be paid, became the *SNL* house style. Aykroyd said that *SNL* was "a television show, but it was also an adult fraternity house, united by bonds of drugs and sex and long hours and emotion and affection that went back years."[35] This was not Albert Brooks's style, of course—rather than affect an indifference to job security, and an animal instinct for the hustle, he displayed his eagerness to please and his need of job security. The performance of desperation that he made his comic métier could not coexist with the *SNL* sensibility; it could only give the lie to it. Michaels's commitment to only pleasing "those people who are like us" on "the presumption" that "there were a lot of people like us" turned out to be the winning hand. Boomers could effectively age with the television set thanks to *SNL*. On screen they could see something of the effect that Siegfried Kracauer described by the "mass ornament," namely a mode of entertainment mirroring their daily modes of labor, but in the political economy of the information society it was not a tightly coordinated assemblage, à la the Tiller Gillers or Busby Berkeley, but rather a recognizable structure now being rolled back to a point that it takes on the appearance of random activity. At this point, whether one's economic activity can be constelled in an ornament—a social pattern beheld from on high—devolves into a debate between Adam Smith's "invisible hand" and Alfred Chandler's "visible hand," between, that is, markets and management. Brooks created comedy on this equipoise. In "The National Audience Research Institute," he begins by bidding goodbye to his audience. "This is my last film in the series for the *Saturday Night* show," he says. "I might be back, but that's not important right now—what is important is you." This is the point of the film, as noted, and the fact that the comedian's lot rests on audience taste gives rise to the two postures outlined above: one a posture of indifference, and the other a posture of anxiousness. Brooks ends the short film by pairing images of these two postures and suggesting the difference between them is trivial. In one test, Test #65, we see the height of expert measurement as an audience member is hooked up to the XR8000, the institute's newest computer, which reads "over two million impulses" from the subject and then translates "these impulses into a critique that can be read and discarded much the same as a typical newspaper review." This is the jaundiced view of information. It can be gathered, processed, and found unhelpful. In the next test, Test #70, Brooks is placed in a small room with a subject who "in an earlier interview expressed an intense dislike for [his] work." The lab techs watch him as he tries to persuade the subject that he is in fact funny, "to bring him around," as he says, to Brooks's "way of thinking," but the test was "designed to show just how deep audience feelings ran." A studied responsiveness and a studied indifference, in this reckoning, amount to the same thing.

But *SNL* could only promote the latter, the posture of indifference, and in doing so they helped lay in place a structure of feeling that would accompany the economic restructuration of the 80s. The show not only lent TV its hip attitude, but in time the movie industry too. The *SNL* players went on to make many of the defining movies of the period. Belushi did *Animal House* (Landis, 1978), then joined Aykroyd in *1941* (Spielberg, 1979) and *The Blues Brothers* (Landis, 1980). Bill Murray did *Meatballs* (Reitman, 1979) and *Stripes* (Reitman, 1981). He also joined Chevy Chase in *Caddyshack* (Ramis, 1980), and Chase as well would be directed by Ramis in *Vacation* (1983). It's easy to trace the network of players in this filmography, and if their domain is the beginnings of Lorne Michaels's media empire, its most significant house writer-director was arguably Harold Ramis. He would help Aykroyd craft *Ghostbusters* (Reitman, Columbia, 1984) for their own and Bill Murray's star turns. The movie can be said to tower over this period, as its soundtrack was ubiquitous in the moment and its box office ranks in the top ten of the decade; it has also been assessed in retrospect, by Reihan Salam among others, as "right-wing propaganda." Salam calls the movie "a powerful brief against 'the reality-based community'," which includes "the academic establishment and the municipal powers-that-be," and it's only a "small, nimble, private-sector cadre" of former *SNL* sketch comics (and a *Second City* one to boot) that "can meet the gathering storm."[36] The movie evinces the kind of magical thinking in which only an unbound marketplace can solve problems. In *National Review*, Steven Hayward approvingly cites the scene in which Drs. Venkman (Bill Murray) and Stantz (Dan Aykroyd) are driven from their university appointments into free enterprise. "I don't know about that," Stantz worries, "I've worked in the private sector—they expect results!" Hayward commends too the use of "a regulation-happy buffoon from the EPA" as the movie's heavy.[37] If Ramis was the writer-director we deserved in the moment of "Reaganite Entertainment," in our counterfactual history Albert Brooks would be the writer-director we needed.

NOTES

1. "*Saturday Night Live* Backstage: Albert Brooks." Available at <https://youtu.be/t3HC42dPQKQ> (last accessed January 9, 2021).
2. *The Tonight Show*, October 25, 1973. NBC. Available at <https://youtu.be/nDO3IJKB-P8> (last accessed December 28, 2020).
3. "The Famous School for Comedians," television episode of *Great American Dream Machine*, dir. Albert Brooks, 1972, PBS.
4. Herbert Zettl, "The Rare Case of Television Aesthetics," *Journal of the University Film Association* 30, no. 2 (Spring 1978): 5.
5. Tom Shales and James Andrew Miller, *Live from New York* (Boston: Little, Brown and Company, 2002), 26.
6. Tony Verna, *Live TV* (Boston: Focal Press, 1987), 171.
7. Timothy White, "Lorne Michaels, Saturday Night Quarterback," *Rolling Stone*, December 27, 1979. Available at <https://www.rollingstone.com/movies/movie-news/lorne-michaels-saturday-night-quarterback-202051/> (last accessed December 28, 2020).
8. Shales and Miller, *Live from New York*, 19.
9. Marc Maron, *WTF with Marc Maron*, "Lorne Michaels," episode 653, November 9, 2015. Available at <http://www.wtfpod.com/podcast/episodes/episode_653_-_lorne_michaels> (last accessed December 28, 2020).

10. Michael Arlen, "A Crack in the Greasepaint," *The New Yorker*, November 24, 1975, 159. Available at <https://www.newyorker.com/magazine/1975/11/24> (last accessed December 28, 2020).
11. Theodor Adorno, "Prologue to Television," *Critical Models*, trans. Henry Pickford (New York: Columbia University Press, 2005), 51.
12. White, "Lorne Michaels."
13. Adorno, "Prologue to Television," 51.
14. Shales and Miller, *Live from New York*, 19.
15. Arlen, "A Crack in the Greasepaint."
16. David Gross, "Culture, Politics, and 'Lifestyle' in the 1960s," in *Race, Politics, and Culture: Critical Essays on the Radicalism of the 1960s*, ed. Adolph Reed Jr. (New York: Greenwood, 1986), 99–118, 108, 112.
17. "A Film by Albert Brooks," segment of television program *Saturday Night Live*, dir. Albert Brooks, October 18, 1975, NBC.
18. John Anthony Moretta, *The Hippies: A 1960s History* (Jefferson, NC: McFarland, 2017), 354.
19. "The Impossible Truth," segment of television program *Saturday Night Live*, dir. Albert Brooks, November 22, 1975, NBC.
20. Shales and Miller, *Live from New York*, 20.
21. White, "Lorne Michaels."
22. Maron, *WTF*, episode 653.
23. "Operation," segment of television program *Saturday Night Live*, dir. Albert Brooks, October 25, 1975, NBC.
24. "Reagan Was a Subject of 60's Screen Inquiry," *New York Times*, September 21, 1986.
25. Shales and Miller, *Live from New York*, 25.
26. "The History of Comedy," Originally aired August 6, 2017, CNN. Available at <https://archive.org/details/CNNW_20170807_020000_The_History_of_Comedy/start/1020/end/1080> (last accessed December 28, 2020). Michaels's comments were originally made in a 1975 interview with Tom Snyder.
27. *Saturday Night Live*, prod. Lorne Michaels, December 17, 1977, NBC.
28. White, "Lorne Michaels."
29. White, "Lorne Michaels."
30. "The National Audience Research Institute," segment of television program *Saturday Night Live*, dir. Albert Brooks, January 10, 1976, NBC.
31. Todd Gitlin, *Inside Prime Time* (Berkeley: University of California Press, 2000), 32. See also Catherine Jurca, "What the Public Wanted: Hollywood, 1937–1942," *Cinema Journal* 47, no. 2 (Winter 2008): 3–25.
32. Shales and Miller, *Live from New York*, 75.
33. Shales and Miller, *Live from New York*, 67.
34. Shales and Miller, *Live from New York*, 67.
35. Malcolm Gladwell, "Group Think," *The New Yorker*, November 25, 2002. Available at <https://www.newyorker.com/magazine/2002/12/02/group-think> (last accessed December 28, 2020).
36. Matt Yglesias, "*Ghost Busters* As Right Wing Agitprop," *The Atlantic*, May 25, 2007. Available at https://www.theatlantic.com/politics/archive/2007/05/-em-ghost-busters-em-as-rightwing-agitprop/42365/ (last accessed December 28, 2020). Reihan Salam originally wrote this on the blog *The American Scene*, but the post is no longer available online.
37. Steven Hayward, "The Best Conservative Movies," *National Review*, February 5, 2009. Available at <https://www.nationalreview.com/magazine/2009/02/23/best-conservative-movies/> (last accessed December 28, 2020).

CHAPTER 4

Irony Ends in Why

Thomas Britt

ANTI-HUMOR

To try to define anti-humor is a losing proposition. As a strand of comedy, its essence is opposition. And practitioners of mainstream comedy, the form to which anti-humor is opposed, are generally reluctant to explain their jokes. So for general audiences, subversive takedowns of straight comedy can be doubly impenetrable. Likely the one constant between mainstream comedy and anti-humor is the desire to end with a laugh, not an anti-laugh. One essential ingredient of anti-humor is irony, which doesn't always warrant a laugh. Irony can shock or disturb a viewer into a changed perspective. In his prophetic 1993 examination of the changing force of irony in literature and television, David Foster Wallace described irony thus: "All irony is a variation on a sort of existential poker-face. All U.S. irony is based on an implicit 'I don't really mean what I say.'"[1]

Comedian, writer, and filmmaker Albert Brooks, often cited as a key influence on the development of anti-humor, defines sarcasm in much the same way in *Looking for Comedy in the Muslim World* (2005).[2] As a comedian abroad, he attempts an American explanation of sarcasm to his bright Indian assistant, saying, "It's when you say one thing but you mean something else." Yet here we return to the constant of distinguishing one type of humor from another: She just wants to know when she's *supposed* to laugh. As a filmmaker, comic, and on-screen persona, Brooks exists in irreconcilable, ambivalent states. Christian Long, situating Brooks's authorial signature within the "American Dream's rhetoric of success" observes that Brooks's directorial efforts conclude with "a kind of success that looks and feels very much like failure."[3] Within this framework, perhaps the postmodern existential poker-face Wallace describes is one of the only powers a man feels he has left.

Where this leaves Brooks the artist and Brooks the persona is as a man, an ironist, waiting for the burdensome business to which he's yoked his life to get more light than heavy. The primary subject matters of Brooks's filmography are Brooks himself and his fate and fortunes within the entertainment industry. Historically, his filmography is framed on either side by the illusion of control, from Captain America in *Easy Rider* to George W. Bush and "I'm the Decider," and the accompanying folly of that illusory control being unmasked.

In *Easy Rider*, a regular reference point for Brooks, Wyatt (Peter Fonda) concludes, "We blew it."[4] Bush, president of the United States during *Looking for Comedy in the Muslim World*, was so haunted by the banner reading "Mission Accomplished" that his speech about successes in Iraq was mostly remembered as a messaging failure of epic proportions. Because Brooks's films so frequently allude to current events and entertainment products, they can be seen as a kind of time capsule containing the larger cultural conceptions of freedom and losing and winning in the postmodern age. Further, there is a certain kind of hope in all of his films, if for no other reason than Brooks's commitment to arguing his way towards controlling the narrative. In a conversation with filmmaker Judd Apatow about his life and career, Brooks attested to the fight for artistic control as an imperative, saying, "You're supposed to. If you're in a position where an argument can win, you're supposed to argue. I mean, I've lost only a few arguments."[5]

In this chapter I examine five films authored by and starring Brooks, including *Real Life* (1979), *Modern Romance* (1981), *Lost in America* (1985), *The Muse* (1999), and *Looking for Comedy in the Muslim World*, as well as one additional film, *Broadcast News* (1987), for which Brooks was nominated for an Academy Award in the Best Actor in a Supporting Role category. Throughout these films, Brooks serves as an embedded satirist or critic savaging entertainment (and news) media formats but simultaneously beholden to and believing in their products for survival. I argue that the Brooks arc from 1979 to 2005 is one in which he, as both a commercial feature filmmaker and a persona within those films, becomes increasingly enmeshed in these institutions and their vagaries, and, not succeeding in blowing them up from the inside, sinks further until his only bitter exit strategy is a weaponized form of anti-humor.

Real Life

Real Life: An American Comedy introduces a structural/storytelling device that becomes common within the Brooks filmography: the opening sequence or first act that pitches the central concept and/or significant theme of the movie.[6] One possible influence for this device is Brooks's parodic approach to more traditional forms of comedy. Among the best known examples of these parodies from Brooks's early comedy and stand-up career was "'Danny and

Dave,' in which Brooks presented himself as a hopelessly inept ventriloquist."[7] A version of this bit from a December 5, 1972 appearance on the *Flip Wilson Show* illustrates the act's economical "reiteration" of the ventriloquist scenario followed very shortly by the "inversion" of that familiar act,[8] with poor Danny dropped to the floor and then water-boarded.[9] The humor here is in the oscillation between the reiteration (Brooks plays Dave as a terrible ventriloquist, but nevertheless a ventriloquist that goes through recognizable motions) and the inversion (Danny becomes dependent and dead; the opposite of what a dummy normally does). An act like "Danny and Dave" trains the Brooks viewer to identify the opening nod to fidelity while also being primed for how Brooks will flip the act to parodic (and then mostly satirical) effect. Thus in *Real Life*, the opening text crawl's reference to PBS's *An American Family* (1973) is a way to predicate the fiction of *Real Life* on top of the actuality of *An American Family*. As with "Danny and Dave," Brooks reiterates the original form (here, a documentary television series) before inverting it.

Within this opening sequence, Albert Brooks appears as Albert Brooks, which is another of the film's variations on grounding the comedic parody within a real-life source. For Brooks the on-screen persona, the goal throughout *Real Life* is to position entertainment media products as a universally desirable end, regardless of the cost. The frequent invocation of science and medicine within the film set up a dichotomy of functions: empiricism vs. entertainment. The strand of empiricism is one of observation and caution, weighing the risks and benefits to the subjects being observed. The strand of entertainment involves careless intervention, forever altering the subjects' circumstances and beings for the sake of the product they've become. This conflict between observing and manipulating is at the center of *Real Life*'s satirical view of Hollywood entertainment, which sees human beings and their lives' projects as content to be upgraded and perfected (indeed, "immortalized") by fictionalizing mechanisms. The character Brooks summarizes this philosophy when he says "To err is human; to film divine." With *Real Life*, filmmaker Brooks satirizes the institution of entertainment media in a number of ways. But the method most pertinent here is his narrative framing of, and cinematographic blurring of, the line between the outer film (*Real Life*) and the inner documentary starring the Yeager family.

An extended sequence at the National Institute of Human Behavior, a key setting for the film's satirical conflation of empiricism and entertainment, includes a description and demonstration of the cameras the character Brooks will use for his documentation of the Yeager family. He introduces a new Ettinauer camera model as "a startling breakthrough in technology. The smallest, most versatile motion picture camera ever made." The technological possibilities of the camera do stoke the imagination. The camera (Figure 4.1) is worn over the head, is operated by body movement and a human-eye like

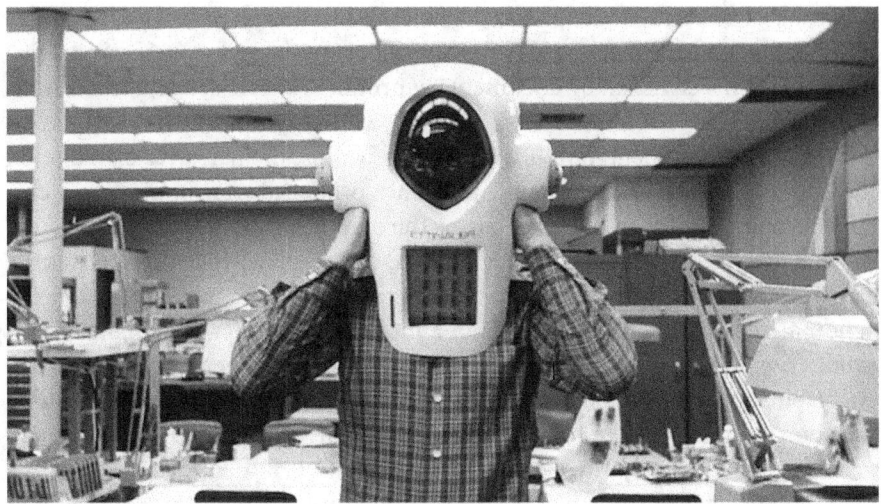

Figure 4.1 Albert Brooks displays the Ettinauer camera, a "startling breakthrough" in observational recording

lens system, uses microphones positioned like human ears, requires no special lighting, and records digitally on circuit chips, eliminating the need for film.

When *Real Life* was produced in 1979, an integrated recording system of this sort was not possible. The direct cinema documentary movement of the 1960s existed within a contradiction of documentary aims with production realities: how could filmmakers possibly claim that their methods were non-interventionist, claim to record real life, when the picture and sound recording devices were so large and obtrusive that the human subject could not ignore their presence?[10] Our present reality has caught up to Brooks's vision for compact recording, a point filmmaker Noah Baumbach mined for comic material in the Brooks-influenced *While We're Young* (2014), which involves a devilishly unscrupulous American millennial artist stealing others' lives with his GoPro camera.[11] Yet what causes *Real Life*'s Ettinauer camera to persist as humorous is not its prophetic properties that now seem plausible, but its alien ones that remain ever strange.

When worn on one's head, the camera transforms its operator's appearance into that of a storm trooper or astronaut or Martian. This is an impression Brooks confirms in a featurette from 2000 included on the DVD edition for *Real Life*, saying said "here was this thing designed supposedly to make as natural a way of photographing people as possible. And yet, in their home, each time they looked up, there was this Martian standing there."[12] Thus, the more critically a viewer thinks about the way the documentary within the film is produced, the more we reflect on fundamental obstructions to filmed reality (like *An American Family*) and the true nature of the character of Brooks's vision for "heightened reality." Thus these so-called Martians remind the Yeagers that their real life has become a performance and reinforce the film's criticism of documentary products advertised as authentic, as something close to actuality.

When the documentation of the Yeagers begins, the narrative explanation for how *Real Life*'s documentary images are produced transitions into a cinematographic approach that transforms the outer film. At an airport, Mr. Yeager (Charles Grodin) stares into the camera, the character Brooks indicates the camera, and then the previously stable outer movie camera begins to follow the action of the documentary subjects in a more fluid manner. The lighting and production values of the outer film and the inner documentary are indistinguishable, but the fluidity of the camera movement and the manner in which the subjects acknowledge the camera are markedly different in the sequences involving documentary coverage of the Yeagers.

The tension, between the quasi-camera ubiquity of the film *Real Life* and the observational shooting done with the Ettinauer within the documentary, corresponds to the narrative tension for much of the rest of the movie. The Yeagers' instant discomfort and seeming regret appears not as compelling material, but rather as cringeworthy exploitation. Brooks the character defends his footage to the scientists, saying, "Tension is action. Don't you ever go to plays?" His entire schema for what to shoot ignores the ethical considerations of what to include and what to omit, instead determining that whatever is "real" is therefore "perfect," because it's "the movie" he's making. The significant professional and personal setbacks experienced by the Yeagers do not affect the Brooks character's aims for the film, even when Dr. Jeremy Noland, project coordinator for the institute, says, "You've strongly altered the reality you're filming. In my opinion, you're getting a false reality here."

Brooks's response to the family's depression is to produce a better life for them through material things, and this action becomes another formal variation on blurring the line between the outer film and the inner documentary. There is a montage of leisure and pleasure, in which the family goes to the mall, to the zoo, and enjoys material comforts. This vision of happiness, of better living through media manipulation occurs in slow motion and has the potential effect of hypnotizing the viewer of the documentary, as well as the viewer of *Real Life*, into believing its vision of happiness. This technique has much in common with the aesthetics of prescription drug commercials and parodies thereof. Here altered reality looks preferable to reality. The insidious pull of the fake as opposed to the real underlies the concluding events of *Real Life*, punctuating the filmmaker Brooks's parodic and satirical aims regarding entertainment and empiricism. The local news outlets, nearly as predatory as the character Brooks plays, assert their right to cover the Yeagers' disintegrating lives. But this newsworthiness damages the commercial appeal of the documentary film, because, as unseen Hollywood producer Martin claims, now the story is something an audience can get for free.

This pressure to maintain the project's commercial appeal, combined with the Yeagers' decision to quit the documentary, motivates Brooks the character to conclude, "The studio is right. The audience loves fake. They crave fake. Reality sucks." He burns down the Yeagers' house, and the ensemble of characters gathers to watch the spectacle. Here, finally, pyromania makes perfect. By blowing up the documentary endeavor from the inside, Brooks the character achieves a kind of truth that his project had falsely claimed from the beginning of the production. This concluding irony of *Real Life* raises the idea that radical action, not scientific precision, is the way to create truth on screen.

Modern Romance

Real Life has earned a reputation as a film that prophesied the rise of reality television programming in later decades. Brooks's subsequent feature, *Modern Romance*, opens with a narrative thread that is a self-fulfilling prophecy for the present movie *Modern Romance*.[13] Brooks is Robert, a film editor, who meets his girlfriend Mary (Kathryn Harrold) for dinner at Hamburger Hamlet. When she asks about his work, he discusses the film he's working on, from "rough mix" to testing or "preview" and the likelihood of having to "recut the whole film". In real life, *Modern Romance* became a target of this same process, with Brooks the filmmaker pressured by executives to change the film based on test audiences' feedback. In his conversation with Judd Apatow, Brooks is cynical about the testing process, recalling that "some of [his] movies tested well enough where they were confused, and others tested so terribly that it's like you killed their children."[14] He says his refusal to make changes requested by Columbia studio head Frank Price resulted in the movie being, for all intents and purposes, abandoned by the studio.

This sad fate only reinforces one of the central themes of *Modern Romance*, that the obsessive search for perfection and approval creates a loop of (darkly comic) despair. From the beginning of the movie, Robert overstates the circumstances of his romantic relationship with Mary. He says they are in a "no win" situation like Vietnam, declaring this will be their last break-up. After the scene ends with her telling him to "drop dead," and his echo of that phrase, the emergence of the credits *Modern Romance*—both the phrase and its placement—provides the first big laugh of the film. The Brooks-influenced Todd Solondz pays homage to this introduction with his own restaurant break-up preceding the title card of *Happiness* (1998).[15]

The connection between Brooks's work and Solondz is worthy of examination because Solondz has earned a reputation for caustic dark comedy that often involves the elision or perversion of truth in commercial literature and film. A few shocking scenes notwithstanding, the most transgressive feature of Solondz's career is what might be called radical honesty in text and subtext. Characters in Solondz's movies say and do things that few audience members seeking entertainment in films would likely think themselves capable of saying or doing. A. O. Scott's assessment of Solondz's approach to narrative in *Life During Wartime* (2010)—that he "allows everyone a chance to be earnestly foolish, unguardedly selfish and also, almost by accident, cruelly honest"—is a fitting description of the characteristic honesty of Solondz's entire filmography. Scott finds in Solondz's films an "almost rabbinical ethical seriousness" that coincides with, or is a key cause and/or effect of, the mordant humor. In addition to *Happiness*, Solondz's *Storytelling* (2001) and *Wiener-Dog* (2016) are particularly indebted to Brooks's uneasy depictions of the form and function of living to create movies about modern life and movies.[16]

Storytelling is a movie in two parts, "Fiction," set in the 1980s, and "Non-Fiction," set in the year 2000. "Fiction" dramatizes the interactions of college students and a professor of creative writing. The protagonist is Vi (Selma Blair), a young woman who wants to prove herself to her merciless professor, Mr. Scott (Robert Wisdom). Because Mr. Scott is a Pulitzer Prize-winning author, his authority is considered absolute. This point, of an industry award serving as life's ultimate goal, is analogous to Brooks's frequent invocation of the Academy Award and other coveted honors. The cold and critical environment of his classroom challenges Vi to write a story that will be received with approval by Mr. Scott and her peers. "Fiction" deals with a number of topics, including race relations and physical disability, in a satirical manner. The aspect of "Fiction" that most resonates with Brooks's inquiry of real life depicted in narrative forms is the act and aftermath of an aberrant sexual encounter between Vi and Mr. Scott (visually censored for theatrical rating and release). Vi sees the sex act as a way to create arresting fiction. When her classmates and Mr. Scott reject the fiction that recounts the act, Vi defends it by saying "But it happened!" prompting Mr. Scott to point out that the act of writing turns real life into fiction. "Fiction" ends with Vi stuck in an irresolvable maelstrom of expression and criticism, one in which the no-holds-barred actuality she put herself through for story content's sake arguably sets her back even further within her peers' critical appraisal. She learns the hard way that audiences love fake; that reality sucks.

Storytelling's "Non-Fiction" was compared unfavorably to *Real Life* at the time of the film's release, with Peter Rainer writing that "Albert Brooks did this art-reality thing a lot better years ago in *Real Life*." But "Non-Fiction" isn't attempting the same satirical/parodic jab as *Real Life*, because "Non-Fiction" is not restricted to a dominant source like *American Family*. In the postmodern "Non-Fiction," everything from Direct Cinema to Dogme 95 and beyond is fodder for Solondz's ideas about the shifting goalposts of truth and reality and success in documentary film. Paul Giamatti stars as Toby Oxman, a man who once had dreams of movie stardom but who now works in a shoe store. Confronting the reality that his teenage dreams are dead, Toby hitches his hopes of post-millennium success to a documentary project that he pitches as a film about "teenage life in suburbia," but whose parameters change for each person he pitches it to throughout the movie.

Toby finds his subject in the aimless Scooby Livingston (Mark Webber). Their introduction to one another in a high-school bathroom occasions the most hilarious dialogue exchange in Solondz's filmography: "You a pervert?" "No, actually I'm a documentary filmmaker." Scooby is a drug-damaged youth, routinely disappointing his father and without any goals except for being on television, like Conan O'Brien. Toby enters Scooby's life with the promise that Scooby will be the star of the film, sealing the Livingston parents' participation in the documentary project. The parallels to *Real Life* are numerous, from the uncomfortable dinner scenes observed by the documentary camera, to Toby pitching the project as "*An American Family* for the new millennium." But the broader connections to Brooks's work occur in the naked ambition of Toby to create a film that will both please an audience as well as bring him personal acclaim. Scenes in an editing room, which focus on the degree to which editors control the narrative of a film, are shot in the tradition of the edit room sequences of *Modern Romance*, to which I will return shortly.

Toby is desperate to see his film with an audience, any audience, from the general public to those with specialized tastes, because he wants to see what they like. This awareness of and apprehension about test screenings has marked Brooks's career and determined the fate of *Modern Romance* as a commercial product. The conclusion of "Non-Fiction" is arguably the most controversial event in the film because it serves as the resolution of a blackly comic (or anti-humorous and offensive) thread of conversation that occurs between Scooby and his parents on the subject of their Jewish identity and the Shoah. The Livingston's maid Consuelo (Lupe Ontiveros) having been betrayed and unfairly exiled by the family, returns to enact the radical revenge of gassing the family to death. Scooby survives because he was away from the house, watching his teenage life turned into a joke at Toby's test screening. Toby and Scooby arrive at the scene of the tragedy to recognize the dramatic ending their documentary now enjoys. "Non-Fiction" ends in real death, one-upping *Real Life*'s derisive ending. The Yeagers lose their house. The Livingstons lose their lives.

Wiener-Dog is also an episodic film, with distinct stories linked by the titular dog who wanders in and out of various human lives.[17] The segment featuring Danny DeVito's Dave Schmerz, a screenwriting professor and stunted screenwriter, is in some ways autobiographical, as Solondz works as an adjunct professor and likely experiences some of the same frustrations as Schmerz. The Schmerz sequence of *Wiener-Dog* sees the old guard of moviemakers as dried up and the new generation of moviemakers as empty. Schmerz, whose next screenplay can't seem to pick up any heat in the industry, is damned to hear pitches from film students whose ideas range from the wholly derivative to non-existent. There are no successful pitches in this section of *Wiener-Dog*, which is all about movies, only sad advertisements for formulas that no longer work. Schmerz's mantra, "What if? Then what?" might have been a successful springboard for ideas in a previous generation, but it is now publicly mocked by a successful returning alum, who is shocked that Schmerz is still around. *Wiener-Dog*'s attention to ideation and pitching and rejection are firmly within the field of film industry anxieties that are Brooks hallmarks.

After realizing his utter isolation and rejection, Schmerz finds a new sense of purpose. He will wire his dachshund to explode and bring down the academic building that houses his enemies. It's no stretch to read this section of *Wiener-Dog* as a darkly comic revenge fantasy of a middle-aged screenwriter whose critics are growing louder and younger and (however undeservedly) more vital than he is. The collision of characters in *Wiener-Dog* is one pitting an old pathetic man against vapid young adults, so there's no traditional human hero to root for. The poor dog is the IED. Through the arc of his joyless ambition, Schmerz is a variation on the Brooks character from *Real Life*. He will succeed, even if the measure of success, his legacy, becomes destruction itself. And the irony of Schmerz's radical action is that it unexpectedly revives his dead mantra. Both the clueless students and Schmerz's eventual encounter with the law, turn on the rhetoric of "What if? Then what?" Here Solondz suggests, through this somewhat autobiographical character, that detractors can be educated, can be made to appreciate the storyteller they overlooked in his time. This theme defines Brooks's later career, including a couple of variations on the acceptability and necessity of bombing.

Brooks and co-writer Monica Johnson structure *Modern Romance* around the parallel activities of film post-production and romantic life. In both his professional and personal pursuits, Robert stays positive just long enough to look/talk/think himself out of satisfaction with the film or lover in front of him. Thus, *Modern Romance* is a romantic comedy to the extent that Brooks appears to want to ground his film in a genre that asks its audience to root for impossible things. He again reiterates certain aspects of the form mostly for the purpose of inverting them, thus our attention to film editing is on the seams, not seamlessness, and the thrust of the romantic plot is towards chaos, not stability.

Unable to continue on in the editing room with the break-up fresh in his mind, Robert takes Quaaludes and waits around his home for the drugs to take effect. The sequence frustrates expectations for any viewer expecting a traditional romantic comedy. One distinguishing feature is the frequency with which Robert talks to himself, conveying the character's situation and feelings to the viewer. This dialogue is not unlike the to-camera address or narration of *Real Life*, yet *Modern Romance* offers no documentary conceit that would motivate a character speaking to the audience in this way. Isolated Robert talking to himself (and the viewer) is a clear example of Brooks bucking screen conventions. Another quality of the film that upends romantic comedy conventions is Robert's unlikableness. This variation on the Brooks persona—let's not forget that Robert is a filmmaker, too—is somewhat duplicitous in his professional relationships. He calls more than one colleague the "best" assistant editor. And in his quest for personal romantic fulfilment, Robert toys with more than one woman. His need is most important, with their emotional lives secondary or comparatively unimportant.

Robert's repeated refrain of "I just broke up with somebody" foregrounds his self-centered nature. That he freely offers the phrase to strangers in public places adds a layer of irony to the pain he's feeling; if he hurts so badly, why announce himself with the very scenario that stung him? But this, too, is part of the film's comic design, as Robert is a character at odds with himself in nearly every way. He cannot stay focused on any course of action, talking to himself and contradicting himself as if the fog of the break-up has clouded his every move. The on-screen narration of his conflicted thought-processes and actions puts the viewer in the middle of that push and pull, a place that is often awkward but also occasionally hilarious. His attempt to date another woman, Ellen, lasts only as long as it takes to drive with her a certain distance from home and then circle back, physically and geographically rendering his circuitous mind state. That *Modern Romance* is structured from self-defeating loops is a form that expertly suits the content of this movie, which is less about romance and more about making (editing) movies.

Halfway through the film, when Mary finally returns to his life in a real sense, Robert proclaims to her in bed that he knows "the difference between movie love and real love." Following this reunion is a long sequence about film editing featuring director James L. Brooks as David, a film director for whom Robert is editing a picture. Robert is certain that he and assistant editor Jay (Bruno Kirby) have improved a sequence of the science-fiction movie they are editing by changing the dialogue and reaction shots of an expository scene. But this is a short-lived victory, as David the director believes that the previous version of the scene was preferable and has the authority to discard the fruit of Robert's potentially film-saving burst of inspiration. In this situation Robert *is* right, but he's not free *to be* right. A later scene about film post-production similarly demystifies the manipulation that takes place before any Hollywood movie reaches an audience. Like the earlier picture-editing scene, the sound-mix discussion and demonstration bring to mind the thankless work that goes into creating a "seamless" experience for a viewer. The amount of obsessive attention given to sound-editing and finding the right sounds of footsteps for an action scene to create an elusively perfect product has the potential to obviate or ruin the obsessed characters behind the product.

The concluding events of *Modern Romance*, in which Robert becomes increasingly obsessed with Mary being his exclusive partner and getting her to admit she's been with other men, bring the film to a scene in which Mary announces "it's over". This declaration is a framing device for the film, which began with Robert's announcement that the relationship was over. Yet Robert argues that his obsessive behavior is a sign that he cares, and this argument works for Mary, who agrees to his proposal of marriage. He responds with, "Perfect. Perfect."

The last joke of *Modern Romance* is text on screen that recounts the couple's marriage, divorce, and plans to remarry. But the lasting impression of *Modern Romance* is to highlight the futility of self-obsessed characters seeking perfection and being temporarily rewarded for their delusions. Saul Austerlitz identifies such a scenario as the common thread of Brooks's career:

> His movies are also all failed experiments. Not for the filmmaker— considering the cohesion of his work, we can only assume that Albert Brooks has accomplished precisely what he had hoped to—but for his characters, who all set out in search of something they are too self-absorbed to find.[18]

Real Life and *Modern Romance* focus the viewer's mind on the ways that Hollywood and the entertainment industry seduce consumers into believing that perfection is possible, despite the reality that every material thing in this world leaves something to be desired. It's no wonder that Brooks the filmmaker is skeptical of test screenings premised on crafting perfect products.

Lost In America

Brooks's next directorial effort, *Lost in America*, at first appears to be a significant pivot away from his earlier preoccupations with the entertainment industry as well as the theme of being fulfilled by material things.[19] *Lost in America* imagines jettisoning the evidence of an American Dream achieved. But this disavowal is another trap. The arc of *Lost in America* is one that sees mobility and freedom from material things as preferable to stability and material comfort. But the conclusion of the film is that freedom in America is predicated on material comfort.

As in the previous films *Real Life* and *Modern Romance*, *Lost in America* utilizes an opening scene that introduces the ideas that will drive the film. The opening images of the film are an exterior shot of a sold home and an interior shot of boxed belongings. These neutral images denote the transition of moving, but could connote an upgrade or a downgrade in status. While the audio that plays under the opening sequence—entertainment critic Rex Reed appearing on a Larry King radio interview—is pertinent to Brooks's view of how comedy films are received, there is also a relationship between Reed's comments and the film's themes of freedom and mobility. Reed, referencing a Mel Brooks quotation, says "I don't need 40 other people to laugh to remind me I should be laughing," explaining that he can attend a comedy film alone and still be qualified to evaluate the merits of the film. Within the framework of *Lost in America* as a comedy about the capriciousness of the American Dream, Reed's comment stands as an ideal that is impossible to live up to; we think of ourselves as earning a place above any social contract, but striking out alone often reveals our indebtedness to others.

The first dialogue scene between protagonists David (Brooks) and wife Linda (Julie Hagerty), the homeowners, expresses this conflict. David cannot sleep because he's conflicted about his status and decisions after having just sold his home. Linda says she wishes they as a couple were more irresponsible and not so controlled. And as he often does in his on-screen avatars, Brooks launches into a pep talk to generate temporary optimism. On the subject of his impending promotion at work, David, who works in advertising, says, "Now I can be irresponsible. I'm in a position of responsibility." Here he imagines the kind of freedom an individual has when they move up the corporate ladder and are less beholden to others. No longer merely an employee, finally in charge of their own destiny. Like Rex Reed going alone to a comedy film in the middle of the day, David asserts his right to step outside of the system and toward individual agency.

For most of the film's first act, *Lost in America* illustrates "First World Problems" like Linda worrying that her life and her new house will be predictable and comfortable to the point of misery, and David facing the complications of selecting features for his new Mercedes. The first significant turning point in the script (again by Brooks with co-writer Monica Johnson) occurs when David does not get the promotion to Senior Vice President he expected to receive. After cursing his boss twice, he gets fired and declares, "How dare you. I want my eight years back" before lamenting his wasted youth.

David's firing is the inciting incident that leads to a plot development most popularly associated with *Lost in America*—selling everything and hitting the road in a Winnebago with a nest egg of $145,000 to provide for the needs of their new lives. Whereas "I just broke up with somebody" was the motif of *Modern Romance*, "My wife and I have dropped out of society" is the phrase David uses to introduce himself in *Lost in America*. It's a portentous phrase; dropping out is only something to brag about when done with freedom and a cushion. Linda uses her freedom to lose their cushion, gambling away nearly the entire nest egg in a single night in Las Vegas that was to inaugurate their life on the road.

Figure 4.2 David Howard (Brooks) proposes a "bold experiment" to get his money back and create positive advertising for Las Vegas

Up until this point in the movie, *Lost in America* appears to be mostly about the American Dream and to have little to do with the entertainment industry, the normal subject of Brooks's critique. However, Brooks injects the film with a satirical view of image making and storytelling central to the advertising industry in scenes such as his plea for redemption from the casino operator (Garry Marshall) (Figure 4.2). David pitches his credentials, not letting the fact that he's in a bathrobe diminish the force of his self-promotion. He continues making references to *Easy Rider*, a film mentioned in his earlier films and that offers an important textual parallel in this film. His pitch to turn "give us our money back" into an advertisement that promotes the Desert Inn casino is already asinine before he elaborates with visions of Santa Claus giving the couple back their nest egg in Las Vegas.

This is arguably the most important scene in the film, because here the concept of freedom and the privilege to live irresponsibly is unmasked to reveal that other sort of privilege that is rife in the entertainment/culture industry: a class of which David is a card-carrying member. In his gall before the casino manager, David makes the case for an unearned individual exceptionalism, the freedom from consequence, redemption without admittance of wrongdoing. In a later sequence, also fundamental to the film's satirical point, David articulates the materialist philosophy that drove his vision of freedom from the opening scene. Lecturing Linda, he explains, "The egg is a protector like a god, and we sit under the nest egg and we are protected by it. Without it, no protection." His anger at Linda for losing their money is justified, but at the foundation of that anger is a hypocrisy that trusts wholly in money to provide the illusion of being free from material concerns. Linda calls him out on his hypocrisy while recasting her folly as a way to stay honest: "If you're really going to drop out, you do it with nothing."

The trail that leads back to society is marked by David's continuing insistence that he deserves better than the common man, a shifting understanding of what *Easy Rider* really had to say about a free life on the open road, and the lure of undeniably shiny objects like a new Mercedes. Perhaps the most striking irony of *Lost in America* is that David ends up being right. He did blow it, but the road back to a secure advertising salary isn't a long one. Being momentarily humbled isn't a high price to pay for re-entry to the kind of lifestyle that a majority of the world's population could only dream of attaining. The final shot of the film brings with it the realization that for guys like David, there is no being lost in America. The viewer wonders if he understands *that* privilege.

Broadcast News

James L. Brooks's *Broadcast News* was neither written nor directed by Albert Brooks, but the film is worth noting because it extends the Brooks persona characterized here and synthesizes the themes of real life versus dreams/freedom that were the substance of Brooks's directorial efforts in the years preceding *Broadcast News*.[20] Brooks plays Aaron, a reporter at a national news network in Washington DC. Though Aaron is arguably a supporting character within the ensemble featuring leads of Holly Hunter (as producer Jane) and William Hurt (as anchorman Tom), it is the somewhat marginalized nature of his role that makes the character ideal for Brooks at this point in his career.

The romantic and professional rivalries in *Broadcast News* would not be one bit out of place in a film written and directed by Albert Brooks. Aaron loses to a born winner who did nothing to earn that winning position. Aaron is wiser than *Lost in America*'s David because he understands that the line between dreams and real life is so tenuous than no promotion ensures permanent victory. When Tom asks Aaron, "What do you do when your real life exceeds your dreams?" Aaron responds "Keep it to yourself." Aaron is also the kind of character Brooks might play in one of his own films because he's once again a man who exists behind a media form. In *Broadcast News*, he's the television news reporter who works to get the story and sometimes plays the voice of God. In this latter function, he makes Tom look better by feeding lines and information into a phone to Jane, who relays that dialogue to Tom, who says Aaron's words live on the air. Aaron marvels, "I say it here, it comes out there."

Aaron is *unlike* a character in an Albert Brooks film because his failures teach him, once and for all, to value the reality over the dream. Tired of being at the mercy of news bosses, he asks for "one shot at anchoring the weekend news," *Broadcast News*'s version of the Brooks pitch. In Aaron's appearance as a weekend anchor, he sweats so profusely that any of his mental assets as an informed reporter recede behind the wet face and body the camera mercilessly exposes. The spectacle of the crew trying to dry him before his next on-camera appearance makes clear that Aaron will not receive a second shot as anchor. This failure, however, results in the clear-eyed realization that he enjoys being the reporter. Aaron's clarity, his honest commitment to be who he is, coincides with a judgment he makes about Tom as the Devil, as a temptation to resist. In this characterization, Aaron warns Jane about devilish Tom's insidious effects on individuals and institutions:

> He will be attractive, he'll be nice, and helpful, he'll get a job where he influences a great God-fearing nation. He'll never do an evil thing, he'll never deliberately hurt a living thing—he'll just bit by little bit lower our standards where they're important. Just a tiny little bit. Just coax along flash over substance. Just a tiny little bit. And he'll talk about all of us really being salesman. And he'll get all the great women.

Aaron's Devil analogy is sounder than the nest egg/God analogy David makes in *Lost in America*. His stance—a critique of American news media becoming indistinguishable from the entertainment media's dream factory—is a moral one. But in "real life," his argument has lost. Decades since *Broadcast News*, American news media now comprises mostly flash and little substance. Albert Brooks the actor is a perfect body for this message in James L. Brooks's film. The warning signs of cultural/artistic decline he offers within his films cohere with Aaron's sage perspective. But as Albert Brooks the filmmaker approaches the new millennium, he risks becoming a figure like Dave Schmerz, lost within the system that once prized his creative premises but now prefers something louder, younger, and more vital.

The Muse

In the 1990s, Albert Brooks wrote and directed *Defending Your Life* (1991) and *Mother* (1996), films that examined the moral courage and familial bonds of the characters Brooks played. But it is *The Muse*, his film from the end of the decade, that offers the most direct evidence of Brooks getting lost in his own arguments about the processes and products of high achievement within the Hollywood system.[21] In *The Muse*, Brooks's character Steven is a Hollywood screenwriter already alienated from the process and product of his labor from the moment the viewer meets him. The opening scene, in which Steven receives a humanitarian prize, gives him the opportunity to point out what's missing from his life: "Being a screenwriter in Hollywood is . . . a lot like being a eunuch in an orgy. The only difference is, the eunuchs get to watch and I'm not even invited to the set." A short time later, when his daughter asks him what a humanitarian is, he answers "someone who's never won the Oscar." Brooks, like his character in *The Muse* has been nominated for an Oscar but never received one and also has a history of making quips about this apparent lack.

Thus the quest from the beginning of *The Muse* is to find a way to earn the ultimate prize of Hollywood, the Academy Award. And the Academy Award is the first of more than a dozen products/brands that are featured so prominently in the film that the plot would not quite hang together without their presence. Product placement is highly conspicuous in *The Muse*, and part of this conspicuousness has to do with advertising trends at the time of the film's production. In *Big Media, Big Money: Cultural Texts and Political Economics*, Ronald V. Bettig and Jeanne Lynn Hall distinguish 1990s movie product placements as proliferating "with the rise of agencies brokering deals between advertisers and film studios, offering sliding scales for background appearances, hands-on use, and insertion into dialogue" and early 2000s product placement as becoming "more central to Hollywood production and promotion budgets."[22] In January 2000, Tim Gray of *Variety* wrote that "When it comes to film product placement, 1999 was a banner year," specifically mentioning *The Muse* as an example of the trend.[23]

Product placement alone isn't a problem that plagues *The Muse*. After all, it's conceivable that this screenwriter who works and lives among filmmakers and wealthy people would encounter Trader Vic's, Paramount, Steven Spielberg, Tiffany, Four Seasons, Spago and Wolfgang Puck, and Universal in his daily life. But for Albert Brooks to indulge in the placement so nakedly and without reflexive critique seems at best like a missed opportunity and at worst a sell-out to the corporate interests that might have otherwise been a target for satire. To give Brooks the benefit of the doubt, it's possible that foregrounding rank materialism is a way of situating Steven within a milieu bereft of spiritual or mystical currency. Yet if that is the point of the film, then why play those elements straight as the filmmaker satirizes Steven's actual leap of faith, which is to trust in a Muse called Sarah (Sharon Stone) to inspire him to write an award-winning screenplay?

The effect of this lopsided approach to satire is that Brooks defangs the greater point his script attempts to make about how investments work in Hollywood. Steven makes it clear that he'll give himself to Sarah completely if she helps him win an Oscar, and Steven's wife Laura (Andie MacDowell) readily accepts the excuse that what Sarah is doing for Steven is (in his words) "mystical. It's magical. It just might save my life." Laura's lack of inquisitiveness and dispassionate acceptance of this mysterious development in Steven's life that involves paying for Sarah's life of luxury creates a family drama free of dramatic stakes. Likewise, the more than $10,000 that Sarah will cost the family *weekly* do not ever appear to strain Steven's comfort. The atmosphere of conspicuous consumption, including the wholesale acceptance of a hustling Muse, isn't funny so much as it is condescending to any viewer who doesn't share the socio-economic buffers enjoyed by the characters in the film. *Lost in America* this is not.

The Muse exists as a satire about investment and inspiration in Hollywood but lacks the sense of counterpoint that made all of Brooks's previous directorial outings included here so successful. *Real Life* contrasts the quotidian existence of the Yeagers with Hollywood's fictionalizing spectacle. *Modern Romance* juxtaposes the struggle of jealousy within romantic relationships with the power to manipulate fictional narratives in an editing room. *Lost in America* entices with the ideal of dropping out of society before intruding with the harsh reality of a bank account running on empty. *The Muse* is, by contrast, completely insular. Steven's story is one that takes place entirely within an elite Hollywood existence where the greatest discomforts include having to take arduous walks to Hollywood business meetings and take a back seat when a wife's business venture is spectacularly successful.

In this way, *The Muse* is influential on later comedies by filmmakers such as Judd Apatow, whose *This Is 40* (2012) critic A. O. Scott reviewed by observing that Apatow "has absorbed some of Mr. Brooks' deadpan, buried-joke filmmaking style, [but] does not share his penchant for anxious introspection." Scott writes that *This Is 40*, which features Brooks in a supporting role, involves protagonists Pete and Debbie, who are "Cushioned by comforts that most of their fellow citizens can scarcely imagine" and "nonetheless feel as if things were starting to go pear-shaped," and that:

> The audience, of course, is free to take up the slack, to despise Pete and Debbie, even at the risk of hypocrisy. Look at those two, fretting about money, with a BMW and a Lexus in the driveway, the kids in private school and enough left over for a romantic resort getaway and a lavish catered birthday party.[24]

The Muse does not encourage any such response nor does it invite us to share in anxious introspection. In the film's third act, an interaction between Steven and an executive varies themes from *Lost in America* and *Broadcast News*, to diminishing effect. The executive says, "Nothing's fair, Steven. That's what life is," and reiterates his advice to take a vacation or go into a different career. Steven calls him the Devil. He begins and ends the picture wealthy, happily married, and longing for an Academy Award. There's no honest way to identify with Steven's outrage because not once in the film has he chosen any pathway apart from the Hollywood system nor has he been challenged to change.

Looking for Comedy in the Muslim World

Brooks's only directorial credit from the new millennium is a war-on-terror-era comedy with the broadest geopolitical setting of the filmmaker's career. The premise, which finds Brooks (playing himself) summoned to join with the State Department as part of a mission "to better understand the Muslim peoples of the world," seems like an ideal way for Brooks to break out of the insular Hollywood mode that deadened the comedy of *The Muse*. At the beginning of the film, a cameo by Penny Marshall, said to be casting a remake of *Harvey*, introduces the comic potential of Brooks bringing his persona to a role originated by James Stewart. Marshall notes that Brooks would be "a different way to go" but that she doesn't want to do "Jewish" for the role. Her dismissal of Brooks before, during, and as he leaves the audition is one of the more concentrated bits of self-deprecation in Brooks's long history of highlighting himself as a "different" sort of leading man. Tom Hanks, not Albert Brooks, is the figure that Hollywood most associates with carrying the mantle of Jimmy Stewart. Describing the "extraordinary ordinariness" of Hanks, Paul McDonald attributes Hanks's popularity to "a particular form of branded identity, combining gender and nationhood as a modern American everyman."[25] Brooks, by contrast, writes a later scene in *Looking for Comedy in the Muslim World* in which Al Jazeera pitches him a vehicle they believe is tailor-made for his persona: a sitcom called *That Darn Jew*.

Brooks is more warmly received at his meeting with government officials to discuss the request of the State Department. Laughter is the new tactic the United States government has chosen to better understand the Muslim population of the world. Brooks's mission would be to go to India and Pakistan and prepare a 500-page report on what makes them laugh. With the memory of the *Harvey* audition in his mind (and in the mind of the viewer), Brooks asks, "How did I get picked?" Their response is, "Quite frankly, our first few choices were working." Ultimately Brooks is not so much prompted by the great service to country, as he is by the promise of receiving the Medal of Freedom, a parallel to *The Muse*'s quest for Oscar gold. Brooks's fixation on awards that grant authority and validation earns fresh inspiration through this attachment to international relations.

On an airplane at the beginning of his journey, one of the men from the State Department discusses Brooks's films, such as *Lost in America*. This is the third scene involving Brooks's film career (following the scene with Marshall and the scene in which he learns why he was picked for the mission) before the second act has truly begun, which creates the impression that *Looking for Comedy in the Muslim World* will squander an opportunity to satirize the vast world beyond the immediate experiences of its director/writer/star. Ryan Bishop argues that this self-centeredness is part of the film's satirical view of American intervention:

Much of the film's humour is self-deprecating, individually for Brooks and collectively for the US. His character, a comedian named Albert Brooks, embodies the somewhat widespread observation that the US was poised at the start of the new millennium for a period of unprecedented global control and yet was completely unprepared culturally and intellectually for it.[26]

Bishop's observation is right, to a point. *Looking for Comedy in the Muslim World* frequently depicts the US Government as inept (they aren't able to make arrangements for Brooks correctly or on time). And Brooks is individually unprepared for his foreign reception. But *Looking for Comedy in the Muslim World* plays as a transitional film in a directing career that has not resumed since the film was released. As a "last" film, it is more ambivalent than his other films, mostly because the filmmaker presents a contradictory view of his own legacy.

Everything in *Looking for Comedy in the Muslim World* circles back to Brooks's failures. Some of these are familiar riffs on his status as a comparatively unknown American film star. Others are more subtle references to his past troubles with test screenings: when his State Department companions argue that a full house at his comedy performance is more important that choosing the right audience members for that performance, Brooks wonders what will happen if the attendees don't speak (understand) English?

A centerpiece of his mission is his stand-up performance in Delhi, which is plagued by technical shortcomings, a cringe-inducing resurrection of his ventriloquist bit, and an aborted attempt to crowdsource ideas for an improvisation, in which he slashes all of the audience ideas (Figure 4.3).

Figure 4.3 Albert Brooks revives "Danny and Dave" for a new audience in Delhi

The "bombing comedian" is a reliable source of humor for anti-comedians who intend the failure as part of the act. Andy Kaufman, Neil Hamburger, and many others have used alienation and confrontation as core techniques of their sets and personas. However, Brooks as an originator of anti-humor required audiences' awareness of the forms he was mocking. How could an act like "Danny and Dave" ever hope to translate to a foreign audience that lacks that foundation of knowledge? By having Brooks the character go through these motions in Delhi as well as resist the audience's suggestions for an improvisation that might relate to their sense of humor, Brooks the filmmaker is admitting to, or asserting, his inability to adapt, regardless of how open his character otherwise appears to be to understanding others.

Looking for Comedy in the Muslim World presents a Brooks character that is no longer as self-absorbed as his characters in *Real Life* or *Modern Romance*. He also lacks the sense of entitlement possessed by his characters in *Lost in America* and *The Muse*. And at one point in the film, he seems to be at peace with the reality that "you don't get punished in comedy . . . you try things, some work, some don't, you're allowed to bomb." Though despite all of these advancements, the film is preoccupied with Brooks's failure to connect with audiences in the way he would choose to if he had more control of his destiny as an entertainer. To reinforce this point, far more people in *Looking for Comedy in the Muslim World* recognize him as a voice from *Finding Nemo* (2003) than they do as an auteur.

One of the most stirring sequences of the film, in which Brooks exhibits rare "bravery," is ultimately an illustration of his small but devoted following: he absolutely kills at a "secret meeting with Pakistani comedians" that isn't broadcast and will never benefit him in any material way. Simultaneously, the geopolitical intrigue of the film imagines Brooks's effects to be impossibly large, outsized to the point that "India and Pakistan have resumed armed conflict" as a result of his peace-making mission. The bombs that explode in his wake are like aftershocks of his resentment, which pale in comparison to the lasting works of political satire, like Stanley Kubrick's *Dr. Strangelove* (1964). Because Brooks the character in the film shares the autobiography (and the stand-up material) of Brooks the real man, it's difficult not to read the scale of this particular backfire as an assertion that the world just didn't appreciate him when he was around.

CONCLUSION

Of course, Brooks's legacy is nothing if not ironic. The conclusion of *Looking for Comedy in the Muslim World* features Amy Ryan as Brooks's wife saying, "I'm so proud of you. What you've done is monumental. You might have changed the world." Years later, in Steven Spielberg's *Bridge of Spies* (2016), the same actress, Amy Ryan, plays the wife of a noble Cold War hero who returns home from a successful mission negotiating an exchange of a captured American pilot for a Soviet spy. This historical hero, James Britt Donovan, actually changed the world. The actor playing the hero is none other than Penny Marshall favorite Tom Hanks.

In 2011, I interviewed Brooks when he was promoting Nicolas Winding Refn's *Drive*, a film for which Brooks received the best reviews of his career as an actor. I asked him about the currency of critical acclaim, and he answered:

> I think if you do something and it leaves a mark, you'll feel it a year later. I don't even know if you'll feel it the week it's happening or the month it's happening. I'm still getting results from movies I made 20 years ago, so if it leaves a mark, it's ongoing. But show business is like this huge slow gobbling machine, and it doesn't—by its very nature, you don't see results in a week. So I don't know.[27]

This quotation brings to mind a defining feature of Brooks's career, which is that he's always been somehow out of sync with historical time—usually ahead of it. He accomplished his mission as a storyteller by satirizing the capitalistic aftermath of the *Easy Rider* ethos. He later blew it by allowing his individual history of frustrated expectations to weigh down his most star-studded or politically fertile productions. But somewhere, perhaps in Pakistan, a young comedian might be taking notes on *Looking for Comedy in the Muslim World*. And years from now he'll show us all how much he owes to Brooks, who brought down the house that time he crossed the border.

Long vocal about how difficult it is to get a movie made, Brooks has been inactive as a director since he released his own speculative story of comedy and foreign policy. That filmmakers like Todd Solondz and Noah Baumbach enjoy a large enough base of support to fund their low-budget movies (most recently through emerging platforms like Amazon and Netflix) suggests there is a continuing market in the post-theatrical, post-cable marketplace for the satirical brand of comedy Brooks pioneered. In mid-2016, Brooks entered that slipstream alongside those filmmakers he helped birth, as Netflix announced the service would be streaming his directing filmography for the first time. The promotional video accompanying the Netflix announcement was familiar in both form (a purposefully awkward commercial of Brooks pitching the films from behind a desk) and content (the conceit was that Brooks had taken the radical action of kidnapping an executive's child to force Netflix to run his movies). While it was interesting to see the films receive new life on a more modern platform, within a year's time none of them were available for streaming until September 2020, when the Criterion Channel programmed a one-month Albert Brooks series but only included one of his films, *Lost in America*, in their permanent collection. This, too, is a perfectly Brooks development. With every industry opportunity, comes another opportunity for disappointment. Or as Dave Schmerz would phrase it: What if every Albert Brooks film were available to stream on Netflix? Then what? They'd disappear.

NOTES

1. David Foster Wallace, "E Unibus Pluram: Television and U.S. Fiction," *A Supposedly Fun Thing I'll Never Do Again: Essays and Arguments* (Boston: Little Brown, 1997), 68.
2. Albert Brooks, dir. *Looking for Comedy in the Muslim World*. 2005; Burbank, CA: Warner Independent, 2006. DVD.
3. Christian Long, "Albert Brooks," *Senses of Cinema* 80 (2016). Available at <http://sensesofcinema.com/2016/great-directors/albert-brooks/> (last accessed December 27, 2020).
4. Dennis Hopper, dir. *Easy Rider*. 1969; Culver City, CA: Columbia Pictures, 2010. Blu-ray.
5. Judd Apatow, *Sick in the Head: Conversations About Life and Comedy* (New York: Random House, 2016), 41.
6. Albert Brooks, dir. *Real Life*. 1979; Los Angeles: Paramount Pictures, 2001. DVD.
7. The Editors of Encyclopædia Britannica, "Albert Brooks," *Encyclopædia Britannica*. Available at <https://www.britannica.com/biography/Albert-Brooks> (last accessed December 27, 2020).
8. Dan Harries, *Film Parody* (London: Palgrave BFI, 2000).
9. "Albert Brooks Ventriloquist Bit." Available at <https://youtu.be/t_me-D6SJK0> (last accessed December 27, 2020).
10. Stella Bruzzi, *New Documentary: A Critical Introduction* (New York: Routledge, 2000), 74.
11. Noah Baumbach, dir. *While We're Young*. 2014; New York: A24, 2015. Blu-ray.
12. "Real Life: A Conversation with Albert Brooks," *Real Life*, dir. Albert Brooks. 1979; Los Angeles: Paramount Pictures, 2001. DVD.
13. Albert Brooks, dir. *Modern Romance*. 1981; Culver City, CA: Columbia Pictures, 2006. DVD.
14. Apatow, *Sick in the Head*, 32.
15. Todd Solondz, dir. *Happiness*. 1998; New York: Good Machine, 2004. DVD.
16. Todd Solondz, dir. *Storytelling*. 2001; Los Angeles: New Line, 2002. DVD.
17. Todd Solondz, dir. *Weiner Dog*. 2016; Santa Monica: Amazon Studios, 2016. Blu-ray.
18. Saul Austerlitz, *Another Fine Mess: A History of American Film Comedy* (Chicago: Chicago Review Press, 2010), 270.
19. Albert Brooks, dir. *Lost in America*. 1985; Burbank, CA: Warner Bros, 2017. Blu-ray.
20. James L. Brooks, dir. *Broadcast News*. 1987; Los Angles: Twentieth Century Fox, 2011. Blu-ray.
21. Albert Brooks, dir. *The Muse*. 1999; Los Angeles: October Films, 2010. DVD.
22. Ronald Bettig and Jeanne Lynn Hall, *Big Media, Big Money: Cultural Texts and Political Economics* (Lanham, MD: Rowman & Littlefield, 2012), 195.
23. Tim Gray, "Plugolas: H'w'd fetes product placement," *Variety*, January 13, 2000. Available at <https://variety.com/2000/voices/columns/plugolas-h-w-d-fetes-product-placement-1117760859/> (last accessed December 27, 2020).
24. A. O. Scott, "Happy Birthday, You Miserable Achievers," *The New York Times*, December 21, 2012. C1.

25. Paul McDonald, *Hollywood Stardom* (Hoboken, NJ: Wiley-Blackwell, 2013), 66.
26. Ryan Bishop, *Comedy and Cultural Critique in American Film* (Edinburgh: Edinburgh University Press, 2013), 156.
27. Thomas Britt, "My Humor is Traced with Dark: An Interview with Drive's Albert Brooks," November 15, 2011. Available at <https://www.popmatters.com/151132-my-humor-is-traced-with-dark-an-interview-with-drives-albert-brooks-2495920015.html> (last accessed December 27, 2020).

PART II

Brooks as Auteur

CHAPTER 5

When Success is Failure

Christian B. Long

Albert Brooks has been called the "West Coast Woody Allen," a nickname which acknowledges the similarities Brooks and Allen share: they both write and direct observational comedies in which they play the lead. However, the nickname misses what distinguishes Brooks from Allen (and most other American filmmakers) and misreads Brooks's films to boot. In a review of the 2005 Albert Brooks film *Looking for Comedy in the Muslim World*, J. Hoberman notes that "Woody Allen may bestride the world like a colossus, but—the brilliance of *Real Life, Modern Romance,* and *Lost in America* notwithstanding—not even the French have shown any interest in Albert Brooks."[1] The films Brooks co-wrote, directed, and starred in—*Real Life* (1979), *Modern Romance* (1981), *Lost in America* (1985), *Defending Your Life* (1991), *Mother* (1996), *The Muse* (1999), and *Looking for Comedy in the Muslim World*—both thematically and formally engage with the Janus-faced nature of success and failure. For Albert Brooks, to succeed is to fail, and to fail is to succeed. For this reason, in this chapter I want to position Brooks as an auteur whose films consistently confront the problem of believing not wisely and guardedly but too well and too deeply in the American Dream's rhetoric of success.

In the late 1960s and 1970s Albert Brooks worked as a stand-up comic. His early comedy albums, *Comedy Minus One* (1973) and *A Star Is Bought* (1975) were part of a larger shift toward meta-comedy. For as popular a guest as Brooks was on *The Tonight Show*, other comics such as Steve Martin and Andy Kaufman had more success with self-aware, meta-comedy (also called anti-comedy). Florian Keller uses Slavoj Žižek's idea of over-orthodoxy or over-conformism, "an excessively literal symbolic identification with an ideological discourse," to argue that by taking the American Dream's valorization of self-reinvention completely literally, Kaufman "actually staged an overconformist caricature of the [American] Dream."² Brooks, on the other hand, takes the American Dream, that of working hard and playing by the rules in the pursuit of happiness as a given. The characters Brooks plays are professionally and economically successful, which leads them to believe in the rules and expectations that the American Dream puts in place. But Brooks's characters exhibit an overconformist position that shows the strangeness and emptiness of the American Dream for its winners: they perceive their upper-middle-class success as a kind of failure.

Writing for the *Chicago Reader* in 1985, Dave Kehr made the most extended case for Brooks as an auteur in a long review of *Lost in America*. Kehr highlights Brooks's love of long takes and distinctive editing patterns, in which "he resists both close-ups and cross-cutting, the two time-honored ways of binding up an identification between character and spectator."³ Rather than provide the comfort of the Hollywood comedy editing style, Brooks uses a style that resembles that of more serious filmmakers. As Kehr sees it, "Brooks' long takes reinforce this feeling of solidity: by resisting the temptation to cut . . . Brooks gives his actors and settings the time they need to exist on the screen, to occupy a place in the film with a weight that goes beyond the immediate demands of the screenplay."⁴ This seriousness of form creates a more serious undercurrent to Brooks's films, and Kehr calls Brooks the great realist comedy filmmaker, placing him in league with Jean-Marie Straub and Danielle Huillet, Buster Keaton, Frank Tashlin, Jacques Tati, and Roberto Rossellini, and in opposition to Allen, Francis Ford Coppola, and Brian DePalma.⁵ Kehr writes that, "Brooks' comedy is above all a comedy of disappointment," which is the logical product of his essential difference from most other comic filmmakers.⁶ As Kehr puts it, Brooks "strives for a perfect normalcy, a seamless unexceptionalness . . . Brooks' comic persona is brazenly average."⁷ Kehr concludes that "the formal system he has found for his films is, almost literally, a system of disillusionment."⁸ In other words, Brooks reveals the disappointment to believing in the promises of the American Dream and success; he shows the disappointment of overconformity.

I want to build on Kehr's reading of *Lost in America* to account for Brooks's entire directorial career. I will take a more or less chronological approach to Brooks's movies, tracing both their consistent engagement with success-as-failure and the ways Brooks represents formally his skepticism about success. I begin with *Real Life* and *Modern Romance*, then turn to *Lost in America*, *Defending Your Life*, and *Mother*. I will then consider *The Muse* and *Looking for Comedy in the Muslim World* before concluding with a second look at *Lost in America*. Albert Brooks's films might seem formally straightforward and uncomplicatedly invested in the status quo, and thus less in need of careful analysis, but their consistent interrogation of how overconformists experience the promises and failings of the American Dream and how film style can position a filmmaker at interesting angles to the rhetoric of success make Brooks a significant figure in American film and comedy who has not received the critical attention his work merits.

REAL LIFE AND *MODERN ROMANCE*

While Kehr bases his case for Brooks as a major filmmaker on *Lost in America*, the formal and thematic identity that he sees in *Lost in America* is present from Brooks's first film, *Real Life*.⁹ In *Real Life*, Albert Brooks played Albert Brooks, an actor directing his first movie, a Loud family-like documentary about a "normal" family in Phoenix, Arizona. For much of the film, Albert's relentless Dale Carnegie-esque positive thinking frequently confuses success and failure. The film crew distracts Dr. Warren Yaeger during a surgery, leading him to accidentally kill the horse he's operating on. But Albert sees things differently, declaring in a voice-over that, "The operation was over at 11:45. Well ahead of schedule." Yaeger does not share Albert's sunny take, clearly recognizing the event as a catastrophic failure. The entire conversation during which Yaeger asks Albert to cut the surgery scene from the film plays out in a single take, in a long shot of Yaeger's office. The more emotionally pained Warren becomes over losing the horse, the more Albert insists it makes him a sympathetic "character." Warren even wonders aloud if Albert would sign an agreement not to include the failed surgery in the film, but Albert dismisses that idea immediately. Warren's failure, after all, could make the movie better, and more likely to succeed at the box office.

Figure 5.1 Dr. Yaeger (Charles Grodin), matador

As *Real Life* presents itself as a documentary, the long take registers as a generically appropriate way to shoot the scene. But *Real Life* is fiction, and a comedy at that, which makes the uncomfortably long take in Yaeger's office different. The Hollywood continuity-style cut for a scene like the one in Yaeger's office would, at some point, cut to a reaction shot of a grinning Albert, inviting the audience in on the joke. By not cutting away from the conversation, Brooks marks Albert's bright-side reaction as nearly pathological in its optimism.

In the end, Albert diagnoses the problem his film faces in terms of what he has learned from Hollywood fictions rather than from the psychological insights his eternally frustrated consultant Dr. Ted Cleary offers. In the film's conclusion, Albert calls himself a failure, calls his movie an abortion, and admits he knows nothing about reality. The movie-based model for success—crowd-pleasing films like *Star Wars*, *Jaws*, and *Gone With the Wind*, all of which end with big satisfying explosions—directs Albert to blow it all up. This explosion takes generic form, as Albert's documentary becomes a (bad) action movie; deadpan becomes the histrionic. For Harvey O'Brien, Albert's breakdown is part of the film's "final, viscously polemical turn" that makes the implicit argument "that the ability to look closely and honestly at the self is beyond the means of American filmmakers."[10] In other words, the only way that the "documentary" *Real Life* can satisfactorily end is in failure. *Real Life* succeeds as comedy because Albert fails in nearly every aspect of "making" "*Real Life*". "*Real Life*'s" formal failure makes *Real Life*'s thematic/ideological success possible.

In a 1984 overview of *Saturday Night Live*'s original cast members' film work, the only cast member Jack Barth praises is the one who never appeared on stage, Albert Brooks: "His *Modern Romance* was so simple and loose that the magnitude of his achievement never sunk in. His character was so awed by his own shortcomings, yet so *normal*, that the jokes were too pathetic and true to laugh at."[11] Even as he praises the film, Barth describes Brooks's film as a kind of failed comedy, "too pathetic and true to laugh at."[12] But *Modern Romance* is not an ordinary comedy.[13] In a short review Gavin Smith uses an often-cited bit of movie trivia, that *Modern Romance* was one of Stanley Kubrick's favorite movies, as a further endorsement of Brooks's work as laudably complex.[14] Smith praises the film as "quietly terrifying" and "almost frighteningly insightful about Bob's compulsive behavior."[15] The frightening, pathetic, and even terrifying nature of the film comes from its treatment of Robert Cole's (Brooks) inability to maintain a relationship with Mary Harvard (Kathryn Harrold) (and it's clear that the fault lies entirely with Robert). At the end of the film, after Robert has stalked Mary and behaved abominably, they get back together. A postscript reveals that, "Robert and Mary were married three weeks later in Las Vegas, Nevada." Then, after two-thirds of the screen has remained empty, a second line appears, "They were divorced the following month." Again, the line scrolls up, leaving two-thirds of the screen without any text. The final postscript provides the grim punchline, "They are currently dating with plans to remarry." By spacing out the make-up-break-up even in the film's postscript, Brooks disrupts the generically appropriate ending: marriage ends up looking like an unhappy ending and divorce a happy ending. Success is failure and failure success. But I want to place the "romance" in *Modern Romance* to the side to concentrate on Robert's work life.

Robert's repeated and extensive failures in forming a romantic couple with Mary contrast strongly with his professional success. Smith notes that "one of the incidental joys of *Modern Romance* is its dead-accurate depiction of a film editor's working life."[16] *Modern Romance* does not simply say Robert is a film editor and leave it at that; nor does it simply have Robert (and others) talk about being a film editor. To accentuate Robert's skill as an editor, Robert explains to his co-editor Jay (Bruno Kirby) the edits he makes in the film-within-the-film, and the changing scene appears four times forwards and once in reverse. After showing Robert's skill as an editor, Brooks ends the scene by having the director (James L. Brooks) demand that Robert return the scene to its previous form. Perhaps appropriately, Brooks's editing of the two halves of the scene—the good re-edit as opposed the director's request to leave the scene as-is—drives home the emptiness of success and the personalization of failure. In the good re-edit section, Brooks uses an over-the-shoulder shot of Robert and Jay at the editing table, a Robert point-of-view shot of the editing table, and a shot of David and Jay looking directly into the camera (with a few insert close-ups of film being cut and pasted together). After making his edits, Robert and Jay look into the camera and the "reverse shot" of their gaze is the new version of the scene. After watching the re-cut scene, Brooks cuts to the over-the-shoulder shot as Robert exclaims "ah ha!" and pumps his fist in excitement, which makes the success of the scene something the audience enjoys, not Robert. Were it Robert's triumph, the logical cut would be to a close-up of Robert.

In the second half of the scene, Brooks does not use the over-the-shoulder shot. Instead, the scene uses the looking-directly-into-the-camera shot, the POV shot of the editing table, and a three-quarter shot of all three men. To show the three men watching the re-edited scene, Brooks first uses the look into the camera shot. Then, in a "reverse shot," the re-cut scene plays. Immediately after Robert's new cut, Brooks cuts back to the three men looking into the camera, as Robert makes a quick sideways glance at David to check for any recognition of the quality of his cut. After the re-edited scene plays, Brooks cuts to a longer, three-quarter shot with David, Robert, and Jay. David does not understand or like the scene in its new form. Robert addresses his fruitless attempt to explain to the editing table, as a direct address to *Modern Romance*'s audience.

But the scene ends with David asserting the power of the director over the editor. He tells Robert, "You may be right. But let's do it the other way." Brooks uses two three-quarters shots, one from behind Robert to begin, followed by a three-quarters frontal shot, to register Robert's pained expression. The scene's content emphasizes Robert is a good editor; its form similarly prefers Robert. When explaining the cut to David, Robert points at the screen on the editing table—where the camera is placed. In this set-up, Robert makes his explanation directly to the audience, not the director. And because the film-within-the-film scene plays through its multiple iterations four times in total, the audience has a chance to see how Robert's edits improved the scene. The switch in shot at the reaction to the re-edited scene places success and failure in different places. Robert shares his success with the audience in the over-the-shoulder shot, but the failure of his edits comes in three-quarter shots that place Robert in the centre of the image. The failure is his from every angle. Robert's success—convincing *Modern Romance*'s audience that the movie would be better the way Robert wants to cut it rather than how the director wants to cut it—is formally and narratively erased. A film editor's working life, and *Modern Romance*'s narrative and formal imagination of it, seems ideally suited to an Albert Brooks character: your success belongs to someone else but any failure is yours alone.

LOST IN AMERICA

Lost in America might be Brooks's best-known film, largely owing to the degree to which it captures yuppie life in Reagan-era America, making it quite useful in overviews of the 1980s' cultural history.[17] But academic film studies tends to use *Lost in America* as a jumping-off point rather than a destination. In "Fear of Flying: Yuppie Critique and the Buddy-Road Movie in the 1980s," Ina Rae Hark argues that "Brooks astutely unmasks the romance of the road as a mere fantasy alternative to high flying," but Brooks is peripheral to her overall argument about road-buddy picture.[18] Similarly, in *Comedy and Cultural Critique in American Film*, Ryan Bishop begins with Brooks, whose films "often work on the theme of people who are self-absorbed (even narcissistic), individuals whose self-contained certainties about the world and how things work within it run into evidence that refute [sic] their viability" but subordinates him to a more critically embraced figure: "in this way, his protagonists are metonymic of the US itself, which means he keeps good company with Spalding Gray and his *Swimming to Cambodia*."[19] Nearly every critic talks about the Winnebago, *Easy Rider*, and the Boomers turning into yuppies; I want to focus on David Howard's (Brooks) understanding of the "rules" of promotion and professional success to show how *Lost in America* troubles both the rhetoric of the American Dream and the Dream itself.

Like *Modern Romance*, *Lost in America* begins with a neurotic man poorly explaining himself to an infinitely patient woman. David admits that his anxiety stems not from moving house, but from his impending promotion at work. He presents the promotion as the key to happiness, telling Linda (and himself) that "After tomorrow everything is gonna be better. I'm positive." Brooks delays getting to the promotion, and the scenes that come between David practicing the promotion experience and the experience itself link David strongly to the fulfillment through consumption that gained force in the 1980s. In the first delaying scene, David practices his promotion acceptance speech—he imagines that he'll be offered an even larger salary—in the bathroom mirror as he brushes his teeth. In the second, David discusses a Mercedes purchase. The things David talks about in the first fifteen minutes of the film—a promotion, a big raise, a new house, and a new car—represent the consumer keys to happiness on which most versions of the American Dream are built. The frequency with which *Lost in America* is called a yuppie movie hinges on this conception of happiness, as one of consumption made possible through climbing the ladder. The promotion plus two new major purchases will, for David, prove that he has finally achieved the Dream.

However, when David finds out that rather than become senior vice president, he will be transferred to New York to work on the firm's biggest and newest account, he reacts as if the rules have been broken, as if he has been demoted. The belief that working hard and playing by the rules will lead to advancement undergirds David's case. First he insists that, "I should get the position I deserve instead of just being shifted to another account . . . you have to keep your promise to me." David's I-quit harangue makes the case for promotion in terms of the implied metrics of time at the job and personal skills and merit: "by being extra clever and by being here longer I get shifted to just other account and he because of his low intelligence and short time with the company [Phil Shabano] gets this job I've been waiting my whole life for." The promise, in this case, is not actually anything Paul said, but the promise of the American Dream. But the promise was only ever implicit—*is* only ever implicit—which breaks David's belief in the ladder-climbing version of the Dream. When the scales fall from his eyes, he recalibrates his description of adhering to the rules to achieve the American Dream:

> I was on the road to nowhere. Do you know the road? It's a nowhere road. It goes nowhere. You're on it. You don't know it? It's a nowhere road. It just goes around in a circle. It's the carrot on the stick and the watch when you're 70.

David thus turns away from the go-nowhere work life in pursuit of the Dream for the vision of the Dream put forward in *Easy Rider* and other 1960s counterculturalnarratives: a purposeful aimlessness divorced from concerns of promotions and raises in corporate America.

DEFENDING YOUR LIFE AND *MOTHER*

Success and failure permeate Brooks's thinking even into the afterlife. *Defending Your Life* begins with Daniel Miller's birthday party.[20] On his way home from the party, the successful and even well-liked Daniel gets hit by a bus and dies. The rest of the film takes place in Judgment City, a way station in the bureaucracy of the afterlife. In *Defending Your Life*, a review of key moments from your life determines the future of your afterlife. The connection of self-worth and net worth that permeates American life seems to extend into the afterlife. With a defense and a prosecutor and a two-judge panel, the film "participates in a long trajectory of texts that depict the adjudication of one's post-mortem destiny using courtroom and trial imagery."[21] In Judgment City's placeless afterlife, everything from housing to food is free, but *Defending Your Life* frequently frames the adjudication of Daniel's ability to deal with fear in terms of money. The prosecutor in Daniel's case homes in on his previous financial decisions—not investing in Casio, not bargaining harder for a better salary—as proof of fear, which Daniel finds both painful and slightly beside the point. Resist though he may, Daniel experiences a Judgment City where the extent to which he doesn't quite stack up appears in consumer terms. When he meets and falls in love with Julia (Meryl Streep), her exemplary life takes the form of consumption: She stays at the Majestic Hotel with a Jacuzzi in her room, she gets crème-filled chocolate swans; Daniel stays in a dingy hotel and only gets mints. *Defending Your Life* engages with the power of conforming to the prevailing value system most consistently in terms of money, but its vision of conformity goes beyond the financial. In his first interview with Diamond, Daniel shows a great deal of interest in how his case stacks up against other cases, historically, starting with how many days that will constitute his review. Daniel's interest in his relative normalcy remains throughout his stay in Judgment City. Diamond notices, "you're very concerned about normal, aren't you? Kinda cute." Daniel's concern over being normal even in the afterlife testifies to his deep-seated belief in the importance of the system he is part of—whether it's Judgment City or the American Dream—as a way to judge his success or failure. When Daniel finally lives his life as he ought to have lived it, it's in the afterlife. *Defending Your Life* turns what looked like a moderately successful life into a failure, but also creates an afterlife in which by dying Daniel learns how he ought to have lived, turning success into failure that in turn becomes success.

Like *Defending Your Life*, *Mother* also begins with a failure, although John Henderson's (Brooks) divorce presents slightly lower stakes than eternity.[22]

After his second divorce, John decides that he needs to sort out his relationship with his mother so that he can improve his relationships in general. This return to origins plays out through the entire film, with John going back to live with his mother Beatrice (Debbie Reynolds) to discover where his troubles with women started. For John, the two things that bring him the most joy—that generate what he takes to be a psychological breakthrough—are being hated and sharing in failure. When John learns his mother wrote a lot of books that she never published, he thinks he can explain his failed relationship with his mother (and thus with women in general), who "raised children who she hated for ruining her life and killing her chances at doing the one thing she loved." A piano quietly plinks, signaling that this is a Touching Moment, and Beatrice says, "Well my goodness. I never heard it put exactly like that, but yes. I'm afraid that's true." John starts to dance around the room at this breakthrough, telling his mother, "We did it. We figured it out, mother. Look what just happened! We know why you hate me. We know why she hates me!" John asks Beatrice about her too-brief writing career. John pop psychologizes, "I just have to be a huge threat to you . . . he doesn't represent the writer. I represent what you had to stop." Beatrice again affirms John's point, admitting, "Maybe you're right. How do you like that?" with a surprised expression.

> Listen to me. I'm sorry mother. I wish I could have done something to change all of this, you know that. But I had nothing to do with it. But for the very first time—for the first time—I don't see you as my mother. I see you as a failure. And it's wonderful!

Kathleen Murphy reads this scene as "easy psychobabble solutions, happy endings that are there because the movie stops short of its blackest humor."²³ Murphy misses how Beatrice dismisses "easy psychobabble solutions" throughout the entire film. Early on, she summarizes the whole situation as, "you're having problems and you're blaming me, is that it?" When John has his breakthrough, her response undercuts its power: "I'm a failure and that's wonderful? Alright honey. If that's what you need" as she laughs softly, which John does not register. The next morning, when John informs her he's moving out now that he's solved his psychological problems, she admits, "My goodness, I didn't get that moment that you did," right before joking with John that she forgets if she's the "blocked and insecure" one or the "stifled and angry" one. In other words, John's success at figuring out his problems is much less successful than it seems.

John's failure comes through clearly through cinematic means. On first glance Brooks's directorial style is anonymous, but the way in which *Mother* questions success and happiness appears in its *mise en scène* consistently. The film's credit sequence testifies to Brooks's ability as a director, representing

John and the situation he faces in one long extended take. John walks into a house's front room, which has only a leather chair and a side table. He drags the chair to every corner of the room, pausing to sit down at each stop, until the chair is back where it was when John entered. The credits say "an Albert Brooks film," but the title is *Mother*, and the film belongs to Debbie Reynolds. The particular way in which John and Beatrice Henderson occupy and control space figures as much of the film's vision of success and happiness as its narrative and dialogue. Whereas John is trapped inside the frame during the credit sequence, Beatrice is never controlled by the frame. Though she struggles with getting into the shot when she uses a video-display phone, Beatrice controls space by moving into the frame that someone else—usually John—already occupies. For example, when she hears loud music playing, Beatrice follows the sound to its source, opening the door to John's room to reveal John dancing with a look of great determination. Exposing John dancing with himself, presents the most spelled-out case of Beatrice sneaking into the frame and taking control of space to become the center of attention. For instance, when John moves all his old things from the garage to his bedroom, he walks down the hallway carrying a lamp. Beatrice's head pops out from behind a corner, and as John disappears into his room, the only person in the frame is Beatrice, shifting the focus of the image from John to her. Similarly, when John pays off the day laborer, Beatrice appears from the rear left of the image and walks into the center of the frame.

The shot begins focused on the money changing hands, but a rack focus shifts attention to Beatrice. Thus *Mother* insistently takes attention away from

Figure 5.2 Beatrice (Debbie Reynolds) sneaking into the frame

what John is doing to shift attention to what Beatrice does. This approach continues through to the film's conclusion, when Beatrice appears as the arbiter of success. Beatrice, on the other hand, immediately starts writing, and her first piece of work tells John's story. In such an ending John's success depends on Beatrice's success as a writer. What's more, that dependence makes his success incidental to hers, a deflating vision of success-as-failure that echoes John's experiences with Beatrice throughout *Mother*.

THE MUSE AND *LOOKING FOR COMEDY IN THE MUSLIM WORLD*

The last two films Brooks made, *The Muse* and *Looking for Comedy in the Muslim World*, both make the same change to the lives of the characters he plays: they give him a wife and kids.[24] Where Brooks once struggled to find and find happiness with a romantic partner, in both *The Muse* and *Looking for Comedy in the Muslim World* he has what seems to be a stable and fairly happy family life. This switch to a more stable, domestic background grants Brooks's characters a measure of success at home that struggles at work obscure. At the beginning of *The Muse* the screenwriter Steven Philips (Brooks) wins a humanitarian award. His acceptance speech describes being a screenwriter as an unsatisfying, outsider experience, "a lot like being a eunuch at an orgy. The only difference is, the eunuchs get to watch and I'm not even invited to the set." Later that night, Steven's older daughter Julie tells Steven she is proud of him, and in thanking her Steven says, "I'm so happy you were there" to see his success. But when his young daughter Mary asks what a humanitarian is, Steven informs her, "It's someone who's never won the Oscar." In Steven's eyes, the award is not a token of successfully helping others, but rather a token of his own professional failure.

The intersections of his happy family life, his drive for screenwriting success, and his wife Laura's (Andie MacDowell) success as a small businessperson create a world in which, as Gore Vidal might have said, every time a friend of Steven's succeeds, something inside him dies. Gavin Smith locates *The Muse*'s similarity to other Brooks films in its problem-solving logic:

> In *The Muse*, as in *Mother* (96) and *Lost in America*, the great central comic conceit is his adoption of an improbable radical solution: When your marriage fails, move back in with your mother to figure out why your relationships with women don't work; when you don't get the promotion you feel you deserve, quit, drop out of society, and go on the road to find yourself; if your writing career goes south, hire a muse and do whatever she instructs, even if you can't shake the feeling you're being shortchanged.[25]

At the heart of the logic Smith describes in terms of *The Muse* in particular is a common thread to Brooks's films in general, a suspicion that everything you do to succeed *still* won't be enough, either in the doing or in the result. Even though Steven hired Sarah the muse (Sharon Stone), a never-ending line of filmmakers occupy her time. Sarah also inspires Laura to commercialize her cooking skills. Steven doesn't take Laura's horning in on the muse well, a fear Laura characterizes as, "If she gives to me she takes from you." Steven's fear of being short-changed, at first, seems accurate. Laura enjoys a far better rate of return—her cookies get sold at Wolfgang Puck's Spago. But Laura's success only makes Steven's inability to finish his screenplay all the more frustrating.

The Muse concludes with Steven briefly enjoying success, only to have it turn into failure. Rather than using end titles, as he does in *Modern Romance* and *Lost in America* (which I will deal with momentarily), Brooks ratchets up the pace to race through a series of highs and lows. First, Steven finally looks to be selling his screenplay, but somehow Rob Reiner has the very same screenplay at another studio, and Steven looks like a fraud. The next scene finds Steven working at Laura's cookie shop, but a phone call from his agent rescues him: his screenplay is getting picked up. Upon arriving at the studio, he learns that the executive who bought his script is Sarah. Gavin Smith, probably the strongest Brooks partisan, writes, that "a cult of personality has deservedly formed around his compact oeuvre."[26] For Smith, the Brooks character is "a specific comic persona: smugly self-confident, oblivious to its own absurdity" "defined by the more complex experience of humbling misfortune and an ensuing struggle to overcome pervasive anxiety and regain existential terra firma."[27] The yo-yoing of Steven's fortunes at the film's conclusion ends at a low point for Steven, not at his success. Even when both Steven and Laura succeed professionally, Brooks makes Steven's success a version of failure. *The Muse* may be a comedy, but its happy ending is attenuated: in the face of constant humbling misfortune, existential terra firma is the comforting inevitability of failure.

Looking for Comedy in the Muslim World made less than one million dollars, making it Brooks's least financially successful film. It made much less money than other 2006 comedies such as *Garfield: A Tale of Two Kitties*, *Clerks II*, and *Larry the Cable Guy: Health Inspector*. The film begins by predicting its own box office failure, with the director Penny Marshall wondering why she's even talking to Albert about her remake of *Harvey* (1950). She sees Brooks not as "the next Jimmy Stewart," merely the star of the inexplicable remake of *The In-Laws*. Similarly, when the State Department comes calling, Albert immediately assumes that they wanted *Mel* Brooks. Since the previous scene shows that Albert has no films to make, when his wife encourages him to talk to State, it's a demonstration of both her love and confidence as well as his less-than-desirable status in Hollywood. Albert's inability to get cast makes him a good hire for the State Department, and recalls Jack Barth's assessment of how Brooks pinpoints Hollywood's feelings about him starting with *Real Life*: "They think he's great—and they think he'll never sell tickets."[28] In Washington DC, fellow actor, sometime senator and State Department Commission chair Fred Thomson admits, "quite frankly, our first few choices were working," but, "as far as I can tell, you're a pretty respected comedian," which makes Albert qualified enough to answer the question State wants answered: "What makes Muslims laugh?" Thompson seals the deal with the suggestion that "the Medal of Freedom would do wonders for your acting price." Unable to find work in Hollywood, Albert hopes to transmute Hollywood failure into nation-serving success.

Albert's investigations lead to his return to stand-up comedy, in an act that rehashes some of Brooks's anti-comedy material from the 1970s. Unsurprisingly, in retaining "his essential gag of being the comedian who isn't funny," Brooks ensures that Albert's act bombs when he performs at the Rajendra School in New Delhi, and while his hyper-competent assistant Maya argues that no one laughed "because they're idiots," her boyfriend wonders "if you do as badly on *The Tonight Show* as you did the other night, are you banned from the show business? Are you still allowed to be an entertainer?" Albert's "set" in Pakistan, which has to be translated for his audience of six, does slightly better, although everyone being high might have helped. But no success can go unpunished in a Brooks film. Albert, by asking so many questions in India and sneaking into Pakistan to perform for half a dozen aspiring comics, is mistaken for a spy, and increases the tensions to the extent that India and Pakistan briefly resume hostilities. *Looking for Comedy in the Muslim World*'s ending echoes *Real Life*'s conflagration, with Brooks toasted as "the Henry Kissinger of comedy" at a celebratory dinner in California while India and Pakistan go into a nuclear alert status that Albert unwittingly started. In a traditional happy-unhappy Brooks postscript, India and Pakistan stand down after "they identified Mr. Brooks as the problem." In successfully doing his part for US soft power, Albert fails to reduce the threat of global violence—in fact he increases it.

While Smith finds Brooks's characters wrestling with humbling misfortune his calling card, Scott Raab tracks the way success often looks like failure throughout Brooks's own career:

> Lorne Michaels asked him to become the permanent host of *Saturday Night Live* in 1975; Albert said no. In 1976, he debuted as an actor in *Taxi Driver*, playing Robert De Niro's dorksome rival for Cybill Shepherd's dainty hand; Martin Scorsese was so impressed by Albert's work that he expanded the role during shooting. It was the perfect Albert Brooks career move, an artistic success leading to implausible failure: He didn't land another role until he directed himself in *Real Life*. Even

after an Oscar-nominated job as the sweat-ruined TV news correspondent in 1987's *Broadcast News*, he has had trouble getting cast in other people's films.[29]

Raab's profile, like Smith's description of the Brooks character, appeared in 1999, when Brooks was promoting *The Muse*. After *The Muse*, Brooks only wrote and directed one film: *Looking for Comedy in the Muslim World*. This failure to make films of his own can be explained, in part, by Brooks's success as an actor. Brooks has continued his voice-over work—*The Simpsons* (1990–2016) and *The Simpsons Movie* (2007), *Doctor Dolittle* (1998), *Finding Nemo* (2003), *Finding Dory* (2016), and *The Secret Life of Pets* (2016)—and comic roles for hire, such as *Out of Sight* (1998), *The In-Laws* (2003), *This Is 40* (2012), and a four-episode guest run on *Weeds* (2008). Brooks has also taken on more dramatic roles, building on his well-received work in *Broadcast News* (1987) in films like *My First Mister* (1999), *Drive* (2011), *A Most Violent Year* (2014), and *Concussion* (2015). Brooks's most popular films, in terms of box office success, are not his own films, but those in which he is an actor-for-hire, not an auteur, an ironic but fitting summary of his career.

"I EAT SHIT," THE ALBERT BROOKS HAPPY ENDING

The ending of *Lost in America*, which Mark in *Looking for Comedy in the Muslim World* thinks is "a little tacked on," encapsulates how Brooks, even in the midst of a happy ending, treats success as a species of failure. After losing the entirety of their early-retirement nest egg at the roulette wheel in Las Vegas, David and Linda park the RV in small town Arizona, grimly set on getting their lives back in order. David finds work as a crossing guard and Linda as a fry cook. One night, David, Linda and her new manager, the teenager Skip, have a brief chat in the RV. Skip's presence in the motor home creates a bizarre "family" in which Skip holds the highest-prestige job in the RV. David admits that, like Linda, he's at the end of his tether. To solve the problem, David and Linda agree that they must get to New York—and the job David quit—as quickly as possible. David and Linda hightail it to New York, and when David arrives at the office in New York, he sees the previously hated Brad, and nearly chases him into the building.

For Michael Boyd, the endings of the Reagan-era films *Something Wild* (1986), *After Hours* (1985), and *Lost In America* "each ridicule middle class complacency even while they provide culturally square, politically conservative 'messages' with happy endings that, despite a deeply felt cynicism, seem to present wholesale sell-out as the only sensible course of action."[30] It seems to me Boyd misreads the ending of *Lost in America*. Generically, *Lost in America*

Figure 5.3 David (Brooks) takes the job in New York and finds his nemesis Brad there

is a comedy, and it so it should end with a wedding and a feast. And it does. David renews his vows with the American Dream by re-marrying his job, and the wedding feast entails eating shit. The postscript tells us that "David Howard got his job back with a 31% salary cut—but with better medical." For Kehr, such an ending shows that "Brooks' characters . . . are allowed to begin again, with healthily diminished expectations."[31] Or, as David puts it, "I eat shit." All of which is another way of saying that in *Lost in America*, as in all of Albert Brooks's films, success is failure.

Brooks's films all begin with some kind of failure, which is not strange—most movies will direct their protagonists through a series of adventures that lead, in the end, to success. But Brooks's films also end with failure—or more specifically, a kind of success that looks and feels very much like failure. Every success—a finished movie, marriage, the Ford account, eternal life, personal growth, a screenplay finally getting picked up, and a completed report for the State Department (as well as a job in Portland, Oregon)—comes in a larger context that it looks much more like failure: a mental breakdown, divorce, a net wealth of zero, being dead, a breakthrough no one else registers, having to work with an unbalanced boss, and almost starting a war (to say nothing of never being anchor and getting stabbed in a parking lot). Dave Kehr points out, "Keaton needed Chaplin, just as Brooks needs Allen: the consensus comic draws off the audience's need for identification and reassurance, leaving the marginal comic free to follow his own lights."[32] Woody's had hits and award-winners. *Annie Hall* (1977) was a top twenty hit and nominated for best picture at the Oscars; *Midnight in Paris* (2010) grossed more on its own than all of

Brooks's (marginal) films combined. Calling Brooks a neglected figure akin to Jerry Lewis misses the mark too. Jerry Lewis was a major box office draw in the 1950s and 1960s, and as a "total filmmaker" has a significant profile in film studies, as Chris Fujiwara's book and Murray Pomerance's edited collection show.[33] Brooks has his champions in popular film criticism, Kehr chief among them. J. Hoberman rates some of Brooks's work as brilliant. Mike Higgins calls Brooks "unfairly neglected"; Robert DiMatteo claims that "no one can represent and redeem obnoxiousness" like Brooks.[34] But Brooks barely registers in academic film criticism, which is a great loss. Brooks's recurrent concerns—the rhetoric and ideology of success, failure, and the unhappy happy ending, and the long-take, long shot style he places them in—position him as an auteur, and one who deserves greater critical attention.

NOTES

1. J. Hoberman, *Film After Film: Or, What Became of 21st-Century Cinema?* (London: Verso, 2012), 125–6.
2. Florian Keller, *Andy Kaufman: Wrestling with the American Dream* (Minneapolis: University of Minnesota Press, 2005), 159.
3. Dave Kehr, *When Movies Mattered: Reviews from a Transformative Decade* (Chicago: University of Chicago Press, 2011), 96.
4. Kehr, *When Movies Mattered*, 98.
5. Kehr, *When Movies Mattered*, 95, 97–8.
6. Kehr, *When Movies Mattered*, 99.
7. Kehr, *When Movies Mattered*, 96.
8. Kehr, *When Movies Mattered*, 99.
9. Albert Brooks, dir. *Real Life*. 1979; Hollywood: Paramount Home Video, 2000. DVD.
10. Harvey O'Brien, "'That's Really the Title?' Deconstructing Deconstruction in *The Positively True Adventures of the Alleged Texas Cheerleader-Murdering Mom* (1993) and *Real Life* (1978)," in *Docufictions: Essays on the Intersection of Documentary and Fictional Filmmaking*, ed. Gary D. Rhodes and John Parris Springer (Jefferson, NC: McFarland, 2006), 202, 203.
11. Jack Barth, "Kinks of Comedy," *Film Comment* 20 no. 3 (May–June 1984): 46–7.
12. Barth, "Kinks of Comedy," 46–7.
13. Albert Brooks, dir. *Modern Romance*. 1981; Culver City, CA: Somy Home Entertainment, 2006. DVD.
14. Gavin Smith, "Editor's Pick: *Modern Romance*," *Film Comment* 42, no. 3 (May/June 2006): 75.
15. Smith, "Editor's Pick: *Modern Romance*," 75.
16. Gavin Smith, "All the Choices: Albert Brooks interview," *Film Comment* 35, no. 4 (July/August 1999). Available at <https://www.filmcomment.com/article/all-the-choices-albert-brooks-interview/> (last accessed January 13, 2021).
17. Albert Brooks, dir. *Lost in America*. 1985; Pyrmont, Australia: Warner Home Video, 2003. DVD.
18. Ina Rae Hark, "Fear of Flying: Yuppie Critique and the Buddy-Road Movie in the 1980s," in *The Road Movie Book*, ed. Steven Cohan and Ina Rae Hark (London: Routledge, 1997), 213.

19. Ryan Bishop, *Comedy and Cultural Critique in American Film* (Edinburgh: Edinburgh University Press, 2013), 155–6.
20. Albert Brooks, dir. *Defending Your Life*. 1991; Burbank, CA: Warner Home, 2001. DVD.
21. Meira Kensky, *Trying Man, Trying God: The Divine Courtroom in Early Jewish and Christian Literature* (Tubingen: Mohr Siebeck, 2010), 3.
22. Albert Brooks, dir. *Mother*. 1996; Hollywood: Paramount Home, 2006. DVD.
23. Kathleen Murphy, "Festivals: Toronto," *Film Comment* 32, no. 6 (November/December 1996): 55.
24. Albert Brooks, dir. *The Muse*. 1999; Universal City, CA: Universal Home, 2010. DVD. Albert Brooks, dir. *Looking for Comedy in the Muslim World*. 2005; Burbank, CA: Warner Home, 2006. DVD.
25. Smith, "All the Choices," 14.
26. Smith, "All the Choices," 16.
27. Smith, "All the Choices," 14.
28. Barth, "Kinks of Comedy," 47.
29. Scott Raab, "Albert Brooks Knows the Whole, Hellish Truth," *Esquire*, September, 1999. Available at <http://www.esquire.com/features/ESQ0999-SEP_ALBERT_BROOKS-2> (last accessed May 17, 2016).
30. Michael Boyd, "Comedy and Perversity: Some American Films of the 1980s," *Bridgewater Review* 9, no. 1 (April 1992): 4A.
31. Kehr, *When Movies Mattered*, 99.
32. Kehr, *When Movies Mattered*, 95.
33. Chris Fujiwara, *Jerry Lewis* (Urbana: University of Illinois Press, 2009); Murray Pomerance (ed.), *Enfant Terrible!: Jerry Lewis in American Film* (New York: NYU Press, 2002).
34. Mike Higgins, "The Muse," *Sight & Sound*, January 2000. Available at <http://old.bfi.org.uk/sightandsound/review/542> (last accessed March 6, 2016); Roberto DiMatteo, "Real Afterlife," *Film Comment* 27, no. 2 (March 1991): 18+.

CHAPTER 6

Modern Romance: Albert Brooks's Anatomy of Love

Enid Stubin

> Movie love is abiding throughout life . . . we're lovers who are let down all the time, and go on loving.
>
> Pauline Kael in a 1998 interview[1]

In his second feature film, *Modern Romance* (1981), Albert Brooks takes that eternal subject of cinema—the love story—and investigates it through the trope of movie-making. His character, hopeless in holding on to a confused but loving girlfriend, attempts to maintain control of her and his increasingly muddled life through the rigorous demands of his work as a film editor. The scenes set in an editing suite, with their discussion of effects, both special and prosaic, and the negotiations between the editor and the studio technicians provide a professional analogue for the chaos of the protagonist's emotional world and the process of establishing order within what Hollywood is pleased to call the creative process. The seductive and elusive possibility of emotional security and stability is tested within the framework of friendship, loyalty, and artistic collaboration, and the hierarchy of the studio both thwarts and reflects the demands of love as played out through the dynamics of trust, authority, and desire. Produced within a decade of Francois Truffaut's *Day for Night* (*La nuit americaine*) (1973), Brooks's film uses the idea and the conventions of self-reflexive art, with its embedded presumptions of aesthetic control, to present a savage, wry, and poignant look at the state of contemporary love.

Truffaut's *Day for Night*, his self-reflexive homage to filmmaking, begins just before the credits appear with a voice-over by Georges Delerue, the film's composer, instructing the soundtrack's musicians. In an establishing shot from above, Jean-Pierre Léaud (Alphonse) emerges from a metro station, encounters a man, slaps his face, and we hear the director's voice: "Cut." Another disembodied voice over a public-address system launches into a series of complaints regarding *mise en scène* ("The beginning was especially off") and continuity, and as the scene is reshot, we see the layers of movie craft, engineering and artifice, required for the simulation of reality. Now we see how the slap has been faked. (That he who was slapped is merely a stand-in for the actor who will assume that role, is also revealed.) When the cast and crew gather to watch the dailies, Alphonse, rapt at his own image, mouths his lines in unison with his on-screen self, and we learn that the day's footage was ruined in the lab and must be reshot. The film-within-the film, *Meet Pamela* (*Je vous présente Pamela*), an anodyne romantic triangle, is eclipsed by the intrigues, long-lost loves, and current erotic preoccupations of the cast and crew. Even Ferrand, *Meet Pamela*'s director, played by Truffaut himself, defers an assignation as a young woman arrives at the hotel where the cast and crew are staying. In a curt phone exchange with the desk clerk, Ferrand sends the woman away: he's simply too busy with work.

In his essay on *Modern Romance*, Jacob Knight sees the film as a "dissection of the romantic comedy" genre and registers "two engrossing scenes where characters explain invisible film craft set inside both an editing bay and a Foley studio."[2] These claustrophobic interiors contrast with a gorgeous Nice as the setting for *Day for Night*, with its sunny exteriors, both city and country, and the ramshackle hotel where cast and crew are housed. And they anchor *Modern Romance*'s self-conscious and subversive stance on movie love: "Brooks is talking about something much bigger than romance or the movies that financially exploit it."[3]

The premise of *Modern Romance* is stated before the opening credits roll. An overhead shot of the restaurant, with its dark wood and red Naugahyde, the dreary suburban coffee shop of one's nightmares, reveals only a handful of customers as Mary Harvard (Kathryn Harrold) slides into a booth across from Robert Cole (Albert Brooks), innocently intent on having dinner with her boyfriend. The ordinariness of the evening, observed in the impassive gaze of the waitress, gives us "real life" as Robert directs his order in terms reflecting his ambivalence: "Mushroom omelette cooked with very little butter—butter on the side." Is the waitress's patient look a silent judgment of Robert, or is she merely waiting to take his order? Or is she musing over her witnessing of yet another troubled couple at her station? The camera rests on her face for just a moment longer than expected.[4] Alone again with Mary, Robert confesses, "I don't feel real good lately," and acknowledges his difficulties at work, the "this" as opposed to "that" making it impossible for him to know how well he's editing a film. Despite her attempts to draw him out and encourage him, Mary recognizes the signs and portents of his pronouncements: "Okay. It's over—again." Her resignation is rendered in her blank stare as Robert breaks up—yet again—with her: "Fine. I'm leaving." The pacing of their argument suggests

Figure 6.1 Robert (Brooks) and Mary (Kathryn Harrold) on a date, breaking up again

that this scenario is an old and familiar one to the couple, and as their quarrel moves out to the restaurant's parking lot, registered in another overhead shot, we see that this conflict encompasses the dynamic of their relationship: "Drop dead!" Mary hurls, and Robert retorts with the sarcastic cover, "Drop dead. Very sweet. That's *exactly* what I'm talking about. That's lovely." They have been here before.

Robert carries the funeral baked meats of their break-up into the next scene, as his Porsche noses into the parking lot of American International Pictures, infamous as the house of cinematic schlock, the nursery of the B-picture and the creative crucible of Roger Corman's oeuvre. Here Robert works with his forbearing assistant Jay (a wonderfully modulated Bruno Kirby), who is delighted to receive not one but two take-out dinners, taking a cheery inventory: "Chef's salad—what kind of dressing is this?" Robert answers, "House dressing. I don't know." The answer is telling—Robert's operative strategy, in life and in love, is to answer any question as he thinks he should and only then admit that he doesn't have the answer (in fact, Mary ordered herb dressing). This mode of prevarication characterizes his work as well: the visual joke of a pile of cans labeled "14 Empty Reels" behind Robert underscores both the arbitrary nature of his work and the haphazard cast of his moods. Jay tells Robert that the film's director is unhappy with a pivotal scene in the clunky sci-fi film they're editing, and Robert bristles at the director's implied criticism of their judgment. But Robert is preoccupied with his personal life and attempts to justify his latest separation from Mary:

Robert. We fought and we fought. Then we had great sex. But did we ever talk?
Jay. You *need* to talk?

It's unclear whether Jay's efforts to follow his friend's thinking are intended to comfort or merely mollify an exasperating workmate. At home, Robert negotiates his neutral bachelor's digs, where several props—the answering machine he's forgotten to turn on, the small-scale globe, and an office-sized Rolodex—underscore his emotional isolation and provinciality. Phoning Jay compulsively, he muses over his newly single status: "It's good to be alone. . . . Alone's kind of a nice place to be . . . One *isn't* the loneliest number—you know what I'm trying to say?" His two-Quaalude-induced recitative provides us with the performative self that Robert presents to those around him: "I'll lay down now," he announces to an empty room before toppling onto his bed and then, within a few seconds, whines "I can't sleep," suggesting the ironic and cinematic "real time" intrusion into the narrative of his life and the film itself. But it also provides a director's self-referential notes. "It's good to be alone," Robert discovers, but of course, Brooks's Robert is never alone: he has turned "real" love into "movie" love, our reference for human feeling, the love we have come to accept and the touchstone for emotional and erotic authenticity. He can no more escape himself and the clogged consciousness that makes him question Mary's devotion than he can escape us, his audience. Moments later, Robert calls Jay, who is shouldering their shared work by himself, again: "I love you—I mean in the right way. I think you're an amazing guy." Do Robert's words reflect real admiration and

Figure 6.2 "I don't want a Quaalude"

appreciation, or does he intend them to disguise his inner state? Jay is loyal but not completely naïve, and he recognizes the source of Robert's sudden devotion: "The 'ludes kicked in."

Lumbering through his living room, Robert shifts from loopy elation ("I love my albums, I love them, I love them") to despondency at the musical adaptation of "A Fifth of Beethoven" ("I don't like this song . . . it's sad") and back again as he riffles through his Rolodex and counts the many "nice friends" he finds there. But when his mother, voiced by Brooks's actual mother, Thelma Leeds, phones, he puts her off with some lame evasion. And although a call from Harry, who asks about work on a John Schlesinger film, appears to promise friendship and a job ("You *got* it, you *got* it," he assures Harry amiably), Robert's mood sours suddenly when Harry, told of their break-up, asks for Robert's permission to date Mary: "You're a scumbag . . . you're trash . . . you're Mr. Trash Man. Don't move in on *my* territory." Robert's genial presentation is constantly undercut by his neediness, jealousy, and possessiveness, and his mood swings expose his isolation. Finding a familiar name in his Rolodex, he phones and schmoozes Ellen in the same wheedling voice he uses to cajole his parakeet Petey:

Robert. El-*len*. Do you know why I'm calling?
Ellen. No.
Robert. Because I have deep feelings for you. And Ellen . . . this could be serious.

His reactions both slowed and heightened by the tranquilizers he's taken, Robert watches himself manoeuver through life, observing himself rather than responding to his actual feelings. Stumbling out of his house to his car in a benighted effort to interrupt Mary's imagined liaison with Harry, Robert can do no more than turn on the radio. We watch his unmoving Porsche and hear top-ten radio as time lapses to the following morning, when he staggers out of the car to re-enter his home and congratulate himself: "You got through the night!" But the all-night radio session has drained the car's battery, and Robert can't get to work, where Jay has managed to complete their assignment.[5] Free to embark on a new self-help regime, Robert chants the mantra "Better, stronger, and healthier," and by now we know how unlikely his transformation will be. The clerk in the health-food market is ready for his sad tale of splitting up and prescribes: "You'll need C, magnesium." The store and the relentlessly merchandising culture are poised for Robert and his vulnerabilities. At his next stop, a sporting-goods store, he browses and finds a box labeled "Runner's Dream," a reasonably priced package of jogging paraphernalia, when a supercilious salesman materializes and looms over him:

Salesman. How're you doing?
Robert. Fine, how are you?
Salesman. How do I *look*?

This is not just *any* Los Angeles sporting-goods salesman; this is a *miles gloriosus* of retail portrayed by Bob Einstein, Albert Brooks's brother also known as "Super Dave Osborne" and a protean master of comic satire. Bumping up the cost of Robert's purchase by substituting pricier items, he proffers a pair of high-end running shoes and refuses to let Robert try them on: "Guaranteed to fit. If not, bring them back." When Robert balks at the price of the rapidly mounting pile of à la carte items, the clerk condescends to him: "I misjudged you. I'm not perfect. Buy the box." Of course, Robert pays for the pile of expensive gear.

On the running track, the joggers really look as if they're running; mistiming his entry onto the field because he's obsessing over his appearance, Robert collides with one of them. His own attempt at racing is shot so that he looks as if he's running in place, going nowhere, and indeed within a few moments he veers off the track and calls Mary from a pay phone, scoffing when the receptionist answers, "Fidelity," the name of the bank where Mary works, and imagining yet another rival for Mary's affections. Determined to cancel his date with Ellen, he confirms it out of cowardice instead and notes ruefully, "I'd better buy some dope. . . . I need new sheets . . . I'm not prepared to get laid." Another call from Mom elicits another string of hopeless lies until she asks about Mary, and he responds, "It's the same continual fight. We don't have enough in common." Preparing for his date with Ellen, Robert warbles an aria of self-encouragement, at one point gloating over the posh dinner Mary will be missing and shifting the lyrics of "It Had to Be You" to "It Could Have Been You," crooning a song of jaunty, taunting aggression. Nevertheless, he drives up to Mary's home unannounced, disapproving of her dress, and accusing her of seeing someone else, contrasting the "chemical" aspect of his assignation with Ellen to the "natural"—and therefore more suspect—evening Mary planned with someone else. "How could she have made a date so quickly?" he muses, suggesting not only his fear of the shift in her affections but the time frame of cinematic convention—how *do* these things happen between scenes? For her part, Mary shuts the door on Robert, and for the first time in the film we see the action from her perspective, the point of view inside her house; a little pocket door within her front door borders the outside as a frame of film—or a prison.[6] At that moment, the film opens out from its comfortable, familiar stance of romantic satire to a recognition of the continuum of human misery, betrayal, and pain. Suffering himself, Robert is about to hurt another player in the game.

Ellen's voice over the intercom betrays reveals an eager, anticipatory pleasure in her date with Robert, who has no idea of who she is. His brusque opening line on picking her up outside her apartment building—"You used to work for Peter Bogdanovich, right?"—suggests that he's trying to place her outside the confines of his Rolodex. As they drive, the car radio offers "a special request," Michael Jackson's plangent "She's Out of My Life," and without warning, Robert turns the car around and takes Ellen back home with the promise of "another" wonderful evening some other time. We see her baffled as he leaves her at the curb and pulls up at the parking lot for a discount store selling liquor, ice cream, and toys. "Do any apologize?" he asks the store clerk before choosing a stuffed giraffe and a talking doll whose grating, high-pitched "I love you *very* much" seems a tone-deaf mockery of the words she articulates and the purpose Robert has enlisted her for. Wrapping and leaving these offerings at Mary's door, he rushes home to play his messages but decides that he "Can't stay home." Brooding on a bridge, illuminated by the stars in a night sky and accompanied by swelling music (Andre Kostelanetz's "My Own Best Friend"), Robert notices a man old enough to be his father in a phone booth, pathetically beseeching *his* love-object: "Why don't I just come over? . . . *He's* there now, right? . . . Please, I wasn't born yesterday." Defeated, the man trudges off, a poignant figure engulfed by bitterness and loss, but Robert, unable to see the analogy to his own situation, dashes home to play his messages, intoning fervently, "This is it, this has *got* to be it." Prepared for the expected slap of rejection, the audience hears Mary's halting, plaintive voice at the same moment Robert does: "I liked the giraffe. . . . Robert, what are we gonna *do*?"

The scene that follows summons up and subverts the love scenes that have informed film culture since its inception. "Sometimes I think you don't know what love is," Mary says as she undresses—so easily!—and slips into bed, lissom and smooth, continuing their conversation chummily. With clumsy effort, Robert wrestles off his plaid shirt and chinos, and his prodigiously hirsute back, chest, and arms establish a comic contrast between these two lovers. James L. Brooks plays on this theme in *Broadcast News*, comparing and contrasting the two rivals for Holly Hunter's affections by their intellectual and physical attributes: William Hurt's superficiality and groomed, handsome looks are set against Albert Brooks's intelligent, supple wit and his hyperhidrosis, when in his big break on national TV, Brooks's character sweats copiously through his shirt and suit, ending his chances for a prime-time newscasting position. "Maybe that's movie love," Mary speculates, and maybe it is, Robert's insistence on editing and idealizing their love and denouncing it when it fails to meet his expectations. "This part is perfect, isn't it?" he sighs, nuzzling her. But she cannot avoid the fact of his ambivalence:

Mary. Yesterday you told me you didn't want to see me anymore.
Robert. Cheap talk. I'm here, aren't I?

Quoting Dennis Hopper's wise-guy retort to a cop in *Easy Rider*, Robert establishes his frame of reference and demonstrates both his mistrust of and inability to see past "movie love."

The morning after, Mary wakes Robert with affectionate kisses while he lolls about in her Laura Ashley bedroom and eyes her clinging dress with anxious outrage: "Don't you have any *wool*?" Cheerful and buoyant, on her way out to work, she laughs off his possessiveness: "You're just saying that because you love me." Alone in her domain, a pink-and-white-curtained bathroom, a hirsute Robert lathers up his face and neck (why stop there?) to shave and, hunting around for a razor with a sharper blade, rummages through her vanity drawers to find a stack of Pacific Bell bills that indicate some late-night phone calls to a number in New York. The shot of the actual bill and his running obligato of commentary, speculating on whom she might have been speaking with, enlists us as confidants even as the scene shifts abruptly to the inane science-fiction potboiler he and Jay must edit, in which George Kennedy plays a crusty old space pro saddled with an inexperienced recruit one consonant shy of proficiency:

> *Zenon*. We've got to have that information!
> *Zeon*. I believe I know the code, Sir.
> *Zenon*. You know *nothing*.

Reviewing the unedited footage with its leaden dialogue and stolid acting, Robert appears confident for the first time in the film. Insisting on cutting the scene, he announces triumphantly to Jay, "I think we double the suspense!" At that moment, David (James L. Brooks), the director of their science-fiction movie, enters and begins a disquisition on the sound of footsteps in the scene, a theoretical consideration that opposes Robert's judgment and that sounds improbable and arbitrary, finishing with the childlike insistence, "That'll make it *better*." They replay the film, and we see David mouthing Zenon's lines with rapt attention. All of Robert's professional authority melts away as a result of David's objections: "I *love* that line," he insists even as David asks for "something subtler." Collecting the shards of his dignity, Robert offers a tortuous justification of his plan, to which David appears to listen and then says sunnily, "Maybe you're right, but let's do it the other way." He beckons Robert outside the editing room to invite him, out of earshot of Jay, a lowly assistant editor, to a party at his home that evening. Robert begins a string of excuses as to why he can't attend, but eventually he accedes, and in the next shot we see Robert and Mary from behind, approaching the glamorously lit house.

On entering, Mary immediately recognizes and is recognized by two men who chat her up sociably, while David sweeps in to introduce Robert to George Kennedy (playing "Himself," as noted in the film's closing credits and promotional material). The party scene comments on the film's "real life" correspondences: the director James L. Brooks playing Robert's passive-aggressive director; the casting for their science-fiction movie of the durable George Kennedy, presaging some environmental disaster; the presence of the Harlem Globetrotters' Meadowlark Lemon (also credited as "Himself"), a reliable B-list Hollywood celebrity, as a casual admirer of Mary's charms. Jovial and expansive, Kennedy asks Robert, who is introduced to him as the film's editor, "My best stuff—is it on the cutting-room floor?" Distracted by Mary's disappearance with the two guys into one of the house's bathrooms, Robert listens perfunctorily while Kennedy tells a good-natured anecdote about getting lost at Universal, a studio considerably more prestigious than American International. David is delighted by the story and suggests that Kennedy use it as fodder for the talk-show circuit when he publicizes their sci-fi movie, but Kennedy asks, not unreasonably, "Why do I want everyone to see how *stupid* I am?" Of course, the convention of the talk-show anecdote is to reveal just how stupid the teller is. But the story Kennedy tells gauges the relative quality and reputation of Hollywood studios; does the ostensibly artless, off-the-cuff account reveal the vulnerable human beneath the veneer of celebrity, or is it a craftily designed narrative intended to fashion another layer of artifice? In 1969, Goldie Hawn, newly minted as an up-and-coming star for her antic girl-next-door energy in *Rowan and Martin's Laugh-In*, arrived at a photo studio for a feature in *Esquire*. Making a point of how unsure of herself she was, Hawn asked throughout the long session for the photographer's guidance in poses. Finally, after hours of suggestions and rejections, she ended up biting her big toe. The photographer and crew exulted in Hawn's wacky audacity—so delightful, so unexpected, so spontaneous! When she left the studio, her manager, waiting in the outer office, asked her, "Did they go for the bit with the toe?"

Crediting both George Kennedy and Meadowlark Lemon as "Himself" is both a nod to the convention of placing fictional characters in movies in quotation marks and a larky, ironic gesture questioning their "realness." Casting well-known actors, athletes, and politicians for their reality quotient and then placing their names in quotation marks suggests their ultimate disillusionment and exposure. The reliably gregarious Meadowlark Lemon is thus reduced to any lascivious party guest ("Hey, that girl you came in with? She's *hot*.") and here one possessed of the ability to fuel Robert's jealousy and resentment. Including James L. Brooks as a hack director, outwardly agreeable but obdurate, must have been a wicked pleasure for Brooks: despite Robert's objections, his belief in his own judgment and taste, the scene stays as it was shot. And the role of Jay figures as our representative following Robert's lead and whims while he registers all around him: the director, the audio technicians, and his own salt-of-the-earth take on matters. Yet he gets enlisted in Robert's benighted Foley experiment, running around to simulate the sounds of their movie characters' footsteps. The Foley technique is yet another aspect of movie "magic"—mimicking the real with the patently unreal. And Brooks's own father, Harry Brooks (né Einstein), famous for a career in radio and film and sensationalized public death from a heart attack while waiting to perform in a roast of Lucille Ball and Desi Arnaz, must have been the source of radio lore, where sound effects did more than accompany or augment dramatic action—they created it.

Cornered and exasperated, Robert sees Mary emerge from the bathroom with the two guys, diffidently brushing her nose, and announces that he'd like to leave. "Well, I don't know, I'm kinda up," she demurs, at once self-conscious about the cocaine she's snorted with the guys and reluctant to go home. We see the beginnings of a bickering contest as she and Robert begin a passive-aggressive tussle: should they go or should they stay? Having wrested Mary from the potential seductions of David's rented house, Robert suggests a role-playing game—that they pretend to be strangers meeting for the first time. Despite her bemused expression, he anticipates a brave new world of renewed faith driven by fantasy and, safely home, gathers Mary up in his arms and exults, "Oh, look at you—I've only just met you!" It's a bit of erotic tomfoolery, a stratagem to spice up the familiar, but it's also a director's choice: Robert directing and editing his life.

This scene, as close as we get to rapture for Robert, cuts immediately to George Kennedy as Zenon, running along a corridor with a bulky "transformer" in his arms. Cut to the studio console where Robert and Jay are joined by two world-weary technicians. In order to give David the "thudding, metallic" sound he wants for the scene, Robert hoists a dispenser water bottle and invites Jay, "Chase me, chase me." It's a child's request begged of an adult during play.[7] The Foley stage, with the uncut footage of the film as backdrop, is seen as an arena of technological fraudulence, and Robert calls out eagerly to the bored technician, "Give us some echo." When the scene is finally recorded, Robert defers to the man and asks, "What do you think?" The technician replies with slow sarcasm, "I think you saved the picture." Missing the man's tone completely, a delighted Robert high-fives Jay as a disembodied voice comes over the studio speakers to announce the next audio project: "*Heaven's Gate*—short version." This allusion to one of Hollywood's most costly and hubristic blunders suggests that the low-cost ineptitude of the film Robert is editing may not be the worst of cinematic sins.

Cheered by this latest success, Robert calls Mary at work and gets what by now is a familiar taunt: "Fidelity." Robert tells shameless lie after lie in order to find her whereabouts, citing a matter of "life or death," and to him everything *is* that momentous, working as he does in a world that trivializes and upends the "real." Seeing Mary as Robert does in a Japanese restaurant, holding court while surrounded by five of her banking clients, the audience might well register the convivial, matey crush around her that contrasts with the largely deserted restaurant of the first scene. Embarrassing her, Robert succeeds in calling her away from her customers and accusing her of disloyalty, and here Mary suddenly matches his outrage with fury of her own: "I mean, what do you expect? That I'm *fucking* these guys? Because that's what I think you think." With no excuse at the ready, Robert claims to have planned a weekend excursion for the two of them, but she sees through this glozing lie. Nevertheless, she agrees to come away with him the next day, and their parting words suggest her new awareness of his manipulations:

> *Robert.* I love you
> *Mary.* I know you do.
> *Robert. (Muttering to himself)* I guess that's close enough to "I love you."

The next scene gives us Robert in his Porsche pulling up to Mary's office building, where she's waiting with her luggage for their weekend together. In his overstruck desire to please her and to mitigate the lie from which their plans sprang, he overwhelms her with a bag of fruit and an insipid basket of flowers, and as his car pulls away we see the mocking sign outside the building: "Fidelity." In the car, Mary tells him with pride and pleasure that she's closed the deal with the five businessmen and signed them up for an exclusive account with her bank:

> *Mary.* They work for Yamaha.
> *Robert.* Pianos?
> *Mary.* Motorcycles.
> *Robert.* Same thing.

This brief exchange illuminates the core of their problem: Robert doesn't hear or register the things that matter to her. A moment later, eager to tug her back to him, he asks what he assumes is a rhetorical question:

> *Robert.* So what are you thinking about?
> *Mary. (Radiantly)* That account.

Until this point, Robert's flailing insecurities have seemed arbitrary, comic exaggerations in a routine. Here we recognize that for all her indecisiveness regarding Robert, Mary has a job she loves and a strong sense of identification with the work she does. His film editing, on the other hand, is subject to the whims of others, the improbable logic of B movies, and his own flawed judgment. When they arrive at the cabin, her pleased surprise ("It's so *nice* here!") takes a turn when, still cheerful, she asks, "Is there a phone in here somewhere?" Her rationale for needing a phone ("I have to call Susan") rings hollow, but by now we're weary of Robert's emotional coercion, his relentless need for control, his micromanagement of every aspect of their modern romance. We remember that as she stooped over him in bed to land chirruping kisses on his face, he could only object to her dress, insisting that she change it before going off to work. And here, as Mary walks to the pay phone outside the cabin, ostensibly walking on grass, she sounds as if she's treading on linoleum. We think back to the scene at American International, where Robert and Jay exhaust themselves creating the right sound for Zenon's footsteps in what looks suspiciously like a carpeted corridor. Brooks gives us a scene reminiscent of that in Stanley Kubrick's *Lolita* (1962), in which James Mason's Humbert watches Sue Lyons as Lo speaking animatedly into a pay phone and understands with dread that for all his attempted control, she has slipped the leash and is arranging an assignation with his nemesis, Clare Quilty, played by a villainously shape-shifting Peter Sellers. And we witness this scene as well, aware, with Robert, of the pleasure Mary is taking in the call, the unalloyed delight in her face and posture and sharing a moment of subversive pleasure in her defiance.

> *Robert.* You seem happy.
> *Mary.* I *am* happy
> *Robert.* But you seem happier after the phone call.
> *Mary.* Why don't you just go through the rest of my fucking mail?

Breaking away from him and their idyllic cabin, enclosed and inviting, she lurches out of his arms and into the darkened woods. "Mary, that's full of snakes!" he warns, and the allusion is apt, exposing the shattered illusion of their Edenic getaway. "We should just go back," she pleads, but when he demands to know who was on the phone, she blurts, "You wanna know who it is? It's my brother's girlfriend, okay?" Sounding as dishonest as Robert, she opens the possibility that she hasn't been faithful, that Robert's demands have pushed her into her own realm of secrecy, evasion, and betrayal.[8]

> *Robert.* I couldn't help calling. I called because I love you.
> *Mary.* We weren't even together then. That was August.

In an attempt to reach through her exasperation and weariness, he offers, "This is how people work out this shit." Unbelieving and desperate, Mary echoes his earlier statement: "I don't think we should see each other anymore." His response, backlit by the fireplace, is the impassioned plea, "Marry me." The camera on his entreating face and her wonder, fear, and eventual acquiescence, free of any cynicism, transforms their world, heretofore one of shabby manipulations and transparent egotism, into a moment of shimmering hopefulness. Harrold's expression as she kisses Brooks redeems the neurotic game-playing that has preceded this moment. But then, as the camera pulls away, we hear his insistent supplication, "You watch, you watch . . . it's gonna be perfect . . . perfect." And we watch—as their figures recede into the darkness of the cabin and the camera rise up over the structure, the piano introduction to a song of the moment, "You Are So Beautiful," warbled by Joe Cocker, reverses our expectations once more, and the final crawl tells us that what we've been watching all along is a shaggy love story: "Robert and Mary were married three weeks later in Las Vegas, Nevada." After a moment, we read, "They were divorced the following month." And in the final statement, violating screen convention but upholding the claims of contradiction, "They are currently dating with plans to remarry."

What makes this *Modern Romance* so human is its refusal to take the claims of "movie love" seriously.[9] Instead, Brooks gives us a parody of romantic comedy rather than a satire, updated for his audience and representing in all their ambivalent anxieties the preoccupations of the moment, the universal concerns: love and work, work and love.

NOTES

1. Quoted in James Harvey, *Movie Love in the Fifties* (New York: Da Capo, 2002), v.
2. Jacob Knight, "The Love Monster: Albert Brooks' *Modern Romance*" Birth. Movies. Death. April 5, 2017. Available at <https://birthmoviesdeath.com/2017/04/05/the-love-monster-albert-brooks-modern-romance#disqus_thread> (last accessed January 14, 2021).
3. Knight, "The Love Monster."
4. In his interview with Brooks, Gavin Smith comments, "In scenes in restaurants or public places you'll cut to a single of an incidental character like a waiter or a store clerk for a moment, giving emphasis to someone we never see again." Brooks responds, "I think that's one of the most fun parts of movies. One of the best reviews of *Lost in America* I got was from Pauline Kael: she said the little characters that come and go in his movie are like candy for the audience. I love little characters." (Gavin Smith, "Albert Brooks Me Generation Everyman," in *Backstory 5: Interviews with Screenwriters of the 1990s*, ed. Patrick McGilligan [Los Angeles: University of California Press, 2009]). 15.
5. Speaking about his writing collaborations with Monica Johnson, Brooks notes, "*Modern Romance* we wrote in a car, with a tape recorder on." Quoted in Smith, "Albert Brooks Me Generation Everyman," 17.
6. "I've always sort of imagined movies as people looking through a window. Sort of peeping in on the goings-on." Brooks quoted in Smith, "Albert Brooks Me Generation Everyman," 15.
7. In her contemporary review of *Modern Romance*, Janet Maslin observes the film's "meandering, heartfelt nuttiness" ("Albert Brooks' 'Romance,'" *New York Times*, March 13, 1981, C8. Available at <https://www.nytimes.com/1981/03/13/movies/albert-brooks-romance.html?searchResultPosition=8> [last accessed January 20, 2021]).

8. In his essay on *Modern Romance*, Craig Williams notes, "The sense of hope that is integral to the rom-com—the inherent faith in the relationship being portrayed—is replaced with despair." He sees the film as a "companion piece" to Martin Scorsese's *Raging Bull* (1982) and acknowledges Kubrick's admiration of *Modern Romance*: "Stanley Kubrick loved it, and told Brooks that it was the movie he'd always wanted to make about jealousy." Williams, "In Praise of *Modern Romance*—Albert Brooks' Masterpiece." Available at <https://lwlies.com/articles/modern-romance-albert-brooks/> (last accessed January 14, 2021).

9. Craig Williams cites Scott Tobias and Nathan Rabin's argument that Brooks's comedy "rests on the duality in his films between scathing satire and celebratory narcissism. *Modern Romance* is his masterpiece, and, not coincidentally, it is the film that best captures this duality." Williams, "In Praise of *Modern Romance*." See also Scott Tobias and Nathan Rabin, "Albert Brooks," *AV Club*, June 16, 2011. Available at <http://www.avclub.com/article/albert-brooks-57634> (last accessed January 14, 2021), for a consideration of *Modern Romance* as "an uncompromising look at the uglier side of love, the one that most movies deny exists." Tobias and Rabin see Brooks, the son of a noted comedian and actor, as uniquely qualified to satirize Hollywood conventions.

CHAPTER 7

Easy Riders, Raging Yuppies: *Lost in America* and the Work of the Professional-Managerial Class

Derek Nystrom

Lost in America opens with perhaps the least cinematic tracking shot in the history of the medium.[1] After a brief, night-time establishing shot of a house with a "SOLD" real estate sign in the yard, the camera tracks slowly through a darkened interior filled with packing boxes, rolled-up rugs, and the general disarray of a house in preparation for a move. Snaking its way through the dimly lit rooms, the camera occasionally stops, seemingly at random, while the film's opening credits are superimposed over images of no real visual interest. The soundtrack to these images, meanwhile, is not a song or musical theme, the conventional means by which a film establishes its mood. Instead, we are treated to a radio broadcast of Larry King interviewing critic Rex Reed. Since they discuss film comedy, and Reed later responds to a caller who protests the depiction of sex in movies, the viewer might wonder if this broadcast is meant to serve as some kind of commentary on the film we are about to see (which is, after all, a comedy, and which eschews any explicitly erotic content). However, the exact purpose of this commentary is not at all clear, its puzzling nature underlined by its non-relation to the banal visual field. Indeed, when the camera finally alights upon our protagonists David and Linda Howard (Albert Brooks and Julie Hagerty) in bed, and David switches off the radio to talk to Linda about matters unconnected to Reed's conversation with King, the viewer can be forgiven for asking what the point of the opening credit sequence was.

Fans of Brooks might observe here that the filmmaker often mocked Reed for misunderstanding his first feature, *Real Life* (1979).[2] Reed apparently mistook the mockumentary for a straightforward imitation of PBS's *An American Family* project, and panned it accordingly ("Why would Paramount Pictures give *this man* the money to do such an important experiment?" Brooks recalls Reed saying).[3] In this light, Brooks would seem to be subtly mocking Reed, who spends most of the interview smugly touting his critical acumen. Reed tells King that his ideal screening scenario is one in which he is alone, so that his evaluation of a film is not affected by others; he bemoans studio screenings in which "they fill the movie house with all the secretaries from the film company and all the secretaries' second cousins," who "scream and yell like they're backers at an opening night." Asked whether comedies require an audience to work, Reed doubles down on his position: "If it's really funny, I'll laugh. I don't need 40 other people to laugh to remind me that I should be laughing." Since Reed clearly didn't get the joke motivating *Real Life*, one imagines that Brooks is needling him by replaying this interview over the opening credits of *Lost in America*, suggesting that an audience might have helped him grasp the humor of the earlier film, while also making clear the comic motivations of this one.

But I would argue that there is more than oblique score-settling at work here. For whatever other purposes Reed's remarks might serve, they also inaugurate *Lost in America*'s examination of middle-class identity and professional labor. When Reed denigrates the studios' attempt to influence critical reaction by packing the theater with those who have a material interest (however attenuated) in a film's success, he situates his work outside the circuits of instrumentalized commercial action: his job, unlike those of the secretaries, is not to serve the studios' bottom line, but to apply independently determined standards of evaluation. These standards, in turn, are what allow Reed to posit that he doesn't need other audience-goers to help him recognize if a film is "really funny." To be a professional critic, in other words, is to have a privileged insight into cultural value, one that is not swayed by either crude material considerations or the (uninformed) opinions of others. The class elitism of this position is emphasized by Reed's sneering dismissal of the reactions of secretaries and their second cousins; while the "screaming and yelling" of the former might be encouraged by their bosses, the latter have only their lack of skills in proper critical discrimination to blame. Insisting on the independence of his expertise, Reed concludes his account of his professional practices by declaring, "I don't respond very well to mass hysteria, anyway."

By distinguishing his labor from the material demands of capital on the one side and the "mass hysteria" of the untutored working class on the other, Reed is firmly locating himself in what Barbara and John Ehrenreich have called the professional-managerial class, their more analytically precise term for what is normally referred to as the middle class. As the Ehrenreichs have written, the professional-managerial class (or PMC) took shape around the turn of the previous century as a mediating force between capital and labor.[4] Growing in size and importance throughout the twentieth century, the PMC served the owners by managing the working class at the site of production; training and tending to this workforce in the various teaching and caring professions; and reproducing the ideological supports of capitalism through the culture industries. Yet despite its central role of disciplining the working class, the PMC also asserted its autonomy from capital's attempts to control its own laboring practices. Professional and managerial workers insisted that the legitimacy of their work depended upon standards of expertise developed independently from capital's bottom-line concerns.[5] (These self-determined and self-regulated professional standards also distinguished PMC labor from that of the working class, whose tasks were most often routinized and closely supervised.) In short, the PMC is situated in what Erik Olin Wright has called a "contradictory class location": like capital, the PMC's class interests lie in their control over workers, but like the working class, the PMC's labor is dominated by and exploited for the benefit of capital—a condition they struggle against through their defense of their professionalized work practices.[6]

This contradictory class location generates a whole host of paradoxes for the members of the PMC. I submit that *Lost in America* is a sustained investigation of many of these lived contradictions, especially those highlighted by the then-widely discussed emergence of a new generation of middle-class subjects: the yuppies. In what follows, I will trace the ways in which *Lost in America* shows how the contradictions embodied by the film's two yuppie protagonists are in fact constitutive of not just their generational experience (as most commentators on the film observed), but also their class position. Moreover, the film's attention to the antinomies of PMC identity is accompanied by a skepticism about the imagined autonomy of professional work. The Howards spend the second half of the film in situations in which they are unable to make use of their specialized skills and expertise. Absented from the specific ecologies of production that enable professional labor to generate value, David and Linda are both unable to restore their lost class privilege and unwilling to consider other uses for that labor. *Lost in America*'s examination of professional labor's ability (or lack thereof) to operate outside of the constraints of capital takes a self-reflexive turn, I conclude, through its persistent references to Dennis Hopper's *Easy Rider* (1969). I will suggest that *Lost in America*'s critical treatment of that film's cultural and cinematic legacy also serves as an opportunity for Brooks to reflect upon his own filmic practices, which are foregrounded by moments of conspicuous yet seemingly unmotivated cinematographic flourishes. If *Lost in America* asks us to be suspicious of professional labor's claims to autonomy, then, it also requires us to think more critically about the conditions that structure Brooks's own professional labor—that is, those of Hollywood filmmaking.

RESPONSIBLE IRRESPONSIBILITY: DELAYED GRATIFICATION AND THE PMC

Lost in America's anatomy of the contradictions of PMC life begins immediately after its inscrutable opening credit sequence. David wakes Linda to air a series of free-floating anxieties about their impending move, but when Linda asserts that at least some of his anxieties come from the fact that they are both "a bit too controlled"—that she wishes that they "were a little more irresponsible"—David loses his temper. He initially seems insulted by the implication that he has become "old or stodgy," but soon ties their overly "responsible" nature to their professional jobs, telling Linda, "You're not the most irresponsible person in the whole world. Look at your job: personnel director is like a Nazi camp. If you hire one person they don't like, they fire you. So how much freedom do you have?" Yet David tries to convince Linda that his hoped-for promotion to senior vice president at his advertising agency will change all of this: "I'll have stock in this agency. That makes me responsible, *genuinely* responsible. So I can fool around now. Now I can be irresponsible, I'm in a position of responsibility."

This hilariously oxymoronic formulation points to one of the key pressures facing members of the PMC: the need to delay gratification. Unlike wealthy elites, whose class position is most often literally inherited, and unlike the working class, whose occupations (thanks to routinization and de-skilling) frequently do not require lengthy apprenticeships, those who pursue professional or managerial work must undergo extended periods of schooling and training. In order to acquire the sort of expert knowledge—and its concomitant forms of institutional certification, such as university degrees—that legitimize the PMC's authority in the workplace, members of this class must engage in a sustained, even lifelong performance of the kind of responsibility and self-control that David and Linda bemoan in their pre-dawn conversation. In fact, as Barbara Ehrenreich argues in *Fear of Falling*, the ability to defer gratification came to be seen as the central character trait that distinguished the middle class from the lower orders, who were thought to suffer from "present-time orientation."[7] This class-specific injunction to unrelenting self-control helps explain why, when David tells Linda, "After tomorrow, everything is gonna be better, I'm positive," he immediately follows this claim by pathetically asking, "Don't you think so?" He is quite literally unable imagine an end to the deferral of gratification.

When David is informed the next day that despite his eight years at the agency, he is *not* getting the promotion he expected, but is instead being transferred to New York to work on a new account, he explodes in anger—an anger based on his expectation that his deferral of gratification would be rewarded. He screams at his boss, "I want my eight years back! I wasted my youth for you!" David then complains that, unlike his "friends in college who went out to find themselves"—which is to say, unlike those who refused to defer their gratification—he "took the business route" only to get "a transfer," something, he sarcastically observes, that does not require his extensive professional training: "I can get that at a bus stop *right now*! I don't need *any* qualifications."

Yet it is not the case that David and Linda had wholly deferred gratification up until this point in their lives. It is clear from the beginning of the film that they are avid, even profligate consumers: one of David's early morning worries is that perhaps they should have bought a home with a tennis court, even though they don't know how to play tennis ("If you have a court, you learn"). And when he objects to Linda's characterization of them as "too controlled," he reminds her that they went out and bought "a $450,000 house and . . . all the things you want and maids and servants and everything else." David cites this extravagance as a sign of the benefits of self-control, but it actually sounds like proof that they are in fact not very disciplined at all, at least when it comes to their expenditures.

This paradoxical stance of rigid self-control in pursuit of professional ascendancy along with seemingly reckless spending is one of the central "cultural contradictions of capitalism" that Daniel Bell identified in the book of the same name. The ever-increasing dominance of consumer capitalism in the twentieth century—that is, the expansion of the economy through the relentless generation of new consumer needs, and the accompanying encouragement to spend rather than save—meant that the producer-centered values of the Protestant work ethic came into conflict with the consumerist injunction to seek pleasure now. As Bell put it, "On the one hand, the business corporation wants an individual to work hard, pursue a career, accept delayed gratification—to be, in the crude sense, an organization man. And yet, in its products and its advertisements, the corporation promotes pleasure, instant joy, relaxing and letting go."[8] Bell's larger argument implies that all subjects of consumer capitalism were subjected to these conflicting directives, but his revealing choice of words here suggests that the PMC experienced this particular contradiction most acutely: "Organization Man" is the title of William Whyte's influential post-war study of middle managers. Bell's terminology is no accident, since the PMC is the one class whose workplace legitimacy depends upon expert credentials that can only be achieved through responsible self-control, even as its members are encouraged to spend with greater abandon.

THE RISE OF THE YUPPIE

In 1985, the year of *Lost in America*'s release, the dominant media used a newly minted buzzword to identify those who willingly, even eagerly, embraced this contradiction: "yuppie." Standing for "young urban professional," the neologism initially became popularized in accounts of Gary Hart's surprising early success in the 1984 Democratic Party presidential primaries (yuppies were thought to be his core demographic). But soon the term became a ubiquitous descriptor of an allegedly new species of middle-class subject. This group was defined with varying levels of sociological precision, depending on which article one read, but the common themes included an unapologetic commitment to working long hours at professional corporate jobs, and an even more unabashed lifestyle of conspicuous consumption. These journalistic accounts spent some time discussing the former, but they took particular relish in describing the latter at length: the yuppies' taste for then-exotic items like Perrier, quiche, sushi, and Brie; their styles of dress for both work (pinstriped suits) and what amounted to play (designer-brand workout clothes, worn in high-end health clubs); their expensive foreign-made cars; their renovated loft condos; their new technological gadgets (such as Sony Walkmans, VCRs, and home computers); and so on. In this way, the yuppies were imagined—as is often the case with lay accounts of class description in American discourse—as a category of consumer taste rather than a location in the relations of production.

To be fair, there was something to the idea that yuppies were best identified by their preference for bottled water and BMWs instead of their role in reproducing the conditions of surplus value extraction. As many commentators at the time noted, the yuppies were said to differ from the "organization men" of the previous generation by their unwillingness to identify themselves with the firm for which they worked. A Harvard Business School professor told *Newsweek* that yuppies approach their jobs "with very high expectations and a minimal degree of loyalty"; a Yale management professor concurred, saying that yuppies are driven "not so much by their willingness to work hard for the corporation, but their devotion to accumulating power and getting rich."[9]

Figure 7.1 The exemplary consumer at his real job: David (Brooks) in his office, discussing the Mercedes leather for his new car

In other words, the yuppie embrace of corporate life was more of a means to the end of enabling their sophisticated consumer tastes. *Lost in America* offers a perfect dramatization of this dynamic: the only time we see David at his ad agency job (right before he gets himself fired for insulting his boss), he is not involved in any productive labor whatsoever. Instead, we see him on the phone, haggling with a Mercedes dealer over the specifics of the new car he plans to buy. As the film devotes substantial screen time to a discussion of the relative merits of a leather interior versus that of thick vinyl ("It's what they call Mercedes leather," the dealer helpfully explains), we clearly see that the real job of a yuppie is being an exemplary consumer.

When *Lost in America* was released, then, it was almost universally described as a film about this new sociological group. Virtually every review deployed the term "yuppie" at some point to describe the film's protagonists and often its expected audience. Gene Siskel's *Chicago Tribune* review used it three times in two sentences.[10] One reviewer told his radio listeners to avoid seeing the film on a Friday or Saturday night, "because they would be overrun by the Yuppie audience."[11] But it was not just the professional occupations and commodity fetishism of the film's protagonists that encouraged this association. The film's plot trajectory—in which David uses the occasion of his firing to persuade Linda to join him in dropping out and "finding themselves" in a way they had not done in their youth—aligned with one of the most crucial features of the dominant media's account of the yuppies: that they somehow both embodied *and* betrayed their generation's countercultural past.

On the one hand, this media narrative suggested that the yuppie embrace of corporate work and conspicuous consumption amounted to a renunciation of the radical political and cultural movements of the 1960s. Exhibit A for this version of the yuppie narrative was Jerry Rubin, the anti-war activist and Chicago Seven member who became a stockbroker in the 1980s; the term "yuppie," some commentators claimed, was a direct allusion to the "yippies" of the theatrically countercultural Youth International Party, which had been founded by Rubin, Abbie Hoffman, and others.[12] Thus, when the Weather Underground activist Bernadine Dohrn emerged from a decade of hiding as a fugitive (during which she was alleged to have participated in multiple bombings of government and corporate targets) and soon joined the litigation department of Chicago law firm Sidley & Austin, her lawyer could explain the transition simply by saying, "She's a yuppie. She has evolved from revolutionary to square."[13]

However, one could also see the yuppie lifestyle as a perverse continuation, rather than repudiation, of the 1960s counterculture. Indeed, commentators often identified something unsettling about these apparently co-opted yuppie figures: despite their apparently new-found adherence to the values of the capitalist marketplace, they were frequently characterized as a disruptive force. *Newsweek* speculated that "the banker who was horrified in 1968 when Columbia students occupied the president's office will not necessarily be reassured to discover that one of those students now has an M.B.A. and an office down the hall from him."[14] Some of this unease was due, no doubt, to the fact that these younger professionals were allegedly less loyal to their employers. But *The New Republic* identified another reason why yuppies were so unnerving to those who otherwise aligned with their worldview: while leftists saw yuppies as sell-outs, the right saw them as "a disgrace to the bourgeois banner—all trivial self-indulgence and consumerist excess, no 'middle-class values' of the sterner sort."[15]

With this in mind, it is worth remembering that one of the main criticisms of countercultural youth during the 1960s, as Barbara Ehrenreich points out, was that they "had lost that indispensable middle-class virtue, the capacity for deferred gratification."[16] By pursuing pleasure in the moment, rather than adhering to the rules of the institutions that would guide them toward professional or managerial occupations, the middle-class followers of the counterculture were engaged in nothing short of class treason; when they "turned on, tuned in, and dropped out" (to borrow Timothy Leary's infamous slogan), they were also refusing to reproduce their parents' class position. Yet, as Ehrenreich notes, "the critics seldom noticed how much the hedonism of the counterculture mirrored and amplified the hedonistic promise of their own, perfectly respectable, consumer culture."[17] Ehrenreich's implication here is that, since the counterculture rejected the terms by which the older cohort of the PMC grappled with the injunction to sacrifice present enjoyment for future rewards even as they were enticed to buy pleasure in the marketplace now, this lived contradiction could perhaps be safely repressed. The emergence of the yuppies—willing corporate denizens who nonetheless pursued an unrestrained hedonism—thrust this contradiction uncomfortably into the foreground.

It is perhaps for this reason that Tom O'Brien, in his review for *Commonweal*, claimed that "Brooks, in effect, plays the old yippie Jerry Rubin, now stockbroker Jerry Rubin."[18] Of course, this gets the film's plot trajectory backwards: the Howards have been dutiful stockbroker-types for their entire lives; it is only after David is fired that they decide to drop out and pursue the 1960s dream of finding themselves. But O'Brien's association of Brooks's character with the apparently Janus-faced Rubin signals how *Lost in America* turns on the tensions within PMC identity that, as Ehrenreich has argued, played a significant role in generating the countercultural rebellion in the first place.[19] David and Linda's unfinished business with their pasts—their unrealized (one might even say deferred) countercultural rebellion—induces the film to explore the PMC's unfinished business with its constitutive paradoxes.

DROPPING OUT, BUT WITH A NEST EGG

One of the central jokes of *Lost in America*, though, is that the Howards do not really want to reject the substantial comforts of their life for a countercultural set of experiences. Indeed, they have little concrete sense of what those kinds of experiences would even be; David, in trying to persuade Linda to quit her job, insists: "It's time to get out. We have to touch Indians. We have to see the mountains and the prairies and the whole rest of that song."[20] This is not to say that the Howards are not genuinely dissatisfied with aspects of their yuppie lives: before David's firing, Linda confesses to a co-worker, "I don't like anything anymore. I don't like my life; I don't like my house; I don't like anything." Moreover, Linda insightfully grasps that David's assumption that his new job will suddenly make them happy is mistaken: "He genuinely believes that this promotion is going to change everything. But you know, he believed that every single promotion. And it never does. Things are always the same." Yet their inability to envision clearly an alternative to their life is signaled early in the film, when David, defending himself from the accusation that he is too responsible, tells Linda, "I'm doing the very best I can. I don't know what else to do."

Thus, when they start to plan in earnest for their new life away from their professional careers, they cannot help but imagine it through the consumerist modality through which they organized their previous existence. Even as they contemplate liquidating their assets and selling their belongings in order to hit the road, they pore over real estate listings for country farmhouses they might buy and discuss the various features of the RV they plan to purchase with the windfall they received from the inflated real estate market.[21] David unintentionally highlights the conflicted nature of their approach—the way it attempts to maintain bourgeois consumer comforts while rejecting the world that makes such comforts possible—when he exclaims, "We can drop out, and we can still have our nest egg!" Wishing to escape from the contradictions of professional life, David and Linda conceive of "escape" in a similarly contradictory fashion: they want to leave it all behind while taking it all with them.

In fact, their alleged countercultural impulses do not survive the first night. Arriving in Las Vegas in their fully stocked Winnebago in order to renew their wedding vows, they decide against camping out and instead stay in an expensive hotel, where they can, as Linda puts it, "have room service" and "watch porno movies," deferring yet again their planned transition into an alternative mode of life. (Linda insists that their material indulgence will be "just tonight, and then that's it, never again.") It is during that night in Vegas, though, that Linda loses the entirety of their savings in a crazed early morning gambling binge that happens off-screen. This sudden plot shift divided critics at the time of the film's release. A few reviewers noted that it served a satirical purpose: Tim Pulleine observed that Vegas is "a parody of the free enterprise ethic," and it is worth remembering that the bulk of David and Linda's nest egg was derived from the casino-like real estate market.²² That said, the film does not emphasize this comparison, which may explain why other critics found this element of the story to be a forced plot device. John Simon offers perhaps the most fully articulated version of this critique:

> To make valid satirical fun of the Howards and the society they suffocate in, *Lost in America* should have made their downfall—or the unviableness of their scheme—hinge on something less capricious, less facilely instantaneous. The nest egg should dwindle away in spite of their best intentions, its evaporation should tell much more about them (us) and their (our) world than that Linda had a rather unprepossessing flaw.²³

I would argue, though, that Linda's "flaw" does in fact tell us a great deal about them (us)—especially if the implied "we" of Simon's review is, as one suspects, the professional-managerial class. Linda explains her gambling binge to David by saying, "I never had this feeling before . . . It was like being on another planet. I didn't care. I didn't need anything. I didn't have any problems."

This experience was profoundly different from her work life: "I sat in that office for seven years without a window. Sometimes I felt like I was going crazy." In other words, Linda found herself unable to defer gratification any more: "I just held things in so long, I just burst." After years of maintaining a sustained performance of responsible self-control in the sensory deprivation tank of her work space, Linda seeks out "another planet," one of present-time orientation. But, in keeping with her yuppie (rather than yippie) inclinations,

Figure 7.2 "I didn't have any problems"

her rebellion from the ethos of delayed gratification comes not in the context of alternative, countercultural practices, but instead in an environment that apotheosizes the anarchy of the capitalist marketplace. This seemingly facile and capricious plot event, then, is better understood as the necessary and perhaps even inevitable detonation of the cultural contradictions that had been driving the protagonists' actions to this point.

THE WHITE COLLAR BOX

If the first half of *Lost in America* is about the tensions between deferred gratification and consumerist hedonism for the professional-managerial class, the second half explores the conditions of their labor's value. This stage of the film is inaugurated by David's attempt to get their nest egg back from the casino, which he does by camouflaging the request as a proposed advertising campaign. To do so, David attempts to deploy all of his professional skills and authority. When he meets with the casino manager (Garry Marshall), he begins by reviewing his credentials: "I was creative director for Ross & McMahon.... So, when I say I have an idea, you know, I'm not a jerk who walked in off the street." Yet despite this proof of his specialized expertise, David's plan is rejected by the casino boss. To a large extent, this is because his proposed campaign is a patently ridiculous one: he suggests that the casino give the Howards their nest egg back and advertise doing so, in order to associate the casino with "warm feeling." But what is striking about the way this scene plays out is that Brooks does not limit the comedy to the ludicrous nature of this plea (e.g. David's suggested jingle: "The Desert Inn has heart/ The Desert Inn has heart/ The Desert Inn has heart"). The scene also involves a series of failed attempts by David to wield his cultural capital effectively. When he explains that he and his wife are modeling their lives on *Easy Rider*, the casino boss does not even recognize the film's title ("Easy what?" he asks). Later, David insists that the advertising campaign would not cause others to demand their money back, because it would make "a clear distinction between the bold, who would be my wife and I, and then all the other schmucks who come here to see Wayne Newton," to which the casino owner responds, "I like Wayne Newton . . . That makes me a schmuck?"

Much of the comedy of these interactions turns on the gap between David's cultural capital and that of the casino manager; even discounting his faux pas regarding Wayne Newton, it is clear that David is assured of the superiority of his range of cultural references, as he declares that *Easy Rider* is "a great film" that "you gotta see" because "it's historic." This kind of cultural literacy—the ability to recognize *Easy Rider*'s historical importance, and confident assertion of the low cultural standing of Wayne Newton—is a crucial feature of the skill set of professional culture workers. Yet in this context, David's display of superior taste fails to perform the function that it normally does in his workplace: that is, translate cultural capital into financial capital. In fact, the second half of *Lost in America* involves a series of scenarios in which the Howards are unable to parlay their professional training and credentials into gainful employment or other kinds of material reward. Turned down for a job as a delivery person in the small Arizona town in which they eventually settle, and unable to land other employment, David finds himself working as a crossing guard. Linda, meanwhile, secures a job that is superficially similar to her previous position, as she is once again a manager; however, her specific title is assistant manager, at a fast-food restaurant (Der Weinerschnitzel), where her superior is a teen named Skippy.

In other words, if David and Linda are lost in America, what they have lost are the specialized locations within the relations of production where their forms of professional labor could generate economic value. This absence is registered most strikingly (and amusingly) in David's meeting with an employment office clerk, who can barely contain his disbelief when David explains that his average yearly salary at his previous job was $100,000. When David asks if he has "something maybe in the executive file—or maybe you have a white collar box or something," the clerk responds "Oh, I know, you mean, the $100,000 box!" and laughs uproariously. Scott Tobias, in a recent essay accompanying the Criterion DVD edition of the film, describes this moment as "a sign of David's hilarious disconnect from ordinary Americans," but I would argue that the satire here is more class-specific.[24] David's hope that there would be a "white collar box" suggests a belief that his professional skills would be valuable in any context, that they have something like intrinsic worth. In other words, it is a belief that assumes the autonomous status of professional labor itself.

To understand the significance of this belief, we must return to the history of the PMC's development as a class within capitalism. Despite the fact that the primary task of this class was to attend to and manage the workforce on behalf of the owners, many professionals argued that the deployment of their specialized skills and knowledge should not be subordinated to the interests of capital, but should instead take the lead in reorganizing the social order. Indeed, as the PMC consolidated itself during the early decades of the previous century, the Ehrenreichs argue, its "leaders envisioned a technocratic transformation of society in which all aspects of life would be 'rationalized' according to expert knowledge."[25] This anti-capitalist orientation was revived during the 1960s, as the largely PMC-born and -bred leaders of the New Left (at least in its early formations) excoriated the older members of their class for having submitted too willingly to corporate and state power, for having failed to direct their professional knowledge and skills toward the public good. What is important about this history for my purposes is that such claims for the liberatory potential of professional expertise rely heavily on a belief in the autonomy of this expertise from its uses under capitalism. These forms of what the Ehrenreichs call "PMC class consciousness" strive to valorize professional labor on its own terms, divorcing their specialized modes of work and forms of knowledge from their usual context of reproducing the conditions of capitalist production.

This might seem to have little to do with David's inability to find a job in Safford, Arizona that would approximate his salary at Ross & McMahon. And indeed, David betrays little in the way of any anti-capitalist beliefs, despite his half-hearted embrace of a canned form of the 1960s counterculture. But the relevance to *Lost in America* of the PMC's historical attempts to valorize its labor as autonomous becomes clearer if we imagine another way that the second half of the film could have unfolded. In this alternative, perhaps more Preston Sturges-like version,[26] the Howards could, after losing all of their money, find themselves in a small town that does afford them jobs that approximate their earlier occupations: David could design ads for local businesses, one of which would be a mom-and-pop clothing store that Linda has been hired to help manage. Despite the fact that these jobs would pay nothing like their previous positions, both David and Linda would come to rediscover the things that drew them to their chosen professions in the first place. David would experience anew the joy he takes in writing, drawing, and directing, while Linda would find herself rejuvenated by the kinds of relationship-building that ground-level personnel management requires. By using their expertise in these new environments, the Howards would come to appreciate the essentially positive wellsprings of creativity and interpersonal connectivity from which their chosen occupations were derived. The film would end happily, as our protagonists would have genuinely "found themselves" by regenerating their faith in the intrinsic value of their professional labor, and thus in their class identity.

But this imaginary, middle-class-affirming film is not the film in front of us.[27] Instead, *Lost in America* ends with David eagerly agreeing with Linda that they should drive to New York as quickly as possible, so he can "eat shit" to try to get his job back. This revelation, on David's part at least, is catalyzed less by a wish to return to his previous mode of work (although the indignities of being a crossing guard are hilariously depicted) and more by his consumerist fantasies: he is haunted by the ghosts of commodities past. After David has been guiding rude children across the street, a Mercedes drives up to him, satirically accompanied on the soundtrack by strings and a heavenly choir; first appearing like a mirage in the distance, the car is essentially the one that David planned on buying at the beginning of the film (although this one has the real leather interior). David's wish to return to his old job, then, is not based on the inherent pleasures of his professional labor. It is a desire to return to a context of production in which that labor is highly compensated. If any kind of PMC class consciousness emerges here, it is a cynical one: the instrumentalized nature of professional expertise is admitted, and submission to corporate power is seen as the only path possible to realizing its value. The final (if unspoken) irony of this cynical recognition is that the work to which David hopes to return entails the excitation of consumer desire that produced the contradictions of PMC identity that bedeviled him and Linda at the beginning of the film.

"JUST LIKE *EASY RIDER*"

Right before David leaves the employment clerk who kids him about "the $100,000 box," he tries, as he has numerous times in the film, to explicate his actions by referring to *Easy Rider*.[28] As is almost always the case in *Lost in America*, this attempt fails (the clerk hadn't seen *Easy Rider*, but did see the 1983 Rodney Dangerfield vehicle *Easy Money*). But this scene is not just another example of David's inability to wield his usually privileged cultural capital effectively; it also constitutes part of the film's ongoing engagement with Dennis Hopper's classic of New Hollywood cinema. It is a common observation in criticism on *Lost in America* that the film uses *Easy Rider* as an intertext in order to satirize the Howards' pretensions toward countercultural rebellion. What is less noted is the way that *Easy Rider*'s supposedly revolutionary status is critiqued in turn.

Richard Schickel's review in *Time* articulates the standard understanding of *Lost in America*'s use of *Easy Rider*:

> Foolish fellows! If they had just waited a few years, Peter Fonda, Jack Nicholson and Dennis Hopper could have been really Easy Riders. Instead of discovering American from the jolting seats of their motorcycles, they could have cruised along in the stolid comfort of an RV. With, maybe, the little woman fixing toasted cheese sandwiches in the microwave.[29]

Schickel's ironic comparison here—mocking the "stolid," domestic nature of the Howards as antithetical to the adventurousness of *Easy Rider*—replicates that of *Lost in America* for much of its running time, perhaps most pointedly in its allusive use of Steppenwolf's "Born to Be Wild" to score the couple's first drive in their Winnebago. (The film underlines this disjunction of sound and image by having an actual biker pull up next to the Winnebago; when David honks to express solidarity with the biker, he gives David the finger: another failed attempt at aligning himself with *Easy Rider*.) And to be sure, David's frequent description of *Easy Rider* as the film he has "based his whole life on" functions similarly to his repeated injunction that he and Linda need to "touch

Indians": that is, as a sign of his limited understanding of what an alternative, countercultural existence actually entails.

But David's invocation of the film as a model for his and Linda's actions is also not entirely mistaken. When Linda claims, during a post-Vegas fight in front of the Hoover Dam, that the protagonists of *Easy Rider* dropped out with "no nest egg," David correctly retorts, "Bullshit! They had a giant nest egg. They had all this cocaine" (which they sold at the start of the film). This exchange could be taken for an incidental joke, were it not followed soon afterward by another discussion of the film that casts doubt on its countercultural politics. After they are pulled over for speeding by a motorcycle police officer who initially appears to be an impassive enforcer of the law, Linda asks him if he has seen *Easy Rider*. David demurs—"I've tried this, it doesn't work"— but the officer enthusiastically responds that it is his all-time favorite movie ("I started riding the motorcycle because of that movie"). In the conversation that follows, though, the policeman's attraction to the film seems politically incoherent at best; he agrees with David, for example, that the commune scene is great, but he also enthuses about the final scene: "Remember the ending, when they got blown away? . . . It made my day!" In a film that continually uses *Easy Rider* as a shorthand reference point for all things countercultural, then, the only person other than the Howards who even recognizes it turns out to be a literal representative of law and order. Dennis Hopper's allegedly radical vision, Brooks suggests, does not just provide its protagonists with a free market-generated payday that is echoed in the Howards' real estate windfall; it is also so ideologically polysemous that it could hail a Clint Eastwood-quoting member of the repressive state apparatus.

Brooks is clearly poking fun at *Easy Rider*'s overly romanticized reputation, especially among the baby boomer generation, but a more serious critique is at play here, a skepticism about the possibility of depicting a truly alternative social vision within Hollywood cinema. Granted, Brooks has elsewhere aligned his filmmaking aspirations with those of New Hollywood directors of the late 1960s and early 1970s. In an interview pegged to *Lost in America*'s release, Brooks told Gene Siskel, "In the early '70s when I was still in college and *The Graduate* and *Carnal Knowledge* were out, that's what made me want to go into moviemaking. It looked like a place to express ideas."[30] But it should be noted that Brooks's approach differs from that of a film like *Easy Rider*, which tries to imagine forms of non-capitalist life, especially in the back-to-nature commune sequence. As David E. James has argued, these radical gestures are undermined by the film's reliance on dominant Hollywood generic formats (like the road movie).[31] Brooks's work instead has more often taken such (presumably unintentional) gestures of ideological containment as their subject. To put it more precisely: Brooks, starting with his early stand-up performances in the 1960s and 1970s, often foregrounded the always-already commodified nature of his cultural productions. In one of Brooks's early 1970s appearances on *The Tonight Show*, Saul Austerlitz recalls, "he announced a going-out-of-business sale of bargain-basement Albert Brooks routines, which he would personally deliver to the purchaser's home."³² Another routine from *The Tonight Show* featured Brooks admitting that he does not have any new material to perform, but since he knows he needs to appear on television in order to promote his first comedy album, *Comedy Minus One*, he engages in a series of clownish slapstick gags, even though "that's not what I'm all about." But it is perhaps his second comedy album that best exemplifies this meta-commentary on his comedy-as-commodity: 1975's *A Star Is Bought*. As the opening cut of the concept album explains, rather than operate in a single musical genre that would be played on only one kind of radio station, each track of the album would engage in a different style (country, blues, classical, novelty song, etc.) in order to maximize the album's radio exposure.³³ The resulting album is both explanation and enactment of this ruthlessly market-driven process of cultural creation. In short, Brooks's mode of critique, from its earliest incarnations, has satirized "the system" from within, rather than attempting (à la *Easy Rider*) to imagine its alternative.

Given Brooks's history of ironizing the commodity status of entertainment, it is notable that, in his interview with Siskel, he complains that it is Hollywood's treatment of films as commodities that has all but extinguished the possibilities explored by the New Hollywood: "We're seeing the movies being transformed from an occasionally artistic business into a supermarket."³⁴ Recounting his struggles to secure funding for his previous films, Brooks suggests that such problems will only get worse with the rise of conglomerate ownership of the studios. "How is [American cinema] supposed to get better when Coca-Cola has all of its controls firmly in place at Columbia? Coca-Cola doesn't make exotic soft drinks; why should they bother to make exotic movies?"³⁵ But he also traces the decline of New Hollywood filmmaking to the success of *Star Wars*-like blockbusters, as well as the infamous box office failure of *Heaven's Gate* (1980): "[W]ith *Heaven's Gate*, the ball officially changed hands. You could almost hear it in this town where they said in effect, 'That's it. We will take it back'."³⁶

Brooks's language here is quite telling; in describing the battle for control between filmmakers and the corporate-owned studios, he is also diagnosing the shifting balance of class power in Hollywood between capital and the PMC. According to Brooks, the film industry's professional culture workers, writers and directors like him, were finding themselves less able to determine the nature of their creative projects. Brooks's objection to these developments is rooted in his desire to exert precisely this kind of creative control. In other interviews, he has frequently recalled a conversation he had with an agent, who told him, "Gee, I don't know why you always take the hard road," to which

Brooks replied, "You think I see two roads?"[37] The implication of this comment is that Brooks's creative vision is generated according to its own principles; it is not measured against the requirements of the marketplace and/or the demands of the studios. What Brooks is articulating here, in other words, is quite simply the PMC desire for its labor to be autonomous.

I am suggesting, then, that *Lost in America*'s persistent citations of *Easy Rider* serve two related purposes: to acknowledge the compromised nature of its social vision, which fails to provide a genuine alternative to the middle-class life that has made the Howards chronically unhappy, but also to emblematize, despite its limitations, a tradition of Hollywood art cinema that is increasingly endangered. In other words, *Easy Rider* operates as a signifier of the desire for autonomous culture work as well as the constraints placed upon this work within Hollywood filmmaking. In these ways, *Lost in America*'s *Easy Rider* fixation acts as a kind of encouragement to think meta-cinematically, to consider Brooks's own cinematic labor. After all, when David says, "This is just like *Easy Rider*, except now it's our turn," one could be forgiven for thinking that the character is also speaking for Brooks himself.

This self-reflexive dimension is reinforced by the film's occasionally conspicuous camerawork. As Gavin Smith observes, Brooks's visual style, while effective, is usually "remarkably discreet and unemphatic; he has a light, deft touch, with a classical precision and economy, shooting and cutting his scenes in smooth, seamless successions of medium shots, with clean, high-key lighting."[38] Yet there are passages in *Lost in America* when the cinematography becomes distinctly more visible *as* cinematography. In particular, as Chuck Bowen notes, there are the Kubrickian flourishes of the "early office sequences, in which employees of an advertising company navigate hallways as chilly and sterile as those in *2001: A Space Odyssey*." *The Shining* is perhaps the more apt reference point here: these sequences involve two long-take (about forty-two seconds each) Steadicam shots, which follow David as he traverses the halls, first to his office, and from there to his meeting with his boss. What is striking about these shots, though, is that they seem largely unmotivated. They are essentially without dialogue, and amount to what is basically narrative dead time: we already know that David is headed to a meeting in which he will learn about the promotion, so there is little story-based justification for devoting almost a minute and a half of screen time to banal movement through office interiors.

One might suggest that we are meant to think of these tracking shots, emphatically noticeable in their difference from Brooks's otherwise unobtrusive shooting and cutting style, when we see a later, also largely dialogue-free Steadicam following shot that takes place at the Hoover Dam. This shot, which is almost exactly the same length as the previous Steadicam shots, features a number of suggestive differences: we follow Linda, not David (who is present but out of the frame); we watch her as she moves not through austere office hallways, but in an exterior setting of considerable natural and man-made grandeur. Where the earlier Steadicam shots were laced with the narrative tension of David's impending meeting, this shot takes place in something like an aftermath, as the couple has not only learned of David's denied promotion and subsequent firing, but has also lost their nest egg. It feels like it could be a significant turning point in the film.

In fact, John Powers argues that the Hoover Dam sequence asks us to note the difference of "this depression-era triumph of the collective spirit" from the other, largely privatized spaces of the film. Indeed, in the alternative, more affirmative version of *Lost in America* I hypothesized earlier, this moment would have been one in which Linda and David begin to imagine different possibilities for their labor as they regard the immensity of the dam, a monument to professional engineering exercised in the service of the public good. Yet such a realization does not occur. Even though the tracking shot ends with a lengthy consideration of the dam's vertiginous height, with the camera tipping precariously over the guard rail to take in the full size of the structure, this image is merely used for some gallows humor: David says, "Nice dam, huh? Do you want to go first, or should I?" In other words, despite the suggestive narrative and thematic possibilities of this long-take Steadicam shot—its cinematographic rhymes with the previous shots in the office sequences, and the ways such an association might comment on the different potential contexts of professional labor—the shot ultimately, like those in David's office, feels extraneous and unnecessary.

But if these conspicuous yet unmotivated following shots do not generate commentary on the professional labor depicted within *Lost in America*, they do serve as commentary on the professional labor involved in making *Lost in America*. David Bordwell has observed that "[b]ravura following shots became a fixed feature of the work of Scorsese, John Carpenter, De Palma, and other New Hollywood directors."[39] Bordwell also notes Paul Schrader's contention that "unmotivated camera movement, so prominent in European directors like Bertolucci, became the hallmark of his generation of U.S. directors."[40] Given Brooks's attraction to this tradition of filmmaking, these Steadicam shots could be seen as a kind of visual objective correlative for his cinematic aspirations, especially since, as I have already noted, the shrinking possibility of pursuing these aspirations was very much on the filmmaker's mind while he made *Lost in America*. In these moments, the Steadicam, detached from any clear narrative or thematic purpose, hovers through the film's *mise en scène*, as if seeking some way of producing meaning. Yet even as these shots are freed from the constraints of conventional, invisible style, they nonetheless fail to generate an alternative form of significance. In their very failure to do so, these passages of the film, so visually redolent of New Hollywood aesthetics, embody a kind of professional culture work that searches in vain for a context in which it might generate value without giving up its autonomy.

In this way, these tracking shots recall the first, which takes place during the film's opening credit sequence. That tracking shot, you will recall, surveys the Howards' various upper-middle-class commodities, but without any kind of consumerist pleasure. Boxed up and poorly lit, these objects are visually robbed of any value, and thus denied any power to motivate action, something confirmed by the random, unmotivated movement of the camera itself. The soundtrack to these images is the voice of a professional critic confidently proclaiming his ability both to discern and to generate cultural value through his autonomously determined labor. Even if we did not know Brooks's history with this critic, we might have guessed that he wants us to laugh at Reed's mistaken belief in his power and mastery. But by the time Brooks has shown us the spectacle of David and Linda scurrying back to their corporate employers to eat shit, we can see the pathos behind Reed's self-delusion as well. And in Brooks's own subtle visual gestures toward a professional labor that seeks the autonomy that Reed fantasizes he already enjoys, we can perhaps see a filmmaker responding to one of his critics to say, "*Hypocrite lecteur,—mon semblable,—mon frère.*"

NOTES

1. Albert Brooks, dir. *Lost in America*. 1985; Warner Bros. Pictures, Criterion Collection, 2017.
2. Albert Brooks, dir. *Real Life*. 1979; Paramount Pictures.
3. Brooks told the *Onion AV Club* in 2006: "[With] *Real Life*, I remember Rex Reed, who I don't even think knew who I was in *Real Life*, and of course hated it. It's one of the reviews that I will never forget as long as I live, because it was so insane. He said, 'Why would Paramount Pictures give *this man* the money to do such an important experiment?'" "Albert Brooks," interview by Scott Tobias, *Onion AV Club*, January 18, 2006. Available at <https://film.avclub.com/albert-brooks-1798208934> (last accessed January 7, 2021). Unfortunately, I have been unable to track down the review in question.
4. Barbara Ehrenreich and John Ehrenreich, "The Professional-Managerial Class," in *Between Capital and Labor*, ed. Pat Walker (Boston: South End Press, 1979).
5. For example, "[e]ven scientific management controls [which rigorously police workers' activities] met with initial resistance from many in the business community, who saw it as a potential threat to their own autonomy from outside surveillance. (Scientific management . . . was originally popularized as a tool for the public to use to judge the fairness of corporate prices)." Ehrenreich and Ehrenreich, "The Professional-Managerial Class," 23.
6. Erik Olin Wright, *Classes* (London: Verso, 1985). While the accounts of the professional-managerial class offered by the Ehrenreichs and Wright are in some tension with each other, my use of their work tends to focus on the significant overlap in their conceptualizations, rather than their points of disagreement. See Derek Nystrom, *Hard Hats, Rednecks, and Macho Men: Class in 1970s American Cinema* (New York: Oxford University Press, 2009), 9–12 for a fuller discussion of this issue.

7. Barbara Ehrenreich, *Fear of Falling: The Inner Life of the Middle Class* (New York: Pantheon, 1989), 48–56.
8. Daniel Bell, *The Cultural Contradictions of Capitalism* (New York: Basic Books, 1976), 71–2.
9. Jerry Adler et al., "The Year of the Yuppie." *Newsweek*, December 31, 1984, 18, 17.
10. Gene Siskel, "'Lost in America': Funny, Touching Snapshot of Real People," *Chicago Tribune*, March 15, 1985, F28A.
11. Linda-Marie Delloff, review of *Lost in America*, dir. Albert Brooks, *The Christian Century*, April 24 ,1985, 425–6.
12. This connection is attributed to columnist Bob Greene in Adler et al., "Year of the Yuppie," 14–16.
13. "Dohrn Again." *The New Republic*, October 14, 1985, 4, 41.
14. Adler et al., "Year of the Yuppie," 14.
15. "Arise, Ye Yuppies." *The New Republic*, July 9, 1984, 4, 41.
16. B. Ehrenreich, *Fear of Falling*, 70.
17. B. Ehrenreich, *Fear of Falling*, 72.
18. Tim O'Brien, "Spunky Punks: Trading Places in America," review of *Desperately Seeking Susan*, dir. Susan Siedelman, and *Lost in America*, directed by Albert Brooks, *Commonweal*, May 17, 1985, 304.
19. B. Ehrenreich, *Fear of Falling*, 57–96.
20. It is worth noting that the film shrewdly recognizes the significant freedom of professional employees from workplace surveillance in this scene: Linda tells David that "I can't quit now. . . . Even if I wanted to, my boss isn't here; there's no one I can quit to."
21. Mike Davis offers a fascinating analysis of how such seemingly non-political occurrences like real estate market inflation during the 1970s were actually part of what he calls an emerging logic of "overconsumptionism": "an increasingly political subsidization of a sub-bourgeois, *mass* layer of managers, professionals, new entrepreneurs and rentiers who . . . have been overwhelmingly successful in profiting from both inflation and expanded state expenditure" (emphasis in original). Mike Davis, *Prisoners of the American Dream: Politics and Economy in the History of the U.S. Working Class* (London: Verso, 1986), 211.
22. Tim Pulleine, review of *Lost in America*, dir. Albert Brooks, *Monthly Film Bulletin*, December 1985, 381.
23. John Simon, "'Near Misses,' review of *Lost in America*, dir. Albert Brooks, and *Camila*, dir. María Luisa Bemberg," *The National Review*, May 17, 1985, 48.
24. Scott Tobias, "*Lost in America*: The $100,000 Box," *The Criterion Collection*, July 25, 2017. Available at <https://www.criterion.com/current/posts/4760-lost-in-america-the-100-000-box> (last accessed January 7, 2021).
25. Ehrenreich and Ehrenreich, "The Professional-Managerial Class," 22.
26. Simon and Pauline Kael both refer to Sturges in their reviews of *Lost in America*, even as they note the ways in which the film is not entirely Sturges-ian. Austerlitz entitles his chapter on Brooks "The Return of Sully Sullivan," in reference to Sturges's 1941 film *Sullivan's Travels*. Pauline Kael, "Coddled," review of *Lost in America*, dir. Albert Brooks, and *The Breakfast Club*, dir. John Hughes, *New Yorker*, April 8, 1985, 120–5. Available at <https://www.newyorker.com/magazine/1985/04/08/coddled> (last accessed January 7, 2021); Saul Austerlitz, *Another Fine Mess: A History of American Film Comedy* (Chicago: Chicago Review Press, 2010).
27. Brooks himself told Janet Maslin that he was initially drawn to the idea of the film's ending, which is about "when people realize what a big mistake they've made and have to cut their losses," as opposed to that of a "standard Hollywood movie . . . [which] would have had these people trout fishing and building their own log cabin." Janet Maslin, "America Discovers Albert Brooks," *New York Times*, June 2, 1985, H20. Available at

<https://www.nytimes.com/1985/06/02/movies/america-discovers-albert-brooks.html> (last accessed January 7, 2021).
28. Dennis Hopper, dir. *Easy Rider*. 1969; Culver City, CA: Columbia Pictures, 2020. Blu-ray.
29. Richard Schickel, review of *Lost in America*, dir. Albert Brooks, *Time*, March 18, 1985, 84.
30. Gene Siskel, "Funny Albert Brooks is Serious About the State of Filmmaking." *Chicago Tribune*, March 3, 1985, L3.
31. David E. James, *Allegories of Cinema: American Film in the Sixties* (Princeton: Princeton University Press, 1989), 12–18.
32. Austerlitz, *Another Fine Mess*, 272.
33. *A Star Is Bought*, performed by Albert Brooks. Asylum Records, 1975; Wounded Bird Records, 2017. CD.
34. Siskel, "Funny," L3, L7, L3.
35. Siskel, "Funny," L7.
36. Siskel, "Funny," L3.
37. Gavin Smith, "All the Choices: Albert Brooks Interview," *Film Comment* 35, no. 4 (July/August 1999): 17. Available at < https://www.filmcomment.com/article/all-the-choices-albert-brooks-interview/> (last accessed January 7, 2021).
38. Smith, "All the Choices," 16.
39. David Bordwell, "Intensified Continuity: Visual Style in Contemporary American Film," *Film Quarterly* 55, no. 3 (Spring 2002): 20.
40. Bordwell, "Intensified Continuity," 20.

CHAPTER 8

Defending *Purgatorio*: Dante, Brooks, and Finding One's Celestial Place

Frank Percaccio

>*and I will sing of that second kingdom /
>in which the human spirit is made clean /
>and becomes worthy to ascend to Heaven.*
>   Canto I, lines 4–6, *Purgatorio*[1]

The opening shot sequence of writer-director Albert Brooks's *Defending Your Life*[2] encapsulates the film's contemporary values concerning material and capital gain over emotional and personal worth. Brooks's film intelligently subverts the norms and values of the conflicted yuppie narrative and its discontents; these films examine the lives of unhappy, successful people. This thematic tendency is traceable in multiple, interrelated American film narratives, such as the satirical-nightmarish violence of predatory capitalism in *American Psycho*[3] set in 1987, and in the amusing horror experienced by the non-titled gentry in *Pacific Heights*.[4] These films' focalizing perspectives alternate between the playfully absurd to the grimly distressful as they comment on the Reagan-Bush era of unabated commercial superficialities; in *Defending Your Life*, director Albert Brooks makes an endless supply of non-fattening omelettes heavenly—more than a refurbished home or embellished business card.

Defending Your Life opens at an office birthday party given in honor of Daniel Miller (Albert Brooks). While office birthday gatherings may be commonplace, they represent friendly and quasi-familial connections in the formal corporate environment that dominates the American landscape of the successful and the urbane.[5] Miller begins the story off-screen with a voice-over noting how he has been with his current employer for nearly ten years and how he regards his co-workers like a family. Miller closes the introduction with the awkwardly insightful comment, "Isn't that tragic?" His co-workers laugh, and Miller follows with an anecdote of a birthday phone call he had received from his mother that morning. Brooks's well-crafted comedic stylings expose how Miller's mother stung him by referencing his stagnant salary. Miller segues with a joke in a similar vein, in a discernibly caustic tone, how his ex-wife would similarly chide him, but she did not call him "honey." Essentially, before *Defending Your Life* begins its visual narrative, Brooks offers commentary on the commonly held notion of a successful corporate professional in the late 1980s. Albert Brooks points out, albeit with humor, that the relatively successful Daniel Miller lacks relationships of any true depth, or even close contact with another human being, evidenced when Miller tells a co-worker about spending his birthday alone, or rather, with his new car.

With the obvious trappings of yuppie success on display in *Defending Your Life*, such as Miller's new BMW convertible with its (then) state-of-the-art compact disc player, to sequences featuring conversations about competitive salary negotiations, with references to broken families and personal declines tied to professional humiliations included, *Defending Your Life*'s focus on Miller's ideas of success, measured by material gains, becomes fodder for what he will answer for after he passes from this world. Albert Brooks's characters engage and cohabitate in the afterlife's prime real estate location, Judgment City, and they are asked to reflect upon their lives to understand what they really should have learned while they were alive on Earth, like an allegorical space for the always desired second chance to be enacted.[6]

Several other films produced in this era focus upon existence beyond death from a variety of perspectives. Some film adaptations invoke familiar images of hellish torment at the hands of demons. *Hellraiser II* (1988),[7] for example, was not considered commercially or artistically successful, but it has become a cult favorite among horror film fans. Similarly, a film such as director Ridley Scott's *Legend*[8] concretely visualizes images of Satan and hell itself but was not critically well received.[9] *Hellraiser II* and *Legend* draw upon contemporary, unimaginative images of the afterlife and the supernatural as their narrative framework engages articulated, concrete binary visions of life beyond: Heaven or Hell on the big screen.

A number of mid-to-late 1980–90s studio releases correspondingly produced a post-mortem existence with a nod toward familiar graphics and experiences of (Hollywood) Heaven, or, if not, the film featured an idealized representation of the afterlife stemming from the Abrahamic tradition rather than an eternal, hellish dystopia. For example, Phil Robinson's *Field of Dreams*[10] posits the mixture of baseball and cornfields as redemptive agencies, and Jerry Zucker's *Ghost*[11] conflates personal loss, pounds of clay, and special demonic effects; both films were commercially successful as they contemporized the afterlife narrative and made their respective messaging accessible to the audience.

W. P. Kinsella's magic-realist novel, *Shoeless Joe*, served as the basis for director Phil Alden Robinson's film adaptation.[12] The book elevates baseball to an Elysian level, with a veritable who's who of baseball lore returning from the beyond to play as young men once again. The baseball diamond becomes a modern, American symbolic vision of the Elysian Fields, where the noblest (at least from Kinsella's perspective, those most favorable) players have an opportunity to return to take the field, akin to ancient warriors battling for honor rather than the faded glory they chased during their earthly lives. Robinson's film adaptation examines America's preoccupation with melodrama (it is a family in debt crisis), nostalgia (for lost family and times past), and in general, for the myths associated with baseball, America's pastime. There is a form of spiritual processing in which characters move from one plane of existence into another—the playing-corn field is the site of transference.

Ghost deploys elements appropriated from pre-Christianity's Orpheus myth, in which the artist departs from this world to save his beloved in the afterlife. The film focuses on Sam Wheat, a yuppie murdered by his business partner. After his death, Wheat, who has not passed on to a traditional, Christian-informed Heaven or Hell, instead engages with the living still on Earth and he works toward saving his wife from impending danger. The audience witnesses Sam Wheat in the prior form and appearance he had when he was alive. On the same ominous streets of New York City the psychotic but successful Patrick Bateman trolled for victims and witnessed these otherworldly exchanges.

The visually stylish and familiar setting in Brooks's *Defending Your Life* is unique: it does not conceptualize or focus on a wholly positive or negative image of the afterlife, as the film is set in a city (resembling Los Angeles) with hotels, cars, and endless supplies of tasty food. *Defending Your Life* and, as I am suggesting, Dante's epic early fourteenth-century poem, *Purgatorio*, may be recognized as situating this negotiable phase of the afterlife in a center position, between both poles of Heaven and Hell, in a transitive state, a state where human reflection, understanding, and personal growth are the measurable expressions of one's humanity, spiritual worthiness, and ultimate salvation: entry into Heaven. Although films recurrently deploy images of hell and heaven whose symbolic and dynamic roots trace back to the Middle Ages or the Renaissance,[13] Brooks's *Defending Your Life* invokes motifs more closely intertextually aligned with Dante's *Purgatorio*. Both narratives comment on the act of male self-awareness, spiritual processing, and panoptic surveillance.

Throughout *Defending Your Life*, one notes the actualization of Foucault's theories concerning surveillance, trial, and ultimately, judgment.[14] In Brooks's film, the building where the trial is being held is called Judgment Center. The exterior establishing shot places the building in the center of the frame and evokes elements of a modern panoptic site; the audience sees the building, which looks like any other ugly modern structure, and the building sees all. While Foucault's original theories were rooted in the technology and architecture of his era and his panoptic vision resembles a turn-of-the-century prison rather than an otherworldly gateway to a higher spiritual plane, the Judgment Center edifice in Albert Brooks's world is recognizable to his film audience in the similar manner in which Dante's medieval readers would have readily accepted the trials and perceived justice meted out in the different levels of Purgatory.

In *Defending Your Life*, Brooks renders the notion that the universe is watching all. Albert Brooks's court scenes in Judgment City are vivid contemporary representations of Foucault's Panopticon theories in practice. In *Discipline and Punish, the Birth of the Prison*, Foucault concludes that: "the Panopticon must not be understood as a dream building: it is the mechanism of power reduced to its ideal form . . . (it) must be represented as a pure architectural and optical system: it is in fact a figure of political technology."[5] In *Defending Your Life*, the courtroom, the building, the city itself, is neither dream-like nor desultory. Souls get processed.

In *Defending Your Life*, surveillance (and later judgment) reveals itself as part of everyday life and beyond; as Daniel Miller learns the real gravity and potential consequences of the constant surveillance he has been under his entire life, it all becomes belatedly more apparent to him once he arrives at the Judgment Center. A long, symmetrical exterior shot of the processing center appears before the shot cuts to Miller exiting a tram. There, he is greeted warmly by a lawyer, Bob Diamond (Rip Torn), Brooks's version of Dante's

Figure 8.1 Judgment City, soul processing center

supportive spirit, Virgil. In the following shot, Diamond tries to make small talk as the action moves indoors. The dolly-mounted camera stays just ahead of Miller and Diamond as they walk in a two-shot down the hallway. This could be any corridor in an office building in a modern city, but it is not.

Once inside the reviewing room, Miller and Diamond are greeted by the prosecuting, but not devilish, attorney, Lena Foster (Lee Grant). Diamond begins the sparring with his counterpart by stating, "I heard you lost last week!" An antagonized Foster returns with a hard stare, a pointed finger, and a clear "I'm going to get you, I promise." A rattled Daniel Miller refers to the feud between the attorneys and immediately requests a mistrial. He states, "There should be a mistrial here. This is a mistrial." Diamond replies, "This isn't a trial." Miller acknowledges that his fate is connected to the outcome of the events that are about to unfold and states, "It's a 'mis' whatever it is." This exchange, and the overall faux-friendly ambiance of the interior setting lend themselves to the notion that Miller is undoubtedly being tried, and that this event is primarily predicated on what was already seen, and soon-to-be judged: Foucault's theories of surveillance and punishment are put to comedic play in Brooks's narrative as a prominent intertextual resource.

Once the two judges walk in, Diamond directs Miller to sit in the chair in the center of the room, an intimidating and strategized positioning recalling Joan of Arc's physical placement on a stool in Dreyer's *The Passion of Joan of Arc*[16] during her trial segment. In *Defending Your Life*, the shot cuts to a wide shot of the reviewing room. The judges, male and female, are shot from behind, the backs of their heads visible as they sit high upon their benches. The two opposing attorneys sit in office chairs and at large, modern desks. Daniel Miller sits in the center of the room in a comfortable contemporary-looking living room lounge chair. Once everyone assembled in the room has cordially greeted each other with a round of routine "good mornings," one of the judges states, "I'm sure your defender has explained all the basics." The audience, and Miller, clearly understand that although Bob Diamond may attempt to reassure Miller that he isn't on trial, the audience knows Miller is being tried for every moment of his life, even though the judge further states, "Although this feels like a trial, it isn't. It's just a process that helps us decide."

This introductory session, like any trial proceeding, allows for Ms. Foster to begin presenting her case as to why Miller should return to Earth; in other words, he is *not* eligible to pass on to the next world. Therefore, Miller's likely return to earth is seen as a punitive decision, and he would be disallowed to advance into the more spiritual plane of potential existence, the afterlife. This pending judgment invokes Foucault's panopticon-punish theories: the individual was seen and will be rendered. When Ms. Foster begins presenting her case by saying, "Could we go to 11-4-19?" Miller appears perplexed. A judge explains, "By the way, Mr. Miller, this signifies you're 11 years, 4 months, and 19 days old." Foucault's real-world practices of surveillance and judgment demonstrably intersect with Dante's supernatural world of spiritual priorities. Throughout Dante's *Divine Comedy*, for which *Purgatorio* is the second volume, every character is inextricably tied to his or her actions on Earth, for they too have been judged by the similarly constant and ubiquitous surveillance of Dante's medieval omniscient God.

After the judge's explanation, in the next shot sequence, Miller sees the moment Ms. Foster called for in her opening statements. The viewing audience and the members of the courtroom see on a large screen the schoolyard scene from Daniel's boyhood, replete with audio and the ambient sound of playground swings and children playing. The camera cuts to a tight shot of Miller, whose only reaction is "Wow." Of course, he is astonished to realize that every moment of his life has been purposefully recorded and could be played back for all to witness. The schoolyard episode depicts a pre-teen Miller, suffering humiliation at the hands of a schoolyard bully, and once the action is complete, the courtroom viewing screen goes blank, Miller's seat swivels back to face the judges, and the lights come up in the room. Miller is then asked what he felt as he engaged his past. Miller responds that it was "strange to watch myself." His reaction shot reveals his embarrassment and anxiety, and the darkness in the background only serves to further highlight his bewilderment as he has had to re-live the juvenile mortification, finally realizing that every moment of his life is now fodder for scrutiny, and ultimately, judgment.

The true role of this judicial system's modern panoptic culture is "intended to correct, reclaim, 'cure.'"[17] In one illuminating montage sequence highlighting Daniel Miller's bad decisions, the audience, judges, and attorneys witness Miller at especially weak times of his life. Clips of skiing accidents and assorted commonplace mishaps provide comic relief for the audience, but it also serves as a reinforcement of Foucault's principles and the prosecutor's case. The pervasive Foucauldian surveillance system created by Brooks in *Defending Your Life* further implies timeless ubiquity with Dante's medieval schema and is complemented by the film's special effects sequence in the Past Lives Pavilion. The Pavilion's major draw involves the visual recycling of self-as-spectacle, so that those on trial may see, and actively retrieve, projected images of how they lived in their former lives since the audio and video invisibly informing our existence has always been in recording mode and has been forever. This replayed, constant surveillance compels Miller to relive those awkward moments that ultimately define human passage.

In Dante's *Purgatorio*, surveillance is advanced and controlled by the medieval Roman Catholic Church's doctrine. Dante's reliance on the Catholic tradition allows his readers to make personal adjustments to the concept and practices of continuous surveillance. Christian children are indoctrinated with the fear of an all-watching, all-knowing God who sits in judgment of a soul's actions. Dante's readers would very likely accept the standardized concept of church-government-godly surveillance that is reinforced by the creatures that inhabit the credible world of the *Divine Comedy*. Myriad demons, angels, and dead souls (historical beings) play administrative roles to assist in his ethereal panoptic landscape.

Brooks's modern audience would accept the parameters of Judgement City's imaginary-technological abilities to tap into anyone's past; the very purpose of Purgatory is arguably the soul's acceptance of its flaws, the desire to correct and to be reclaimed, and all with the understanding that these errant deeds have been accounted for since relentless surveillance has placed these souls in their current situation. Similarly, when Marc Cogan points out in *The Design in the Wax* that "souls of the sinful but redeemed must be made healthy, they must be released from sin not by pardon, but by therapy,"[18] he reinforces a corollary, interpretive reading of Foucault.

Whether set in medieval Italy or postmodern Los Angeles, Dante and Brooks similarly illustrate the concept that a soul experiences an evolutionary process of transmigration and as a result, both narratives illustrate elements of hylomorphism. In Thomas M. Ward's "Transhumanization, Personal Identity, and the Afterlife: Thomistic Reflections on a Dantean Theme," he takes "inspiration from Dante's concept of transhumanization," and argues "that the metaphysics of the afterlife according to which a human person in the interim phase between death and resurrection is not a mere disembodied soul."[19] Ward goes on to state, "Hylomorphism, by contrast, promises an account of human nature that makes our flesh and blood animality part of what we really are, part of our essence, while still offering resources for a philosophically satisfying account of immortality."[20] With this in mind, Dante and Brooks's interpretive reading of the afterlife in their respective narratives vividly provide a hylomorphic conceptual "take" of the next stage of existence, the liminal stage. With regard to Dante, the poet and his characters behave how people would behave during their era, and he encounters many types such as politicians, poets, figures from antiquity; they are characters that Dante's readers would recognize. Brooks creates a similar theoretical construct in his screenplay when he envisions the sights and sounds of Judgment City. Here, too, easily identifiable characters inhabit the otherworldly landscape. These figures include hotel workers, cheery waiters and waitresses, banal office workers, and dreadful stand-up comedians. These static inhabitants of Judgment City provide further insight into the temporary pilgrims who are there only for their trial.

The liminal stage of existence is essentially the middle phase of existence, the "act two," the fulcrum in the middle of the story whereby an individual is no longer uninitiated; the journey has begun, but the individual has not yet reached the desired destination. Pilgrims on the journey know the immediate details they are traversing and the steps necessary to reach their goal, but they have not yet surmounted all of the obstacles, both within and without themselves, to truly achieve the transfigured state they will attain upon the completion of their tasks, in whatever form they may take. It is here, in the liminal state, where Dante and Brooks thematically intersect.

Dante's *Divine Comedy* clearly enunciates the concept of the liminal state of existence. *Purgatorio* is the second text codifying three phases. Dante's pilgrim begins his journey in what most would consider the most miserable place in the medieval universe, the Inferno. Pain and punishment abound in each level of hell, and as Dante moves through each level, he learns more about the afterlife and its rules. It is not long before Dante understands the system's construction and what he must do to achieve happiness. In this specifically Roman Catholic example, Dante learns that the key to happiness is to become closer to God and his love and that each sin turns a soul further away from God and, ultimately, his love.

However, it is not until Dante exits from the Inferno's trappings that he begins to realize that he is in control of his destiny. The concept of Purgatory was a later—and now, abandoned—addition to Christian thought. In *The Medieval Imagination*, Jacques Le Goff fixes the inception of the liminal spiritual state the Roman Catholics called Purgatory to a specific period. Le Goff concludes: "Purgatory as a spatial and temporary entity was formed between the third and the thirteenth century. It was an elaboration of the Christian belief that certain sins could under conditions be redeemed after death."[21] When Dante, the literary character, enters Purgatory, he describes what he sees in his immediate environment, while Dante, the writer, adds his perspective for us to analyze as a kind of ongoing metacommentary. In a similar manner Albert Brooks, the actor, reacts to the imaginary spectacles in the environment that Albert Brooks, the filmmaker, creates in order to reveal the comical-dramatic of one's life as potential agencies of self-reformation. Both characters soon learn that they are in the middle of their journey and share the desire to complete the trials set before them and to move on to a higher spiritual plane.

The liminal state of being centers on engaging in a transformative stage in order to pass onto the final stage of the character's rite of passage. In *The Divine Comedy*, Dante, the pilgrim-character, desires to move beyond the liminal stage of Purgatory and then on to Paradise, while in *Defending Your Life*, Brooks's Daniel Miller, the neo-pilgrim-character, seeks to move on to a higher state of being as well, but one in which spiritual salvation (as promulgated via Roman Catholic doctrine) has been replaced by a humanist, temporal wisdom, an enlightened understanding of the universe, which is readily quantified by commodified brain usage. In Dante's medieval world, the currency of the earthly and spiritual realm is boundless love. Sin turns us away from God's love, and purging the sins while in Purgatory[22] would lead Dante's readers to the awareness of spiritual elevation they so desire. Brooks's message is consistent with Dante's in *Defending Your Life*; however, Brooks's world is no longer a medieval tapestry of competing religious and humanist narratives. In Brooks's film, Miller's single greatest fault is a kind of spiritual cowardice—fear—and its various manifestations, such as fear to commit to people and to self, to fail others and self, and generally, to be a man capable of serious introspection in which he generates feelings other than self-loathing. Miller must evolve and learn that he cannot hide, since everything is witnessed, and not to hate himself, since God loves him.

The shot sequence immediately following Daniel Miller's accidental death from a head-on collision with a bus while he is driving distractedly in Los Angeles, signals a shift in narrative space and time to Judgment City. New, dead arrivals are seated in wheelchairs, taken in energy-efficient trams, and eventually, many arrive at the Continental Hotel. Once in the lobby, the groggy newcomers are directed to go to their rooms, enjoy a restful night's sleep, and informed that fuller explanations will be provided in the morning. While symbolic and literal comparisons may be drawn between *Purgatorio* and *Defending Your Life*, both texts exhibit structural similarities at the beginning of our protagonists' respective journeys towards self-actualization and, ultimately, redemption.

Just as Daniel Miller is instructed that the evenings are for rest and reflection, when Dante arrives at the gates of Purgatory, he too will be instructed that he must wait until morning before proceeding. Dante and Virgil spend a restful night before they begin to comprehend what lies ahead of them. Dante, the writer, has afforded his protagonist the luxury of a guide in the form of Virgil for two-thirds of his epic *Divine Comedy*, for Virgil cannot enter Paradise, the final spiritual space. Brooks's initial shot sequences in Judgment City weave comedy, both visually and in spoken dialogue, into this expository portion of the film, and Brooks provides his own Virgilian guide, Bob Diamond, who encourages Daniel to engage in all the city has to offer. Hell has its own punishments, mostly ironic; Brooks's city-space has comedy clubs, hotels, and fine restaurants in Judgment City, but along with the comedic points, *Defending Your Life* features noteworthy character development and performances in its exposition. There is one, "free" night when Miller and his attractive, compassionate, and yet somewhat troubled Julia (Meryl Streep) visit the aforementioned Past Lives Pavilion: a technological condensation of useful or useless moments, but they are also expressive moments which define our inner beings via symbolic inference. This attraction to see and experience one's former selves fuses technology with Eastern philosophy and religion. Those staying in Judgment City can step before a screen in a private booth and see who they were in past lives. With a nod toward the modern, participants are reminded that a time limit must be adhered to if other souls are waiting to use the machine.

By combining media projection technology readily available at the time of the film's creation with the concept of reviewing our past lives as a principled spectacle, Brooks creates something comedic and informative for the audience. Dante's pilgrims spend the reflective night outdoors, apropos to the era, whereas Brooks's Daniel and Julia spend a night on the town, overeating food associated with guilty pleasures. The night-time becomes a period for reflection and an attempt for the respective protagonists to try and make sense of their new, semi-celestial landscape. Both Miller and the pilgrim Dante are not quite sure of the afterlife game's rules, and with each evening's pause there is a potential to revisit the day's events and to contemplate what the new day will bring.

Structurally, Dante and Brooks use the evenings for expositional purposes that signal the space and time of reflection, desire, and the effects of their immersive visual experience. In Canto VII, Dante uses the evening setting to suggest similar spiritual moments and insights for the reader: "But see, already the day is going down/ and no one can go up at all at night./ We should be thinking of a good place to rest in."[23] Dante, the pilgrim, is instructed that there is no possible means of going forward in the evening and his guide suggests he speak with some of his fellow travelers, "there are souls off on the right, over here./ If you allow, I will lead you to them/ and they will be known to you, not without great pleasure."[24] *Defending Your Life*'s Past Lives Pavilion employs comedic cause and effect "replays" of past Miller escapades that led to his usual failure-to-act routine. Brooks's character development is reinforced in these shot sequences to illustrate the main flaw in Daniel's character: fear. Miller is depicted as tribesman in one former life. His race is different, the era is different, but the inherent Daniel Miller trait persists: cowardice. Conversely, Julia is thrilled to see her former lives. She sees how she lived in various noble past lives that exhibit her fearlessness across her lifetimes.

Purgatorio and *Defending Your Life* inhabit a shared space regarding how we should lead our lives. Beatrice says of Dante, "such, potentially, was this man . . . but the more vigor there is in the ground,/ the more rank and tangled grows the land/ if the seed and tilling left undone."[25] Just as Beatrice implies that wasted talent and potential goes counter to the true purpose of our lives, attorney Bob Diamond chides Daniel Miller for reliving and expressing his fear-based indulgent anxieties. Bob Diamond says Daniel is "cheap with himself," suggesting that whatever Miller really needed when he was alive, he denied himself. Throughout *Defending Your Life*, Brooks illustrates how the most important thing not to do while alive is to live a life fraught with fear but rather to live life with passion, whether successful or failed (ironically, as did Dante's restrained passion for Beatrice in their personal histories).

In the reviewing room, when Miller is forced to witness the replay of morally instructional, significant scenes in this past life, prosecuting attorney Foster cleverly chooses moments—director Brooks's comedic shot sequences—to exhibit Miller's cowardice. Specifically, the first episode from Daniel Miller's series of replayed failures focuses on his fear of investing in a new start-up company, Casio. At the outset of this shot sequence, Lena Foster refers to this moment in Miller's life when he received "information which comes along once every five, six lifetimes." Miller saved some money that he planned on investing. Unsure of which direction to go, Miller listened to a strong pitch from "a good friend from school who was the son of an executive of the Casio Corporation." In this flashback sequence, Daniel Miller attempts to mask his fear with comedy, mocking the very concept of a Japanese company being able to produce a quality timepiece. Daniel Miller passed on this opportunity and instead chose to invest in cattle whose "teeth fell out." Fear held Miller back. Fear was his undoing in this case, but of course, the joke is on Miller when the judge presiding over his case rolls up his sleeve to show his Casio watch, and then again when Foster points out that Miller's original investment of $10,000 would now be worth $37.2 million.

To further add to Miller's humiliation, his substitute defender for the day, Dick Stanley (Buck Henry), cannot help but exclaim, "Wow!" The immediate cut to Miller's stunned reaction shot and Stanley's refusal to rebut the information, followed by yet another cutaway shot of a dumbfounded Miller and a sarcastic reply of, "Boy, you are good," begins to get Miller anxious, riled up, and presumably past his fears. Perhaps Stanley and Diamond, serving as Miller's mentors, elicited the very response they hoped for from Miller via this spectacle of a past humiliation. Brooks's camera remains on Miller as he takes the initial steps toward getting over his fears when he speaks up for himself and states: "Does this make me defective because I didn't make money on this? I can't believe the whole point of the universe is to make money." Lena Foster responds that the purpose is to evaluate Miller's judgment and his motivations regarding his choices. The struggle is not over capital but over a form of self-actualization, with a trial pressing forward.

In another revealing instance of his fear to act, Miller immediately folds during a salary negation. Prior to Miller's interview with his new potential firm, he speaks with his wife about how he will negotiate his salary. The action cuts from the afterlife reviewing room to the living couple dining in their kitchen. Daniel insists that his wife play the role of his boss at the bargaining table. The husband and wife go verbally back and forth, and with each demand from his wife, Miller holds firm that he will not take the position for any offer less than $65,000. The image of Miller confident and reserved after his rehearsal with his wife contrasts with the later frozen face of a frightened yuppie who grabs the first offer his prospective boss makes. Brooks's wide shot zooms in on the bargaining action. As the two men are seated and the action is framed in two-shot, Miller is offered a paltry $48,000. Before the two men settle into their seats, Miller immediately blurts out, "I'll take it!" The camera cuts to a tight reaction shot of the new employer who appears surprised how easily Miller had taken the first offer. When asked in the courtroom why he had given in so quickly, Miller impotently returns to the issue of money and values.

Defending Your Life's thematic preoccupations involve how humans experience and learn to cope with fear, happiness, and how to overcome adversity, to achieve a form of spiritual worth: the space and time beyond purgatory, which is the site of Miller's preparatory cleansing. In this film text, Brooks's philosophical overview is to exhibit readiness for the next plane of spiritual existence, one must learn to confront and even overcome one's sense of (real or unreal) fear, and instead move toward a life of personal and spiritual fulfillment.[26] *The Divine Comedy* adheres to medieval Roman Catholic dogma as Dante informs sinners in *Purgatorio* that they are expected to continue their spiritual development beyond their current stunted state in order to achieve Paradiso. When Bob Diamond states how much of his brain he uses to note that he is still a work in progress, he does so in order to explain to Miller that, although a successful afterlife lawyer, Diamond too has not yet "arrived" and is still evolving.[27] Diamond also makes comparisons to relative brain size among his contemporaries in Judgment City to make a point to Miller. Likewise, in the *Divine Comedy*, Dante learns from Virgil that he too is not yet able to pass on to the highest level. Upon reaching the entry into Purgatory, Cato of Utica greets Virgil and Dante and explains how systems function in this incorporeal realm; in *Defending Your Life*, spirit-guides come in many forms and serve to express different instructional designs. In 1990, director Adrian Lyne's film *Jacob's Ladder*[28] also centered on the spiritual passage from life-to-death and beyond in the case of a haunted Vietnam war veteran, Jacob Singer. Louis, the masseuse, facilitates a special effects journey that goes beyond the earthly sphere, and Singer's guide-angel's strong hands heal yet another lost male.[29]

Throughout Dante's trip through *Purgatorio*, poets, philosophers, and sinners alike assist Virgil in Dante's tutelage. Brooks's guides are stand-up purveyors of comedic routines. In *The Divine Comedy*, Dante reflects the late-medieval, relatively proscriptive moral and spiritual views held by the Roman Catholic Church. Brooks conveys his perspective on a soul's level in an intellectual, humorous, and measured narrative that could be readily accepted by a data-driven Western audience that more readily identifies with, and is likely to accept, the visual-as-real rather than the ethereal-as-plausibly real.

It is nearly impossible to consider any aspect of *The Divine Comedy* without considerable attention granted to Dante's vision of spiritual musing and personal longing: Beatrice. Beatrice's death is the source of Dante's initial suffering, and this death occurs before his journey into Purgatory. It is Beatrice, and his love for her, that serves as a beacon for Dante as he travels through hell with Virgil. Moreover, Beatrice provides a key compositional strategy in Dante's *Purgatorio* as she represents the feminine, the virtuous, the redeemed, and in many ways, the poet's conception of idealized love. She makes the journey complete. Albert Brooks offers his viewers a contemporary reading of Dante's Beatrice in the lovely, laughing, yet imperfect Julia (Meryl Streep). Julia is smart, independent, honest, and, most importantly, as humorous as she is fearless. Julia and Daniel connect one evening in Judgment City's comedy club. Initially, the scene focuses on a banal, stereotypically unfunny comedian performing his act. The performer offers his audience B-grade comedic material. Daniel Miller heckles the comic. The comedian and Miller exchange a few barbs, Julia laughs, and she and Miller leave the club to find another source of asexual entertainment.

Julia and Miller's attraction begins to develop soon after their first interaction, and it is clear to the characters and the audience that they are drawn to one another. They share laughs, discuss their lives, and compare notes on their trials. Brooks provides his viewers with some critical details about Julia during the first conversation she has with Miller after they leave the club. The audience learns that Julia was a mother and had even adopted a child. However, beyond the sharp quips and the budding relationship, the audience discovers that Julia has to be in Judgment City for four days, compared to Daniel's nine days of trial. Julia also reveals that Sam, her lawyer, thinks that she will move on and not have to return to Earth. Conversely, Daniel's body language indicates that Bob Diamond has not offered any real encouragement to him other than to visit local restaurants and recreational facilities.

It becomes clear to Brooks's audience that living a life without regard to false fears and moral cowardice is the intended purpose of existence on Earth. Dante and Brooks both reinforce this message throughout their respective narratives. For Brooks, in one shot sequence, the audience and Miller learn about the formerly living Julia, and why her lawyer, Sam, believes she will move on to the next level during an episode at her trial. The audience watches Miller when he goes to Julia's trial. He slips into the reviewing room, where he finds Julia sitting comfortably curled up in her chair as the judges, Sam, and the prosecuting attorney watch a video replay of her life. A burning house fills the screen; the gravity of the situation is immediately apparent. Julia heroically emerges from the flames with a kitten in her hands, into the welcoming arms of her loved ones. The lights come up in the courtroom, and everyone in the room fights back cliché tears.

Julia's courtroom experience sharply contrasts with Miller's because she is the enlightened one of the two formerly living beings now on trial. Julia, although not living a perfect, sin-free life, is the one who lives without irrational fear and, instead, fills her time with an engaging, expressive *agape*, whereas Daniel has no such presence. Similarly, when Dante meets Beatrice in *Purgatorio* in Canto XXXIII, it is she who is enlightened, free from fear, and the one who urges Dante on when she says, "disengage yourself from fear and shame."[30] The prominent, strong feminine forces in both texts offer (then) contemporary perspectives on self and moral-spiritual advancement.

Near the end of their respective journeys in purgatory, Dante and Miller begin to comprehend the space and time they are experiencing from both philosophical and personal perspectives. At this late point in the narratives, the redeemed characters of Julia and Beatrice have moved beyond the realm of their male counterparts and encourage these two men to overcome their final, self-imposed hurdles. In Dante's case, he must move through the curtain of fire in Canto XXVII and in effect be reborn through the fire. Dante exhibits fear and reluctance, and Virgil must tell him, "now look my son,/ this wall is between you and Beatrice"[31] and again later in Canto XXX, in a moment of fear, Dante "turned to the left with the confidence that/ a little child shows, running to its mother/ when something has frightened it or troubled it."[32] Like Miller, Dante's fear is acknowledged by those closest to him. Beatrice herself petitions Dante with: "do/ not weep yet, do not weep even yet."[33] Dante, the soul-presence on its journey toward Roman Catholic redemption, must conquer its complex former fears and pass through the flames to be able to spiritually "advance." In *The Divine Comedy*, it is love, in its myriad human and spiritual forms, that empowers Dante to summon the fortitude to brave the scorching heat. Once he passes through, he can pass on enlightened.

In Brooks's exceptional reworking of Dante's scenario, Miller too must travel a similar path. Miller's epiphany occurs in the lobby of Julia's hotel after the two have had a wonderful evening together in Judgment City. As Julia and Daniel's evening begins to draw to a close, the dramatic focus shifts from the comedic when Julia asks Daniel to come up to her room to spend the night. In a series of reverse close-up shots that focus on the speakers, Daniel first states: "I'm afr–. I'm tired of being judged." The camera cuts to the rejected yet smiling Julia who states, "It's OK." The camera cuts back to Miller, who provides a rational, albeit weak and fear-driven explanation for turning her down. Once again, Daniel Miller denies himself a meaningful and perhaps life-changing experience due to fear. Julia's calm reaction to Daniel's rejection, particularly after she had professed her love for him moments earlier, is a tribute to her understanding of her place in the universe and what is asked of her: courage to face life and failure. All at once Julia exhibits her unfolding bravery by stating strong feelings to Daniel, her maturity in accepting his rejection, and mostly, her wisdom in the comprehension of Daniel's fear. Like Beatrice intuits Dante's failings, Julia also serves as a teacher to Daniel. It will be the discovery of unabated love, their love for one another that serves as the stimulus for Daniel's climactic action and salvation.

Daniel later does muster a semblance of courage when he arrives at his hotel room. He rings the Majestic Hotel where Julia is staying and asks for her. The person on the other end of the phone informs Miller that two Julias are residing in the hotel and that both have left instructions not to be disturbed. Brooks uses this bureaucratic obstacle for comedic set-up purposes, and Daniel leaves an impassioned romantic note for both Julias. As he hangs up the phone, Daniel is shot in side-angle profile. Bob Diamond is heard in off-screen voice-over, "Has Mr. Miller overcome his fears, your honors?" Then, the shot cuts to the courtroom, and Diamond continues in his voice-over segue as the audience sees the judges seated on their bench: "I believe that my final summation scene will prove to you that he has." Diamond's final words do not move the judges to react favorably; their expressive facial contortions and body language suggest skepticism.

Bob Diamond then offers a compelling scenario from Daniel's life that Diamond believes shows Miller's freedom from fear. Daniel's marriage had recently failed, and he was at a low point in his life. Checking in at the airport for a flight to Asia, Daniel uses a third of his money after his divorce to upgrade to a first-class seat. Diamond goes on to point out how Daniel has learned much and is ready to move on to something spiritually advanced. The prosecutor, Ms. Foster, is given an opportunity to present a closing argument. In her closing statement, she replayed the Majestic Hotel lobby scene and paid particular attention to Daniel's struggle to utter the word "afraid." In this scene, unlike the first time the audience witnesses the near-lovers moments in the hotel lobby, Brooks cuts to Miller's affective reaction shot close-up to reveal to the audience how Miller has behaved: discouraged, defeated, and fearful. When Miller's chair swivels around, and the lights come up in the reviewing room, he realizes that fear holds him back from advancing and experiencing love for others, including himself, and that the judges will not allow him to advance. The damning point is confirmed when Ms. Foster forces Daniel to confess, "I was afraid!" in open court.

Immediately after learning that he is to be sent back to Earth, Miller and Diamond are outside, in a tram station where souls depart for different destinations. With an ongoing series of monotonous, ignored announcements and people milling about queuing for transportation, the environment is all too familiar to the modern traveler. Dynamic intertextualities may be made with Dante's *Purgatorio* and its form of spiritual transportation (an exit strategy) as the souls depart into another realm. Artists have interpreted Dante's passing into a spiritual elsewhere as an extended, elaborately decorated medieval conception of a supernatural tram; similarly, in *Defending Your Life*, the contemporary representation of the bus serves as the means of transport beyond.

As Diamond and Miller make their way to Daniel's tram, Bob offers some final words of legal advice as he hands over the documents Miller will need to make his way back to Earth to live again and later spiritually ascend if possible. Diamond, similar in his knowledge as Virgil as it concerns his limitations regarding travel and degrees of spiritual cleansing, leaves Daniel with some last words and a knowing glance, "Good luck kid. I got a lot of faith in you." Daniel initially goes along with his undesired, seemingly inescapable fate and follows those instructions. Miller allows himself to be buckled in for his tram ride back toward Earth. As soon as the doors close, Julia calls out, off-screen, "Daniel! Daniel!" With the camera still fixed on Miller, he turns to follow the voice. Miller sees Julia and calls her name out to her. As the trams pull out from their parking spaces, the music begins to swell, and the shot sequence may be viewed as emblematic of film's traditional race-to-the-finish-line scene.

Knowing it is his last chance for love and happiness with Julia, Daniel exhibits true courage by breaking out of his seatbelt, forcing open the tram doors, and jumping out onto the pavement. This specific moment is Daniel Miller's wall of fire. He is moving toward his love, facing his fear, and in dodging the other running trams, Miller is besting his demise on Earth. If a car accident lead to his death, a fast exit from a running bus can save him. When Miller painfully reaches Julia's tram, he endures electric shocks and tries to pry open the doors so he can join Julia. In Brooks's compelling romantic closure sequence, a revealing panoptic surveillance, signalling the completion of the liminal state, suggests the intertextual reading of both the literary and film texts. Director Brooks cuts back to the reviewing room, where the audience sees lawyers Diamond and Foster in silhouette. Daniel and Julia's romance now exists, and is visible in real time. Diamond tellingly comments on Miller's bravery, while Foster smiles approvingly, and the judges allow him to pass. Dante, the medieval pilgrim in the world beyond space and time, and Brooks's Daniel Miller, the sad figure from the West Coast, learn from their experiences and ultimately transcend their anxieties and offer their respective audiences points to reflect upon as we hasten along on our pilgrimage, bravely or not.

NOTES

1. Dante, *Purgatorio*, trans. William S. Merwin (New York: Knopf, 2000), 3. Canto I lines 4–6.
2. Albert Brooks, dir. *Defending Your Life*; perf. Albert Brooks, Meryl Streep; US: Geffen Pictures, 1991, film.
3. Mary Harron, dir. *American Psycho*; perf. Christian Bale; US: Lions Gate, 2000, film.
4. John Schlesinger, dir. *Pacific Heights*; perf. Melanie Griffith, Matthew Modine; US: Morgan Creek, 1990, film.
5. Rachel Owen, "The Image of Dante," *Dante on View: The Reception of Dante in the Visual and Performing Arts*, ed. Antonella Braida and Luisa Cale (Aldershot: Ashgate, 2007), 86. Owen notes how artists often portrayed Dante as an Everyman, "showing his allegorical role, his role representing mankind itself." Brooks's Miller is similarly depicted as a successful Everyman, consistent with the accepted contemporary norms and concerns.
6. R. K. Fenn, *The Persistence of Purgatory* (Cambridge: Cambridge University Press, 1996), 130. Fenn analyzes the concept of Purgatory from a number of American perspectives.

When discussing the Unitarian, William E. Channing, Fenn offers: "At the very least, life after death takes on the aspect of a continual self-improvement, with or without the agonies of self-accusation that he envisages for those whose penitence arrives too late in this life to forestall purgatorial torments in the next."

7. Tony Randel, dir. *Hellraiser II*; perf. Doug Bradley; US: New World Pictures, 1988, film.
8. Ridley Scott, dir. *Legend*; perf. Tom Cruise, Mia Sara; US: Embassy International Pictures, 1985, film.
9. Eileen Gardiner, *Visions of Heaven and Hell before Dante* (New York: Italica Press, 2000). Gardiner's text explores influential visions of Heaven and Hell created before Dante's *Divine Comedy*. Gardiner points out that many of the visions of those souls barred from Heaven suffered from fire, cold, sharp objects, and were subjected to eternal torture and suffering.
10. Phil Alden Robinson, dir. *Field of Dreams*; perf. Kevin Costner, James Earl Jones; US: Gordon Co., 1989, film.
11. Jerry Zucker, dir. *Ghost*; perf. Patrick Swayze, Demi Moore; US: Paramount, 1990, film.
12. W. P. Kinsella, *Shoeless Joe Jackson: A Novel* (Boston: Mariner Books, 1999).
13. Amilcare A. Iannucci, *Dante, Cinema, and Television* (Toronto: University of Toronto Press, 2004), 18. Iannucci's book is a collection of essays that examine the myriad ways Dante has been appropriated in film. He concludes his essay with "Throughout the history of Hollywood, therefore, Dante has been a sustained and continued influence. He has contributed to filmic vehicles of every sort and has fed the imagination of countless directors who, once they enter Dante's world to retrieve a single detail, scene, or idea, often become ensnared in the web of interrelated references that his rich and varied parallel poetic universe provides."
14. Michel Foucault, *Discipline and Punish: The Birth of the Prison* (New York: Vintage Books, 1995). Foucault's text is composed of four parts: Torture, Punishment, Discipline, and Prison.
15. Foucault, *Discipline and Punish*, 205.
16. Carl Theodor Dreyer, dir. *The Passion of Joan of Arc*; perf. Maria Falconetti; France: Gaumont, 1928, film.
17. Foucault, *Discipline and Punish*, 9.
18. Marc Cogan, *The Design in the Wax: The Structure of the Divine Comedy and Its Meaning* (Notre Dame, IN: University of Notre Dame Press, 2007), 77.
19. Thomas M. Ward, "Transhumanization, Personal Identity, and the Afterlife: Thomistic Reflections on a Dantean Theme." *New Blackfriars* 96, no. 1065 (September 2015): 564–75.
20. Ward, "Transhumanization."
21. Jacques Le Goff, *The Medieval Imagination* (Chicago: University of Chicago Press, 2001), 67.
22. Jacques Le Goff, *The Birth of Purgatory* (Chicago: University of Chicago Press, 1991), 2–3. Le Goff's text traces the concept of Purgatory, and when looking at the historical precedents notes how it became a spiritual place where "certain sinners might be saved, most probably by being subjected to a trial of some sort, a new belief was born, a belief that gradually matured until in the twelfth century it became the belief in Purgatory."
23. Dante, *Purgatorio*, 65. Canto VII lines 43–5.
24. Dante, *Purgatorio*, 65. Canto VII lines 46–8.
25. Dante, *Purgatorio*, 295. Canto XXX lines 115–20.
26. Carol Zaleski, *Otherworld Journeys: Accounts of Near-death Experience in Medieval and Modern Times* (New York: Oxford University Press, 1988), 45. Zaleski points out a familiar element in stories about the afterlife: "The otherworld journey narrative usually begins

by describing how the soul is severed from the body before departing for the next world. Through illness or injury, ecstasy or dreaming, the tie to the body is loosened."
27. Lloyd Howard, *Virgil the Blind Guide: Marking the Way through the Divine Comedy* (Montreal: McGill-Queens University Press, 2010). Howard's text closely examines Virgil from multiple perspectives, at times noting Virgil's power and competence, and conversely his shortcomings and impotencies.
28. Adrian Lyne, dir. *Jacobs Ladder*; perf. Tim Robbins, Elizabeth Pena; US: Carolco, 1990, film.
29. Iannucci, *Dante, Cinema, and Television*, 11. Iannucci states: "Adrian Lyne has used Dantean material to shape his cinematic vision of Hell of a disordered mind in *Jacob's Ladder* (1990)."
30. Dante, *Purgatorio*, 295. Canto XXXIII line 32.
31. Dante, *Purgatorio*, 265. Canto XXVII lines 35–6.
32. Dante, *Purgatorio*, 295. Canto XXX lines 43–5.
33. Dante, *Purgatorio*, 295. Canto XXX lines 55–6.

CHAPTER 9

Albert Brooks Channeling the Feminine

Rebecca Bell-Metereau

The charm of Albert Brooks as an actor defies easy categories. With a face a bit too bemused and bland to be called classically handsome, hair a tad too frizzy and voice a mite too modulated for the standard masculine hero, Brooks is nevertheless far too normal to be deemed a misfit. He occupies liminal territory in his physical and comedic type, and the characters he creates as a screenwriter and director often occupy a gender no man's land as well. Indeed, an essential element of Brooks's comedy is his ability to channel the feminine, regardless of which film genre he chooses or whether he is director, star, bit player, writer, or disembodied voice. In *Real Life* (1979), the early groundbreaking mockumentary he co-authored with Monica Johnson, Brooks plays an exaggerated version of himself as a documentarian attempting to capture the domestic life of a fictional family.[1] In the screenwriting duo's more conventional fictional work, *Modern Romance* (1981), Brooks plays Robert, a neurotically agonizing suitor who is torn between desire and jealousy, commitment and hesitation, establishing a blueprint for the indecisive and often annoying aspects of the characters he creates and plays, caught between the opposing responses of stereotypical gender roles.[2] *Defending Your Life* (1991), written and directed by Brooks, features a protagonist who suffers in his postmortem afterlife from terminal indecision and quakes with fear opposite the foil of Meryl Streep's effortlessly brave and seemingly flawless character.[3]

As director, lead, and co-screenwriter with Johnson again, Brooks created his most financially successful film, *Mother* (1996), as well as his second-worst box office movie, *The Muse*, but in both, he brought powerful women into his productions.[4] In *Mother*, Brooks managed a comeback opportunity for both Debbie Reynolds and himself. This tale of John Henderson (Brooks), a successful writer who moves in with his mother Beatrice (Reynolds) after his second divorce, lays bare the competition in their relationship and inserts a feminist message, revealing that Beatrice has not simply been a mother, but has also secretly been an aspiring writer for years. In *The Muse* (1999), another Brooks and Johnson screenplay, a similar reversal occurs when Sarah (Sharon Stone)—the eponymous muse—becomes Steven Phillips's (Brooks) boss by winning the final contract to direct an ill-fated screenplay that was originally Steven's creation.

All of these films contain several common denominators, including powerful women, but critics are perennially puzzled by Brooks as they seek patterns in his work. Gavin Smith's interview describes Brooks as a "Me Generation Everyman":

> Whether it be the smug, callow filmmaker's perfect experiment in documentary in *Real Life* (79), the impossible fantasy of "true love" in *Modern Romance* (81), the way a life of complacent materialism is exchanged for an equally deluded freedom of the road in the anti-Reagan-zeitgeist *Lost in America* (85), or ended altogether by the ultimate bummer of sudden death at the start of *Defending Your Life* (91), the Brooks protagonist is oblivious until too late. In *The Muse*, as in *Mother* (96) and *Lost in America*, the great central comic conceit is his adoption of an improbable radical solution: When your marriage fails, move back in with your mother to figure out why your relationships with women don't work; when you don't get the promotion you feel you deserve, quit, drop out of society, and go on the road to find yourself; if your writing career goes south, hire a muse and do whatever she instructs, even if you can't shake the feeling you're being shortchanged.[5]

Smith's Every*man* configuration misses slightly in its gendered terminology, for Brooks defies masculine stereotypes by working with women like co-screenwriter Monica Johnson to problematize gender. Male protagonists in their co-authored films often carry burdens traditionally assigned to female characters: indecision, resentment, hesitation, feelings of inadequacy, and a simultaneous and contradictory desire for both affiliation and liberation. Meanwhile, the female characters are often more bossy, edgy, or unconventional than one usually encounters in American comedies. For example, when the wife in *Lost in America* goes off the rails by gambling away their entire life savings, she violates a female stereotype and a statistical probability. Meanwhile, her husband forgives her, stays by her side, and avoids the standard macho response of simply abandoning a disappointing wife and leaving her stranded.

Nowhere is this pattern of Brooks's feminized male protagonist more clearly demonstrated than in the work in which he disappears visually, leaving only the shadows of his gentle physical gestures (as captured by animators) and the plaintive and modulated tones of his multifaceted voice. If Albert Brooks is the unappreciated genius in his numerous roles as the lucky failure, he is the Albert Einstein (his actual original name) of voice work in his performance in *Finding Nemo*, as the unsung heroic parent in the seventh highest-grossing animated film worldwide.[6] Through the spoken words of Nemo's father, Marlin, Brooks must express both maternal and paternal concerns in tones that switch in an instant from hectoring to anxious or frantic at each turn of the plot. Taking on sole responsibility for parental duties after the death of Nemo's mother, the neurotic widower fish is bereaved and spooked at any hint of independence. He is terrified that his son might follow in his mother's fated fin-prints and venture beyond the safe coral reef to the big ocean, where Mother Fish had met her watery doom. Brooks's worried tone is pitch-perfect for the traumatized father, saddled with raising by himself a physically challenged son who has a stunted dorsal fin. One can hardly devise a clearer visual metaphor for fears of phallic inadequacy than Nemo's small, wilted fin. Both Nemo and his anxiety-ridden father represent variations on impotence—young Nemo in terms of insecurity about his physical disability and Marlin in terms of his psychological post-traumatic state. As they are swept out into the powerful womb of water beyond the reef, Dory (voiced by Ellen DeGeneres), their forgetful companion, is coded as beyond gender constraints, with her devil-may-care attitude couched in the familiar voice of DeGeneres, famous for her openly lesbian stance as a performer. An archetype of the wise fool, Dory carries androgynous authority and timeless moral wisdom.

In the works created by Brooks and Johnson, Brooks's characters are often caught between delusions of grandeur and utter abjection, between the brashness of hypermasculinity and the self-erasure of classic female stereotypes of insecurity and inadequacy. In analyzing highlights of Brooks's career, one may trace his characters' vacillations, grandiose bravado, and depths of despair as exquisitely nuanced stages of a highly gendered comedic vision that manages to simultaneously foreground and challenge stereotypes. He uses voice and gesture, costuming and language to stretch boundaries and create jarringly unexpected comic contrasts, drawing from the kinds of gendered insights and observations that were no doubt shaped by his relationship with women who influenced and enriched his work, in particular his long-time screenwriting partner, Monica Johnson.

A CAREER OF COLLABORATION WITH WOMEN

When Brooks began his screenwriting work with Johnson, he already had an established reputation in groundbreaking short television bits. Their first co-authored film, *Real Life*, established a new genre of mockumentary that numerous comedians subsequently imitated. Taking a page from *Candid Camera* and anticipating Sasha Baron Cohen's mind-blowing blend of real life and documentary performance, Brooks played with the line between real life and performance. *Real Life* features Brooks playing a version of himself as a comedian who decides to follow the fictional family of veterinarian, Warren Yeager (Charles Grodin), his wife Jeannette (Frances Lee McCain), their daughter Lisa (Lisa Urette) and son Eric (Robert Stirrat). The clever and absurd format of *Real Life* may have grown out of Brooks's intertextual performance experience, but some of the funniest bits would seem to come from Johnson, his relatively little-acknowledged writing partner. A perfect example, typical of female-centered humor, occurs when the wife comes to the dinner table with a heating pad on her belly. Her husband criticizes her for bringing an unsanitary device to the table, but she is not the least bit intimidated by his comment, replying, "I have terrible cramps, I am bleeding profusely and I want to vomit on the table." While Warren demonstrates a conventional masculine attempt to suppress and control female trouble, Brooks's character demonstrates empathy, validating his female subject by praising the openness, bravery, and authenticity of her expression of emotions.

Brooks's male protagonists often careen between extremes of manic aggressive behavior and despondent inaction, while women in his films usually take the lead, breaking out of feminine stereotypes of passivity or coyness. Encouraged by Albert's sympathetic demeanor, Jeannette initiates an awkward seduction. Unlike a typical masculine hero, he is the one who demurs and sets boundaries on their relationship, a cautious response that is often coded as feminine within the standard social paradigm of American culture. Jeannette violates another common pattern by being the one to leave the house to spend time alone, forcing her husband to manage child-rearing. Once she is gone, the precocious teenaged Lisa (Lisa Urette) follows in the footsteps of her transgressive mother and even challenges incest taboos by dressing up, putting on make-up and role playing with her father, claiming, "I'm fantasizing. You are my lover. Take me in your arms and kiss me like you've never kissed me before." In one of the funniest lines of the film, Grodin closes the scene by replying with a deadpan serious tone: "This is your confirmation dress." In contrast to Brooks's character, Warren stolidly resists the transgressiveness of the females in his family.

Throughout *Real Life*, breakneck dialogue repeats this pattern of unexpected and outrageous contrasts that cascade out of Brooks's mouth in a kind of absurdist dialectic. As Jeannette continues her efforts to seduce Albert, she comes into his arms and says, "You're such a sensitive man." He makes a motion as if to pat her without actually touching her and when she kisses him, he reacts nervously by saying he has no charisma: "No kissing, I'm a shallow fellow; I didn't do it." When she insists, "I trust you," he answers, "No, no, no trust."

Figure 9.1 "Such a sensitive man"

Later on, when the African American psychologist Dr. Cleary (J. A. Preston) questions Albert about Jeannette's choice to call him about an emergency with her grandmother, Brooks says, "You gotta lighten up here. Her grandmother had a stroke." Then he tries to suggest that the psychiatrist may be uncomfortable in Phoenix because the doctor is African American. Growing defensive, Albert prattles on, digging his own grave, saying, "I know you're going to take over the world. You're stronger, you're faster." These wild swings between positions of dominance and submission contribute to the depth and humor of Brooks's depictions of gender and racial power dynamics.

Without calling special attention to costuming but using it to superb comic effect, Brooks creates humor through juxtaposition of contrasting categories, including gender. In the scene in which a reporter comes for an interview, Albert wears a long tan robe with a furry brown collar and cuffs, his absurd costume contrasting with his hypermasculine tirade against the reporter. He spews forth unrelated comments criticizing the reporter with lines like: "He wore far too much cologne." When the parents say, "The children are afraid to go to school," he responds, "That's normal. Take a week, I'll get a high colonic," and then concludes, "Let's think about me for a minute," resorting to a sort of infantile self-centeredness. As the documentary process depicted in the film begins to unravel, Brooks's character decides to appear in a colorful clown suit, wearing whiteface make-up and a curly wig, supposedly to cheer up the family. In this role, he furthers the pattern of gender role reversals, telling Warren, "I cried the other night." Using a stuffed rabbit as a puppet, Albert makes the bunny puppet embrace Warren's knee. These absurd costumes create the comedy of farce, as they more subtly suggest the gender fluidity of the central character.

Wild vacillations continue as Albert, desperate to turn his disaster into success, brainstorms for an example of the most successful movie ending ever made as an inspirational model for his hapless documentary. Rejecting the two most masculine alternatives he comes up with—*Star Wars*, where they blow up a planet, and *Jaws*, where they blow up a shark—Albert falls into momentary despair, suggesting, "I'm mentally ill," as if deliberately gaslighting himself. Then, he suddenly brightens as he settles on *Gone with the Wind*, a film with a female protagonist who refuses to accept defeat, even in the face of utter devastation. By this point in the film, his clown outfit resembles a muumuu dress, further feminizing Brooks's absurd character. Recalling *Gone with the Wind*'s dramatic ending, Albert tells his camera operator: "It was spectacular. They only burned down Atlanta." As *Gone with the Wind*'s famous soundtrack plays in the background, Albert runs through the Yeagers' house, lighting curtains with torches. Delighted, he yells, "A gigantic fire. We did it. The most spectacular ending anybody could ever have. Their house is really burning." The final shot shows everyone sitting on the ground in front of the burning house, as if watching a television set, Albert cross-legged in his floppy clown costume covered with large garish flowers. Over this shot, a scroll slaps a satirically materialistic happy ending on the narrative, informing viewers that the Yeagers received their $25,000 to rebuild their house and even add a tennis court. Dr. Cleary's tell-all book is mentioned as selling less than 400 copies, as the music transitions from the *Gone with the Wind* theme into the breezy whistling of the fifties jazz soundtrack of the film's opening. This conclusion returns to Brooks's common pattern of turning disaster into success.

Real Life was intended to make a much broader comment on what constitutes success and its relation to media images within the larger society, with an anthropological comment embedded in Brooks's humor. Dave Walker observes:

> He and Shearer (who had co-produced one of Brooks' comedy records) and Johnson had begun work on a script lampooning the then-hot "est" self-improvement seminar system, but veered into "Real Life" when Brooks discovered a quote by cultural anthropologist Margaret Mead about the 1973 PBS documentary series "An American Family." That project, a dead-serious, inside-out examination of a California family named the Louds, had been one of its decade's pop culture milestones. Mead said the Loud project, which detailed the collapsing marriage of mom and dad Pat and Bill Loud as well as their son Lance's gay coming-out, was "as new and significant as the invention of drama or the novel—a new way in which people can learn to look at life, by seeing the real life of others interpreted by the camera."[7]

Giving credit to Margaret Mead for the inspiration, Brooks claimed, "The quote deserved a movie."[8] This quoting of Mead is noteworthy because it foregrounds the prescience of her observation, wherein Brooks and Johnson acknowledge the insight and wisdom of a foundational female theorist in a traditionally male-dominated field.

ROM-COM, COM-ROM, OR MODERN BIO-DRAMEDY

In *Modern Romance*, Johnson and Brooks establish another narrative pattern that recurs throughout their films: a dissatisfied character tries to abandon his past and take a leap of faith into a world of new relationships. As movie editor Robert Cole, Brooks's protagonist has great aspirations and an overinflated sense of self-worth, but it quickly becomes apparent that this bravado conceals deep insecurity and a kind of crazed impulsiveness. It is in the details, though, that we recognize Brooks's devil—a paralyzing fear of failure. In analyzing the film, Craig Williams calls on us to consider "relatability" and to "broaden the way we think about gender" and its connection to genre in *Modern Romance*:

> With this in mind, *Modern Romance* may be a film about male ego, but, like Elaine May's *The Heartbreak Kid* or Mary Harron's *American Psycho*, the execution—the directing, writing, editing—lacerates that very ego. Part of Brooks' brilliance is in creating a monster by exaggerating certain traits that will be very real to a big proportion of his audience.[9]

This explanation of connections between characters and viewers' experience leaves out mention of Johnson's possible influence and also misses the essential contradiction in Brooks's character—his ping-ponging between hypermasculine narcissism and the passive aggressive trope often associated with stereotypes of femininity. As for the issue of "relatability," this paradigm ignores the fact that viewers often identify with characters—or not—based on the gender of the viewer. It also contradicts Williams's own assertion that "the very notions of relatability and compromise were anathema to Brooks as a comedian and an artist." Brooks and Johnson's films feature characters who contain multitudes and offer multiple points of identification, in keeping with audiences who identify with these characters because of a taste for complexity and liminality.

Brooks punctures the dream of dominant masculinity throughout *Modern Romance*. As Brooks's character Robert Cole tries to hash out his on-again-off-again romance with Mary Harvard (Kathryn Herrold), he enacts the common pattern of a controlling male at some points, employing everything from bullying tactics to stereotypically feminine passive-aggressive guilt trips. At the same time, Robert DiMatteo claims that in *Modern Romance*, Brooks "limns a unique portrait of masculine vulnerability."[10] When he tries to patch up the relationship, he cajoles, begs, and threatens, and interferes with his girlfriend's career, even barging in on her business dinners. Here, he seems less like a macho man than like a spoiled child, appealing to Mary's sympathetic instincts. His final pitch is a standard romantic and unrealistic vision of a perfect relationship that requires a stereotypical female partner. Mary has already demonstrated that when it comes to her career in the boardroom, neither virile bullying nor female-coded manipulative tactics work, but in the domestic setting of her home, Robert's willingness to beg overrules her better judgment. Ultimately, in the film's conclusion, comedy deflates the ridiculous hyperbole of their Harlequin romance dream of perfect love, as the closing scroll describes their subsequent divorce, reunifications, and separations.

SENTIMENTAL ENLIGHTENMENT

Defending Your Life was not co-authored by Monica Johnson, but the presence of Meryl Streep bends the production toward a liberating depiction of gender in several ways. According to Brooks, it was sheer serendipity that brought her into the production, since he first talked about the project with her at a party and was then delighted when she expressed interest in the role. Just as Johnson seems to have exerted a subtle yet powerful influence on Brooks's portrayal of gender in *Real Life*, it appears that Meryl Streep's sunny persona contributed significantly to the tenor of *Defending Your Life* in ways that are not generally credited.

A look at how Streep inserted her own thinking, dialogue, and point of view when she was a relative unknown vying for the part of Joanna Kramer opposite the powerhouse star, Dustin Hoffman as Ted Kramer, is instructive in this regard. Initially drawn to her apparent vulnerability after the death of her spouse, Hoffman wanted Streep in *Kramer vs. Kramer* (1979), but he ended up with a more powerful figure than he bargained for. Streep was determined to convince Hoffman and director Benton that her take on the female lead was more authentic and powerful than the original script's version. Method actor Hoffman demanded at one point that Streep "stop carrying the flag for feminism and just *act the scene*," and at one point he admitted he "hated her guts," even though he admired her ability to get the job done.[11] Benton later described her influence on the character and the film: "This picture started out belonging to Ted Kramer, and by the end it belonged to both of them," Benton recalled. "And there was no way Dustin could shake her. No way he could do anything to shake her. She was just there, and she was an incredible force."[12] In spite of friction on set between the two actors, Streep maintained her equanimity and eventually came to Hoffman's rescue in real life. After the film's debut, when Rona Barrett was attacking Hoffman's portrayal as a "slap" to feminists, Streep came bounding into the press conference, saying, "Here comes a feminist." She stated with aplomb that the "basis of feminism is something to do with liberating men *and* women from prescribed roles."[13]

In a similar if more congenial way, Streep offered input and inspiration that could flourish in Brooks's *Defending Your Life*. Brooks did his part by being willing to accept her contribution to her character and the film, perhaps in part because he was in a vulnerable position, feeling his own career had seemed to stall at that point. As he describes it in a *Rolling Stone* interview, he found himself like the cartoon *Road Runner*'s Wile E. Coyote figure, looking down and realizing he had run off a cliff. Landing at a point of desperation and seeming in awe of Streep's reputation, he came up with a schtick that would entice her to accept a part in his film:

> I met Meryl Streep at a party years and years and years ago. I think it was at Carrie Fisher's house. Meryl brought so much reputation to her life because of all these iconic roles, but when you met her, she was just so easy-going and natural. She was aware of my work, and she asked what I was doing. I told her I was making this movie, and she sort of jokingly said, "Is there a part in it for me?" I went home and thought, "Okay . . ." It took a lot more from the producers to make that happen, but the person that I wanted for that role was the person that I sat and talked to at that party. So my job was to provide an environment where she could just hang out. She's the greatest character actress that ever lived, and she didn't get a lot of opportunities just to hang out, so that's what I thought could be great. She's playing somebody who's had a perfect life, and she automatically brings to that someone who is as close as you could get, someone who seemingly has had a perfect life. So all of that worked overall.[14]

In addition to his intuitive typecasting of Streep, Brooks successfully resuscitates successful techniques used in *Real Life* by capitalizing on humorous costuming for the recently deceased Daniel and his fellow walking corpses. Dressed in gown-like costumes, all the ambulatory dead in *Defending Your Life* wear robes called "toopas" that make them look like a cross between hospital patients and novice angels: "Looking at you in that Toopa. You look good in it," says Rip Torn, playing an afterlife bureaucrat named Bob Diamond with all the oily good cheer and breeziness of a salesman or late-night show producer. Diamond explains how "little brains" (people living on Earth) use only 3 percent of their brains, with most of their mental energy absorbed by fear. Daniel says, "So I'm on trial for being afraid," a laugh line that summarizes the film's plot and resembles the dilemma of real-life males in American society in

Figure 9.2 Watching Daniel (Brooks) watch Julia (Meryl Streep) watching her life

a nutshell. In contrast, the easy good humor of Streep's character, Julia, in this film typifies her star persona, but it also plays on her actual toughness, strong will, and heft as a real-world creative artist. Even though she doesn't come across as a particularly feminist lead, her cheerfulness, modesty, and unselfconscious bravery in the face of death all place Brooks's character Daniel at a disadvantage. He clearly envies her self-confidence and record of courageous acts, the likes of which social convention would expect from a typical manly figure. Brooks milks these situations for comedy, for example, when his character attends the movie compilation of Julia's life. He wipes his face and looks down in dismay as he watches clips of her not only rescuing her children from their burning home, but returning to the house and emerging with the family cat. Here, Brooks's use of newsreel or *cinéma vérité* style adds a comedic self-reflexive element to the scene, as the viewer watches Brooks watch himself, agonizing in his own hell of humiliation and envy.

The final scene has all the suspense and drama of an action movie, when Daniel sees Julia leaving on another bus, never to return to earth for a repeat round of life as a "little brain." Taking his own life in his hands, he leaps out the door of his accelerating bus and races over to her vehicle, clinging to the door as it slams in his face and screaming for the driver to stop as it takes off. Meanwhile, Diamond, observing this scene with the prosecutor and judges through a supernatural surveillance device, says, "Brave enough for you?" As Brooks pulls the doors apart and runs to embrace Streep, the entire busload of afterlife witnesses applauds and the music rises triumphantly. As is the case with many of successful Hollywood endings—from *It's a Wonderful Life* to

Dirty Dancing—the couple's embrace is witnessed by others, who vicariously experience and intensify their climactic moment. The masculine fantasy of the film is fairly basic: Meryl Streep, "a human being who is effortlessly superior in every way . . . could love Albert—though only on another plane of existence."[15] It is ironic that Brooks's character is able to behave with the stereotypical masculine attribute of bravery when he abandons himself completely to a woman and imitates the unself-conscious bravery she has demonstrated throughout her life.

TWO COMEBACK PERFORMANCES IN *MOTHER*

Mother features another quietly powerful woman in a low-key comic narrative that allows Albert Brooks and Debbie Reynolds to shine in equal measure, enacting characters who wriggle from the grip of restrictive familial and gender expectations. The film plays on the nostalgia of its audience with its opening soundtrack, beginning with parody lyrics for the "Mrs. Robinson" soundtrack from Mike Nichols's *The Graduate* (1967), substituting the name of the protagonist's mother, "Mrs. Henderson." Target audiences might be recalling Nichols's thirty-year-old film and identifying in some ways more with Mrs. Robinson than with Benjamin, but in *Mother*, Brooks reinserts himself into the identity of the boy who occupied a room in his mother's house in the late sixties. Instead of dating women, he courts his mother, alternating between challenging her and egging her on to break out of the stodgy life he imagines she experiences. Female viewers might be looking at actor Debbie Reynolds as a role model who stages a successful comeback in later life, playing an older female lead who has independence, an active sex life, and a passion for creative writing.

The film's opening finds Brooks's protagonist, John Henderson, finalizing his divorce from Karen Henderson (Laura Weekes), who "came with a lot of nice furniture." Discussing with a friend the possibility that all the women he's gone out with were basically the same woman, he gives a trendy nod to gender reversals, wondering whether the scenario of falling in love with a transgender man, as depicted in David Cronenberg's film version of *M. Butterfly*, could be possible, in a non-sequitur reminiscent of the montage of absurd comments about incest in *Real Life*. With a similar sort of free association, Brooks's character goes on to complain that his wives did not really believe in him and wonders why he is drawn to such women. As if in answer to this query, the scene cuts to Beatrice Henderson (Debbie Reynolds) asking a repairman if the color on the new television set he just installed looks a little green, a query that typifies her demanding and dissatisfied attitude. As soon as John arrives at his mother's house, he and Beatrice begin to argue about food. He doesn't

Figure 9.3 Food as one of the mediators of John (Brooks) and Beatrice's (Debbie Reynolds) relationship

eat meat, and she keeps food forever in her refrigerator. After a few minutes of bickering, he tells her that he wants to move back in with her until he can figure out why he has such a bad relationship with her. She snaps back, "If you talk to these women the way you talk to me, I can see why they leave you." The musical soundtrack rises: "And here's to you Mrs. Henderson," adapted from Simon and Garfunkel's score for *The Graduate*, self-consciously playing with the Oedipal motif.

John's character is further emasculated and infantilized when their shopping spree turns into a romantic montage, with John declaring, "We have a date . . . a special evening." When he complains that his mother always tells clerks about his recent divorce and case of writer's block, she responds, "People are just curious why a grown man and his mother would be in an underwear store together." At a pet store, the realistic film style morphs into a surreal scene in which Reynold's face is pictured in extreme close-up, the voice artificially lowered with slight slow motion, telling the clerk the life story of her son's failed marriages. John says, "What difference would it make? What if we were man and wife," to which his mother replies, "Honey please," with obvious impatience. These incest jokes constitute an amplified echo of *Real Life*'s father-daughter dialogue with a scene in which John takes his mother into a Victoria's Secret store and says his mother wants a pair of crotchless panties. The clerk replies, "Wonderful," leaving John more embarrassed than his mother appears to be.

The competition between mother and son is also cast within the context of sibling rivalry between the two sons. In order to demonstrate his closeness to his mother, Jeff shows John a picture of a phone he plans to give their mother, but John insists it will not work with her, either underestimating her intellect or reveling in her imminent failure. He explains to his brother, "I feel estranged from my own mother and it affects everything in my life, including my relationships with women. . . . I'm going to move back in with mother." Jeff is shocked, but John counters: "You sound a little jealous." As if to show that failure is contagious, the younger son Jeff's apparently happy marriage eventually frays when John competes for their mother's attention. Jeff gets into a fight with his wife, who tells him, "You talk to her every goddammed day of your life," adding, "You're a momma's boy" who doesn't know his mother any better than John does: "You just cling more." This scene then cuts to a shot of Brooks and his mother at a zoo looking at an elephant, while his mother comments that "these animals have a better memory" than humans do. Harkening back to *Real Life* in suggesting incestuous attachment, *Mother* takes the topic several steps further, as Beatrice shows little of the prudery expected from a middle-aged woman. When his mother tells him about a man she has sex with on a regular basis, he asks why she never spoke about someone with whom she has an intimate relationship, to which she replies, "We're not intimate, we just have sex." During Jeff's visit, the two men get in a fight in Beatrice's driveway as a neighbor overhears their conversation. John ends up shouting, "I love my mother and I love having sex with her," a line that gets laughs because of its sheer outrageousness. The film's happy resolution occurs when Beatrice finally admits her resentment of her children, describing a story she wrote in which a woman "raised children whom she hated for killing her chances of doing the one thing that she loved." At this point, John is overjoyed: "For the first time I don't see you as my mother. I see you as a failure, and that's wonderful." This comic line is rich with possibilities. It reveals how his sense of inadequacy as a male child was created in part by his mother's hyper-critical attitude toward him, but also by his own mistaken sense that she was invulnerable. Once he is able to view her as an equal or perhaps an inferior, his enslavement to gender categories is loosened and he can see his mother as just another struggling, imperfect human being.

INTERSECTIONS OF RACE, RELIGION AND GENDER

Returning to the comic framework established in *Real Life*, Brooks's mockumentary *Looking for Comedy in the Muslim World* (2005) opens with a bluesy jazz soundtrack and the dream of receiving a big award like a Nobel prize.[16] As humor ambassador to India and Pakistan in *Looking for Comedy in the Muslim World*, Brooks's character brags to his fictional wife about the possibility of a Nobel Prize for comedy—an echo of the boast he makes in his first film—only to find that no one laughs at a single joke he makes. This gloomy debut is overturned when the protagonist gets a local translator and discovers the crucial importance of language in successful comedic delivery. At the film's opening Albert Brooks's fictionalized version of himself enters a State Department building to meet with actor Fred Thompson, playing a slightly fictionalized version of himself as well. The actor explains that he has summoned Brooks to head up a commission to understand Muslims, initiated by President Bush, who, "as you well know . . . has a pretty good sense of humor." Brooks's reaction shot, a quick look of puzzlement when he hears this unlikely description, is one of many subtle comic bits peppered throughout the film. When Brooks asks, "Why me?" Thompson answers, "Quite frankly, our first few choices were working," but also dangles the prospect of receiving a Medal of Freedom award. The ego bait works, and the next scene shows Brooks ready to head to India, a predominantly Hindu country with 150 million Muslims, and then to Pakistan. Moving from a traveling shot of serene first-class luxury down the aisle to coach class and the sound of a crying baby, a tight shot of Brooks shows two State Department assistants beside him, advising him, "Relax, we only have nineteen hours and ten minutes left." Here, Brooks's failure to receive a first-class seat increases his frustrated helplessness, and the stolid bureaucratic stoicism of his companions stands in stark contrast to Brooks's aura of beleaguered victimhood.

The film weaves intertextual references and cultural in-jokes throughout, as Brooks tries to establish himself as a comedian and celebrity and make professional connections in his new environment. A series of deadpan encounters demonstrate the futility of his character seeking common ground. In his tiny cramped office, Brooks interviews for an assistant, but the first few applicants do not even know how to type. The next candidate seems well qualified, but then she asks him if he is Jewish and her open anti-Semitism disqualifies her as well. When he asks a rather effeminate man what his aspirations are, he answers, "One day I would like to become a woman," to which Brooks replies, "Well, good luck with that." This heteronormative response is part of Brooks's conventional persona, which appears to be more conformist than those of characters he plays in earlier films. It may also harken back to his riff in *Mother* about transgender issues in *M. Butterfly*. He asks an employee at the hotel what he finds funny, and the clerk responds, "I like it when animals act like people." Brooks says, "Oh, like Stupid Pet Tricks," a phrase that delights the employee, who fails to recognize the American popular culture reference.

Brooks ends up hiring a young woman named Maya who seems highly qualified but laughs at none of his jokes, in spite of his attempts to "mansplain" sarcasm to her. As she becomes more comfortable with him, she complains to him about Mageed, her possessive, unemployed Iranian boyfriend. He tells her he once made a movie about jealousy, a self-reflexive allusion to *Modern Romance*, declaring that it "never seems to get better." When she reacts with alarm, he shrugs, in a typically self-serving Brooksian reversal, and responds, "It might get better." As obsequious apprentice to his bumbling character, Maya admires and trusts him without reservation, responding to him in a way that resembles his wife's attitude. In this film, though, instead of the edgy treatment of male-female relationships we witness in *Real Life*, Brooks has his protagonist encounter pretty females who simply reflect naïve admiration for him. Rather than complicate their encounters with the temptation of marital infidelity, he takes the safer route of undercutting the self-imagined nobility and success of his bumbling Mr. Magoo by showcasing disastrous news reports and conversations that follow in his wake and contradict his overblown sense of himself. The masculine bravado and clumsy brashness of Brooks's character epitomize American presence and influence abroad.

Brooks manages to milk humor from the repeated humiliation of his character, and the use of an increasingly absurd-looking set of elaborate embroidered costumes that feminize his bland looks. As Maya and the State Department assistants pass out flyers to advertise his comedy concert, Brooks tries to identify people who speak English. Meanwhile, his handlers—a big bureaucrat named Stuart (John Carroll Lynch) and a younger one named Mark, played with suave self-confidence by handsome advertising madman type, Jon Tenney—hand out announcements indiscriminately to people who obviously speak no English, in the midst of Old Delhi. They manage to fill a school auditorium with people whose grasp of English is questionable, and the location has no dressing room or stage lights. On the night of his big performance Maya goes out into the courtyard to fetch Brooks, who is getting ready in a tipi. He emerges in an exaggerated traditional Indian outfit, looking like a bridegroom in white festooned with gold braided embellishments. His awkward attempts to imitate the local culture make him appear somewhat self-conscious, feminized, and totally absurd. When Brooks comes on stage, he begins his routine and fails to get a single laugh. Out of desperation, he then decides to perform an improvisation exercise, requesting suggestions from the audience, noting them on a chalk board, and then changing and disregarding all their suggestions. This comic strategy simply bewilders the audience and, at another level, imitates a masculinist and imperialist attitude of superiority and disregard for the input of those he considers inferior.

As his protagonist does in *Real Life*, Brooks's comic character picks himself up and keeps trying after his abysmal failure in India. This time, he sneaks across the border illegally to perform for a group of Pakistani comedians. With the assistance of an interpreter, Brooks manages a hilarious performance, in part because they truly understand his comedy and in part because they all share a few tokes from their communal pipe before the show. On the drive back, he asks a question that arouses knowing laughter from the film audience: "Can we stop for a milk shake?" He is thrilled when Al Jazeera wants to interview him the next day, and he daydreams aloud: "This is how you win a Nobel prize." Again, Brooks uses effeminate costuming to heighten comic effect, with his character claiming he needs to shop for something special to wear to the interview. He emerges wearing a fancy kaftan and absurd embroidered shoes with curly toes. His flashy garb contrasts with the professional clothing of the three Indian reporters, who are all dressed in sophisticated, masculine-looking Western style (both male and female), thus making his character look especially ridiculous. He mistakenly believes they are interested in his project, looking for comedy, but it turns out they want him to do an Al Jazeera E-style program. The premise for the series is an American Jewish man living in an apartment in India, with the title, "That Darned Jew." When he refuses their offer, they counter: "Do you know how to get ahold of Jerry Seinfeld? Get us another Jew." Although he declines, his wife—oblivious to the insulting nature of this proposal—tells him on the phone that he should think about it. This brilliant throwaway bit is a jab at anti-Semitism, at those who do not recognize it, and also at a reality television craze in which people willingly humiliate themselves for money and short-lived fame.

In his last failure to make a real cultural connection in India, he finds himself so distracted talking to his wife on the phone about his problems that he does not even notice the Taj Mahal he is supposed to be visiting. In what might turn out to be his only real contribution to someone in India, he advises Mageed on the telephone: "Jealousy is unattractive." Then, immediately switching back to his own situation, he mutters to himself, "It's OK to bomb; it's not the end of the world." Misinterpreting this series of random comments, the government spies who have been surveilling his call post a "level three" security alert, as Brooks is sent home by the ambassador. Maya promises to write everything up in a final report, and cross-cutting shows Brooks leaving as troops head for the border to deal with the non-existent crises he inadvertently precipitated.

The scroll at the film's conclusion expresses Brooks's self-pitying thoughts when it states: "No medal, no phone call, no nothing." The commentary broadens to include a critique of social priorities: "July 2nd America's looking for comedy program was put on hold. In its place is a new bomber that can fire its weapons without ever leaving the hangar." The closing scene returns the protagonist to the Western version of traditional gender roles, at a homecoming celebration with Albert's fictional wife Emily proposing a toast "to my husband, the Henry Kissinger of comedy." Her blind admiration for him contrasts with a dose of reality, as a traveling camera zooms in on a shot of a small television running in the kitchen with a newscaster (Linden Soles) saying, "After two years of peace, India and Pakistan have resumed armed conflict. Both countries, nuclear powers, have gone on high alert." In a perfect dialectic, the next shot shows his adoring wife saying, "I'm so proud of you . . . You might have changed the world." The closing scroll adds that the conflict subsided "once they identified Mr. Brooks as the problem." His character combines the neediness of an overgrown child with the brashness of masculine bravado in a hilariously toxic stew, always threatening to splash back on him where it will hurt the most. His character is the ultimate failed macho American comedian, legend only in his own mind, and ambassador only of the absurd. By showcasing disastrous news reports and demeaning conversations that follow in his wake, Brooks does more than simply undermine his character's overblown sense of himself. In his bumbling carelessness, Brooks's character comes to personify American influence and thoughtless destructiveness overseas.

EPILOGUE AND TRIBUTE TO MONICA JOHNSON

Circling back to Brooks's earlier work, I argue that *The Muse* may be one of Brooks's most biographical films—in spite of its whimsical elements bordering on magical realism. It is worth asking whose biography it represents. In a 1999 review of the film, Janet Maslin skirts a crucial issue that many reviewers fail to consider at all—the nature of Brooks and Johnson's writing collaboration. After Johnson's death from cancer at 64, Brooks described his co-author as "an extraordinary person. Funny, smart, and so much fun to work with. The world has lost a great sense of humour."[17] Johnson worked on an array of groundbreaking proto-feminist television shows in the 1970s and 1980s, including *The Mary Tyler Moore Show*—featuring the first never-married career woman as the eponymous lead—and *Laverne & Shirley*, based on the friendship of two working-class women, played by Penny Marshall and Cindy Williams. Johnson took the initiative to have Penny Marshall arrange a meeting with Brooks, and they instantly became "each other's first audience."[18] Brooks describes their relationship:

> I play all the parts and the stage direction and Monica has all the ideas and lines she can think of. She provides this place where comedy can live. She's very muselike in that sense. From the very beginning, when you talk about the Albert Brooks character, she understands that character innately. Not me, him. She understands that guy very well. It was a challenge for me to do it without her. . . . I know if I can't make Monica laugh, it won't go any further than that.[19]

In the person of Sharon Stone's muse, we see the clearest articulation of the notion that Brooks's character is not as successful or powerful as he imagines himself to be. He really owes his success to some woman in the background who judges his every move and makes unfathomable demands on him. In Stone's lines, echoes from various strands of Brooks's other films take shape, whether in the curt rationalizations of his unpredictable compulsive gambler wife from *Lost in America*, his argumentative career-centric girlfriend in *Real Romance*, or his stubborn and critical eponymous antagonist in *Mother*. These women all demand of Brooks's character a combination of respect, obedience, and utter fidelity.

From a materialist perspective, *The Muse* is a sort of success report card, representing Brooks's most lavish display of Hollywood connections, with a soundtrack written for the film by Elton John, cameo appearances as themselves from Jennifer Tilly, Rob Reiner, Wolfgang Puck, James Cameron, Lorenzo Lamas, and Martin Scorsese, and Sharon Stone playing Sarah Little, a part that garnered her a Golden Globe nomination, but no win. The Hollywood Press Association demanded their members return gift watches back to Stone or October Films, in order to avoid the appearance of bribery. As his most expensive and least financially successful film, costing $15 million and making only $11 million, *The Muse* failed the financial test, but it offers a sly and trenchant critique of the industry's commercialism. It even exposes the exploitive and stingy doling out of screen credits, including the old joke about someone who was happy to have an elf write his screenplays until the elf demanded a screen credit. At least Johnson managed to get screen credit.

Like Sharon Stone's eponymous character in *The Muse*, Johnson may well have been Brooks's largely unsung muse, flitting from one comedy partnership to another, and from one marriage to the next. Johnson was survived by her only daughter, Heidi Johnson, and her seventh husband Charles Lohr. Today, she lives on in her contributions to the films and television work she collaborated to create as author, inspiration, and producer. Regardless of the degree of her contribution to Brooks's films—which can only be surmised—it was Brooks's ability to see her value, along with that of the many other women who sent him on guilt trips or inspired his greatest work, an ability that contributes to the fascination and global appeal of a funny man who knew better than most how to channel his inner female.

Monica Johnson co-wrote screenplays for *Real Life*, *Modern Romance*, *Lost in America*, *Mother*, and *The Muse*, and although they had varying degrees of success, they all exhibit a similar pattern of violating or testing such common boundary categories as incest taboos, marriage customs, and gender identities. Her final collaboration with Brooks, *The Muse*, reads as Johnson's wish-fulfilment allegory for their relationship and perhaps for her entire career. Johnson did not co-write for *Defending Your Life*, *Finding Nemo*, or *Finding Dory* (2016), but Brooks was joined by strong female influencers in these cases as well. In his solo effort, *Looking for Comedy in the Muslim World*, Brooks failed to push back against gender stereotypes, although he bravely attempted to stretch cultural and ethnic boundaries. Perhaps without Johnson at his side, though, he was unable to identify what was truly edgy, outrageous, or funny.

He ended up with a female version of the fawning "native" flunky instead of a transgressive local wild card. Perhaps he lost the androgynous side of Albert Brooks when Johnson was no longer around to recognize the challenging absurdities and laugh lines that would reveal his true character.

All of this is not to argue that Albert Brooks simply mooched off the talent of women. Rather, it is to say that one of his greatest gifts was to recognize his muses, whether they were women, marginalized ethnic or social groups, or neglected family members who may have seemed to him more like sibling rivals than partners. He channeled his internal female spirit when he experienced, recognized, and exploited the position of the underappreciated, the ignored, even the dead. At one point in his career, when he did not receive an Academy Award nomination, he paraphrased Sally Fields's famous line, "You like me, you really like me," delivered to and later ridiculed by her fellow Hollywood stars and the general public. Brooks tweeted, "You really don't like me, you really don't like me," a funny line expressing how he felt as a creative artist, but a sentiment that no doubt resonates with anyone who has missed out on acknowledgement that was passionately desired and perceived as deserved. This sense of being underestimated and undervalued may well be the emotional core of Brooks's ability to channel the female experience, the wellspring of pain, fear, and stubborn courage at the root of his comic genius.

NOTES

1. Albert Brooks, dir. *Real Life*. 1979; Hollywood: Paramount Pictures.
2. Albert Brooks, dir. *Modern Romance*. 1981; Culver City, CA: Columbia Pictures.
3. Albert Brooks, dir. *Defending Your Life*. 1991; Burbank, CA: Warner Bros.
4. Albert Brooks, dir. *The Muse*. 1999; USA: October Films; Albert Brooks, dir. *Mother*. 1996; Hollywood: Paramount Pictures.
5. Gavin Smith, "All the Choices: Albert Brooks Interview," *Film Comment* 35, no. 4 (July/August 1999). Available at <https://www.filmcomment.com/article/all-the-choices-albert-brooks-interview> (last accessed January 7, 2021).
6. Andrew Stanton and Lee Unkrich, dirs. *Finding Nemo*. 2003; Burbank, CA: Pixar.
7. Maria C. Montoya, "Albert Brooks 'Real Life' Film Is an Unexpected Classic," *NOLA.com*, February 28, 2009.
8. Montoya, "Albert Brooks."
9. Craig Williams, "In Praise of Modern Romance—Albert Brooks' Masterpiece." *Little White Lies*, August 5, 2016. Available at <https://lwlies.com/articles/modern-romance-albert-brooks> (last accessed January 7, 2021).
10. Robert DiMatteo, "Real Afterlife," *Film Comment* 27, no. 2 (March/April 1991): 18, 20.
11. Michael Schulman, *Her Again: Becoming Meryl Streep* (New York: Harper, 2017), 232, 252.
12. Schulman, *Her Again*, 254.
13. Schulman, *Her Again*, 258.
14. Jennifer Wood, "'Defending Your Life' at 25: Albert Brooks on Making a Comedy Classic." *Rolling Stone*, March 22, 2016. Available at <www.rollingstone.com/

movies/movie-news/defending-your-life-at-25-albert-brooks-on-making-a-comedy-classic-178596/> (last accessed January 7, 2021).
15. Stuart Klawans, "Films," *The Nation*, April 22, 1991, 534.
16. Albert Brooks, dir. *Looking for Comedy in the Muslim World*. 2005; Burbank, CA: Warner Independent.
17. Albert Brooks, "Albert Brooks Pays Tribute To Monica Johnson," *Female First*, November 3, 2010. Available at <www.femalefirst.co.uk/movies/movie-news/Albert Brooks Pays Tribute To Monica Johnson-86779.html> (last accessed January 7, 2021).
18. Patrick McGilligan (ed.) *Backstory 5: interviews with screenwriters of the 1990s* (Berkeley: University of California Press, 2010), 16.
19. McGilligan, *Backstory 5*, 15–16.

PART III

Brooks as Cultural Figure

CHAPTER 10

Finding Brooks: Animating the Baby Boomer Generation in *Finding Nemo*

Dietmar Meinel

In his look at the re-release of *Lost in America* (1985) in 1999, film journalist David Sims characterizes Albert Brooks as "America's most pessimistic comedian."[1] Feeling stuck in their professional career and suburban house, *Lost in America*'s David and Linda Howard (Albert Brooks and Julie Hagerty) are an upper-middle-class couple who long for some sort of emotional, spiritual, or intellectual liberation. Inspired by *Easy Rider* (1969), the couple decides to quit their managerial occupations and embrace life on the road but quickly awakes from their dream of living free to experience the harshness of life without money when they gamble their savings away. As co-writer, co-star, and director of *Lost in America*, Brooks pokes biting fun at the white, (upper-) middle-class fantasy of escaping the confines of modern life and finding emotional, spiritual, or intellectual enlightenment in a life on the road in the 1980s; the "happy ending for Brooks" in *Lost in America* is nothing but "a depressing return to the status quo."[2] Rather than finding some form of enlightenment after forsaking their wealth, the protagonists of *Lost in America* eventually return to their staid life and professional occupations. The exposition of "the triumph of modern narcissism in all its cringe-worthy hilarity" (Powers) in *Lost in America*, as film journalist John Powers writes for *NPR*, is a main feature of the Brooks oeuvre.[3] In his review of another Brooks film, *The Muse* (1999), Gavin Smith poignantly highlights the continued engagement with yuppie materialism in the comedian's work:

> Once again, a Me Generation Everyman occupies an ideal lifestyle or system, blissfully unaware of its underlying precariousness. Whether it be the smug, callow filmmaker's perfect experiment in documentary in *Real Life* (79), the impossible fantasy of "true love" in *Modern Romance*

(81), the way a life of complacent materialism is exchanged for an equally deluded freedom of the road in the anti-Reagan-zeitgeist *Lost in America* (85), or ended altogether by the ultimate bummer of sudden death at the start of *Defending Your Life* (91), the Brooks protagonist is oblivious until too late.[4]

These recurring qualities of characters played by Albert Brooks speak to a broader engagement with "the contradictions, compromises, and neuroses of the Baby Boom generation" and its "overdeveloped sense of entitlement and unapologetic materialism."[5] Such entertaining, albeit often unbecoming portrayals of the baby boomers depict a generation "narcissistic and controlling yet insecure and resigned, reflexively self-analytical yet lacking emotional self-honesty,"[6] while also illustrating Brooks's talent to "wring laughs out of the psychological concerns of [a] generation."[7] For Margy Rochlin, writing in 1999, the films of Albert Brooks not only function "as time capsule chapters in the life of a funny, curly-haired, emotionally fitful man as he moves from his late 20's to his early 50's" but also for an entire generation.[8] Long-time collaborator and co-writer for many Albert Brooks films, Monica Johnson similarly explains that "I've always been proud of the fact that as far as comedy goes, we're maybe the only people tracking the baby boomer thing [. . .]. Our movies have evolved as we have. Basically, the story we pick is about wherever we are in life."[9] To tell these often unflattering stories of the baby boomer generation, Johnson and particularly Brooks extensively use irony and self-referential humor in which "the ultimate joke is on viewers" since most may not be "too different from [Brooks's] protagonist."[10]

From the beginning of his career as a comedian, Brooks paved the way for comedy about comedy. Already in his "Albert Brooks' Famous School for Comedians" (1971) essay for *Esquire*, his similarly titled short film *Albert Brooks' Famous School for Comedians* (1972), and the subsequent *Saturday Night Live* contributions Brooks "explod[ed] the schticks and traditions of standup comedy"[11] and eventually "dismantled the familiar, seemingly moribund comedy formats" popular in the early 1970s.[12] This practice of drawing attention to and commenting on the medium and the art form continued to be a mainstay of the Brooks oeuvre from his stand-up albums to his films. His comedy album *A Star Is Bought* (1975), for example, tells the story of one Albert Brooks attempting to produce a popular music album by composing tracks for various radio stations, all of which is presented as a radio documentary including narrations and celebrity interviews. In his directorial debut for the silver screen, *Real Life* (1979), Brooks also features as an aspiring filmmaker named Albert Brooks who attempts to succeed in the industry by shooting a documentary. Similarly, *Lost in America* opens with a Rex Reed interview about whether the viewer needs a laughing movie theatre audience to appreciate the humor of a comedy. Throughout the film, the yuppie couple continuously cites *Easy Rider* as a motivation for their decision to leave their suburban life behind and travel America. When the two are departing from Los Angeles, the extra-diegetic soundtrack plays the Steppenwolf song "Born to be Wild" from *Easy Rider* while a biker flips off a giddy and exuberant Albert Brooks waving from behind the wheel of his expensive motor-home. These are only a few examples of Brooks's "self-reflexive metacomedy" that highlight how he utilizes irony, intertextuality, and self-referentiality to qualify as "America's most pessimistic comedian."[13]

The Pixar animated film *Finding Nemo* (2003) introduces viewers to yet another archetypal Brooks's character.[14] In the opening scene the clownfish protagonist Marlin, voiced by Brooks, excitedly chats with his wife about the new suburban home the father-to-be acquired for the two and their unhatched offspring. However, as he loses his wife and almost all of his brood in a barracuda attack on their suburban home shortly thereafter, *Finding Nemo* takes a decidedly sombre tone. The trauma of the assault haunts Marlin as he becomes fearful of the world outside his home and constantly worries about potential threats to the well-being of his only surviving son, Nemo. While Marlin's seemingly hyperbolic behavior offers plenty of instances for irony or "self-reflexive meta-comedy,"[15] *Finding Nemo* hardly ever pokes fun at middle-class life. Instead, when a human scuba diver captures Nemo, the situation compels Marlin to face his largest fear and venture into the ocean world to attempt saving his son. Although Nemo eventually escapes his imprisonment in an aquarium without the help of his father, in journeying through the ocean and finding a variety of interspecies friends along the way, Marlin nonetheless overcomes the trauma of his family's death. Whereas the shift from ironic meta-comedy to family drama may merely signal a deviation from previous Brooks films, the figure of the clownfish father actually constitutes a development of the Brooks persona. This chapter, therefore, examines the integration of a sense of "new sincerity"[16] into his established persona. Described as discarding "any form of irony,"[17] this mode of cinematic narration highlights the dynamic shift occurring in *Finding Nemo*. At the same time, this notion of a "new sincerity" also speaks to broader cultural changes in the United States at the time of the film's production and release in the early 2000s.

The following chapter will first situate its close reading of the Albert Brooks persona within the numerous approaches to the study of stars, in particular the notion of stars as professionals who enact a coherent persona on and off the screen. Because Brooks embodied the baby boomer generation from the beginnings of his career,[18] questions about the shift in his persona from meta-comedy to sincerity complement this approach to star studies. The animated nature of *Finding Nemo* furthermore necessitates an exploration of the ways in which voice-acting functions to foster a star persona and its "sphere of intertextual discourse."[19] This framework allows us to read Marlin in the opening scene as yet another personification of the Brooks persona. When *Finding Nemo* shifts in tone, however, the figure of the clownfish father also adds a further layer to the Brooks persona, indicating a potential change in its longstanding character. Eventually Marlin learns to cope with, even overcomes, the trauma of violence and befriends a "virtual ocean menagerie of cooperative species"[20] beyond the coral reef. This chapter concludes by highlighting the cultural work the Brooks's persona engages in. Transcending fear and valuing cooperation, Brooks-as-Marlin challenges the predominant cultural climate in post-9/11 America and addresses the parents and grandparents, particularly the baby boomer generation, in *Finding Nemo*'s audience.[21]

ANIMATING THOSE HEAVENLY BODIES

In his seminal work, *Stars* (1979), Richard Dyer conceptualizes stardom as a "signification [. . .] realized in media texts"[22] manufactured by two competing strategies: stardom as "an image of the way stars live" and stars as people "independent of their screen/'fiction' appearances."[23] Consequentially, Dyer proposes to read stars as "characters in stories" and as "representations of people."[24] Most stars (attempt to) reconcile this dualism of private personality and star persona, minimizing notions of a possible conflict "between the general lifestyle and the particularities of the star."[25] While the practices and means of managing a star persona have followed broader shifts in the film industry from before the Hollywood studio system to the present, as Dyer details in his second book-length engagement with stardom, *Heavenly Bodies* (1986), the star persona is always "extensive, multimedia, intertextual"[26] blending star performances, public appearances, and (the enactment of) private life:

> The star phenomenon consists of everything that is publicly available about stars. A film star's image is not just his or her films, but the promotion of those films and of the star through pin-ups, public appearances, studio hand-outs and so on, as well as interviews, biographies and coverage in the press of the star's doings and "private" life. Further, what people say or write about him or her, as critics or commentators, the way the image is used in other contexts such as advertisements, novels, pop songs, and finally the way the star can become part of the coinage of everyday speech.[27]

Such an encompassing framework for the study of stars invited questions about stardom beyond the exclusivity of the Hollywood film industry as scholarship increasingly began to examine the production of stars in various entertainment industries and professional sports. While these areas of inquiry would continue "to denote a dialectic between on/off-screen presence,"[28] the notion of celebrity moves beyond explorations of a star persona established in individual texts to examine the "state of 'being famous'"[29] when "fame rests predominantly on the private life of the person, as opposed to their performing presence."[30] As "the ambiguity between skill and popularity" gradually leans in favour of the latter, performers from all fields of public life—from music to sports, literature, and politics—participate in the production of stardom "through the media via appearances in diverse media forms and formats."[31] With the rise of social media and video-hosting websites, celebrity status is not necessarily tied to a particular cultural text or commercial product but to the performance of a public persona itself—in "a rhizomatic space of celebrity."[32] Whereas Dyer examines stardom in the context of the (dissolution of the) Hollywood studio system, Barry King draws attention to the entrepreneurial dimension of stardom as "[p]roduct sponsorship and advertising have gained equal or greater weight in the star's income, and fame as the result of excellence in a specific sphere has become, whether through choice or eagerly embraced necessity, an abstract glue of presence binding together a portfolio of performances."[33] Today, stardom and particularly celebrity depends on paratextual or extra-cinematic appearances of a star in advertisement or publishing campaigns, television, radio, magazines, and internet shows, ceremonies, philanthropic work, professional databases and fan-produced websites, and numerous social media platforms (to refer to the most prominent examples). This "commodity stardom," as Pam Cook asserts with reference to Nicole Kidman, "is displayed across a bewildering array of media forms and commercial activities"—and preferably functions globally.[34]

Albert Brooks is not Nicole Kidman. Brooks rarely features in the paratexts so vital for establishing and promoting a "personal brand" today.[35] Rather than epitomizing the contemporary media culture of digital natives and streamed content, Brooks harkens back to the era of vinyl, cassettes, and video stores. As the fleeting introduction of his star persona at the beginning of this chapter indicates, Brooks build his persona and his commercial success through his intermedia work in stand-up, television, and film without expanding his "commodity stardom" into more popular and profitable areas.[36] While Brooks ventured into stand-up comedy, he recorded only two albums in the 1970s, produced one six-part series of shorts for *Saturday Night Life* also in the 1970s, appeared in minor television roles in that same decade before working in the film industry as writer, director, and actor. Celebrated for his directorial output (as well as his performance in *Taxi Driver* [1976], his Oscar-nominated performance in *Broadcast News* [1987], his guest-work in *The Simpson* [1989—to present], and his award-winning appearance in *Drive* [2011]) with an oeuvre of only seven films in more than forty years, Brooks never became a global brand or commodity and to this day, to adapt Smith, "stands outside this mainstream."[37]

Of course, not being Nicole Kidman or standing outside the mainstream is yet another possibility to shape a star persona. Brooks has done so as a (Hollywood) professional combining "a particular star image with a particular film context" and "a particular genre."[38] Christine Geraghty roots her notion of this form of professionalism in the star practices of the Hollywood studio system "in which the actor appears to be playing himself or herself."[39] Similarly, Barry King describes this approach as "personification" since an actor's personality is consistent with the character or role.[40] Personification denotes an understanding of stars less as competent actors and more as continuously enacting their personality with "the pleasurably recognisable repertoire of gestures, expressions and movements [being] the property of the star [and] not of any individual character."[41] Organizing his comedy "around a distinct personality-type,"[42] Brooks personified his characters sometimes with surprising consequences:

> When I played Albert Brooks in *Real Life* I learned how confusing that [telling jokes about one's own experience] gets, because people didn't know me very well then. I was reading reviews like, "This Albert Brooks should never be allowed to make another film, and he doesn't know how to handle a family. How dare he be so rough with children." And I'm going, Holy shit, don't people get it? So unless you play something so bizarre and unrealistic, you're always going to get mixed up with your work, which is just the way it is.[43]

This personification of a particular character throughout an oeuvre—whether in stand-up, television, or film—indicates the stability of the star persona, functions to orient audiences in their viewing expectations, and figures in the (commercial) success of a star as every deviation from the established persona "may lead to disappointment for the intended audience."[44] While the constant performance of the same personality on and off the screen narrows an actor's repertoire, the practice also provides a sense of stability or continuity for audiences usually reserved to television series. Stars working within a (professional) personification approach eventually offer their viewership "the pleasures of stability and repetition and the guarantee of consistency in the apparent plethora of choice offered by the expanding media."[45] As irony and meta-comedy are absent from most of *Finding Nemo*, the clownfish Marlin presents an instance of instability and profoundly deviates from the Brooks persona. Instead of reading his performance of a sombre and frightened father as a decision to simply cast Brooks against his type or persona (as happened, for example, in *Drive* where Brooks plays a ruthless gangster), this chapter explores the implications for a story animated not only for children and adolescents but particularly for the adult viewership of *Finding Nemo*.

From its inception, star studies were interested in the cultural or ideological work of stardom. Already in *Stars* (1979) and *Heavenly Bodies* (1986), Dyer situates his explorations of film stars within the broader framework of contemporary notions of individualism as "the star phenomenon reproduces the overriding ideology of the person in contemporary society."[46] His exploration of stardom eventually asks "what it is to be a human being in contemporary society" and an individual, however, not as "straightforward affirmations of individualism" but rather as "both the promise and the difficulty that the notion of individuality presents for all of us who live by it."[47] In particular, his readings originate from the idea that "stars play out some of the ways that work is lived in capitalist society."[48] Dyer complements this neo-Marxist approach with questions about gender, race, and sexuality to further capture the "ideological function" of stars highlighting similarities observable in a star persona and "the ideological tensions of a period."[49] As theoretical frameworks multiplied, scholarship increasingly asked questions about the "network[s] of ideological discourses"[50] to move from complex, albeit often coherent notions of the ideological function of star personas to those involving "strange and awkward cases."[51]

Arguably, animation films constitute one such strange and awkward instance since the digital protagonists only ever appear in person at themes parks or in parades. Mickey Mouse or Betty Boop or, indeed, Marlin, the clownfish father, never appear as public figures to promote the work they star in, walk the red carpet at award ceremonies, or have a large following on social media. Instead, voice-actors not only literally embody their animated characters at public events but also shape their animated appearance as well. As Colleen Montgomery explains in "Pixarticulation: Vocal Performance in Pixar Animation," in the production process at Pixar voice-acting is often recorded before the completion of all computer-animation so that the "performers' particular vocal qualities (register, intonation, accent, etc.) and their delivery of the dialogue frequently inflect the development of the animated characters."[52] Through their voice-acting, stars furthermore link their persona to a character via an intertextual "matrix of vocal allusions"[53] or "a sphere of intertextual discourse"[54] blending "the filmgoer's knowledge of these actor's personas, past work, and vocal qualities."[55] Consequentially, Brooks speaks to his audience as clownfish Marlin and simultaneously as an animated iteration of "America's most pessimistic comedian" in *Finding Nemo*.[56] Because animated character and star persona intersect in their shared voice, Brooks-as-Marlin fosters "appeal among groups who might generally regard animation, or Disney-backed animated features, as outside of their cultural domain" and thereby contributes to the "consistent commercial success" of Pixar films, yet draws in particularly those viewers familiar with the Brooks persona.[57]

FINDING NEMO AND THE NEW SINCERITY OF ALBERT BROOKS

In starring Albert Brooks, *Finding Nemo* draws on the irony, meta-comedy, and cultural commentary so prominent in his previous work immediately in its opening scene. Life in the reef, for example, is animated "from a fish-eyed perspective that is thoroughly annexed to the anxieties of middle-class suburbia, as Marlin extols the virtues of their new home to his wife in terms of the space, neighbourhood and quality of amenities that it offers."[58] At the same time, the clownfish seeks constant "verification from Coral about his ability to provide for his woman by 'delivering' a choice piece of property"[59] and expresses further uneasiness about their life as a family with children, particularly whether his offspring will like him. By depicting the clownfish couple as overtly immersed in "the neighborhood, the quality of the schools, and the view" of their home, *Finding Nemo* highlights their "suburban values" to possibly exaggerate and mock its anthropocentrism as Lynne Dickson Bruckner maintains.[60] Casting Brooks in the role of the anxious suburban father further strengthens reading the opening shots as ironically animating middle-class life. While Marlin evokes the "narcissistic [. . .] yet insecure" part of the Brooks persona,[61] the introduction of parenting in *Finding Nemo*, however, also complicates its portrayal.[62] Eventually, the opening scene of *Finding Nemo* appropriates the talkative humor and the anxious middle-classness of the Brooks persona to introduce the clownfish father, yet also widens the "intertextual density"[63] of the former with the inclusion of fatherhood.

Before the narrative further delves into "the contradictions, compromises, and neuroses of the Baby Boom generation" and its "overdeveloped sense of entitlement and unapologetic materialism" so characteristic for previous Brooks performances,[64] however, an unprecedented violence intrudes the suburban space. A barracuda assault wipes out almost the entire clownfish family; solely Marlin and his son Nemo survive. The faded colors, the subdued soundtrack, and the promise to "never let anything happen to you, Nemo" emphasize the sincerity and gravity of the scene. From this moment, *Finding Nemo* shifts in tone to narrate a story about "the aftermath of the traumatic attack that ruptures this suburban idyll" in which the return to the status quo would be anything but depressing.[65]

For the time being, however, Marlin devotes all his attention to raising Nemo as the narrative sets in with the young clownfish getting ready for his first day of school. Marlin exhibits genuine care for his son as he plays with, tickles, and races Nemo yet also grooms the child or holds his fin when the two travel the reef. In "Men at the Heart of Mothering: Finding Mother in *Finding Nemo*," Suzan G. Brydon qualifies this behavior as mothering since "getting children up for day-care or school, feeding, bathing, organization of the daily schedule, caring for sick children, emotional labor are 'activities more traditionally associated with a mothering role'.[66] Similarly, when Marlin reprimands his son with expressions such as "You take one more move, mister" or "You are in big trouble, young man," the clownfish father also "uses phrases stereotypically attributed to mothers' policing of children."[67] Whereas this behavior may derive from the concerns of a parent for their only child and, in particular, from the fact that Nemo lives with the physical disability of having a small left fin, Marlin experiences distress continually throughout *Finding Nemo* as "he is repeatedly shown trembling, shrinking back in fear, and closing his eyes in the face of danger."[68] Indeed, in promising to "never let anything happen to" his son, Marlin has developed deep-seated anxieties about any kind of thinkable and unthinkable threats outside his suburban home constantly reminding Nemo that the ocean is "not safe" and worrying about the danger of "charging snails" at the petting zoo.[69] However, *Finding Nemo* avoids exploiting male mothering and even hypersensitive behavior for cheap laughs. Consequentially, the motherly Marlin functions neither as a source of comedy nor as social commentary about the "blissful" unawareness of "a Me Generation Everyman."[70]

Even when *Finding Nemo* uses meta-comedy, the scene further highlights Marlin's deviation from the Brooks persona. When other parents ask Marlin to tell a joke, presuming that he, as a clownfish, has to be particularly humorous, he begins to ramble incoherently and eventually fails to deliver a witty punchline. Contrary to the humor derived from such a moment of social awkwardness and meta-commentary in previous Brooks films, the ensuing silence in this moment emphasizes Marlin's inability to function within the social parameters of the reef community; he is not a character to be laughed at.

Figure 10.1 Marlin the clownfish (Brooks) tells a joke

Although Marlin eventually decides to leave his home in order to find his son, the journey through the Pacific worsens his anxieties. Together with his friend Dory, Marlin barely escapes the teeth of rampaging, albeit good-hearted, vegetarian sharks and hostile, carnivorous sea creatures. While these life-threatening encounters strengthen Marlin's view of a hostile ocean world, his worries eventually lead the clownfish to act as violently. In his desire to reach Sydney, where Nemo is held captive, Marlin tricks Dory into traveling a shorter but highly dangerous path. Exploiting her inability to remember any short-term information, the clownfish leads his friends into a field of jellyfish. The venomous creatures quickly poison Dory with their trailing tentacles while Marlin, thanks to his partial immunity, easily passes through the soft-bodied animals. At the last moment, the clownfish realizes his mistake and saves Dory, but the scene encapsulates both the "narcissistic and controlling" yet simultaneously "insecure and resigned" sides of Marlin's character. The film avoids mocking the clownfish, his idiosyncrasies, or the sheltered quality of middle-class life, however, by animating Marlin's motivation for manipulating Dory and exposing her to a life-threatening situation. In showing the rationale behind his fear and egoism, *Finding Nemo* invites sympathies for a traumatized father struggling to find his son in an environment he experiences as deeply hostile and frightening.

The near-death experience as much as the destructive consequences of his actions lead Marlin to question his behavior. From that moment on, *Finding Nemo* shifts in tone once more as Marlin eventually transcends his anxieties by bonding with friendly turtles, giant whales, and helpful albatrosses who all help the clownfish to re-unite with his son.[71] Marlin, Dory, and Nemo do more

Figure 10.2 Marlin (Brooks) lies to Dory (Ellen DeGeneres) to get through the jellyfish

than come home to the coral reef. When Marlin eventually shares a funny joke with his friends and neighbours, he appears to have learned to cope with his traumatic experiences. With its merry return to the status quo, *Finding Nemo* is anything but a critique of the American myth of suburban life. In fact, animating the fragility and vulnerability of middle-class fatherhood after an assault on the suburban home, *Finding Nemo* engages not in ideological critique but in cultural work through Albert Brooks's voice acting.

In telling the story of an anxious-ridden father who faces his fears after a traumatizing attack, *Finding Nemo* appears to mediate the cultural climate of its production context. At the time, American culture was still wrestling with its experience of vulnerability after the terrorist attacks on September 11, 2001. While the shock fostered a climate of imperialist jingoism and masculine bravado in American society,[72] *Finding Nemo* animates the possibility to cope with experiences of anxiety and vulnerability in the journey Marlin undertakes. To do so, the film utilizes the suburban allusions of the Brooks persona but minimize its meta-comedy quality. The absence of self-referential humor from the Brooks character illustrates one example of a "sincerity that avoids any sort of irony or eclecticism"[73] and thereby resonates with prevalent notions about the role of fiction after the attacks of September 11 when commentators diagnosed an "end of irony" and even the "death of postmodernism."[74] In blending the trauma of violence with his reference to (a mostly absent meta-comedy critique of) middle-class suburbia, the "intertextual density" of the Brooks persona addresses those viewers familiar with its previous characterization and simultaneously responds to the climate of anxiety and hostility in post-9/11 America. As Marlin learns to overcome his fears of the outside world, sees the consequences of his (unintentionally) cruel actions, and befriends a "virtual ocean menagerie of cooperative species," *Finding Nemo* further envisions an alternative to the unilateral politics of the "War on Terror" the United States pursued after September 11. Given the history of the Brooks persona, the figure of the clownfish father, to adapt Colleen Montgomery, "becomes a semiotic tether which [. . .] sutures the abstract animated character"[75] to the cultural climate after September 11 and to the baby boomer generation in particular.[76]

Such a sweeping reading of *Finding Nemo* and its audience, however, needs to acknowledge the overwhelming whiteness of a film set in the southern hemisphere in which all characters are "marked as anything other than white and Western (based on the voice-over dialects, our knowledge of the actors who perform those voices)."[77] Contrary to the idea that Brooks has been "tracking the baby boomer thing," the cultural work of the Brooks persona is limited in scope because he cannot capture the diverse experiences of all people from that generation. Most obviously, neither the barriers of segregation nor patriarchy impacted a white, male performer as immediately as others from his cohort.[78] In a climate of imperialist chauvinism and male backlash, the Brooks persona hence embodies the white, male privilege of being seen as the American "Everyman," yet also animates an obliviousness to the vicious consequences of his trauma and egoism until almost too late.

Even as the cultural work of the Brooks persona did not bear fruits since the Bush administration and a majority of Americans did not opt for an introspective approach at the time, *Finding Nemo* challenged the predominant cultural climate of its production period. Brooks-as-Marlin voiced the sincerity of the early 2000s, yet also maintained a link to the depressing qualities of suburban American life his previous work satirized. In doing so, Marlin functions as an adaptation of the Brooks persona for the post-9/11 era and allowed *Finding Nemo* to speak critically to the parents and grandparents in its audience.

From the perspective of star studies, the introduction of fatherhood as well as the shift from meta-comedy to sincerity add further complexity to the Brooks persona. In this sense, *Finding Nemo* exemplifies a (potential) turning point for Brooks expanding the range of his persona. Instead of radically breaking with his previous work, *Finding Nemo* adopts and carefully expands his persona. Whether and how this transformation played out only an examination of Brooks's following works and productions can tell.

NOTES

1. Albert Brooks, dir. *Lost in America*; US: Warner Bros., 1985, film. David Sims, "The Brutal Cynicism of *Lost in America* Still Resonates," *The Atlantic*, July 25, 2017. Available at <https://www.theatlantic.com/entertainment/archive/2017/07/lost-in-america-albert-brooks-criterion/534777/> (last accessed January 14, 2021).
2. Sims, "The Brutal Cynicism."
3. John Powers, "Albert Brooks' *Lost in America* Remains Piercingly Relevant 32 Years Later," *NPR*, August 7, 2017. Available at <http://www.npr.org/2017/08/07/542028917/albert-brooks-lost-in-america-remains-piercingly-relevant-32-years-later?platform=hootsuite/> (last accessed January 14, 2021).
4. Gavin Smith, "All the Choices: Albert Brooks Interview," *Film Comment* 35, no. 4 (July/August 1999). Available at <https://www.filmcomment.com/article/all-the-choices-albert-brooks-interview/> (last accessed 7 January 2021).
5. Smith, "All the Choices."
6. Smith, "All the Choices."
7. Margy Rochlin, "A Funnyman Whose Muse Is in the Mirror." *The New York Times*, August 22, 1999. Available at <http://www.nytimes.com/1999/08/22/movies/film-a-funnyman-whose-muse-is-in-the-mirror.html/> (last accessed January 14, 2021).
8. Rochlin, "A Funnyman."
9. Johnson quoted in Rochlin, "A Funnyman."
10. Sims, "The Brutal Cynicism."
11. Powers, "Albert Brooks' *Lost in America* Remains."
12. Smith, "All the Choices."
13. Smith, "All the Choices."
14. Andrew Stanton and Lee Unkrich, dirs. *Finding Nemo*; US: Pixar, 2003, film.

15. Smith, "All the Choices."
16. I loosely borrow this term from what Jim Collins dubbed the "New Sincerity genre." See Jim Collins, "Genericity in the Nineties: Eclectic Irony and the New Sincerity." In *Film Theory Goes to the Movies*, ed. Jim Collins, Hilary Radner, and Ava Preacher Collins (New York Routledge, 1993), 242–64. While a reading of *Finding Nemo* as part of this "New Sincerity genre" is beyond the scope of this chapter, the previous list also indicates some of the potential pitfalls of categorizing the Pixar film as such. David Foster Wallace examines American television to similarly introduce a notion of "new sincerity" as the absence of irony. I thank Rafael Azevedo for drawing my attention to the concept. See David Foster Wallace, "E Unibus Pluram: Television and U.S. Fiction," *A Supposedly Fun Thing I'll Never Do Again: Essays and Arguments* (Boston: Little Brown, 1997).
17. Collins, "Genericity in the Nineties," 243.
18. Fittingly, scholars have also registered a general fascination with the 1950s at Pixar Studios. Jason Sperb in *Flickers of Film: Nostalgia in the Time of Digital Cinema* (New Brunswick, NJ: Rutgers University Press, 2016) or Colleen Montgomery in "Woody's Roundup and Wall-E's Wunderkammer: Technophilia and Nostalgia in Pixar Animation," *Animation Studies Online Journal* 6 (September 2, 2011), available at <https://journal.animationstudies.org/?s=colleen+montgomery> (last accessed January 14, 2021) are only two of the examples that explore the omnipresence of the 1950s in many Pixar films.
19. Barbara Klinger, "Digressions at the Cinema: Reception and Mass Culture." *Cinema Journal* 28, no. 4 (1989): 5.
20. Jack Halberstam, *The Queer Art of Failure* (Durham, NC: Duke University Press, 2011), 80.
21. I refer to cultural rather than ideological work because critical debates since the 1960s have highlighted the predetermining logic inherent in the idea of cinema as an ideological apparatus. While the study of stardom explores the tensions a star persona manages to conceal and asks about its "ideological function" (Martin Barker, "Introduction," *Contemporary Hollywood Stardom*, ed. Martin Barker and Thomas Austin [London: Bloomsbury, 2003], 6), scholarship also explores the failures to resolve the inherent tensions. As star studies furthermore pay particular attention to audience responses and explore the manifold ways in which viewers and fans participate in the meaning production of a star, the notion of cultural work captures the openness and volatility of stardom as a text. See Barker and Austin "Introduction," *Contemporary Hollywood Stardom*.
22. Richard Dyer, *Stars* (London: Palgrave Macmillan, 1998), 1.
23. Dyer, *Stars*, 35, 20.
24. Dyer, *Stars*, 20.
25. Dyer, *Stars*, 35.
26. Richard Dyer, *Heavenly Bodies: Film Stars and Society* (London: Macmillan Education Ltd, 1987), 3.
27. Dyer, *Heavenly Bodies*, 2–3.
28. Su Holmes, "'Starring . . . Dyer?': Re-visiting Star Studies and Contemporary Celebrity Culture," *Westminster Papers in Communication and Culture* 2, no. 2 (2015): 9.
29. Holmes, "Re-visiting Star Studies," 9.
30. Christine Geraghty, "Re-Examining Stardom: Questions of Texts, Bodies and Performances," in *Reinventing Film Studies*, ed. Christine Gledhill and Linda Williams (New York: Oxford University Press, 2000), 187.
31. Barry King, "Stardom, Celebrity, and the Money Form," *The Velvet Light Trap* 65 (2010): 9.
32. King, "Stardom, Celebrity, and the Money Form," 9.

33. King, "Stardom, Celebrity, and the Money Form," 9. With the collapse of the studio system in Hollywood, stars became increasingly individual entrepreneurs having "to labour, as 'sub-contractors' [. . .] maintaining and upgrading their personae" (Barker, "Introduction," *Contemporary Hollywood Stardom*, 4). For a detailed introduction to the historical development of the star persona in the context of the changing modes of production in Hollywood see Barker and Austin, *Contemporary Hollywood Stardom*, and Barry King "Stardom as an Occupation," in *The Hollywood Film Industry: A Reader*, ed. Paul Kerr (London: Routledge, 1986), 154–94.
34. Pam Cook, "Revisiting Performance: Nicole Kidman's Enactment of Stardom," in *Revisiting Star Studies: Cultures, Themes and Methods*, ed. Sabrina Qiong Yu and Guy Austin (Edinburgh: Edinburgh University Press, 2017), 25.
35. Cook, "Revisiting Performance," 27.
36. On social media, Brooks has about 1.7 million followers on Twitter to date. While his profile admits to joining in the desire to "promote my book" and mentions of his work appear in-between, his postings primarily comment on current political events. While Brooks thereby continues to build his star persona, the account neither advances any discernable promotional campaigns nor provides glimpses into his "private" life.
37. Smith, "All the Choices."
38. Geraghty, "Re-Examining Stardom," 189.
39. Geraghty, "Re-Examining Stardom," 190.
40. Barry King, "Articulating Stardom," *Screen* 26, no. 5 (1985): 30.
41. Geraghty, "Re-Examining Stardom," 190–1. The "repertory or Broadway style" (Dyer, *Stars*, 156) is the counterpart to the professionalism of the Hollywood studio style or personification. In the former "a clear distinction between actor and character" (Dyer, *Stars* 156) exists.
42. Smith, "All the Choices."
43. Brooks quoted in Smith, "All the Choices."
44. Geraghty, "Re-Examining Stardom," 189.
45. Geraghty, "Re-Examining Stardom," 191.
46. Dyer, *Heavenly Bodies*, 12.
47. Dyer, *Heavenly Bodies*, 8.
48. Dyer, *Heavenly Bodies*, 5.
49. Barker, "Introduction," 6, 14.
50. Holmes, "Re-visiting Star Studies," 8.
51. Barker, "Introduction," 13. Consequentially, I prefer to refer to cultural rather than ideological work, as critical debates since the 1960s have highlighted the predetermining logic inherent in the idea of cinema as an ideological apparatus.
52. Colleen Montgomery, "Pixarticulation: Vocal Performance in Pixar Animation," *Music, Sound, and the Moving Image* 10, no. 1 (2016): 9.
53. Montgomery, "Pixarticulation," 16.
54. Klinger, "Digressions at the Cinema," 5.
55. William Whittington, "The Sonic Playpen: Sound Design and Technology in Pixar's Animated Shorts," in *The Oxford Handbook of Sound Studies*, ed. Karin Bijsterveld and Trevor J. Pinch (Oxford: Oxford University Press, 2013), 383.
56. Sims, "The Brutal Cynicism."
57. Montgomery, "Pixarticulation," 15, 16. In his essay "Performance Design: An Analysis of Film Acting and Sound Design" (2006), Starr Marcello demonstrates how these considerations are already part of the casting process (see Marcello, "Performance Design: An Analysis of Film Acting and Sound Design," *Journal of Film and Video* 58, no. 1/2 [2006]: 64). The decision to cast famous stars as lead voice-actors in animated

film is, however, a fairly recent phenomenon: For a look at Brooks's contribution to this development through his work in *The Simpsons*, see the introduction to this volume.
58. David Whitley, *The Idea of Nature in Disney Animation* (Aldershot: Ashcroft, 2008), 130.
59. Suzan G. Brydon, "Men at the Heart of Mothering: Finding Mother in *Finding Nemo*," *Journal of Gender Studies* 18, no. 2 (2009): 138.
60. Lynne Dickson Bruckner, "*Bambi* and *Finding Nemo*: A Sense of Wonder in the Wonderful World of Disney?" in *Framing the World: Explorations in Ecocriticism and Film*, ed. Paula Willoquet-Maricondi (Charlottesville: University of Virginia Press, 2010), 196.
61. Smith, "All the Choices."
62. Although *Finding Nemo* is the second film to portray a Brooks character as a father, in contrast to *The Muse* (1999), the animated film centers around the father-son relationship.
63. Montgomery, "Pixarticulation," 14.
64. Smith, "All the Choices."
65. Whitley, *The Idea of Nature*, 130.
66. Brydon, "Men at the Heart of Mothering," 139.
67. Brydon, "Men at the Heart of Mothering," 139.
68. Brydon, "Men at the Heart of Mothering," 139.
69. Stanton and Unkrich, dirs, *Finding Nemo*.
70. Smith, "All the Choices."
71. Halberstam highlights the vital role Dory plays in finding Nemo and helping Marlin to transcend his anxieties about the ocean world: "Dory is not relegated to the margins of the story but ends up 'knowing' all kinds of things that go against received wisdom but that facilitate Marlin's quest to find his son. So while Dory suffers from short-term memory loss, she also reads human texts, speaks whale, charms sharks, and understands the primacy of friends over family" (79).
72. Susan Faludi, *The Terror Dream: Fear and Fantasy in Post-9/11 America* (New York: Metropolitan Books, 2007), 1–15; and Naomi Klein, *The Shock Doctrine: The Rise of Disaster Capitalism* (New York: Metropolitan/Henry Holt, 2007), 3–23.
73. Collins, "Genericity in the Nineties," 257.
74. See Birgit Däwes, *Ground Zero Fiction: History, Memory, and Representation in the American 9/11 Novel* (Heidelberg: Universitätsverlag Winter GmbH, 2011), 10.
75. Montgomery, "Pixarticulation," 8.
76. The "intertextual density" of the Brooks persona further complicates any straightforward equation of the Pixar film with the predominant ideology of its production period. See, for example, Bob Rehak, "2003: Movies, 'Shock and Awe,' and the Troubled Blockbuster," in *American Cinema of the 2000s: Themes and Variations*, ed. Timothy Corrigan (New Brunswick, NJ: Rutgers University Press, 2012), 83–103.
77. Brydon, "Men at the Heart of Mothering," 135.
78. For an extensive examination of the challenges black performers and women of color face in building their star persona in Hollywood, see Diane Negra *Off-White Hollywood* (New York: Routledge, 2001), contributions to *Revisiting Star Studies: Cultures, Themes and Methods* (2017) ed. Sabrina Qiong Yu and Guy Austin, or Richard Dyer's analysis of Paul Robeson in *Heavenly Bodies* (1987).

CHAPTER II

Debt, Payback, and Economics in Nicolas Winding Refn's *Drive*

Tom Ue

In an interview regarding Nicolas Winding Refn's *Drive* (2011),[1] Albert Brooks describes his character Bernie Rose, formerly a film producer and now a full-time mobster:

> I would imagine that Bernie Rose probably had not been violent for 25 years. Probably had not had to actually physically take someone down for 25 years. And you know, once capable, always capable. But no longer, that wasn't his life. He had his nice life; he made his money, that's what he wanted ... he wanted his business. This was thrown into his lap, and he was more upset about that than anything. But obviously as he said, if he didn't do it, they'd take him down. So when it comes down to your life or his life, he chose his own life.[2]

Brooks's remarks provide us with a glimpse of yet another aspect of his extensive preparations for a performance, preparations that manifest in ways beyond physical transformation. For Bernie, he had a hairpiece made, adopted the flavor of a New York accent, created a tick whereby his character regularly blinks, and even removed his eyebrows.[3] Furthermore, Brooks's performance of, and back story for, Bernie suggest the propensity for monetary transactions to frame the film's understanding of individual agency and circumstances. According to Brooks, Bernie is pressured into violence as a means of self-preservation and he thus encourages us to think more about the story's financial exchanges.

Brooks's against-type performance is an important milestone. The film, both a critical and a commercial success, had its premiere at the Cannes Film Festival, where it won Best Director; and it went on to earn nominations from the British Academy Film Awards for Best Film, Best Supporting Actress (Carey Mulligan), Best Editing, and Best Director. For his performance, Brooks earned his first Golden Globe nomination and he was recognized with accolades from major professional organizations including the Austin Film Critics Association, the Boston Society of Film Critics Awards, the National Society of Film Critics Awards, and the New York Film Critics Circle Awards. In this chapter, I reveal how primary Bernie is to *Drive* notwithstanding his limited share of narrative time, and how Bernie makes pronounced the challenges of successfully reconciling with the story's criminal system. My central claim is that Bernie's narrative offers fresh commentary on Driver's and that, by attending more closely to the mobster, we can learn more about both the central protagonist and his world. I begin by analyzing the dialogic relationship between the two characters; and I go on to argue that Refn uses Bernie's narrative to call into question both characters' autonomy and to offer insights into the film's understanding of monetary exchanges and its criminal world. I juxtapose *Drive* with *The Godfather* (1972, 1974, 1990) to show how Refn's borrowings and exploration of similar concerns help us understand both Driver's and Bernie's positions; and look ahead to Brooks's performance in J. C. Chandlor's *A Most Violent Year* (2014) to suggest the prevalence of monetary concerns in his more recent films.[4]

A getaway driver by night, Driver works, by day, as a stunt driver and as a mechanic for Shannon (Bryan Cranston). Near the start of the film, Shannon approaches Bernie for funds to get into the race car business, explaining to the mobster that he had only made $30,000 the previous year. Shannon wishes to buy a car for Driver, and he assures Bernie that they will be recompensed with millions once he is in the show. Meanwhile, in his new apartment, Driver befriends and becomes increasingly close to his neighbour Irene (Carey Mulligan) and her son Benicio (Kaden Leos). Irene's husband Standard (Oscar Isaac) is in prison. Shortly after Standard is released, Driver finds him badly beaten up by gangsters. He had owed $2,000 of protection money and the value of this debt has repeatedly multiplied until he is now pressured into robbing a pawnshop in the Valley. Despite an explicit warning, Driver decides to help Standard and his accomplice Blanche (Christina Hendricks). During the heist, Standard is killed, while Driver and Blanche escape with a million dollars. They are ambushed and the latter is killed. Driver murders the attackers and sends a message to Cook (James Biberi) and Bernie's mobster partner Nino (Ron Perlman) that he has the money and wishes to return it. Private conversations between Bernie and Nino, to which I will return, trace this money to the East Coast mob, who had set up and who continue to patronize Bernie and Nino. Bernie attempts to take control of the situation by killing all those involved with this robbery. Driver's motivations may differ from Bernie's—he hopes to keep Irene and Benicio safe—but his means are largely the same.

Driver tracks down and kills Nino. The end of the film finds Driver driving away after he kills Bernie, leaving behind the money, and it remains unclear whether or not he survives the wound inflicted by the mobster.

At first glance, Driver and Bernie seem substantially different. Driver is "a nameless, past-less, future-less character often hidden behind masks, shades, the theatrical costumery for the film parts he plays, or—if nothing else—Gosling's impassive gaze."[5] By contrast, as we have seen, Brooks had imagined a past for Bernie. Driver's name implies movement and agency; and as Michael Gott writes, "all four of [Driver's] pursuits are linked quite literally to mobility and allow the film to explore the variety of ways in which mobility is experienced, consumed, and aspired to in contemporary American culture."[6] Driver is comfortably in control from the start, the establishing sequence dramatizing multiple senses of the term "drive." It means, for instance, "[t]o force (living beings) to move on or away"; "[t]o carry on vigorously, 'push,' prosecute, conduct, practise, exercise (a custom, trade, etc.); to carry through or out, to effect; to bring to a settlement, conclude (a bargain);" and "[t]o go through, endure, pass, prolong."[7] Synchronized with a cacophony of Chromatics' "Tick of the Clock," sounds of cars whizzing by, and sirens from police cars, he dictates his terms on a disposable phone in the opening sequence, as the camera surveys the room through a tracking shot, moving from a map of downtown LA with copious annotations, to Driver in a medium shot, to a television set showing the basketball game, to his duffle bag, and finally to a view of the city through his window. "There's 100,000 streets in this city," Driver says,

> You don't need to know the route. You give me a time and a place, I give you a five-minute window. Anything happens in that five minutes and I'm yours. No matter what. Anything happens a minute either side of that and you're on your own. Do you understand? Good. And you won't be able to reach me on this phone again.

As both the driver and the watch, he assures his passengers of his reliability providing that his instructions are precisely followed, and in the very next scene, we see him positioned behind the wheel. During the heist, Driver will drive California's most popular car—a late model, silver Chevy Impala, what Shannon calls a "Plain Jane Boring"—so that he can better camouflage; and he will effortlessly weave past police cars and helicopters alike. By contrast, Bernie, the money behind Shannon's racecourse project, moves more sparingly. The mobster operates from Nino's Pizzeria in two of his eight sets of scenes. In the others, he watches Driver on a racetrack; visits Shannon at his garage twice; cleans and puts away the knife with which he kills Shannon; is phoned by Driver; and in a pair of scenes in a single location, confronts Driver at a Chinese restaurant and in its parking lot.

Yet the film's effective play on doubles dispels such superficial differences. Doubling is instantiated by our very first glimpse of Driver in a reflection on the window. That he is faced away from us so that we see Gosling's face only through the mirrored image makes apparent his obscurity as a character, while foregrounding the insights that can be gained through exploration of this narrative device. Instances of doubles multiply, one being Driver's and Bernie's reluctance to resort to violence. Our first indication of Driver's brutality comes quite late, when, at a diner, he encounters a former passenger who now offers him a job. Both the greeting and the promise of a heist violate Driver's terms: his use of a disposable phone is meant to disengage himself from further communication. Driver replies: "How about this? You shut your mouth. Or I'll kick your teeth down your throat and I'll shut it for you." The ferocity of Gosling's expression, on which the camera dwells, moves the thief to utter hastily, before leaving, "Nice seeing you again." If, in this instance of delayed decoding, we perceive his reluctance to resort to violence, then, in Bernie, we find a useful analogue. Brooks describes in greater detail the backstory that he had invented for Bernie and that he had shared with Refn:

> Well, Bernie grew up with Nino . . . the only two Jews in an Italian neighborhood. And, I would say, never rose to any real important level [in the crime world], made enough money where he came out to Hollywood and, as he said, he made movies but not for the glory of the movies but because there was some money in it. You could turn a profit. You make these cheap exploitation films and you could make a hundred grand and you're done. And that didn't go well. We always thought that Bernie was divorced, that he had two kids that never came out anymore, grown kids that he just basically didn't talk to. I mean, I could go on and on. I thought he had two hookers that he probably saw regularly.
>
> One of the things that I thought was interesting was exporting cars illegally, cause that's a very big business. Range Rovers in China sell for a quarter of a million dollars and you're not legally allowed to go buy a Mercedes in Manhattan and send it to Singapore, but you can do that with some manipulation. So that, and loaning money, a very staid, quiet life. That's why the violence in this movie, that is so irritating that it has to come to him. He's not getting up looking for these issues. He's upset about it.[8]

In material not shown in the film, Bernie is revealed to reside "on Wilshire Boulevard, near downtown Los Angeles, in one of these old, grand apartment buildings that still have beautiful architecture."[9] Driver, we might think, has similarly adopted a "staid, quiet" lifestyle and, notwithstanding his effectiveness, his violence is in response to his urge to protect Irene and Benicio just as

Bernie's is to himself and Nino. The juxtaposition of Driver and Bernie makes especially pronounced the limited amount of control that they seem to have: Bernie aims to repair the damages wrought by Nino, whereas Driver's desire for anonymity is derailed, as we have seen, by a chance encounter. The proximity of Bernie and Driver is suggested, furthermore, through the film's treatment of handshakes, an event that occurs or is evoked in three pivotal scenes. The two characters first meet in a racetrack where Driver shows off his driving skills to encourage Bernie's investment. Following a successful demonstration, Driver initially declines Bernie's offer to shake his hand: "My hands are a little dirty." Refn puns on the senses of dirty as "[c]haracterized by the presence of dirt; soiled with dirt; foul, unclean, sullied," and "[m]orally unclean or impure; 'smutty'."10 Where Driver refers to the former sense, Bernie clearly has the latter in mind when he replies, "So are mine." From Bernie's vantage point, the camera takes the position of a high-angle shot, with Bernie looking down at Driver (Figure 11.1); but interestingly, the characters appear much closer together and to stand in equal footing from Driver's point-of-view (Figure 11.2). What appears to be a continuity error is a revealing instance of their proximity. After Bernie and Shannon agree on the terms of the former's support, Bernie refuses to shake Shannon's hand—only to do so in a later scene, when Bernie takes advantage of this gesture to slit Shannon's wrist. Finally, in the confrontation at the Chinese restaurant, Bernie suggests that they shake hands over their deal and that Driver return the money before driving away. However, both Bernie and Driver will seize this opportunity, ostensibly one for reconciliation, to carry out their assassination attempts.

Bernie operates as our vantage point into the film's criminal world. When he first visits Shannon's garage with Nino to inspect their car, he asks Driver how he is, when their first race is, and if he is going to be ready. Bernie takes

Figure 11.1 The handshake between Bernie (Brooks) and Driver (Ryan Gosling) from their different viewpoints

Figure 11.2 The handshake between Bernie (Brooks) and Driver (Ryan Gosling) from their different viewpoints.

Driver's brief responses as evidence of "false modesty," spurring him, after a pause, to recount how he and Shannon had first met:

> I used to produce movies. In the 80s. Kind of like action films. Sexy stuff. One critic called them European. I thought they were shit. Anyway, he arranged all the cars for me. Did all the stunts. I liked him. I liked having him around. Even though he overcharged the shit out of me. His next business venture, he got involved with some of Nino's friends. They didn't go for the overcharging bit. They broke his pelvis. He's never had a lot of luck. The reason I'm telling you this is that he has a lot invested in you. And so do I.

In this often discussed scene, Bernie may be turning to the past to explain how important Driver is to them, but what he says is ironic and deprives Driver of some individuality: Driver is replacing the now retired Shannon, and at different stages in their careers, they stand in for film actors by performing dangerous feats. As Shannon says to Driver prior to telling him that the director wanted a roll over: "You're doubling for the star. You're not a day player or anything." This instance of triple deferral—from the character to the actor, from the actor to Shannon, and from Shannon to Driver—exposes how dispensable Driver is and the limited amount of autonomy that he has. Todd McGowan's arguments regarding agency and capitalism are relevant here:

> Though subjects within the capitalist universe experience themselves as free (free to make money, free to consume what they want, and so on), the system spares them the weight of the decision. We make numerous decisions every day concerning what to do, where to go, and what to buy,

but none of these decisions occurs outside the confines of the narrow limits of our given possibilities."

In fact, when Shannon first proposed his project to Bernie, and assures him that they will be more successful than the big professional race teams because they have "the driver," Bernie's lack of enthusiasm arises out of Driver's very replaceability: "You just told me they had half a dozen drivers." After all, Driver is not, by name at least, individualized. This constant threat of becoming substituted threatens Driver, who, should he fail to deliver Shannon's promises, would be overcharging Bernie. Bernie may insist to Driver that "We're a team now," assuring him of support and protection, but he had once failed to help Shannon. In fact, Shannon continues to live with the injuries that he had sustained. It is unsurprising, then, that the meeting leaves Driver visibly worried as Bernie ushers away Nino.

For all his swagger, Bernie is similarly re/displaceable. The conflict between the East Coast mob and Bernie's on the West Coast is an informing presence. As Gabrielle O'Brien writes, all of the male characters have criminal connection and are familiar "with violence as a means of power and control."[12] During the heist at the start of the film, Driver hears, on the police dispatch, of a possible gang shooting-in-progress in another area; and Bernie mentions to Shannon, in passing, that the city sees 2,000 heists a year. Justin Vicari sums up the film's setting succinctly:

> Refn's mostly unglamorous L.A. is vaguely dystopian, presided over by a West-coast Jewish mafia network who take their orders from the East-coast Italian heads of the family, and are therefore driven by a frustrated "second-rank" status. Bitterness curdles the air around these glorified Bagmen, Bernie Rose ... and Nino ... ersatz and deracinated, eating Chinese takeout in the little pizza joint that they use as a front.[13]

By attending to Bernie's and Nino's interactions, we are privileged to their insecurities, insights to which Driver is not. Nino explains to Bernie (and us) that the heist money comes from the East Coast mob. When the incredulous Bernie wonders at Nino's audacity, Nino explains: "No. I stole from some jumped-up punk who was trying to step on our action." Bernie tells Nino that they are now deeply involved, and that their lives would be endangered should it be discovered that Nino had stolen from the family, in response to which Nino protests: "What fucking family? The family who still calls me a fucking kike! To my face! Yeah, I'm 59 years old, Bernie. They still pinch my cheek like I'm some fucking kid. Family." This conversation, as Vicari has argued, registers the mobsters' frustrations, which emanate at least partially from the knowledge that their positions are threatened and that they will be displaced imminently by a new generation of West Coast mobsters. If Bernie had suggested to Driver that his role is replaceable, then this vulnerability extends similarly towards Nino and himself. The family metaphor—analogous to the "team" one that Bernie employs—offers no security, notwithstanding Bernie's and Nino's years of committed service. Bernie intimates as much when he reminds Nino: "The money always flows up, Izzy. You know that."

The concentrated energy here—on both the dispensability of people and the social organization of a criminal world populated by doubles—is more prominent than that we find in Walter Hill's *The Driver* (1978), both an important influence and a useful point of contrast.[14] The earlier film involves a battle of wits between The Detective (Bruce Dern) and The Driver (Ryan O'Neal), where the former banks his career on the apprehension of the latter. In a crucial scene, The Driver's accomplice The Player (Isabelle Adjani) accuses him of wanting to prevail over The Detective rather than to benefit materially from a bank robbery, to which the Driver confesses: "I might even mail [the money] to him."[15] On screen at least, Driver shares this indifference towards the pecuniary: he leaves behind the money after all. *Drive* is closer to, and in fact evokes, *The Godfather* (1972) in its understanding of organized crime. In a scene that appears in *Drive*'s screenplay, but not the film, Driver tells Irene that he is leaving and that he hopes Irene and Benicio would join him: he promises to leave behind his criminal past after he "straighten[s] out this thing" and that they will go somewhere. Irene is not optimistic: "It doesn't work like that. . . . Because people like you never get out. And I don't want my son to grow up like that . . ."[16] In the film, Irene never gets an opportunity to respond to Driver's offer. Driver and Irene are attacked in an elevator, and Irene watches in horror as Driver, after kissing her, violently attacks and kills the assailant.[17] O'Brien has usefully drawn attention to the lighting techniques that liken the two men:

> [Driver's] intention is to shield [Irene] from the threatening stranger even though he is visually inscribed as part of the noir tradition. The men are matched to the lift's color palette; their jackets both reflect and mirror the light inside the elevator and the browns of its newly claustrophobic interior.[18]

The closing of the elevator doors alludes to *The Godfather*, which frequently finds Kay (Diane Keaton) distanced from Michael (Al Pacino) physically and emotionally. Midway through the film, Michael encloses himself in a telephone booth, and thus shuts out Kay, when he calls Sonny (James Caan) after learning that their father Vito (Marlon Brando) had been shot. In the film's iconic ending, Kay is again shut out of Michael's and his family's meeting after he promises her that he had no hand in his brother-in-law Carlo's (Gianni Russo) murder. The trilogy makes persistent reference to closing doors: in *The*

Godfather: Part II (1974), Michael shuts the door on Kay when she visits their children; and in *The Godfather: Part III* (1990), Kay watches as Michael discusses retaliation for Tommasino's (Vittorio Duse) murder and disparages over his promises, and his inability, to change. What is striking about this final scene is that it is Kay who walks out of the frame. Such barriers do not entirely mitigate the damage Michael wrought on Kay. She is attracted to, as much as she is repulsed, scared, and ultimately hurt by, his criminal activities: their daughter (Sofia Coppola) dies in the final instalment.

Following Shannon's and Nino's deaths, Bernie offers to meet Driver, explaining to him, "Well, you, me, and your girlfriend are the only players left." At the Chinese restaurant, the mobster tells Driver:

> Here's what I'm prepared to offer. You give me the money, the girl is safe. Forever. Nobody knows about her. She's off the map. I can't offer you the same. So, this is what I would suggest. We conclude our deal. We'll shake hands. You start the rest of your life. Any dreams you have, or plans, or hopes for your future . . . I think you're going to have to put that on hold. For the rest of your life you're going to be looking over your shoulder. I'm just telling you this because I want you to know the truth. But the girl is safe.

What is ironic about these two scenes is how Bernie singles out the stakeholders and how he is dictating the terms of their exchange: the refrain on "I" and "you" firmly establishes their subject positions—in ways analogous to Driver's opening monologue where he sets out his five-minute rule. Yet Bernie is in no position to make such offers, and Driver does not know this: when he questioned Cook regarding who the money belongs to, he was merely assured, "Don't worry. They're going to come get it." Cook finally directs Driver to Nino. We can read Driver's leaving behind the stolen money as his rejection of the mobster activities and his attempt to bring an end to the trail of crime that brought it to the East Coast. Bernie's and Nino's deaths belie significant regeneration: they serve only to hasten the new guard's arrival, ushering in the new doppelgängers who will replace them. Edgar Wright's recent film *Baby Driver* (2017) harkens back to *Drive*: the getaway driver Baby (Ansel Elgort) is coerced into rejoining Doc's (Kevin Spacey) operations even after he repays his debt, so that he too is unsuccessful in his attempt to start afresh.[19] But the films differ in significant ways: *Baby Driver* shifts our attention from money to romance: Doc is sufficiently moved by Baby and Debora (Lily James), the latter is a waitress like Irene, and by his own experiences with love to help them in their attempt to escape Buddy (Jon Hamm), who seeks vengeance for his lover Darling's (Eiza González) death.[20] Doc's warning recalls Bernie's: "The good news is you like driving, because you can't take your foot off the gas for the next

25 years." Shannon's and Standard's examples dispel the notion of emancipation. When Nino provokingly asks Shannon how his leg is, Shannon replies, "I paid my debt." Of course, his limp forcefully reminds him (and us) of how he continues to pay for it. Standard never gets his second chance despite Driver's attempt to make a pact: "When you get your money, his debt's paid. He's out for good. And you never go near his family again." In fact, Bernie promises Driver that, even if the money is repaid, he will always be hunted. In light of the film's many doubles, we might wonder, what are the West Coast mobsters the doubles of?

In *A Most Violent Year*, a more recent film similarly structured around monetary exchanges, Brooks plays the lawyer Andrew Walsh who shares many of the challenges faced by the central protagonist Abel Morales (Oscar Isaac). Brooks's performance was largely unrecognized, though the film earned awards in top categories from the National Board of Review, including Best Picture, Best Actor, and Best Supporting Actress (Jessica Chastain). *Year* opens in New York in 1981, and we are immersed, early in the film, in a climate of perpetual violence. A morning radio broadcast reports that three NYPD officers were shot in the span of an hour the night before, and in a subsequent scene, D.A. Lawrence (David Oyelowo) reports: "There were more murders and rapes in this city last year than there have ever been." *Year* introduces us to two storylines that routinely converge. Morales, with the help of Walsh, is signing an agreement to purchase land to expand his Standard Heating Oil Company; and Julian (Elyes Gabel), one of his truck drivers, is attacked by armed robbers and had his vehicle stolen. The character doubling is clear: both Morales and Julian are Latin American and, like Julian, Morales was once a driver. On the surface, Morales seems to epitomize the American Dream: he married Anna (Chastain), now his accountant; purchased his business from her father, a gangster; and, with his family, have become new occupants of a large house. After paying his deposit, Morales has thirty days to deliver the remaining sum, but he is pressured on multiple fronts. The attack on Julian is one of a series of truck robberies and Morales has taken substantial losses in stolen fuel; meanwhile, Lawrence comes down on him with a 14-count indictment, including three pending legal cases and one with sixteen counts of misconduct ranging from fraud to tax evasion. The safety of Morales's home, furthermore, is compromised in ways more severe than it had been in the past. An intruder spies on the family and leaves behind a loaded gun with its safety switch off—which his daughter (Giselle Eisenberg) finds.[21] In defense, Morales's drivers begin to carry handguns illegally, and Julian becomes involved in a shoot-out. His successful escape from the authorities, combined with the indictments and the armed drivers, leads Morales's banker Arthur (John Procaccino) to deny him the capital to close the deal. He is pressured into borrowing from his competitor Saul (David Margulies) and his granddaughter (Annie Funke) and into mortgaging the house that he shares with his younger brother (Pico Alexander). Morales follows one of his hijacked trucks, learns where the hijackers have sold his oil, links it to his competitor Arnold (Glenn Fleshler), and successfully gains repayment from him. Finally, Morales uses the money that Anna had skimmed from the company over the years so that he no longer needs to borrow from the mafia. Erstwhile, Julian is brought to the police by Morales but he again escapes, only to return, after Morales completes the transaction, to commit suicide in front of Morales, Anna, and Walsh.

Morales's name implies morality but it leaves his moral stance unclear. Suggestions of his malpractice and his social Darwinism pepper the film. In a meeting between Morales, Walsh, and Lawrence, the D.A. categorically sums up Morales's and his competitors' business practice:

> As you know, we've been investigating industry-wide corruption in your business . . . that seems to have been going on for years. So you're right. That means you're all stealing from each other . . . which as far as I can tell is just a refreshing new take . . . on what you've been doing to your customers and fellow taxpayers . . . for the last fifteen years."

Morales may insist that his business operates differently, yet as Walsh tells Morales and Anna, after learning the nature of Lawrence's charges: "We've just pushed it a little too far, that's all. Let's look at it like a badge of honor. Huh? We're big enough now they even give a shit about us." Walsh and Morales are at one, and the latter's aggressiveness in his business dealings is gradually but prominently exposed. Throughout the film, he is routinely asked why he wishes to purchase the land which, after all, is a "polluted, dirty piece of earth." To Josef Mendelsohn (Jerry Adler), with whom he makes this deal, he replies enigmatically, "I imagine I want it for the same reason you did." Mendelsohn, however, operates a garment business and he had only inherited it from his uncle. When pressed about why he wishes to buy instead of rent, Morales replies, simply, "I like to own the things I use." To Walsh, Morales is scarcely more forthcoming: "That place has just been sitting right across that fence mocking me." Yet, at the dinner with Arthur and one of the bank's new VPs Ian Thompson (Jason Ralph), a meeting orchestrated by Walsh and from which he is notably absent, Morales confidently sums up its advantages:

> This property gives us many things. First, access to the river . . . so I can bring in my fuel directly from any provider in the world . . . straight to my tanks. Second, it has over 10 million gallons of storage capacity . . . so I can buy in the summers when the price is low . . . and sell to my customers and, more importantly, my competitors . . . when the price is high. I will no longer just drive trucks. I will control my fate.

The affordances of the property are recognized by at least one of Morales's competitors, "who," Mendelsohn relates, "has been after us almost as badly as you have." Morales triumphs only because of his contract's very favourable terms. In this meeting with Arthur and Ian, Morales demonstrates his ambition and foresight, qualities that are attractive to the bank, and also his competitiveness and his aggressiveness in displacing and replacing competitors. In taking control of his own fate, he is deciding that of his employees, his competitors, and those who work for them. Morales's survival-of-the-fittest mentality is also intimated in his treatment of his sales employees. During a demonstration for interns, Morales makes clear the competition in which they are embroiled on a day-to-day basis: "But the problem is, by hiring you . . . they need to fire someone else. And that's never easy. So after you show them the number . . . you look at them and stare. Stare longer than you should." When one of his employees snickers, he answers:

> This is not a joke. You will only keep this job if you close, and that's not funny to you. I'm only interested in this company growing . . . and when it isn't, it's not very funny to me at all. These people work very hard for their money. And these other guys are ripping them off . . . treating them poorly because they don't know. So when you look them in the eye . . . you have to believe that we are better.

Whether the services and the goods offered by Standard Heating Oil Company are, indeed, better or, as Lawrence claims, the entire industry is pervasively exploitative, Morales's teaching is imbricated with a threat. The statement beginning "These people work very hard" may be suggestive of sympathy with the potential customer, but this is a pretense: the statement concluding "believe we are better" indicates that this understanding is predicated on self-delusion and performance.

Morales is fierce towards his competitors. The assembly that he calls refers to *The Godfather*, where Vito brings together the heads of Five Families following the murder of Sonny. The parallel is used to remarkable effect here: Vito's move allows him both to learn that Emilio Barzini (Richard Conte) is his enemy and to brings peace, which enables Michael to return home safely to New York; but by the end of the film, Michael will order the murder of the heads of the rival families. In *A Most Violent Year*, Morales similarly works to supplant his competitors. Saul's granddaughter reminds Morales he had tried to buy their company. At the meeting, he demands his competitors to stop buying from or authorizing those stealing fuel from him; and when Morales insists that Arnold pay for all of the fuel that was stolen, Arnold claims that he had only bought some and that he may now be ruined. Morales goes so far as to confess: "My goal was to have you out of business by the end of next year. But if you're this fucking desperate . . . I imagine it won't even take that long." Walsh is an active participant in, and privy to the inner workings of, Morales's operations, even if their characters are different. In contrast to Morales, Walsh is more cautious and more strategic. As Morales and Walsh are about to meet Mendelsohn to sign the thirty-day agreement, Walsh says: "I woke up this morning feeling very good about this." Morales, however, reminds him that his support was not always consistent: "You've been telling me not to do this for two years." He urges Morales against overreaction when Lawrence makes clear his intent to bring a case against them and, when he discovers the nature of the charges, Walsh sets up the meeting with Albert to provide Morales with an opportunity to incite confidence in his investors. Walsh knows far more than Morales: he is privy to the plans of Bill (Peter Gerety), the head of the Teamsters, to arm Morales's drivers. He warns Morales of the effect that the attacks have on drivers and on the company's finances and, realizing that Bill can shut down their operations, tries to convince Morales to accept that they need to operate like gangsters. Walsh is similarly aware of Anna's stealing from their company, which he keeps from Morales. In fact, he anticipates Brooks's character, The Businessman, in Mark Osborne's *Le Petit Prince* (2015).[22] This character's utilitarianism is repressive and exploitative: he possesses stars and converts them from objects "that set lazy men to idle dreaming" into sources of energy. Brooks will win a shared Behind the Voice Actors Award for Best Vocal Ensemble in a TV Special/ Direct-to-DVD Title or Theatrical Short. In such performances, Brooks comments on both the central protagonist and the narrative proper, showing us that Morales and his competitors, and The Businessman and his supporters, much like Driver and the mobsters in *Drive*, are multiples of multiples.

NOTES

1. I am enormously grateful to Christian B. Long for his reading and commentary. Discussion with students in my "Self and Other in Literature and Film" course at the University of Toronto Scarborough in 2017 sharpened my thinking in numerous ways, as did conversations with presenters and audiences in the *Crime and the City* symposium at City University of London and the *Debt in History* conference at the University of Toronto Scarborough. I owe particular thanks to Christine Ferguson, Michael Saler, and Neil ten Kortenaar for their help, and to Todd McGowan for his insights and encouragement. I thank Frank Tong and the staff of Dalhousie University Libraries and the University of Toronto Libraries for their research help; and Dalhousie University, the Social Sciences and Humanities Research Council of Canada, and the University of Toronto Scarborough for their support. Nicholas Winding Refn, *Drive* (Montréal: Alliance Vivafilm, 2012), DVD. All references, unless indicated otherwise, are to the film.
2. Thomas Britt, "My Humor is Traced with Dark: An Interview with Drive's Albert Brooks," *Pop Matters*, November 15, 2011. Available at https://www.popmatters.com/151132-my-humor-is-traced-with-dark-an-interview-with-drives-albert-brooks-2495920015.html (last accessed January 14, 2021).

3. Kristopher Tapley, "Interview: Albert Brooks on 'Drive' As A Chance to Prove Something," *HitFix*, September 28, 2011. Available at <http://www.incontention.com/hitfix/2011/09/28/interview-albert-brooks-on-drive-as-a-chance-to-prove-something> (last accessed January 14, 2021). In his interview with Christopher Bell, Brooks comments on his preparation more generally: "I fill out the background of somebody. I make a chart—where this person went to school, who was his first girlfriend—just so when I'm sitting there that I have a background that I know about." Bell, "Albert Brooks Says He Knows His 'Drive' Character's Entire Backstory," *IndieWire*, September 16, 2011. Available at <https://www.indiewire.com/2011/09/albert-brooks-says-he-knows-his-drive-characters-entire-backstory-116293> (last accessed January 14, 2021).
4. Francis Ford Coppola, *The Godfather: 3-Movie Collection* (Hollywood: Paramount Pictures, 2014), DVD. J. C. Chandor, *A Most Violent Year* (Toronto: Elevation Pictures, [2015]), DVD.
5. Tim Edwards, "Lone Wolves: Masculinity, Cinema, and the Man Alone," in *The Routledge Companion to Media & Gender*, ed. Cynthia Carter, Linda Steiner, Lisa McLaughlin (Oxford and New York: Routledge, 2014), 46.
6. Michael Gott, "Between *Noir* and Sunshine: *Drive* As An Ambivalent Urban Road Movie," *Transfers* 2, no. 2 (Summer 2012): 139.
7. "Drive, v." *OED Online* (Oxford: Oxford University Press). According to Anna Backman Rogers and Miklós Kiss, Driver alternates "between being the agent of action as delineated by Deleuze as someone who always knows how to act, who is in command of the space he inhabits, and a not-quite 'seer'." Although he successfully navigates LA, "in the moments 'in between' he seems to come slowly to life." Rogers and Kiss, "A Real Human Being and a Real Hero: Stylistic Excess, Dead Time and Intensified Continuity in Nicolas Winding Refn's *Drive*," *New Cinemas: Journal of Contemporary Film* 12, no. 1&2 (June 2014): 53.
8. Mike Anton, "[Interview] Albert Brooks Discusses 'Drive'," *The Film Stage*, September 15, 2011. Available at <https://thefilmstage.com/interview-albert-brooks-discusses-drive/> (last accessed January 14, 2021).
9. Anton, "[Interview]."
10. "Dirty, adj. and adv." *OED Online* (Oxford: Oxford University Press).
11. Todd McGowan, *Capitalism and Desire: The Psychic Cost of Free Markets* (New York: Columbia University Press, 2016), 71.
12. Gabrielle O'Brien, "Hero in the Shadows: Film Noir, Fairytale and Postmodernism in Drive," *Screen Education* 79 (Spring 2015): 111.
13. Justin Vicari, *Nicolas Winding Refn and the Violence of Art: A Critical Study of the Films* (Jefferson, NC: McFarland, 2014), 181.
14. Walter Hill, dir. *The Driver* ([France]: The Corporation: L'Atelier d'Images, 2015), DVD.
15. Rogers and Kiss offer an insightful analysis of Refn's play on pastiche, and O'Brien on the convergence between fantasy and the film noir.
16. Hossein Amini, *Drive*, 64. Available at <https://www.scribd.com/document/319839165/Drive-Screenplay-by-Hossein-Amini> (last accessed January 14, 2021).
17. For a compelling discussion of this moment of narrative crisis, see Chapter 3 of McGowan's *Capitalism and Desire*. According to McGowan, this scene registers the impossibility of Drive's and Irene's co-existence; locates its gaze within the elevator; and criticizes violence in cinema through violence. I explore a similar tendency in: Tom Ue, "The Question of Closure in James Sallis' and Nicolas Winding Refn's *Drive*," *Journal of Adaptation in Film & Performance* 13, no. 1 (2020): 91–6.
18. O'Brien, "Hero in the Shadows," 116–17.
19. Edgar Wright, dir. *Baby Driver* (Culver City: Sony Pictures Home Entertainment, 2017), DVD.

20. As Garry Leonard has argued in his reading of genre romances *It Happened One Night* (1934) and *Pretty Woman* (1990), "The purpose of the Hollywood genre is to 'drive' the modern self from negotiation, which is a way of being in the modern market economy, to intimacy, which is a commercial-free oasis in this same sea." Leonard's terms may dexterously be applied to *Baby Driver*. Vulnerability, central to emotional intimacy, separates romance from pecuniary aspects of modernity: "In economic terms, intimacy offers something without certainty of reciprocity; intimacy does not ask for a receipt." I am grateful to my student Jesse Gosnell-Mowat for urging me to think about *Baby Driver* alongside *Drive*. See Leonard, "Let's Get Fiscal: Hollywood Romance and the Mechanism of the Self in Modernity," *Film International* 9 no. 5 (December 2011): 16, 20.
21. When Anna angrily reproaches Morales for saying that he "[wi]ll take care of it," she gestures towards a lengthier history of violence that has plagued the family: "It's not a brick through a car window . . . or another of the cute little warnings over the past few years."
22. Michael Osborne, dir. *Le Petit Prince* (Toronto: Entertainment One, [2016]), DVD.

Bibliography

Adler, Jerry et al. "The Year of the Yuppie." *Newsweek*, December 31, 1984.
Adorno, Theodor. *Critical Models*, trans. Henry Pickford. New York: Columbia University Press, 2005.
Amini, Hossein. *Drive*, September 24, 2010, <https://www.scribd.com/document/319839165/Drive-Screenplay-by-Hossein-Amini> (last accessed January 14, 2021).
Anderson, Paul Allen. "Neo-Muzak and the Business of Mood." *Critical Inquiry* 41 (Summer 2015): 811–40.
Anderson, Tim J. "Listening to the Promise of a Better You: Considering the Instructional Record." *Leonardo Music Journal* 26 (2016): 28–31.
Antin, David. *Talking*. Chicago: Dalkey Archive Press, 2001, 151.
Anton, Mike. "[Interview] Albert Brooks Discusses 'Drive.'" *The Film Stage*. September 15, 2011, <https://thefilmstage.com/interview-albert-brooks-discusses-drive/> (last accessed January 14, 2021).
Apatow, Judd. "Our Mr. Brooks." *Vanity Fair*, January 2013, <http://www.vanityfair.com/hollywood/2013/01/albert-brooks-this-is-40> (last accessed December 27, 2020).
Apatow, Judd. *Sick in the Head: Conversations About Life and Comedy*. New York: Random House, 2016.
"Arise, Ye Yuppies." *The New Republic*, July 9, 1984. 4+.
Arlen, Michael. "A Crack in the Greasepaint." *The New Yorker*, November 24, 1975, <https://www.newyorker.com/magazine/1975/11/24> (last accessed December 28, 2020).
Arnold, William. "Brook's 'Muslim World' Comedy is Hit-and-miss." *Seattle Post-Intelligencer*, January 19, 2006, <https://www.seattlepi.com/ae/movies/article/Brook-s-Muslim-World-comedy-is-hit-and-miss-1193212.php> (last accessed December 27, 2020).
Ausiello, Michael. "Weeds Scoop: Albert Brooks is Nancy's 'Dad'." *TV Guide*, April 14, 2008, <https://www.tvguide.com/news/weeds-scoop-albert-8084/> (last accessed December 27, 2020).
Austerlitz, Saul. *Another Fine Mess: A History of American Film Comedy*. Chicago: Chicago Review Press, 2010.
Barker, Martin. "Introduction," in *Contemporary Hollywood Stardom*, ed. Martin Barker and Thomas Austin, London: Bloomsbury, 2003, 1–24.

Barth, Jack. "Kinks of Comedy." *Film Comment* 20, no. 3 (May/June 1984), 44–7+.
Bell, Christopher. "Albert Brooks Says He Knows His 'Drive' Character's Entire Backstory." *IndieWire*. September 16, 2011, <https://www.indiewire.com/2011/09/albert-brooks-says-he-knows-his-drive-characters-entire-backstory-116293> (last accessed January 14, 2021).
Bell, Daniel. *The Cultural Contradictions of Capitalism*. New York: Basic Books, 1976.
Benchley, Robert. "Why We Laugh—Or Do We?" *The New Yorker*, January 2, 1937, 14.
Bettig, Ronald and Jeanne Lynn Hall. *Big Media, Big Money: Cultural Texts and Political Economics*. Lanham, MD: Rowman & Littlefield, 2012.
Bishop, Ryan. *Comedy and Cultural Critique in American Film*. Edinburgh: Edinburgh University Press, 2013.
Booker, M. Keith. *Dystopian Literature: A Theory and Research Guide*. Westport, CT: Greenwood, 1994.
Bordwell, David. "Intensified Continuity: Visual Style in Contemporary American Film." *Film Quarterly* 55, no. 3 (Spring 2002): 16–28.
Boyd, Michael. "Comedy and Perversity: Some American Films of the 1980s." *Bridgewater Review* 9, no.1 (April 1992): 2A–5A.
Box Office Mojo. "1996 Domestic Gross," <https://www.boxofficemojo.com/yearly/chart/?yr=1996&p=.htm> (last accessed December 27, 2020).
Bradshaw, Peter. "Taxi Driver review—Scorsese's sleaze is still the bee's Knees." *The Guardian*, February 10, 2017, <https://www.theguardian.com/film/2017/feb/09/taxi-driver-review-scorseses-sleaze-is-still-the-bees-knees> (last accessed December 27, 2020).
Britt, Thomas. "My Humor is Traced with Dark: An Interview with Drive's Albert Brooks." *PopMatters*, November 15, 2011, <https://www.popmatters.com/151132-my-humor-is-traced-with-dark-an-interview-with-drives-albert-brooks-2495920015.html> (last accessed January 14, 2021).
Bruckner, Lynne Dickson. "*Bambi* and *Finding Nemo*: A Sense of Wonder in the Wonderful World of Disney?" in *Framing the World: Explorations in Ecocriticism and Film*, ed. Paula Willoquet-Maricondi. Charlottesville: University of Virginia Press, 2010, 187–208.
Bruzzi, Stella. *New Documentary: A Critical Introduction*. New York: Routledge, 2000.
Brydon, Suzan G. "Men at the Heart of Mothering: Finding Mother in *Finding Nemo*." *Journal of Gender Studies* 18, no. 2 (2009): 131–46.
Buchloh, Benjamin. "Conceptual Art 1962–1969: From the Aesthetic of Administration to the Critique of Institutions." *October* 55 (Winter 1990): 105–43.
Canby, Vincent. "Film—'Unfaithfully Yours'." *The New York Times*, February 10, 1984.
Canby, Vincent. "Film: 'Broadcast News,' Comedy." *The New York Times*, December 16, 1987.
Canfield, David. "*Mother,* Albert Brooks' Biting Mother-Son Comedy, Featured Debbie Reynolds' Last Great Performance." *Slate*, December 29, 2016, <http://www.slate.com/blogs/browbeat/2016/12/29/debbie_reynolds_gave_one_of_her_greatest_performances_in_albert_brooks_mother.html?platform=hootsuite> (last accessed December 27, 2020).
Cedrone, Lou. "'Defending Your Life' Albert Brooks' new movie is almost heaven." *The Baltimore Sun*, April 5, 1991, <https://www.baltimoresun.com/news/bs-xpm-1991-04-05-1991095207-story.html> (last accessed December 27, 2020).
Chomsky, Noam and Daiv Lightfoot. *Syntactic Structures*. Berlin and Boston: De Gruyter Mouton, 2009.
Cogan, Marc. *The Design in the Wax: The Structure of the Divine Comedy and Its Meaning*. Notre Dame, IN: University of Notre Dame Press, 2007.
Collins, Jim. "Genericity in the Nineties: Eclectic Irony and the New Sincerity," in *Film Theory Goes to the Movies*, ed. Jim Collins, Hilary Radner, and Ava Preacher Collins. New York: Routledge, 1993, 242–64.

Cook, Pam. "Revisiting Performance: Nicole Kidman's Enactment of Stardom," in *Revisiting Star Studies: Cultures, Themes and Methods*, ed. Sabrina Qiong Yu and Guy Austin. Edinburgh: Edinburgh University Press, 2017, 25–44.
Dante. *Purgatorio*. Trans. William S. Merwin. New York: Knopf, 2000.
Davis, Mike. *Prisoners of the American Dream: Politics and Economy in the History of the U.S. Working Class*. London: Verso, 1986.
Davis, Mike. *Ecology of Fear: Los Angeles and the Imagination of Disaster*. New York: Metropolitan Henry Holt, 1998.
Däwes, Birgit. *Ground Zero Fiction: History, Memory, and Representation in the American 9/11 Novel*. Heidelberg: Universitätsverlag Winter GmbH, 2011.
Delloff, Linda-Marie. "Review of *Lost in America*, directed by Albert Brooks." *The Christian Century*, April 24, 1985.
Demers, Joanna. *Steal This Music: How Intellectual Property Law Affects Musical Creativity*. Athens: University of Georgia Press, 2006, 76–8.
DiMatteo, Roberto. "Real Afterlife." *Film Comment* 27, no. 2 (March/April 1991): 18+.
"Dohrn Again." *The New Republic*, October 14, 1985.
Dyer, Richard. *Heavenly Bodies: Film Stars and Society*. London: Macmillan Education, 1987.
Dyer, Richard. *Stars*. London: Palgrave Macmillan, 1998.
Eastman, Max. "To Diagram a Joke." *Enjoyment of Laughter*. New York: Simon & Shuster, 1936, 279–89.
Ebert, Roger. "Taxi Driver." <https://www.rogerebert.com/reviews/great-movie-taxi-driver-1976> (last accessed May 26, 2020).
Ebert, Roger. "The Scout." *RogerEbert.com*, <https://www.rogerebert.com/reviews/the-scout-1994> (last accessed May 26, 2020).
Ebert, Roger. "Looking for Comedy in the Muslim World." RogerEbert.com, January 19, 2006, <https://www.rogerebert.com/reviews/looking-for-comedy-in-the-muslim-world-2006> (last accessed May 26, 2020).
The Editors of Encyclopædia Britannica. "Albert Brooks." *Encyclopædia Britannica*, <https://www.britannica.com/biography/Albert-Brooks> (last accessed December 27, 2020).
Edwards, Tim. "Lone Wolves: Masculinity, Cinema, and the Man Alone," in *The Routledge Companion to Media & Gender*, ed. Cynthia Carter, Linda Steiner, Lisa McLaughlin. Oxford and New York: Routledge, 2014.
Ehrenreich, Barbara. *Fear of Falling: The Inner Life of the Middle Class*. New York: Pantheon, 1989.
Ehrenreich, Barbara and John Ehrenreich. "The Professional-Managerial Class," in *Between Capital and Labor*, ed. Pat Walker. Boston: South End Press, 1979, 5–45.
Eisenberg, Lee. "Back Stage with Esquire." *Esquire*, February 1971, 8.
Faludi, Susan. *The Terror Dream: Fear and Fantasy in Post-9/11 America*. New York: Metropolitan Books, 2007.
Fenn, R. K. *The Persistence of Purgatory*. Cambridge: Cambridge University Press, 1996.
Foucault, Michel. *Discipline and Punish: The Birth of the Prison*. New York: Vintage Books, 1995.
Friedman, Drew. "Co Star, The Record Acting Game." *drewfriedman* (blog), November 8, 2011, <http://drewfriedman.blogspot.com/2011/11/co-star-record-acting-game.html> (last accessed December 28, 2020).
Fujiwara, Chris. *Jerry Lewis*. Urbana: University of Illinois Press, 2009.
Gardiner, Eileen. *Visions of Heaven and Hell before Dante*. New York: Italica Press, 2000.

Geraghty, Christine. "Re-Examining Stardom: Questions of Texts, Bodies and Performances," in *Reinventing Film Studies*, ed. Christine Gledhill and Linda Williams. New York: Oxford University Press, 2000, 183–202.

Gitlin, Todd. *Inside Prime Time*. Berkeley: University of California Press, 2000.

Gladwell, Malcolm. "Group Think." *The New Yorker*, November 25, 2002, <https://www.newyorker.com/magazine/2002/12/02/group-think> (last accessed December 28, 2020).

Gleiberman, Owen. "I'll Do Anything." *Entertainment Weekly*, February 4, 1994, <https://ew.com/article/1994/02/04/ill-do-anything-2/> (last accessed December 27, 2020).

Gleiberman, Owen. "Looking for Comedy in the Muslim World." *Entertainment Weekly*, January 27, 2006, <https://ew.com/article/2006/01/27/looking-comedy-muslim-world-2/> (last accessed December 27, 2020).

Gott, Michael. "Between *Noir* and Sunshine: *Drive* As An Ambivalent Urban Road Movie." *Transfers* 2, no. 2 (Summer 2012): 139.

Graham, Dan. "Homes for America." *Arts*, December 1966/January 1967, 21–2.

Graham, Dan. *For Publication*. Los Angeles: Otis Art Institute, 1975, 17–20.

Graham, Dan. "Dean Martin/Entertainment as Theater." *Rock My Religion*. Cambridge, MA: MIT Press, 1993, 56–65.

Graham, Dan and Sabine Breitwieser. "Dan Graham." *Museum of Modern Art Oral History Program*, November 1, 2011, <https://www.moma.org/momaorg/shared/pdfs/docs/learn/archives/transcript_graham.pdf> (last accessed December 28, 2020).

Gray, Tim. "Plugolas: H'w'd fetes product placement." *Variety*, January 13, 2000, <https://variety.com/2000/voices/columns/plugolas-h-w-d-fetes-product-placement-1117760859/> (last accessed December 27, 2020).

Gross, David. "Culture, Politics, and 'Lifestyle' in the 1960s," in *Race, Politics, and Culture: Critical Essays on the Radicalism of the 1960s*, ed. Adolph Reed Jr., New York: Greenwood, 1986, 99–118.

Halberstam, Jack. *The Queer Art of Failure*. Durham, NC: Duke University Press, 2011.

Handelman, David. "The Ambivalent-About-Prime-Time-Players." *The New York Times Magazine*, December 28, 1997, <http://www.nytimes.com/1997/12/28/magazine/the-ambivalent-about-prime-time-players.html?pagewanted=all> (last accessed December 27, 2020).

Hark, Ina Rae. "Fear of Flying: Yuppie Critique and the Buddy-Road Movie in the 1980s," in *The Road Movie Book*, ed. Steven Cohan and Ina Rae Hark. London: Routledge, 1997, 204–32.

Harries, Dan. *Film Parody*. London: Palgrave BFI, 2000.

Harris-Birtill, Rose. *David Mitchell's Post-Secular World: Buddhism, Belief, and the Urgency of Compassion*. London: Bloomsbury, 2019, 137–66.

Harvey, James. *Movie Love in the Fifties*. New York: Da Capo, 2002.

Hayward, Steven. "The Best Conservative Movies." *National Review*, February 5, 2009, <https://www.nationalreview.com/magazine/2009/02/23/best-conservative-movies/> (last accessed December 28, 2020)

Hess, Thomas. *The Art Comics and Satires of Ad Reinhardt*. Rome: Marlborough, 1975, 23.

Higgins, Mike. "The Muse." *Sight & Sound*, January 2000, <http://old.bfi.org.uk/sightandsound/review/542> (last accessed March 6, 2016).

"The History of Comedy." Originally aired August 6, 2017, CNN, <https://archive.org/details/CNNW_20170807_020000_The_History_of_Comedy/start/1020/end/1080> (last accessed December 28, 2020).

Hoberman, J. "35 Years Later, Taxi Driver Still Stuns." *Village Voice*, March 16, 2011, <https://www.villagevoice.com/2011/03/16/35-years-later-taxi-driver-still-stuns/> (last accessed December 27, 2020).
Hoberman, J. *Film After Film: Or, What Became of 21st-Century Cinema?* London: Verso, 2012.
Hoberman, J. *Make My Day: Movie Culture in the Age of Reagan*. New York: The New Press, 2019.
Holmes, Su. "'Starring . . . Dyer?': Re-visiting Star Studies and Contemporary Celebrity Culture." *Westminster Papers in Communication and Culture* 2, no. 2 (2015): 6–21.
Horkheimer, Max and Theodor Adorno, *Dialectic of Enlightenment*, trans. Edmund Jephcott. Palo Alto, CA: Stanford University Press, 2007, 97.
Howard, Lloyd. *Virgil the Blind Guide: Marking the Way through the Divine Comedy*. Montréal: McGill-Queens University Press, 2010.
Howe, Desson. "'Defending Your Life'." *Washington Post*, April 5, 1991, <https://www.washingtonpost.com/wpsrv/style/longterm/movies/videos/defendingyourlifepghowe_a0b2e7.htm> (last accessed December 27, 2020).
Iannucci, Amilcare. *Dante, Cinema, and Television*. Toronto: University of Toronto Press, 2004.
James, David E. *Allegories of Cinema: American Film in the Sixties*. Princeton: Princeton University Press, 1989.
Jameson, Fredric. *Archaeologies of the Future: The Desire Called Utopia and Other Science Fictions*. London: Routledge, 2005.
Joselit, David. *Feedback: Television Against Democracy*. Cambridge, MA: MIT Press, 2007, xi.
Jurca, Catherine. "What the Public Wanted: Hollywood, 1937-1942." *Cinema Journal* 47, no. 2 (Winter 2008): 3–25.
Kael, Pauline. "Coddled." Review of *Lost in America*, dir. Albert Brooks, and *The Breakfast Club*, dir. John Hughes. *New Yorker*, April 8, 1985, <https://www.newyorker.com/magazine/1985/04/08/coddled> (last accessed January 7, 2021).
Kauffman, Stanley. "Messing Around." *The New Republic*, March 7, 1994, 30.
Kehr, Dave. "As A Director, The Comedian Turns Into A Ruthless Realist." *Chicago Tribune*, March 31, 1991, <http://articles.chicagotribune.com/1991-03-31/entertainment/9101280875_1_modern-romance-first-short-film-comedy> (last accessed March 17, 2017).
Kehr, Dave. *When Movies Mattered: Reviews from a Transformative Decade*. Chicago: University of Chicago Press, 2011.
Keller, Florian. *Andy Kaufman: Wrestling with the American Dream*. Minneapolis: University of Minnesota Press, 2005.
Kensky, Meira. *Trying Man, Trying God: The Divine Courtroom in Early Jewish and Christian Literature*. Tubingen: Mohr Siebeck, 2010.
Kiefer, William W. "Writing Instructors Want Better Status, Conditions." *Hartford Courant*, August 12, 1971, 24.
King, Barry. "Articulating Stardom." *Screen* 26, no. 5 (1985): 30.
King, Barry. "Stardom as an Occupation," in *The Hollywood Film Industry: A Reader*, ed. Paul Kerr. London: Routledge, 1986, 154–94.
King, Barry. "Stardom, Celebrity, and the Money Form." *The Velvet Light Trap* 65 (2010): 7–19.
Kinsella, W. P. *Shoeless Joe Jackson: A Novel* (Boston: Mariner Books, 1999).
Kirsch, Bob. "Talent in Action: Albert Brooks; Kenny Rankin." *Billboard*, July 21, 1973, 58.
Klawans, Stuart. "Films." *The Nation*, April 22, 1991.
Klein, Naomi. *The Shock Doctrine: The Rise of Disaster Capitalism*. New York: Metropolitan/Henry Holt, 2007.

Klinger, Barbara. "Digressions at the Cinema: Reception and Mass Culture." *Cinema Journal* 28, no. 4 (1989): 3–19.

Knight, Jacob. "The Love Monster: Albert Brooks' *Modern Romance*." *Birth. Movies. Death*, April 5, 2017, <https://birthmoviesdeath.com/2017/04/05/the-love-monster-albert-brooks-modern-romance> (last accessed January 14, 2021).

Kosuth, Joseph. *Art After Philosophy and After*. Cambridge, MA: MIT Press, 1993.

Kratka, Irv. "Q + A." *Music Trades*, May 2015, 48–53.

Krutnik, Frank. *Hollywood Comedians: The Film Reader*. London: Routledge, 2003.

Lanza, Joseph. *Elevator Music: A Surreal History of Muzak, Easy Listening, and Other Moodsong*. Ann Arbor: University of Michigan Press, 2004, 219–20.

LaSalle, Mick. "Odd couple amplified / 'The In-Laws remake brings wildly different dads Together." *SFGate*, May 23, 2003, <https://www.sfgate.com/movies/article/Odd-couple-amplified-The-In-Laws-remake-2646259.php> (last accessed December 27, 2020).

Le Goff, Jacques, *The Birth of Purgatory*. Chicago: University of Chicago Press, 1991.

Le Goff, Jacques. *The Medieval Imagination*. Chicago: University of Chicago Press, 2001.

Leonard, Garry. "Let's Get Fiscal: Hollywood Romance and the Mechanism of the Self in Modernity." *Film International* 9, no. 5 (December 2011).

Limon, John. *Stand-Up Comedy in Theory, or, Abjection in America*. Durham, NC: Duke University Press, 2000.

Long, Christian. "Albert Brooks." *Senses of Cinema* 80 (2016), <http://sensesofcinema.com/2016/great-directors/albert-brooks/> (last accessed December 27, 2020)..

McCall, Cheryl. "Psst! Albert Brooks Isn't Kin to Mel Except in Comedy—he was Born, and Sort of Is, An Einstein." *People*, April 16, 1979, <https://people.com/archive/psst-albert-brooks-isnt-kin-to-mel-except-in-comedy-he-was-born-and-sort-of-is-an-einstein-vol-11-no-15/> (last accessed December 27, 2020).

McCarthy, Todd. "My First Mister." *Variety*, January 18, 2001, <https://variety.com/2001/film/markets-festivals/my-first-mister-1200466323/> (last accessed December 27, 2020).

McDonald, Paul. *Hollywood Stardom*. Hoboken, NJ: Wiley Blackwell, 2013.

McGilligan, Patrick (ed.) *Backstory 5: interviews with screenwriters of the 1990s*. Berkeley: University of California Press, 2010.

McGowan, Todd. *Capitalism and Desire: The Psychic Cost of Free Markets*. New York: Columbia University Press, 2016.

Marc, David. *Comic Visions: Television Comedy & American Culture. Second Edition*. Malden: Blackwell, 1997.

Marcello, Starr. "Performance Design: An Analysis of Film Acting and Sound Design." *Journal of Film and Video* 58, no. 1/2 (2006): 59–70.

Maslin, Janet. "Screen: Albert Brooks Turns 'Real Life' Into Movie: Family is the Lens." *The New York Times*, March 2, 1979, <https://www.nytimes.com/1979/03/02/archives/screen-albert-brooks-turns-real-life-into-moviefamily-is-the-lens.html> (last accessed December 27, 2020).

Maslin, Janet. "Albert Brooks' 'Romance.'" *New York Times*, March 13, 1981, C8. <https://www.nytimes.com/1981/03/13/movies/albert-brooks-romance.html?searchResultPosition=8> (last accessed January 20, 2021).

Maslin, Janet. "America Discovers Albert Brooks." *New York Times*, June 2, 1985, <https://www.nytimes.com/1985/06/02/movies/america-discovers-albert-brooks.html> (last accessed January 7, 2021).

Masters, Robert E. L. and Jean Houston. *Psychedelic Art*. New York: Grove, 1968.

Mitford, Jessica. "Let Us Now Appraise Famous Writers." *The Atlantic Monthly*, July 1970, <https://www.theatlantic.com/magazine/archive/1970/07/let-us-now-appraise-famous-writers/305319/> (last accessed December 28, 2020).

Montgomery, Colleen. "Woody's Roundup and Wall-E's Wunderkammer: Technophilia and Nostalgia in Pixar Animation." *Animation Studies Online Journal* 6 (September 2, 2011), <https://journal.animationstudies.org/?s=colleen+montgomery> (last accessed January 14, 2021).

Montgomery, Colleen. "Pixarticulation: Vocal Performance in Pixar Animation." *Music, Sound, and the Moving Image* 10, no. 1 (2016): 1–23.

Montoya, Maria. "Albert Brooks 'Real Life' Film Is an Unexpected Classic." *NOLA.com*, February 28, 2009.

Moretta, John Anthony. *The Hippies: A 1960s History*. Jefferson, NC: McFarland, 2017.

Murphy, Kathleen. "Festivals: Toronto." *Film Comment* 32 no. 6 (November/December 1996): 53–7.

Nachman, Gerald. *Seriously Funny: The Rebel Comedians of the 1950s and 1960s*. New York: Back Stage Books, 2004.

National Commission on Fiscal Responsibility and Reform. *The Moment of Truth* (Washington, DC: The White House, 2010), <https://web.archive.org/web/20121214121412/http://www.fiscalcommission.gov/sites/fiscalcommission.gov/files/documents/TheMomentofTruth12_1_2010.pdf> (last accessed December 27, 2020).

Negra, Diane. *Off-White Hollywood*. New York: Routledge, 2001.

Noel, Daniel G. (ed.) "Jung's anti-modern art of the mandala." *Picturing Cultural Values in Postmodern America*. Tuscaloosa: University Alabama Press, 1995, <https://philpapers.org/rec/DOTPCV> (last accessed December 29, 2020).

Nuttycombe, Dave. "Albert Brooks and the Rise of 'New Humor." *Vulture.com*, February 9, 2011, <https://www.vulture.com/2011/02/albert-brooks-and-the-rise-of-new-humor.html> (last accessed December 28, 2020).

Nystrom, Derek. *Hard Hats, Rednecks, and Macho Men: Class in 1970s American Cinema*. New York: Oxford University Press, 2009.

Obama, Barack. "National Commission on Fiscal Responsibility and Reform," in *Executive Order 13531 Sec. 4*, <https://obamawhitehouse.archives.gov/the-press-office/executive-order-national-commission-fiscal-responsibility-and-reform> (last accessed December 27, 2020).

O'Brien, Gabrielle. "Hero in the Shadows: Film Noir, Fairytale and Postmodernism in *Drive*." *Screen Education* 79 (Spring 2015).

O'Brien, Harvey. "That's Really the Title?" Deconstructing Deconstruction in *The Positively True Adventures of the Alleged Texas Cheerleader-Murdering Mom* (1993) and *Real Life* (1978)," in *Docufictions: Essays on the Intersection of Documentary and Fictional Filmmaking*, ed. Gary D. Rhodes and John Parris Springer. Jefferson, NC: McFarland, 2006, 191–204.

O'Brien, Tim. "Spunky Punks: Trading Places in America." Review of *Desperately Seeking Susan*, dir. Susan Siedelman, and *Lost in America*, dir. Albert Brooks. *Commonweal*, May 17, 1985.

The Onion. "Romantic-Comedy Behavior Gets Real-Life Man Arrested." April 7, 1999, <https://local.theonion.com/romantic-comedy-behavior-gets-real-life-man-arrested-1819565117> (last accessed December 27, 2020).

O'Toole, Lawrence. "Taking potshots at U.S. crockery." *Macleans*, March 26, 1979.

Owen, Rachel. "The Image of Dante," in *Dante on View: The Reception of Dante in the Visual and Performing Arts*, ed. Antonella Braida and Luisa Cale. Aldershot: Ashgate, 2007, 83–94.

Pattison, Michael. "Albert Brooks' 'Modern Romance'." *MUBI.com*, February 17, 2017, <https://mubi.com/notebook/posts/love-actually-close-up-on-albert-brooks-modern-romance> (last accessed December 27, 2020).

Peary, Gerald. "Dropouts of the middle class," *Maclean's*, April 8, 1985.

Peterson, Richard A. and Russell B. Davis, Jr., "The Contemporary American Radio Audience." *Popular Music and Society*, 3 no. 4 (1974): 299–313.

Pfeiffer, Prudence. *Routine Extremism: Ad Reinhardt and Modern Art*. PhD diss., Harvard University, 2010, 104.

Phipps, Keith. "My First Mister." *The AV Club*, March 29, 2002, <https://film.avclub.com/my-first-mister-1798196050> (last accessed December 27, 2020).

Pomerance, Murray (ed.) *Enfant Terrible!: Jerry Lewis in American Film*. New York: NYU Press, 2002.

Powers, John. "The Big Casino." *Sight and Sound*, November 1, 1996.

Powers, John. "Albert Brooks' *Lost in America* Remains Piercingly Relevant 32 Years Later." *NPR*, August 7, 2017, <http://www.npr.org/2017/08/07/542028917/albert-brooks-lost-in-america-remains-piercingly-relevant-32-years-later?platform=hootsuite/> (last accessed January 14, 2021).

Pulleine, Tim. "Review of *Lost in America*, directed by Albert Brooks." *Monthly Film Bulletin*, December 1985, 381.

Quart, Leonard. "A Slice of Delirium: Scorsese's 'Taxi Driver' Revisited." *Film Criticism* 19, no. 3 (1995): 67–71, <www.jstor.org/stable/44075823> (last accessed December 27, 2020).

Raab, Scott. "Albert Brooks Knows the Whole, Hellish Truth." *Esquire*, September 1, 1999, <http://www.esquire.com/features/ESQ0999-SEP_ALBERT_BROOKS-2> (last accessed May 17, 2016).

Rabin, Nathan. "*The Dissolve* on . . . the directors we want to get career-spanning box sets." *The Dissolve*, July 30, 2014, <http://thedissolve.com/news/2856-the-dissolve-on-the-directors-we-want-to-get-caree/> (last accessed December 27, 2020).

Radano, Ronald M. "Interpreting Muzak: Speculations on Musical Experience in Everyday Life." *American Music* 7 (Winter 1989): 448–60.

Rainer, Peter. "Movie Review: Brooks Hits Fly Ball in 'The Scout,' but Not Over Fence." *Los Angeles Times*, September 30, 1994, <https://www.latimes.com/archives/la-xpm-1994-09-30-ca-44660-story.html> (last accessed December 27, 2020).

"Reagan Was a Subject of 60's Screen Inquiry." *New York Times*, September 21, 1986.

Rehak, Bob. "2003: Movies, 'Shock and Awe,' and the Troubled Blockbuster," in *American Cinema of the 2000s: Themes and Variations*, ed. Timothy Corrigan. New Brunswick, NJ: Rutgers University Press, 2012, 83–103.

Reinhardt, Ad. "How to Look at Modern Art in America." *ARTnews*, Summer 1961, 36–7.

Reinhardt, Ad. *Art-as-Art: The Selected Writings of Ad Reinhardt*. New York: Viking, 1975, 188.

Rochlin, Margy. "A Funnyman Whose Muse Is in the Mirror." *The New York Times*, August 22, 1999, <http://www.nytimes.com/1999/08/22/movies/film-a-funnyman-whose-muse-is-in-the-mirror.html/> (last accessed January 14, 2021).

Rogers, Anna Backman and Miklós Kiss. "A Real Human Being and a Real Hero: Stylistic Excess, Dead Time and Intensified Continuity in Nicolas Winding Refn's *Drive*." *New Cinemas: Journal of Contemporary Film* 12, no. 1&2 (June 2014).

Rogin, Michael. "Blackface, White Noise: The Jewish Jazz Singer Finds His Voice." *Critical Inquiry* 18, no. 3 (1992): 417–53.

Rosenbaum, Jonathan. *Movie Wars: How Hollywood and the Media Limit What Films We Can See*. London: Wallflower, 2000.

Rozen, Leah. "Picks and Pans Review: *Looking for Comedy in the Muslim World*." *People*, January 30, 2006, <https://people.com/archive/picks-and-pans-review-looking-for-comedy-in-the-muslim-world-vol-65-no-4/> (last accessed December 27, 2020).

Ruoff, Jeffrey. "'Can a Documentary Be Made of Real Life?': The Reception of *An American Family*," in *The Construction of the Viewer: Media Ethnography and the Anthropology*

of Audiences, ed. Peter Ian Crawford and Sigurjón Baldur Hafsteinsson. Copenhagen: Intervention Press, 1996, 270–96.
Schickel, Richard. "Review of *Lost in America*, directed by Albert Brooks." *Time*, March 18, 1985.
Schulman, Michael. *Her Again: Becoming Meryl Streep*. New York: Harper, 2017.
Schwartz, Gretchen. "'You Talkin' to me?': Robert DeNiro's Interrogative Fidelity and Subversion of Masculine Norms." *The Journal of Popular Culture* 41, no. 3 (2008): 443–66
Scott, A. O. "Sometimes Politics Simply Won't Do." *The New York Times*, January 20, 2006, <http://movies2.nytimes.com/2006/01/20/movies/20musl.html> (last accessed December 27, 2020).
Scott, A. O. "Happy Birthday, You Miserable Achievers." *New York Times*, December 21, 2012.
Scott, Peter. "Grahamarama." *artnet*, July 7, 2009, <http://www.artnet.com/magazineus/features/scott/dan-graham7-7-09.asp> (last accessed December 28, 2020).
Seitz, Matt Zoller. "Garry Shandling Was One of American Television's Greatest Artists." *Vulture*, March 24, 2016, <http://www.vulture.com/2016/03/garry-shandling-american-tv-great-artist.html#> (last accessed December 27, 2020).
Shales, Tom and James Andrew Miller, *Live from New York*. Boston: Little, Brown and Company, 2002.
Shargel, Raphael. "Confusing Success with Profit." *New Leader*, September 20, 1999.
Simon, John. "'Near Misses,' review of *Lost in America*, directed by Albert Brooks, and *Camila*, directed by María Luisa Bemberg." *The National Review*, May 17, 1985.
Sims, David. "The Brutal Cynicism of *Lost in America* Still Resonates." *The Atlantic*, July 25, 2017, <https://www.theatlantic.com/entertainment/archive/2017/07/lost-in-america-albert-brooks-criterion/534777/> (last accessed January 14, 2021).
Sims, Judith. "Comedy Prof Albert Brooks Spits It Out." *Rolling Stone*, January 17, 1974, <http://www.rollingstone.com/culture/features/comedy-prof-albert-brooks-spits-it-out-19740117> (last accessed December 27, 2020).
Siskel, Gene. "Funny Albert Brooks is Serious About the State of Filmmaking." *Chicago Tribune*, March 3, 1985.
Siskel, Gene. "'Lost in America': Funny, Touching Snapshot of Real People." *Chicago Tribune*, March 15, 1985.
Slansky, Paul. "Albert Brooks Is Funnier Than You Think." *Deadspin*, May 9, 2014, <http://thestacks.deadspin.com/albert-brooks-is-funnier-than-you-think-1573238010> (last accessed December 28, 2020).
Slaymaker, James. "'To Err is Human, to Film Divine': The Films of Albert Brooks." *MUBI.com*, October 5, 2018, <https://mubi.com/notebook/posts/to-err-is-human-to-film-divine-the-films-of-albert-brooks> (last accessed December 27, 2020).
Smith, Gavin. "All the Choices: Albert Brooks interview." *Film Comment* 35, no. 4 (July/August 1999), <https://www.filmcomment.com/article/all-the-choices-albert-brooks-interview/> (last accessed January 7, 2021).
Smith, Gavin. "Editor's Pick: *Modern Romance*," *Film Comment* 42, no. 3 (May/June 2006): 75.
Smith, Gavin. "Albert Brooks Me Generation Everyman," in *Backstory 5: Interviews with Screenwriters of the 1990s*, ed. Patrick McGilligan. Los Angeles: University of California Press, 2009, 5–20.
Sperb, Jason. *Flickers of Film: Nostalgia in the Time of Digital Cinema*. New Brunswick, NJ: Rutgers University Press, 2016.
Sterne, Jonathan. "Sounds like the Mall of America: Programmed Music and the Architectonics of Commercial Space." *Ethnomusicology* 41 (Winter 1997): 22–50.

Stewart-Halevy, Jacob. "California Conceptualism's About-Face." *October* 163 (Winter 2018): 71–101.
Strickler, Jeff. ""I'll Do Anything" Has Split Personality." *Star Tribune*, February 4, 1994, 4E.
Tapley, Kristopher. "Interview: Albert Brooks on 'Drive' As A Chance to Prove Something." *HitFix*, September 28, 2011, <http://www.incontention.com/hitfix/2011/09/28/interview-albert-brooks-on-drive-as-a-chance-to-prove-something> (last accessed January 14, 2021).
Teicholz, Tom. "When Reality Was a Joke: The Making of Albert Brooks' *Real Life*." *Los Angeles Review of Books*, November 5, 2016, <http://blog.lareviewofbooks.org/arts-culture/film/reality-joke-making-albert-brooks-real-life/> (last accessed March 17, 2017).
Tobias, Scott. "Albert Brooks," interview. *Onion AV Club*, January 18, 2006, <https://film.avclub.com/albert-brooks-1798208934> (last accessed January 7, 2021).
Tobias, Scott. "What "Albert Brooks" says about Albert Brooks." *The Dissolve*, September 18, 2013, <http://thedissolve.com/features/movie-of-the-week/162-what-albert-brooks-says-about-albert-brooks/> (last accessed March 17, 2017).
Tobias, Scott. "*Lost in America*: The $100,000 Box." *The Criterion Collection*, July 25, 2017, <https://www.criterion.com/current/posts/4760-lost-in-america-the-100-000-box> (last accessed December 27, 2020).
Tobias, Scott, and Nathan Rabin, "Albert Brooks." *AV Club*, June 16, 2011, <http://www.avclub.com/article/albert-brooks-57634> (last accessed January 14, 2021).
Travers, Peter. "Looking for Comedy in the Muslim World." *Rolling Stone*, January 12, 2006, <https://www.rollingstone.com/movies/movie-reviews/looking-for-comedy-in-the-muslim-world-128137/> (last accessed December 27, 2020).
Tunny, Tom. "Video Reviews." *Sight and Sound*, January 1, 1998.
Turner, Chris. *Planet Simpson: How a Cartoon Masterpiece Documented an Era and Defined a Generation*. London: Ebury Press, 2004.
Ue, Tom. "The Question of Closure in James Sallis' and Nicolas Winding Refn's *Drive*," *Journal of Adaptation in Film & Performance* 13, no. 1 (2020): 91–6.
Venel, Hervé. *Triple Entendre: Furniture Music, Muzak, Muzak-Plus*. Champaign: University of Illinois Press, 2013, 47.
Verna, Tony. *Live TV*. Boston: Focal Press, 1987.
Vicari, Justin. *Nicolas Winding Refn and the Violence of Art: A Critical Study of the Films*. Jefferson, NC: McFarland, 2014.
Wallace, David Foster. *A Supposedly Fun Thing I'll Never Do Again: Essays and Arguments*. Boston: Little Brown, 1997.
Ward, Thomas M. "Transhumanization, Personal Identity, and the Afterlife: Thomistic Reflections on a Dantean Theme." *New Blackfriars* 96, no. 1065 (September 2015): 564–75.
White, Timothy. "Lorne Michaels, Saturday Night Quarterback." *Rolling Stone*, December 27, 1979, <https://www.rollingstone.com/movies/movie-news/lorne-michaels-saturday-night-quarterback-202051/> (last accessed December 28, 2020).
Whitley, David. *The Idea of Nature in Disney Animation*. Aldershot: Ashcroft, 2008.
Whittington, William. "The Sonic Playpen: Sound Design and Technology in Pixar's Animated Shorts," in *The Oxford Handbook of Sound Studies*, ed. Karin Bijsterveld and Trevor J. Pinch. Oxford: Oxford University Press, 2013, 367–86.
Williams, Craig. "In Praise of *Modern Romance*—Albert Brooks' Masterpiece." *Little White Lies*, August 5, 2016, <https://lwlies.com/articles/modern-romance-albert-brooks> (last accessed January 14, 2021).
Williams, Mason. "Original Classical Gas Video '3000 Years of Art'," <http://www.classicalgas.com/gasvideo.html> (last accessed June 2, 2020).
Wolf, Alexandra. "Dan Graham's *Homes for America* re:visited." *all-over*, 2015.

Wood, Jennifer. "'Defending Your Life' at 25: Albert Brooks on Making a Comedy Classic." *Rolling Stone*, March 22, 2016, <www.rollingstone.com/movies/movie-news/defending-your-life-at-25-albert-brooks-on-making-a-comedy-classic-178596/> (last accessed January 7, 2021).

Wright, Erik Olin. *Classes*. London: Verso, 1985.

Wurter, Tracy. "Comedy Jokes: Steve Martin and the Limits of Stand-Up Comedy." *Studies in American Humor* 3, no. 14 (2006): 23–45.

Yglesias, Matt. "*Ghost Busters* As Right Wing Agitprop." *The Atlantic*, May 25, 2007, <https://www.theatlantic.com/politics/archive/2007/05/-em-ghost-busters-em-as-rightwing-agitprop/42365/> (last accessed December 28, 2020).

Yu, Sabrina Qiong and Guy Austin (eds) *Revisiting Star Studies: Cultures, Themes and Methods*. Edinburgh: Edinburgh University Press, 2017.

Zaleski, Carol. *Otherworld Journeys: Accounts of Near-death Experience in Medieval and Modern Times*. New York: Oxford University Press, 1988.

Zettl, Herbert. "The Rare Case of Television Aesthetics." *Journal of the University Film Association* 30, no. 2 (Spring 1978): 3–8.

Zinoman, Jason. "No Real Hurry to Tell the Joke." *The New York Times*, May 26, 2014, <https://www.nytimes.com/2014/05/27/arts/television/bob-newhart-master-of-the-one-sided-conversation.html> (last accessed December 27, 2020).

Zoglin, Richard. *Comedy at the Edge: How Stand-up in the 1970s Changed America*. London: Bloomsbury, 2017, 110–11.

Filmography

Brooks, Albert, dir. *Real Life*. 1979; Hollywood: Paramount Home Video, 2000. DVD.
Brooks, Albert, dir. *Modern Romance*. 1981; Culver City, CA: Sony Home Entertainment, 2006. DVD.
Brooks, Albert, dir. *Lost in America*. 1985; Pyrmont Australia: Warner Home Video, 2003. DVD.
Brooks, Albert, dir. *Defending Your Life*. 1991; Burbank, CA: Warner Home, 2001. DVD.
Brooks, Albert, dir. *Mother*. 1996; Hollywood: Paramount Home, 2006. DVD.
Brooks, Albert, dir. *The Muse*. 1999; Universal City, CA: Universal Home, 2010. DVD.
Brooks, Albert, dir. *Looking for Comedy in the Muslim World*. 2005; Burbank CA. Warner Home, 2006. DVD.

Apatow, Judd, dir. *This Is 40*. 2012; Sydney: Universal Sony Home Entertainment, 2013. DVD.
Brooks, James L., dir. *Terms of Endearment*. 1983; Los Angeles: Paramount, 2017.
Brooks, James L., dir. *Broadcast News*. 1987; New York: Criterion Collection, 2011. DVD.
Brooks, James L., dir. *I'll Do Anything*. 1994; Culver City CA: Sony Pictures Home, 2003. DVD.
Chandor, J. C., dir. *A Most Violent Year*. 2014; Toronto: Elevation Pictures, 2015. DVD.
C. K., Louis, dir. *I Love You, Daddy*. 2017; unreleased.
Fleming, Andrew, dir. *The In-Laws*. 2003; Sydney: Roadshow Entertainment, 2003. DVD.
Lahti, Christine, dir. *My First Mister*. 2001. Los Angeles: Paramount, 2002. DVD.
Landesman, Peter, dir. *Concussion*. 2015; Culver City, CA: Sony Pictures Home Entertainment, 2016.
Landis, John, dir. *The Twilight Zone: The Movie*. 1983; Burbank, CA: Warner Home Video, 1997.
Osborne, Michael, dir. *Le Petit Prince*. 2016; Toronto: Entertainment One. DVD.
Refn, Nicholas Winding, dir. *Drive*. 2011; Arundel Australia: Pinnacle Films. DVD.
Renaud, Chris and Yarrow Cheney, dirs. *The Secret Life of Pets*. 2016; Universal City, CA: Universal Pictures Home Entertainment, 2016.
Ritchie, Michael, dir. *The Scout*. 1994; Los Angeles: Twentieth Century Fox, 2001. DVD.
Scorsese, Martin, dir. *Taxi Driver*. 1976; Culver City, CA: Sony Pictures Entertainment, 2004. DVD.

Silverman, David, dir. *The Simpsons Movie*. 2007; Los Angeles: Twentieth Century Fox, 2007. DVD.
Soderberg, Steven, dir. *Out of Sight*. 1998; Universal City, CA: Universal Home, 1998. DVD.
Stanton, Andrew and Lee Unkrich, dirs. *Finding Nemo*. 2003. Burbank, CA: Buena Vista/Pixar. DVD.
Thomas, Betty, dir. *Doctor Dolittle*. 1998; Los Angeles: Twentieth Century Fox, 2012.
Zieff, Howard, dir. *Private Benjamin*. 1980; Burbank, CA: Warner Home Video, 1997.
Zieff, Howard, dir. *Unfaithfully Yours*. 1983; Los Angeles: Twentieth Century Fox, 2005.

Recordings

Brooks, Albert. *Comedy Minus One*, Rhino/WEA B000008DSV, 1993, compact disc. Originally released in 1973.
Brooks, Albert. *A Star Is Bought*, Wounded Bird Records B06XKNZRMG, 2017, compact disc. Originally released in 1975.
Brooks, Albert. "Real Life: A Conversation with Albert Brooks," *Real Life*, dir. Albert Brooks, 1979; Los Angeles: Paramount Pictures, 2001, DVD.
Foundas, Scott and Albert Brooks. "An Evening With Albert Brooks," in *Film at Lincoln Center*, YouTube video, 1:02:14, <https://youtu.be/ZgXN6venczo> (last accessed January 20, 2021).
Kondabolu, Hari. *Waiting for 2040*, Kill Rock Stars, 2014.

Television

Brooks, Albert, dir. "Albert Brooks' Famous School for Comedians." 1971; *The Great American Dream Machine*, S'More Entertainment, 2015. DVD.
Brooks, Albert, dir. "Sick in bed." 1975; *Saturday Night Live: Season 1, 1975–1976*, Universal City, CA: Universal Pictures Home Entertainment, 2006. DVD.
Brooks, Albert, dir. "NBC Super Season." 1975; *Saturday Night Live: Season 1, 1975–1976*, Universal City, CA: Universal Pictures Home Entertainment, 2006. DVD.
Brooks, Albert, dir. "The National Audience Research Institute." 1976; *Saturday Night Live: Season 1, 1975–1976*, Universal City, CA: Universal Pictures Home Entertainment, 2006. DVD.
Brooks, Albert, dir. "A Film by Albert Brooks," segment of television program *Saturday Night Live*, October 18, 1975, NBC.
Brooks, Albert, dir. "The Impossible Truth," segment of television program *Saturday Night Live*, November 22, 1975, NBC.
Brooks, Albert, dir. "Operation," segment of television program *Saturday Night Live*, October 25, 1975, NBC.
Saturday Night Live, produced by Lorne Michaels, December 17, 1977, NBC.
"*Saturday Night Live* Backstage: Albert Brooks," <https://www.youtube.com/watch?v=t3HC42dPQKQ> (last accessed January 9, 2021).

Anderson, Bob, dir. *The Simpsons*. Season 5, episode 7, "Bart's Inner Child." Aired November 11, 1993, on Fox.
Anderson, Mike B., dir. *The Simpsons*. Season 8, episode 2, "You Only Move Twice." Aired November 3, 1996, on Fox.
Carson, Johnny, host and Albert Brooks, guest. *The Tonight Show*. Aired June 6, 1973, on NBC, <https://youtu.be/nDO3IJKB-P8> (last accessed December 27, 2020).
Carson, Johnny, host and Albert Brooks, guest. *Tonight Show*, Aired February 24, 1983, on NBC, <https://youtu.be/y7Q5T7hSa5Q> (last accessed December 27, 2020).
Kohan, Jenju, series creator. *Weeds Season 4*. 2008; Sydney: Sony Home Entertainment, 2010. DVD.

Rock, Chris, host. *77th Annual Academy Awards*. Performed February 27, 2005, on ABC. https://youtu.be/JerPfHYro1U

Silverman, David, dir. *The Simpsons*. Season 1, episode 9, "Life on the Fast Lane." Aired March 18, 1990, on Fox.

The Tonight Show, October 25, 1973, <NBC, <https://youtu.be/nDO3IJKB-P8> (last accessed December 28, 2020).

Writing

Brooks, Albert. (@AlbertBrooks), twitter.com.
Brooks, Albert. "Albert Brooks Pays Tribute To Monica Johnson," *Female First*, November 3, 2010, <www.femalefirst.co.uk/movies/movie-news/Albert Brooks Pays Tribute To Monica Johnson-86779.html> (last accessed January 7, 2021).
Brooks, Albert. *Twenty Thirty: The Real Story of What Happens to America.* New York: St Martin's, 2011.

Britt, Thomas. "My Humor is Traced with Dark: An Interview with Drive's Albert Brooks," November 15, 2011, <https://www.popmatters.com/151132-my-humor-is-traced-with-dark-an-interview-with-drives-albert-brooks-2495920015.html> (last accessed December 27, 2020).
Tobias, Scott, interview, "Albert Brooks," *Onion AV Club*, January 18, 2006, <https://film.avclub.com/albert-brooks-1798208934> (last accessed January 7, 2021).

Index

Note: **bold** signifies illustration

@AlbertBrooks, 36–7, 224
1960s counterculture, 38, 39, 78–92, 125–6, 156–60, 162–4

A Most Violent Year (Chandor 2014), 17, 18, 132, **227**, 235–8
A Portend of the Artist as a Yhung Mandala (1956), 67, **68**; see also Reinhardt, Ad
A Star Is Bought (1975), 3–4, 10, 19, 56, 69–72, 119, 165, 212
Academy Award, 36, 100, 109, 110, 207
advertising, 20, 22, 25, 55–8, 74, 75, 81, 84–8, 105–9, **106**, 153–4, 160, 214–15
afterlife, 25–6, 39, 126, 171–86, 189, 197
"Albert Brooks' Famous School for Comedians," 21–2, 52, 55, 56–9, 62, 63, 73, 212
Al Jazeera, 30, 111, 203–4
All That Jazz (Fosse, 1974), 4

Allen, Woody, 6, 8, 11, 17, 40, 119, 133–4
Annie Hall (1977), 133–4
Midnight in Paris (2011), 40, 133–4
Alvarez, Santiago, 64
American Dream, 32–3, 94, 104–6, 119–20, 124, 126, 132–4, 235–6; see also failure, success
American Time Capsule (Braverman, 1969), 64
An American Family (Gilbert, 1973), 22, 96, 97, 100–1, 150–1, 194–5; see also *Real Life*
Animal House (Landis, 1978), 91
anti-humor, 18, 38, 94–5, 101–3, **112**, 112–14, 119, 131
Antin, David, 55–6, 61–3; see also "Talking at Pomona" (1972)
Apatow, Judd, 10, 14, 18, 41, 95, 99, 110, 132
40-Year-Old Virgin, The (2005), 10, 18

INDEX

Freaks and Geeks (1999–2000), 10
Knocked Up (2007), 10, 18
This Is 40 (2012), 10, 18, 110, 132
Undeclared (2001–2), 10
auteurism, 29, 38–9, 113, 119–21, 133–4
AVP: Alien v Predator (Anderson, 2004), 9
Aykroyd, Dan, 90–1, 92; see also Saturday Night Live

Baby Boomer Generation, 32–3, 35, 39, 81, 83, 88, 91, 124, 164–5, 211–14, 218, 221–2; see also Me Generation
Baby Driver (Wright, 2017), 234–5, 240
Bacall, Lauren, 27
baseball, 172–3
Baumbach, Noah, 97, 114
Belushi, John, 81, 85, 90, 91; see also Saturday Night Live
Ben Stiller Show, The 10
Benchley, Robert "Why We Laugh—Or Do We?," 66–7
Best of Pardon My Boner! Vol. 8, The 70–1
Big (Marshall, 1988), 37
Big Chill, The (Kasdan, 1983), 54, 55
Blue Collar Comedy Tour: The Movie (Harding, 2003), 30
Blues Brothers, The (Landis, 1980), 92
Boogie Nights (Anderson, 1997), 37
box office, 13, 14, 15, 16, 18, 21, 23, 24, 25, 27, 28, 29, 31, 40–1, 92, 121, 130, 132, 134, 165, 189; see also commercial appeal, test screening
Broadcast News (James L. Brooks, 1987), 13–14, 55, 95, 107–8, 110, 131–2, 142, 215

Brooks, Albert, 12, 24, 26, 97, 106, 112, 121, 128, 133, 138, 139, 155, 159, 193, 198, 200, 219, 230, 231
A Star Is Bought (1975), 3–4, 10, 19, 56, 69–72, 119, 165, 212
"Albert Brooks' Famous School for Comedians," 21–2, 52, 55, 56–9, 62, 63, 73, 212
@AlbertBrooks, 36–7, 224
biography and family, 2–3, 9, 14, 64
Comedy Minus One (1973), 3–4, 6, 8, 19, 52, 59–63, 69–70, 79, 119, 165
Defending Your Life (Brooks, 1991), 2, 19–20, 21, 25–7, **26**, 30, 32, 39, 108, 119, 126, 171–86, **174**, 197, **198**, 206, 212
Famous Comedians School (Brooks, 1976), 8, 37, 51, 52, 55, 71, 73, 79, 212
Looking for Comedy in the Muslim World (Brooks, 2005), 2, 21, 29–32, 36, 94–5, 111–15, **112**, 119, 120, 129, 130–2, 201
Lost in America (Brooks, 1985), 20, 21, **24**, 24–5, 31–2, 38–9, 55, 95, 104–8, **106**, 110, 111, 113, 114, 119–20, 121, 124–6, 129–30, 132–4, 148, 150–68, **155**, 190, 206, 211–12
Modern Romance (Brooks, 1981), 16, 21, 23–5, 27, 29, 32, 35, 38, 40, 55, 95, 99–105, 110, 113, 119–20, 121–6, 130, 134, 136–48, **138**, **139**, 189, 195–6, 202, 206–7, 211–12
Mother (Brooks, 1996), 2, 21, 27–8, 32, 108, 119, 120, 126–9, **128**, 189–90, 199–202, 200, 206–7

Brooks, Albert (*cont.*)
  Muse, The (Brooks, 1999), 2, 25, 28–30, 32, 95, 108–11, 113, 119–20, 129–32, 190, 205–7, 211–12, 225
  Real Life (Brooks, 1979), 2, 8, 11, 21, 22–4, 25, 27, 28, 29, 30, 31, 32, 55, 95–9, **97**, 100–4, 110, 113, 119, 120, **121**, 121–2, 131, 134, 150–1, 168, 189, 190, 191–6, **193**, 197, 199, 200, 201, 203, 206, 211, 212, 216
  Saturday Night Live (*SNL*) short films, 78–9, 83–92, **87**
  Twenty Thirty: The Real Story of What Happens to America, 32–6
  voice acting 14–15, 132, 224–5
Brooks, James L.
  Broadcast News (1987), 13–14, 55, 95, 107–8, 110, 131–2, 142, 215
  Terms of Endearment (1983), 13, 15
Bruce, Lenny, 4, 6, 51, 79; *see also* stand-up comedy
Buchloh, Benjamin, 53, 58–9, 74
Burn Hollywood Burn (Hiller/Smithee 1997), 28
Bush, George H. W., 171
Bush, George W. 95, 202, 222

Caddyshack (Ramis, 1980), 92
Cameron, James, 28, 29, 206
Candid Camera (Funt, 1948–92), 192
Cantor, Eddie, 3, 9, 79
capitalism, 39, 114, 151–6, 160–5, 171, 181, 217, 231–2, 235–6
Carlin, George, 3–4, 6, 51, 78–9, 81–2, 84; *see also* stand-up comedy
Carson, Johnny, 3, 6, 66, 79, 81, 85; *see also* Tonight Show, The
Casino (Scorsese, 1995), 28

casino, 25, 106, **106**, **159**, 158–61; *see also* gambling
Cassavetes, John, 13, 20
  Husbands (1970), 13
  Minnie and Moskowitz (1971), 13
Chase, Chevy, 6, 90, 92; *see also* Saturday Night Live
Chicago Seven, 82
China, 35, 40, 229
Chronicles of Riddick (Twohy, 2004), 9
cinéma vérité, 198
class politics, 9, 15, 18, 23, 25, 33, 34, 37, 38–9, 40–1, 55, 56, 79, 84, 87, 106–7, 119–20, 132–3, 150–68, 211–13, 220–1; *see also* identity, class
Cohen, Sasha Baron, 192; *see also* cringe comedy
collaboration, 11, 14, 18, 26, 28, 39, 102, 103–4, 105, 108, 123, 144, 148, 189–91, 196, 205–7, 212; *see also* Johnson, Monica
Comedy Minus One (1973), 3–4, 6, 8, 19, 52, 59–63, 69–70, 79, 119, 165
commercial appeal, 5, 83, 99, 101, 151, 171, 172, 206, 215–17, 226–7, 240; *see also* box office, test screenings
conceptual art, 3, 37, 53–62, 67–9, 73
Concussion (Lanesman 2015), 17, 132
conformity *see* over-orthodoxy
contemporary US art, 51–73
cringe comedy, 98, 112, 211
Criterion Collection, 25, 114–15, 161
Cross, David, 10
Crystal, Billy, 84
Cusack, Joan, 13

INDEX 261

Dante, 25, 39, 41, 171–86
David, Larry, 19, 20, 29, 37
Day for Night (Truffaut, 1973), 136–7
Dead Poets Society (Weir, 1989), 37
Death Becomes Her (Zemeckis, 1992), 26
Debord, Guy 5
debt, 32–35, 39, 41, 173, 226–38
Defending Your Life (Brooks, 1991), 2, 19–20, 21, 25–7, **26**, 30, 32, 39, 108, 119, 126, 171–86, **174**, 197, **198**, 206, 212
Degeneres, Ellen, 1–2, 191, **220**
DeVito, Danny, 101
Dick (Fleming, 1999), 18
Dick Van Dyke Show, The (Reiner, 1972), 12
Direct Cinema, 97, 100–1
Dirty Dozen, The (Aldrich, 1967), 13
Doctor Dolittle (Thomas, 1998), 15, 132
Dr. Strangelove (Kubrick, 1964), 113
Dogme 95, 100
Drive (Refn, 2011), 17, 18, 39–40, 114, 132, 215, 216, 226–35, **230**, **231**, 238
Driver (Hill, 1977), 233
Dyer, Richard, 214–15, 217, 225
dystopia, 33–6, 172, 232

Easy Rider (Hopper, 1969), 25, 39, 95, 106–7, 114, 124, 125–6, 152, 160–1, 163–6, 211, 213; *see also* Jack Nicholson
Ebersol, Dick, 78, 80, 81–2; *see also Saturday Night Live*
economic restructuration, neoliberal, 36–8, 92
Ehrenreich, Barbara, 153, 157

Ehrenreich, Barbara and John Ehrenreich, 151, 161–2, 168; *see also* professional-managerial class (PMC)
Einstein, Bob (Super Dave Osborne), 3, 64, 141
Einstein, Harry 5 (Parkyakarkus), 3, 9, 14
Enjoyment of Laughter (Max Eastman, 1936), 66

failure, 5, 23, 38, 41, 94–5, 107–8, 112–13, 119–34, 167–8, 181, 184, 191, 195, 201, 202–4; *see also* American Dream, success
Famous Artists, 57–9, 79
Famous Comedians School (Brooks, 1976), 8, 37, 51, 52, 55, 71, 73, 79, 212; *see also Great American Dream Machine*
femininity, 39, 182–4, 189–207; *see also* identity, gender
Field of Dreams (Robinson), 172
film editing, 22, 28, 30, 38, 56, 99, 101–4, 110–11, 120–4, 136–8, 142–6, 166, 174, 175, 176, 181, 184–6, 199, 201, 204
Finding Dory (Stanton and MacLane, 2016), 132, 206
Finding Nemo (Stanton and Unkrich, 2003), 1–2, 15, 39, 113, 132, 191, 206, 213–14, 216–22, **219**, **220**, 223
Finding Neverland (Forster, 2004), 9
Fleming, Andrew, 16, 18
  Dick (1999), 18
  Hamlet 2 (2008), 18
  In-Laws, The (2003), 16, 29, 130, 132
Flip Wilson Show, 52, 79, 96
Fraser, Brendan, 2; *see also Scout, The*

gambling, 25, 105–6, 158–60, **159**, 161, 190, 206, 211; *see also* casino
Garofalo, Janeane, 10
genre, 23–4, 27, 28–9, 33–4, 69–72, 102, 103, 137, 143, 144, 148, 189, 191–2, 195, 216, 240; *see also* romantic comedy
Gere, Richard, 37
Ghost (Zucker, 1990), 172, 173
Ghostbusters (Reitman, 1984), 92
global financial crisis (GFC), 34–5
God is Dog Spelled Backwards, 63–4
Godfather, The (Coppola, 1972), 40, 227, 233–4, 237
Godfather: Part II, The (Coppola, 1974), 233–4
Godfather: Part III, The (Coppola, 1990), 234
Golden Globe, 27, 206, 227; *see also* Academy Award
Gone with the Wind (Fleming, 1939), 122, 194
Goodman, Thelma, 2–3, 140
Gosling, Ryan, 39, 228–231, **230**, **231**; *see also* Drive
Graduate, The (Nichols, 1967), 164, 199, 200
Graham, Dan (*Homes for America* (1965)), 58–9, 75
Great American Dream Machine, The, 21–2, 57–8, 75, 79–80
Gregory, Dick, 79
Grodin, Charles, 6, 98, **121**, 121–2, 192; *see also* Real Life
Guerrilla Television (Shamberg, 1971), 54–5

Hagerty, Julie, 105, 150, 211; *see also* Lost in America
Hamburger, Neil, 113; *see also* stand-up comedy
Hamlet 2 (Fleming, 2008), 18

Hanks, Tom, 37, 111, 114
happiness, 98–99, 119, 125–6, 127–8, 178, 186; *see also* American Dream, failure, success
Harrold, Kathryn, 99, 122, 137–8, **138**, 148; *see also* Modern Romance
Heaven's Gate (Malick, 1980), 145, 165
Heidecker, Tim, 10
Hellraiser II (Randel 1988), 172
Hinduism, 202
Homes for America (Dan Graham, 1965), 58–9, 75
Hoover Dam, 21, 164, 166–7
Hunter, Holly, 13, 107, 142; *see also* Broadcast News
Hurt, William, 13, 55, 107–8, 142; *see also* Broadcast News
hypermasculine narcissism, 191, 193, 195; *see also* identity, gender

identity
  class, 9, 15, 18, 23, 25, 33–4, 37–8, 40–1, 55, 79, 84, 87, 106, 120, 132–4, 151–4, 157, 161–3, 165–8, 168, 205–6, 211, 213, 218, 220–1
  gender, 23–4, 39, 111, 189–207, 217, 218–22
  Jewish, 8, 9, 16, 34, 47, 53, 101, 111, 201–5
I'll Do Anything (James L. Brooks, 1994), 13–14; *see also* failure, genre
In Living Color (Wayans, 1990–4), 10
In-Laws, The (Fleming 2003), 16, 29, 130, 132
India, 30–1, 111, 113, 131, 201–4
irony, 23, 51, 84–5, 94, 98–9, 103, 107, 162–3, 212–13, 216, 218
Islam, 131, 202

Jacob's Ladder (Lyne, 1990), 182
job, 4, 12, 23, 29, 37, 52, 99,
    101, 103–4, 105, 107, 109,
    111, 123, 129, 130, 131, 132, 133–4,
    136–40, 141, 142,
    146, 148, 165, 177, 226,
    227
Johnson, Monica, 11, 14, 26, 39, 102,
    105, 189–92, 195–6, 205–7, 212;
    see also *Lost in America; Modern
    Romance Mother; Muse, The;
    Real Life; Scout, The*
Joke (1956); see *A Portend of the
    Artist as a Yhung Mandala*
    (1956)

Kaufman, Andy, 3–4, 6, 113, 119–20;
    see also anti-humor, stand-up
    comedy
Kissinger, Henry, 30, 131, 204
Klein, Robert, 3, 51, 78, 85
Kondabolu, Hari, 10; see also
    stand-up comedy
Kramer vs. Kramer (Benton, 1979),
    196–7
Kubrick, Stanley, 22, 113, 122, 147,
    149, 166

La La Land (Chazelle, 2016), 17
Landis, Jonathan
    Animal House (1978), 91
    Blues Brothers, The (1980), 92
    Twilight Zone: The Movie, The
        (1983), 6, 13
Las Vegas, 25, 63, 105–7, 106,
    122, 132, 148, 158–60, **159**;
    see also casino, gambling
Legend (Scott, 1988), 172
Lenny (Fosse, 1974), 4
Little Prince, The / Le Petit Prince
    (Osborne, 2015), 15, 238
Lolita (Kubrick, 1962), 147

*Looking for Comedy in the Muslim
    World* (Brooks, 2005), 2, 21,
    29–32, 36, 94–5, 111–15, **112**, 119,
    120, 129, 130–2, 201
Los Angeles, 30, 32–6, 40, 53, 60,
    83, 85, 141, 173, 177, 179, 213, 229;
    see also see also dystopia
Lost in America (Brooks, 1985), 20,
    21, **24**, 24–5, 31–2, 38–9, 55,
    95, 104–8, **106**, 110, 111, 113,
    114, 119–20, 121, 124–6, 129–30,
    132–4, 148, 150–68, **155**, 190,
    206, 211–12

Marshall, Penny, 30, 37, 111, 114,
    130, 205
Martin, Steve, 3–5, 6, 7, 8, 11, 119
    A Wild and Crazy Guy, 5
    Let's Get Small, 5, 7
Me Generation, 190, 211, 219;
    see also Baby Boom generation
Mead, Margaret, 22, 194–5
Meatballs (Reitman, 1979), 92
media critique, 21, 23, 37–8, 53–7,
    64, 69, 71–3, 75, 80, 88–92,
    96–8, 107–8, 194–5
meta-comedy, 4–11, 53, 69–70, 78–80,
    119–20, 213, 216, 218–22; see also
    stand-up comedy
Michaels, Lorne, 38, 78–80, 81–2,
    84–5, 87–8, 90–2, 131–2
Million Dollar Baby (Eastwood,
    2004), 9
Mirror Has Two Faces, The
    (Streisand, 1996), 27
mobile camera 21, 98, 150, 166–8;
    see also Steadicam shot, tracking
    shot
Modern Romance (Brooks, 1981),
    16, 21, 23–5, 27, 29, 32, 35,
    38, 40, 55, 95, 99–105, 110,
    113, 119–20, 121–6, 130, 134,

136–48, **138**, **139**, 189, 195–6, 202, 206–7, 211–12
Moonlight (Jenkins, 2016), 17
Mother (Brooks, 1996), 2, 21, 27–8, 32, 108, 119, 120, 126–9, **128**, 189–90, 199–202, 200, 206–7; see also Reynolds, Debbie
Murray, Bill, 92
Muse, The (Brooks, 1999), 2, 25, 28–30, 32, 95, 108–11, 113, 119–20, 129–32, 190, 205–7, 211–12, 225; see also Stone, Sharon
Music Minus One recording series, 3, 61–3, 63
Muzak/Easy Listening, 72–3
My First Mister (Lahti, 2001), 16, 132

National Commission on Fiscal Responsibility and Reform (Simpson-Bowles), 33, 35–6
Netflix, 114–15
New Comedy, 37, 51–3, 69–70, 73, 79
New York, 22, 38, 40, 60, 67, 85, 125, 132–3, **133**, 143, 153, 162, 173, 235, 237
Nicholson, Jack, 13, 163; see also Easy Rider
Nielsen Ratings, 89; see also commercial appeal
Nobel prize, 22–3, 30, 201
Now! (Alvarez, 1964), 64

occupation see job
Odd Couple, The (Belson and Marshall, 1970–5), 12
Odenkirk, Bob, 10
O'Donoghue, Michael, 82
Organization Man, 154, 155
Original Kings of Comedy, The (Lee, 2000), 30

Oscar see Academy Award
Out of Sight (Soderbergh, 1998), 15–16, 132
over-orthodoxy, 9, 38, 79, 119–20, 126, 202

Pakistan, 30–1, 111, 113, 114, 131, 201–2, 203, 204
Parallax View, The (Pakula, 1974), 64
parody, 51, 71, 96, 148, 158–9, 199
Passion of Joan of Arc, The (Dreyer, 1928), 175
passive aggressive, 12, 23, 144–5, 195
pilgrimage, 177–8, 180, 186
Player, The (Altman, 1992), 29
post-9/11 America, 39, 214, 221–2; see also War on Terror
Postcards from the Edge (Nichols, 1990), 26
Pretty Woman (Marshall, 1990), 37, 240
Private Benjamin (Zieff, 1980), 13
product placement, 109
professional mores 15, 23, 26, 37, 38, 56–63, 80, 85, 92, 123–5, 139, 151–2, 153–4, 155–6, 159, 160–3, 168, 169, 171, 228
professional-managerial class (PMC), 151–4, 157, 161–3, 165–8, 168; see also identity, class; Ehrenreich, Barbara and John Ehrenreich
promotion, 25, 105, 107, 124–6, 153, 158, 166–7, 190
Pryor, Richard, 3–4, 6, 51, 78–9, 82; see also stand-up comedy
Public Broadcasting System (PBS), 21–2, 56, 58, 71, 75, 79, 96, 150–1, 194
Purgatorio, 25, 39, 171–86; see also Dante

Quaalude, 16, 102, 139–40, **139**

Raindance/*Radical Software* (Shamberg, 1970–4), 54
Ray (Hackford, 2004), 9
Reagan, Ronald, 27, 86, 190, 212
Reagan era, 35, 92, 124, 132–3, 171
Real Life (Brooks, 1979), 2, 8, 11, 21, 22–4, 25, 27, 28, 29, 30, 31, 32, 55, 95–9, **97**, 100–4, 110, 113, 119, 120, **121**, 121–2, 131, 134, 150–1, 168, 189, 190, 191–6, **193**, 197, 199, 200, 201, 203, 206, 211, 212, 216; *see also* Grodin, Charles
Redford, Robert, 27
Reiner, Carl, 3
Reiner, Rob, 3, 28, 79, 87, 130, 206
   This Is Spinal Tap (1984), 87
Reinhardt, Ad, 56, 67–9, **68**, 76; *see also A Portend of the Artist as a Yhung Mandala*
religion, 8, 9, 16, 34, 47, 53, 101, 111, 131, 201–5; *see also* Hinduism; identity, Jewish; Islam
replacement, 22, 52, 63, 88, 149, 178, 232–4
Reynolds, Burt, 37
Reynolds, Debbie, 2, 27–8, 127–9, **128**, 189–90, 199–201, **200**; *see also* Mother
River Wild, The (Hanson, 1994), 26
Rock, Chris, 9
romantic comedy, 18, 23–5, 102–3, 137, 148; *see also* genre
Rosemary's Baby (Polanski, 1968), 13
Rowan and Martin's Laugh-In (Wolfe, 1967–73), 54, 144
Rubin, Jerry, 82–4, 156–7

satire, 13, 28–9, 109–10, 113, 141, 148, 149, 161
Saturday Night Live (*SNL*) (Michaels, 1975–2021), 5, 12, 21–2, 38, 51, 55, 78–92, **87**, 122, 131, 212
Saturday Night Live (*SNL*) short films, 78–9, 83–92, **87**
Saw (Wan, 2004), 9
Schafer, Kermit
   Pardon My Blooper! (1974), 71
science 8, 22–3, 28, 35, 37, 88–9, 96, 98–9, 168
Scorsese, Martin, 12, 18, 28, 29, 131, 149, 167, 206
   Aviator, The (2004), 9
   Taxi Driver (1976), 12–13, **12**, 45, 55, 131, 215
Scout, The (Ritchie, 1994), 2, 14, 20
Secret Life of Pets, The (Renaud and Cheney, 2016), 15, 132
Seinfeld (David and Seinfeld, 1990–8), 19–20
self-actualization, 173, 179, 181
Serra, Richard and Carlota Fay Schoolman, 56, 71–3; *see also Television Delivers People* (1973)
Shandling, Garry, 6, 19
She-Devil (Seidelman, 1989), 26
Sideways (Payne, 2004), 9
Simpsons, The (James L. Brooks, Groening, Simon, 1989–2021), 14–15, 18
Simpsons Movie, The (Silverman, 2007), 15, 132
Smothers Brothers Comedy Hour, The (Chambers, 1967–9), 63–4
Solondz, Todd, 99–102, 114–15
   Happiness (1998), 99, 100
   Life During Wartime (2010), 100
   Storytelling (2001), 100–1
   Wiener-Dog (2016), 100, 101–2

Spartacus (Kubrick, 1960), 22
Spielberg, Steven, 29, 113–14
1941 (1979), 92
stand-up comedy, 1–5, 8–11, 14, 19, 30, 51–2, 56, 61, 69, 79, 95–6, 112–13, 119–20, 131, 137, 164–5, 177, 182, 212, 215–16; *see also* Carlin, George; Kondabolu, Hari; Martin, Steve; Pryor, Richard
star persona, 1–2, 6, 10–11, 13, 16–18, 19–23, 26, 31, 36–7, 39, 94–6, 103, 107, 111, 120, 130, 196–8, 202, 213–22, 223, 224, 225
Steadicam shot 166–8; *see also* mobile camera, tracking shot
Steve Allen Show, The, 51, 52, 54, 87
Stiller, Ben, 10
Stone, Sharon, 2, 28–9, 109, 130, 190, 205–6; *see also* Muse, The
Streep, Meryl, 2, 26–7, 39, 126, 179, 183, 189, 196–9, 198; *see also* Defending Your Life
Stripes (Reitman, 1981), 92
success, 9, 23, 25, 29, 33, 36, 38, 41, 69, 94, 95, 100–1, 102, 110, 114, 119–34, 145, 169, 171–3, 180, 182, 186, 189–90, 194–5, 199, 203, 205–6, 232; *see also* American Dream, failure

"Talking at Pomona" (1972), 55–6, 60–1
technocracy 37, 41, 58, 161, 174
technology, appeal of 96, 97, 155, 177, 179–80
Television Delivers People (Serra and Schoolman, 1973), 56, 71–3
Terms of Endearment (James L. Brooks, 1983), 13, 15

test screenings, 13, 27, 88–90, 99, 101, 104, 112, 151; *see also* box office, commercial appeal
Tim and Eric Awesome Show, Great Job! (Heidecker and Wareheim, 2007–10), 10
Tonight Show, The (Allen, Habach, Hemion and Weaver, 1962–92), 6–8, 19, 51, 64–9, 76, 79–80, 119, 131, 165; *see also* Carson, Johnny
Top Value TV (Shamberg, 1972–7), 54
tracking shot 21, 150, 166–8, 228; *see also* mobile camera, Steadicam shot
Turn-On (Schlatter and Friendly, 1969), 54–5, 64
Twenty Thirty: The Real Story of What Happens to America (Brooks), 32–36
Twilight Zone: The Movie, The (Landis, 1983), 6, 13

Unfaithfully Yours (Zieff, 1983), 6, 13
Up Close and Personal (Avnet, 1996), 27

Vacation (Ramis, 1983), 92
voice acting 14–15, 132, 224–5; *see also* Doctor Dolittle; Finding Dory; Finding Nemo; Little Prince, The; Secret Life of Pets, The; Simpsons, The; Simpsons Movie, The; Terms of Endearment
Shoeless Joe (W. P. Kinsella), 173

Waiting for 2040 (Hari Kondabolu), 10

War on Terror, 39, 111, 221; *see also* post–9/11 America
Wareheim, Eric, 10
Weeds (Kohan, 2005–12), 16–17, 132
While We're Young (Baumbach, 2014), 97

White Chicks (Wayans, 2004), 9–10
whiteness, 4, 9–10, 211, 221–2
Williams, Robin, 37

yuppie, 39, 41, 82–3, 124–5, 150–69, 171–3, 181–2, 211–13

EU representative:
Easy Access System Europe
Mustamäe tee 50, 10621 Tallinn, Estonia
Gpsr.requests@easproject.com

43668CB00013B/2002

www.ingramcontent.com/pod-product-compliance
Lightning Source LLC
Chambersburg PA
CBHW051606230426